D1175902

THE SCHOOLS

OF

MEDIEVAL ENGLAND

WINCHESTER COLLEGE, c. 1460

FROM A DRAWING BY WARDEN CHANDLER IN MS. LIFE OF WYKEHAM, AT NEW COLLEGE, OXFORD

THE SCHOOLS OF
MEDIEVAL ENGLAND

BY

A. F. LEACH

WITH FORTY-THREE ILLUSTRATIONS

BARNES & NOBLE, Inc.
New York
METHUEN & CO. Ltd
London

First Published, 1915

Reprinted, 1969
by
Barnes & Noble, Inc., New York
and
Methuen & Co. Ltd, London

Printed in the United States of America

PREFACE

THIS is the first attempt at a history of English Schools before the Reformation, reckoned from the accession of Edward VI. It is surprising and yet not surprising that such a history has never been attempted before. It is surprising in view of the interest of the subject and the wealth of illustrative material; but it is not surprising when it is remembered that, before the year 1892, few guessed and fewer knew that there were any public or grammar schools—two terms for the same thing—in England at all, except Winchester and Eton, before the reputed creation of schools by that boy king. If anyone was pressed with the problem how learned persons from John of Salisbury in the twelfth to Cardinal Wolsey in the sixteenth century obtained the schooling which fitted them for their university careers, the solution was invariably sought in some monastery near their birthplace, which was, without the smallest proof, credited with keeping a school. If one asked what was taught in these monastic schools one was told, psalm-singing and a little elementary Latin grammar : a fine preparation truly for the Polycraticus, or the statutes of Cardinal College.

Dr. Furnivall, the author of the best historical account of education and schools of England, in the introduction to his *Babees' Book*, published by the Early English Text Society in 1868, informed me in 1892, in answer to a request for help in research into the history of grammar schools, that there were no grammar schools in England before Edward VI. Soon convinced to the contrary, he was always ready to impart instances of earlier schools which he came across in his wide reading in ancient manuscripts and books.

Yet long after the facts had been published, when the

47534

Head Master of a certain considerable Midland school asked for information as to its origin and history and was told that there was evidence of its existence in the days of Edward the Confessor, he responded by entreating me not to try and make a fool of him.   Yet I found he firmly believed in the fable of the foundation of Oxford University by Alfred the Great; the demonstration of its absurdity by Parker, and the revelation of the true origin of universities by Denifle and Rashdall not having reached him.

Some idea of the true history of our schools has now penetrated to scholastic circles, but it has certainly not reached most antiquaries or historians, still less the general public, in spite of the detailed stories, beginning before the Conquest in many cases, already published in the *Victoria County History of England* of more than a dozen counties.   So the invitation to contribute this volume to Messrs. Methuen's popular series of *Antiquary's Books* was readily accepted.   The plan of these books, however, excludes references to authorities : an exclusion peculiarly unfortunate for historical statements, many of which are so contradictory to received opinions that they will appear at first sight incredible to a great many people, and which rest largely on manuscripts still for the most part unprinted and unpublished.   There is, however, not a single statement in this book not founded on verifiable authority. The relevant extracts from many of the manuscript and other recondite sources have now been printed verbatim, or detailed references given, in previous publications.   A list of these in which the authorities, so far as they are not given in the text, can be verified in detail, is appended.

ARTHUR F. LEACH

34 ELM PARK GARDENS, S.W.

BIBLIOGRAPHY

Works on the history of schools, by Arthur F. Leach, formerly Fellow of All Souls' College, Oxford.

GENERAL

Educational Charters and Documents. lii and 582 pp. Cambridge University Press, 1911.
  Gives the text and translation of salient documents illustrating the existence and conduct of schools from the first mention by Bede of the institution of a grammar school in East Anglia in 631, copied from that at Canterbury, to the scheme for Andover Grammar School in 1909. Of the 161 documents printed, 142 relate to the period before 1547, and 19 of these to the period before the Norman Conquest.

  English Schools at the Reformation. xvi, 122, and 346 pp. Archibald Constable & Co., 1894.
  Part I sums up and explains by reference to previous history, Part II; which contains the Certificates made under the Acts for the dissolution of Colleges and Chantries, so far as they relate to schools, and the warrants issued under Edward VI for the re-grant of endowments to the few schools which were re-endowed by him as Free Grammar Schools.

Free Grammar Schools. *The National Observer*, September, October, 1896. An explanation of the origin and true meaning of the term. *See also* The True Meaning of Free Schools. *Journal of Education*, June, July, 1908.

Edward VI: Spoiler of Schools. 21 pp. *Contemporary Review*, September, 1892.

School Supply in the Middle Ages. 9 pp. *Contemporary Review*, November, 1894.

Memorandum on the History of Endowed Schools. 19 pp. *Report of the Royal Commission on Secondary Education*, V, 57-76, 1895.

The School Boys' Feast. 15 pp. *Fortnightly Review*, January, 1896.

The Origin of Oxford. 11 pp. and 2 pp. *National Review*, September, 1896. *The Oxford Magazine*, May, 1912.

Schools. 43 pp. *Encyclopædia Britannica*, 11th ed., 1911.

The Ancient Schools in the City of London and Christ's Hospital, in Sir Walter Besant's *London, The City*. (The Survey of London.) 11 and 44 pp. (pp. 300-19 and 385-429). Adam & Charles Black, 1910.

The Medieval Education of Women. *Journal of Education*, October, November, December, 1910.

The Humanists in Education. *The Classical Review*, August, 1910.

Education, the Church in relation to. *Dictionary of English Church History*. Mowbray, 1912.

Articles in the *American Cyclopædia of Education*. New York. The Macmillan Company, 1911-13.

Abbey Schools.
Archdeacon.
Boy Bishop.
Busby.
Canon Law on Education.
Chancellors' Schools.
Chantry Schools.
Choristers' Schools.
Church Schools.
Clerk.
Cloister Schools.
Colet, John.
College.
Collegiate Church Schools.
Commonwealth and Education.
Edward VI.
Endowments.
Eton College.
Exhibition.
Fagging.
Fees.
Free Schools.
Glomery.

Grammar School.
Harrow School.
Henry VI.
High School.
Hospital Schools.
London, Education in.
Middle Ages, Education during.
Milton as Educator.
Prefect.
Primer and Primarian.
Reformation, The, and Education in England.
Rugby School.
School.
Udal, Nicholas.
Usher.
Waynflete, William.
Winchester College.
Wolsey, Thomas.
Women, Higher Education of.
Wykeham, William of.
York School.

PARTICULAR SCHOOLS

A History of Winchester College. 14 and 561 pp. (illustrated). Duckworth & Co., 1899.
[See also Winchester College, 1393 and 1893. 18 pp. *Contemporary Review*, June, 1893. Wykeham's Models in the Quingentenary volume, *Winchester College, 1393-1893*. 9 pp. Edward Arnold, 1893. Winchester College in the *Victoria County History of Hampshire*, II, 251-366 and V, 14-19, illustrated.]

Southwell Grammar School in *Visitations and Memorials of Southwell Minster*. A.D. *c*. 950-1542. cxi and 234 pp. Camden Society, N.S. 487, 1891.

Our Oldest School [York]. 20 pp. *Fortnightly Review*, November, 1892.
[But see under Canterbury School, *post*.]

Canterbury (the King's) School. *The Times*, 12 September, 1896; 7 September, 1897. Which is our oldest school? Canterbury *v.* York. *The Guardian*, 12 and 19 January, 1898. Our oldest Public School. *The Times*, Educational Supplement, 3 January, 1911. *The Times*, 4, 6, 16 January, 1911.

Sherborne School. Before, After and Under Edward VI. 83 pp. *The Archæological Journal*, March, 1898.
[See also The Oldest Minutes of the Governors of Sherborne School, by W. B. Wildman. 3 pp. *The Archæological Journal*, December, 1898.]

The Foundation and Refoundation of Pocklington Grammar School. 52 pp. *Transactions of the East Riding Antiquarian Society*, V, 63-144. 1897.

Beverley Grammar School in *Memorials of Beverley Minster*, with text of the Beverley Chapter Act Book, A.D. 1286-147. cxiii and 424 pp. Vol. I, Surtees Society, No. 98, 1898. cxii and 389 pp. Vol. II, Surtees Society, No. 108, 1903, and

Early Yorkshire Schools. Vol. I, York, Beverley, Ripon. lxxiv and 252 pp. *The Yorkshire Archæological Society Record Series*. Vol. XXVII, 1899.

Early Yorkshire Schools. Vol. II, Pontefract, Howden, Northallerton, Acaster, Rotherham, Giggleswick, Sedbergh. lxxxvii and 458 pp. *The Yorkshire Archæological Society Record Series*, Vol. XXXIII, 1903. [See also in Victoria County History of Yorkshire, I, 415-501, for history of the Yorkshire schools brought up to date.]

History of Warwick School. viii and 262 pp. illustrated. Archibald Constable & Co., 1906.

Early Education in Worcester. 685-1700. xc and 341 pp. Worcestershire Historical Society, 1913.

St. Paul's School, London. St. Paul's Girls' School and its Pedigree, and The Foundation of St. Paul's School. *The Times*, 2 and 12 April, 1904.
Colet's Place in the History of Education. *Journal of Education*. June, 1904.
St. Paul's School. *Journal of Education*, July, 1909.
Milton as Schoolboy and Schoolmaster. 14 pp. *Proceedings of British Academy*, III, 1909.
St. Paul's School before Colet. 46 pp. Read before the Society of Antiquaries 25 November, 1909, printed with extracts from original documents. *Archæologia*, LX, 1910.
[See also The Ancient Schools in the City of London, above, and *The Times*, 7, 14 July; 3 August, 1909.]

Durham School, The Pedigree of. *Journal of Education*, October, 1905; April, 1906.
        [See also Victoria County History of Durham, II, 207 *seq.*]

Stratford-on-Avon Grammar School. *Shakespeare's School. Journal of Education*, January, March, 1908.
        [See also Victoria County History of Warwickshire, II.]

The Origin of Westminster School. *Journal of Education*, January, 1905.
        [See also Nicholas Udal in *Encyclopædia Britannica*. Ed. 1911.]

Lincoln School. *Journal of Education*, August, 1906.

The History of Schools in the *Victoria History of the Counties of England*, viz., in the counties of:—
Hampshire—Vol. II, 261-408. 1903; Vol. V, 14-19. 1912.
Surrey—Vol. II, 155-243. 1904.
Durham—Vol. I, 365-415. 1905.
Lincolnshire—Vol. II, 421-93. 1906.
Berkshire—Vol. II, 245-81. 1907.
Derbyshire—Vol. II, 207-81. 1907.
Essex (by Miss Fell Smith, ed. A. F. L.)—Vol. II, 501-64. 1907.
Gloucestershire—Vol. II, 313-448. 1907.
Sussex—Vol. II, 397-440. 1907.
Suffolk (partly by Miss E. Steele Hutton—ed. A. F. L.)—Vol. II, 301-57. 1907.
Yorkshire—Vol. I, 415-501. 1907.
Bedfordshire—Vol. II, 149-85. 1908.
Buckinghamshire (Eton College, 60 pp.)—Vol. II, 147-221. 1908.
Hertfordshire—Vol. II, 47-102. 1908.
Lancashire (partly by Rev. H. J. Chaytor, ed. A. F. L.)—Vol. II, 561-614. 1908.
Warwickshire—Vol. II, 297-374. 1908.
Nottinghamshire—Vol. II, 179-250. 1910.
Somersetshire (Wells: the rest by Rev. T. Scott Holmes, ed. A. F. L.)—Vol. II, 435-65. 1911.

CONTENTS

LIST OF ILLUSTRATIONS

xiii

THE SCHOOLS OF MEDIEVAL ENGLAND

CHAPTER I

OUR OLDEST SCHOOL—CANTERBURY

SCHOOLS in England are coeval with the coming of Christianity. Before its introduction a school, whether word or thing, was unknown. Schools no doubt existed in Roman Britain both before the introduction of Christianity and after. For already, in the latter part of the first century, Juvenal relates that eloquent Gauls are teaching the Britons to plead causes and Thule is discussing the establishment of a Rhetoric School. But whatever other institutions of Britain, if any, survived its conversion into England, churches and schools did not.

For 150 years after the Conquest the English remained heathen, and no traces of Roman culture are to be found among them. They held no intercourse, except in war, with the Britons in the west of the island. If any Britons remained in Saxon England, they were a remnant saved as slaves and serfs, and there is no evidence that they remained Christian. For the rest, says the latest investigator of the subject, Professor Oman, " the unconquered Britons of the West and North made no effort to convert their adversaries. . . . The only reference to the English that can be detected in the surviving notes of British Church-Councils is a clause in the Canons of the Synod of Lucus Victoriæ (569 A.D.), imposing a penance of thirteen years on a man who shall have acted as guide to the barbarians. Even in later days, in spite of Saxon exiles at British Courts, there is no attempt at conversion. Not one solitary legend survives to hint at such an endeavour."

When, at the end of the sixth century, Christianity came to

England, it came, not from the Celtic Britons, nor even from the neighbouring and kindred Franks, but, " bret hot from Rome," a direct importation from Italy.   The Frankish wife of King Ethelbert of Kent, with her Christian chaplain, had no doubt prepared her husband's mind for the admission of the Roman missionaries.   But it was the prestige of the missionaries direct from Rome and from Pope Gregory the Great himself, under the leadership of Augustine, the Prior of Gregory's own monastery of St. Andrew on the Cælian Hill, which caused Kent, and through Kent England, to become part of the " Holy Catholic Church," to establish Christian churches, and, as a necessary concomitant, schools.   For not only were the ceremonies of the new religion a foreign product imported by foreigners speaking Latin, but the language in which the ceremonies were performed had itself by 500 years' usage acquired as the language of the religion of Rome the halo of immemorial antiquity and therefore of sanctity. To understand the rudiments of the new religion, to take part in the new religious worship, it was necessary for the English to learn Latin.   The modern missionary, the Protestant missionary at all events, endeavours to adapt the religion he imports to the understanding of his hearers.   Though the Authorized Version of the Bible and the Common Prayer Book are sanctified by a usage twice as long as that of the Vulgate when first introduced into England, the missionary of to-day does not seek to impose them on his converts in the English tongue.   He presents them with a translation in their vernacular, so that the Gospel is preached to each man, as in the Acts of the Apostles, in the tongue in which he was born.   Not so acted Augustine, " the Apostle of the English ".   The whole of Western Europe had been Romanized first and Christianized long afterwards.   Hence the Roman service had been naturally performed in the Roman tongue which had become the official, if not the vernacular, tongue.   When the barbarians in successive hordes invaded Gaul they adopted the language as well as the religion of the conquered.   It never seems to have occurred to St. Augustine or Gregory the Great that in this respect England differed from Italy and from Gaul, that, in a word, England was no longer Britain.   Augustine therefore imported and was successful in imposing on the English the Roman ritual and the Roman religious books in " the veray Romain tongue," as Dean Colet called it, as it was spoken, or supposed to be spoken in the days of St. Paul, of Jerome, and of Gregory.

To do this, the missionaries had to come with the Latin service-book in one hand, and the Latin grammar in the other. Not only had the native priests to be taught the tongue in which their services were performed, but the converts, at least of the upper classes, had to be taught the elements of grammar before they could grasp the elements of religion. They could not profitably go to church till they had first gone to school. So the Grammar School became in theory, as it often was in fact, the necessary ante-room, the vestibule of the church. But, as there were no schools any more than there were churches in England, Augustine had to create both.

There is every reason to believe that he established the first school in England at Canterbury at the same time with, and as part and parcel of, the first church. Augustine landed in the spring of the year 597. On 2 June that year Ethelbert was baptized. Later, Augustine went over to Gaul and was consecrated bishop by the Bishop of Arles. When he returned, probably in the spring of 598, " Ethelbert," says Bede, " did not delay giving his teachers a place befitting the dignity of their seat in Canterbury his metropolis, and at the same time conferring on them necessary possessions of various kinds ". That is to say, he endowed the archbishop and his see. Augustine, " as soon as he had obtained his episcopal see in the royal city, with the King's assistance, recovered possession of a church which had been formerly built by the work of Roman Christians, and dedicated it in the name of Jesus Christ," and Christ Church the cathedral has been called ever since.

It may be safely asserted then, that in this year, 598, as an adjunct to Christ Church Cathedral, or rather as part of it, and under the tuition of himself and the clerks who came with him and whom Ethelbert endowed, Augustine established the Grammar School which still flourishes under the name of the King's School, not from its original founder, Ethelbert, but from its re-founder, Henry VIII. It cannot, indeed, be proved directly that the school was established in 598. But the inference that it was rests on the unimpeachable evidence of Bede, speaking of a time little more than thirty years later, in which the school appears as a model for a new school founded in another English kingdom.

"At this time," i.e. 631, according to Mr. C. Plummer in the latest and most learned edition of Bede, " Sigberct presided over the kingdom of the East English.   He, while in exile in Gaul . . . received baptism.   After his return, as soon as he had obtained the kingdom, wishing to imitate what he had seen well done in Gaul, he founded a school in which boys might be taught grammar (scolam in qua pueri litteris erudiantur), with the assistance of Bishop Felix, whom he had got from Kent, who provided them with ushers and masters (pedagogos ac magistros) after the custom of the Canterbury folk."   The word in the original is *Cantuariorum*, which may be also translated Kentish folk.   It is, however, immaterial whether we translate "Kentish" or "Canterbury" folk, since Canterbury, as the metropolis of the Kentish kingdom, and as the royal and archiepiscopal city, was naturally the seat of the chief school, as it was also, by the express testimony of a Saxon writer, "of the Supreme Court of the Kentish kingdom".   But if the school had already a custom of its own and was established enough to become a model for other kingdoms in 631, by whom could it have been established except by Augustine, or at what epoch could it have been established except at the first establishment of the see ? Felix was a Burgundian who had come over to England and been consecrated by Archbishop Honorius, one of the last survivors of Augustine's original band of missionaries.   That Sigberct and Felix should have thought it necessary to establish a school on the christianization of East Anglia and the founding of the East Anglian see, in 631, strengthens the inference that St. Augustine and King Ethelbert had done the same in the establishment of the see at Canterbury in 598.

We need not discuss and dissect the unwarrantable claim that Sigberct's school was at Cambridge.   The East Anglian see was settled at Dunwich—and Dunwich has been rightly claimed by the East Anglian historians as the seat of Sigberct's school, and, wrongly, as therefore the oldest school in England.   But this is through the default of the Canterbury historians who went astray seeking the founder of their school in the Greek archbishop Theodore, of whom more hereafter. It is obvious that the school which was taken as the model, and which furnished the first masters to the school founded on its model, like Winchester to Eton 800 years later, must be older than the copy. Even if Dunwich School had not perished, the primary place among the schools, as among the churches, of England must be assigned to Canterbury.

The vexed question of which is "Our Oldest School" is therefore settled in favour of the ancient Grammar School of the city or cathedral church of Canterbury—the terms are convertible—known, though only since the eighteenth century, as the King's School, Canterbury.

Recently, the claim of Canterbury, generally accepted since its first assertion in *The Times* of 14 September, 1896, reinforced by detailed exposition in articles in the same paper of 7 September, 1897, and in *The Guardian* of 12 and 19 January, 1898, has been questioned, and the priority sought to be assigned to Rochester Cathedral School. The basis of the Rochester claim was eventually reduced in a letter to *The Times* of 4 January, 1911, to a statement in "an old history of Rochester," that "in the year 604 Justus endowed six secular priests for the instruction of youth" there. This statement, involving a school with five assistant masters, a number unheard of and undreamt of in English schools before the eighteenth century, is absolutely incredible. Even if the "old history" —the date and provenance of which have been asked for but have not been vouchsafed—were accepted as an authority comparable to that of Bede, it could not make us accept Rochester as the older school. To do so would be to set the disciple above his master. For the See of Rochester was an offshoot of and subordinate to Canterbury. "In 604," says Bede, "Augustine, Archbishop of Britain, ordained two bishops, Mellitus and Justus, the first as bishop of the East Saxons with his see at St. Paul's, London, and the other as bishop at Rochester; in which the king built St. Andrew's church, and he gave to the bishops of each of those churches many gifts as he had done at Canterbury; and added lands and property for the use of those who were with the bishops"—their clerks or chapters.

If it is inferred from this—and it is a perfectly fair inference—that Rochester School and, by parity of reasoning, St.
Paul's School, London, were established as a part of those
episcopal establishments in 604, from the very same inference,
and on the authority of the same record, it must be admitted
that Rochester and London were later than Canterbury, their
mother, mistress, and model, by six years.

Two years after the establishment of Dunwich Grammar
School on the model of Canterbury, we hear of the establishment of a Song School at York, for which also Canterbury
was the model. When Paulinus, one of Augustine's Canterbury
mission, after Christianizing King Edwin and York in 627, fled
from it after the battle of Heathfield, in which Edwin was
defeated and killed by an unholy alliance between the heathen
Penda of Mercia and the Christian Welsh in 633, he left behind him James, the deacon who " though an ecclesiastic, was
also a saint ". Bede, writing as a monk, thought none but
monks really holy. When peace was restored in the province
—i.e. after Oswald had recovered it by the battle of Heaven-
field in 635—" when the number of the faithful increased,
James acted as master to many in church chanting after the
Roman or Canterbury fashion," i.e. the Gregorian as distinguished from the Ambrosian or Milanese chant.

These Song Schools became even more general than the
Grammar Schools. The Song School at Rochester is expressly
mentioned by Bede in Theodore's time as being derived from
Canterbury. Putta, whom Archbishop Theodore found at
Rochester, and made bishop there, is described " as well instructed in ecclesiastical learning, . . . and especially skilled in
the art of chanting in church after the Roman fashion, which he
had learnt from the pupils of the blessed Pope Gregory himself ". This Putta, when Rochester was ravaged by the King
of Mercia in 675, settled down as a simple parish priest in
Mercia and went about " teaching church singing (ecclesiae
carmina) wherever he was asked ".

The twin schools of Grammar and Song, which have often
been confounded as if they were one school, are found side by
side in connexion with all the great churches, that is in all the
great centres of population, from the age of Augustine and
Ethelbert to the age of Cranmer and Edward VI, as distinct

foundations, completely differentiated in function as they were in their teaching, and generally in their government. In small places they were sometimes united under one master. Though as late as 1519 a school-author, who had been Headmaster first of Eton and then of Winchester, William Horman, asserted in echo of Quintilian, himself copying the Greeks, that, without a knowledge of music, grammar cannot be perfect, yet the teaching of singing and music, so often rashly asserted to be the main work of the pre-Reformation school, and the Song Schools which gave it, were always subordinate and secondary to the teaching of grammar and the Grammar School. To a large extent the Song Schools performed the function of Elementary Schools, while the Grammar Schools were the Secondary Schools, and, before the days of Universities, gave university or higher education as well. Our main task is to follow the foundations and fortunes of the Grammar Schools.

For the Song Schools were in essence special or professional schools for those engaged in the actual performance of the services, and useful mainly for them, whereas the Grammar Schools gave a general education, as much needed by the statesman, the lawyer, the civil servant, and the clerk as by the priest or cleric. For a Grammar School meant a school which taught the classics, especially the Latin language and literature ; the terms being interchangeable. All schools, in the ordinary parlance, schools *simpliciter*, schools without an epithet, schools other than special schools, such as schools of law, of medicine, or later, of theology, or of song, or writing, or of arms, or dancing, or of needlework, were Grammar Schools, *scole gramaticales, ludi literarii.* These schools descend direct from Rome and indirectly from Alexandria.

They were no creation of Christianity or of Christian times : no development of catechetical schools or of church officers. For it is certain that our schools are not derived, as sometimes alleged, from the catechetical schools, beginning with that of St. Mark at Alexandria, whom the learned nun, Miss Drane, depicted as teaching a sort of elementary school in which the grey barbarian learnt the rudiments side by side with the Christian child. The smallest study of the meaning of catechumen and the object of catechetical teaching should have prevented this hypothesis from ever being presented, or rather, such a wild guess from ever having been made.

Catechetical schools, so called, were nothing more than courses of lectures to catechumens, who, whether they were new converts or long-standing Christians, were grown-up people being prepared for baptism by catechesis, that is oral instruction, in the principles of the Christian faith.   In the first three centuries of the Christian Church no one dreamt of baptizing infants.   To do so would have seemed not so much profane,   though it would have been that, as preposterous. Baptism was the supreme rite, the admission to the highest grade in the Christian gild, not as now the first initiation into it.   Tertullian, writing in the third century on Baptism, exhorts the faithful to get over the business of marriage and founding families before they incur the awful responsibilities of baptism, a regeneration, a new birth of the soul, which was freed from all sin thereby, a " baptism of repentance ".   He asks, referring to the proposal made by some that children of three or four years old—no one had suggested new-born babies— should be baptized, why should the age of innocence be in a hurry to get its sins remitted?   A century and a half later, when Augustine, at the age of fourteen, clamoured to be baptized, his mother told him to wait until he was older and had a deeper sense of responsibility.   To be baptized was to be illuminated, and a passage in the Epistle to the Hebrews had given rise to, or perhaps rather expressed, the current belief that mortal sin committed after baptism could not be forgiven. " For as touching those who have once been illuminated . . . but then have fallen away it is impossible to renew them again unto repentance."   The age of thirty, the traditional age at which Christ was baptized, was regarded as the normal age for baptism, but many put it off to their death-beds, and then risked being unable to receive it because through physical or mental weakness they were unable to repeat or understand the formulas.

Catechumens therefore were grown persons being informed or instructed in the mysteries of Christianity, translated by the Latin *audientes*, hearing or audience.

There are two sets of early catechetical lectures extant. The famous Didache or Teaching of the Apostles, now recog-

nized as being a guide to catechists, is simply an exposition of
the doctrines and services of the Church, a theological treatise.
The Catechetical Lectures of Cyril of Alexandria, Bishop of
Jerusalem, delivered in 347, are eighteen homilies or expository
sermons, addressed to grown-up congregations. The title of
the first is " To those to be enlightened," the illuminandi. The
second is on the necessity for " Repentance and remission of
sins," and the third expounds that " Baptism gives remission ".
The last thirteen go steadily through the Creed, expounding
and explaining the meaning and importance of its articles.
There is not a word in them to suggest that this catechist
is educating the young.   Chiefly he is arguing against the
heathen as a missionary nowadays might in preaching to
Hindoos, Brahmins, or Chinese sages.

The Great Catechism of Gregory of Nyssa, written about
380, was lately cited in the *American Cyclopædia of Education*
(1912) as giving him " a place in the realm of pedagogy ".
Nobody who had ever looked at it could possibly claim it as a
pedagogical work. Like Clement of Alexandria's *Pedagogue*
of 150 years before, it is a theological textbook pure and simple,
which did not even, as the *Pedagogue* had done, treat the Church
under the metaphor of a school, of which the tutor was Christ.
So too Augustine of Hippo's work *On catechizing beginners* (*De
catechizandis rudimentis*), written in the year 400, is no treatise on educational method, but a handbook of that which is
called, in the title of one of the divinity professors at Oxford,
pastoral theology, a series of hints how to meet the difficulties
presented to or by catechumens of varying degrees of education and intelligence.   Its object may be seen at once from
the opening words, " You said that when you were a deacon at
Carthage, you often had those brought to you who were to be
instructed in the Christian faith ".

There was not even any building set apart for the catechizing, which could be called a Catechetical School. When
Origen in 203 was employed at the age of eighteen as catechist by
Bishop Demetrius of Alexandria, he is said to have been given
the duty of teaching in the church. By Ambrose of Milan
in 380 the baptistery itself was appropriately used for the
purpose. He relates how when, after reading and expounding
the lessons, he had sent away the bulk of the catechumens,

he taught the competent (*competentes*), the advanced cate-chumens who were candidates for actual baptism at the ensuing Easter, the Creed itself.

The early Church as a whole was opposed to education, be-cause the usual school education, being based on the study of the poets, was necessarily mixed up with the pagan mythology, and the higher education in the "philosophy of the Greeks" was mistrusted.   So though the Church was wise enough to make use of learned converts when it got them, these were often compelled to defend themselves and apologize for their education and learning.   Thus Gregory of Nazianzus in his Panegyric on his friend St. Basil, delivered about 382, while descanting on their life together at the University of Athens, has to defend "that external culture which many Christians ill-judgingly abhor as mischievous and dangerous and keeping us afar from God".   "As we compound healing drugs from reptiles, so from secular literature we receive principles of inquiry and speculation while we reject their idolatry.   They aid us in our religion by our knowledge of the difference between the worse and the better.   We must not then dishonour education because some do so, but rather set down those who do as boorish and uneducated, desiring all to be as they are in order to escape the detection of their want of culture."

So elaborate a defence of education and culture in a bishop could hardly have been needed if there were schools of the church itself which gave this very education and culture.   With scarcely an exception all the early Fathers who made their mark in Christian literature and apologetics are known to have been educated in the ordinary pagan grammar and rhetoric schools.   Thus the first recorded so-called master of the Alexandrian Catechetical School, Pantænus, who taught in the reign of the Emperor Severus, A.D. 181, had been himself a Stoic philosopher, and is said by Jerome to have been sent to India as a missionary to the Brahmins and philosophers there.   Eusebius places him "finally at the head of the Alexandrian school,"—doing what? giving a general education to the young?   No — but "commenting on the treasures of God's truth, both orally and in writing".   Clement of Alexandria, his colleague and successor, had also been a student in the philosophy schools of Greece and Italy before he became the convert of Pantænus. His *Stromata*—patch-work or miscellanies—are full of classical and philosophical learning acquired in his pagan days. His disciple and successor as catechist, Origen, had been a pupil of Ammonius Saccas, the Neo-Platonist philosopher, and was supporting himself and his mother and six brothers as master of a Greek grammar school when he was made master of the catechetical school on the flight of Clement from persecution. We are expressly told that he thereupon gave up his school and sold his library. Later he had to leave Alexandria and went to Athens and Rome, and on his return appointed as assistant-catechist, " Heracles the priest, who continued to wear the dress of a philosopher ". The phrase shows that Heracles' learning too was derived from the ordinary schools. Origen afterwards taught a school of philosophy at Cæsarea. Dionysius, the next in succession, in 232, was also a heathen, and brought up in the heathen schools before being converted by Origen ; he continued to act as catechist until he became Bishop of Alexandria in 247. Little appears to be known of their successors as given by Jerome. But it can hardly be doubted that they had one and all been educated in their youth in the public schools.

For in the next century precisely the same education in the grammar, rhetoric, and philosophical schools was enjoyed by the two great Fathers, Basil and Gregory of Nazianzus. They, unlike those before mentioned, were born Christians. But they went to school at Cæsarea in Cappadocia under Carterius. Of Basil, Gregory says that he was brought up by his father a " common," i.e. public, teacher of virtue, but he was brought up in religion by his grandmother Macrina. Basil afterwards went to Cæsarea in Palestine to study Greek and Latin literature, i.e. to a grammar school. Here, according to Jerome, Origen, who after his flight from Alexandria had set up a school of philosophy, " gradually introduced the matter of faith in Christ ". But this sounds legendary. Basil's contemporary Gregory makes no mention of Origen or Christian teaching there. If true, the story shows, not that the school kept by Origen was a catechetical school giving general education, but that he took a mean advantage as teacher of a professedly undenominational school of philosophy to use it for denominational propaganda.

When Gregory and Basil met again as students at Athens, Gregory tells how "two ways were known to us, the first of greater value, the second of smaller consequence, the one leading to our sacred building and to our teachers there, the other to secular instruction". So speaks the bishop in after years. We may be pretty sure that as the object of their going to Athens was to learn the classics, rhetoric, and philosophy, the road to the secular schools was the important one at the time. Even in the funeral oration on Basil, from which these facts are derived, this peeps out. While Gregory tells us nothing about their going to church or their catechetical instruction, he enlarges on their University life, their initiation as freshmen, being subject to a mock debate and argument, ending with a triumphant procession to and sham storming of the Public Bath. Gregory extols the abilities and application of Basil, not in Christian but in pagan learning, his knowledge of languages, acquired before his arrival at Athens, his powerful rhetoric, his attainments in grammar "which perfects our tongues in Greek, compiles history, presides over metres and legislates for poetry, and in philosophy, practical and speculative, and particularly that part of it concerned with logical demonstration called Dialectic". Basil was, however, no mathematician. Astronomy and geometry he grasped, but "excessive application to these he despised as useless for those who sought after piety". Medicine he learnt, both theory and practice, because of his own physical delicacy and with a view to visiting the sick.

This prodigy, "whose ship was loaded with all the learning attainable by man," though he is represented as treating rhetoric as a by-work merely to assist him in Christian philosophy, was, like Gregory himself, not baptized till after he had been a student at Athens for five years, though Gregory had, during a storm on his way to the University, vowed to be baptized, if he escaped shipwreck.

Even after leaving Athens Basil spent some time as master of a public rhetoric school before he became a priest and an ascetic, when he inflicted on the world and himself the first cœnobite ·ule. Though he himself confessed the failure of his monastic life, "though I have left the city as the source of innumerable ills, yet I have not learned to leave myself . . . so I have got no great good from my retirement"; yet in his later days he wrote, "The choice lies between two alternatives, a liberal education, which you may get by sending your children to the public schools, or the salvation of their souls, which you may secure by sending them to the monks. Which is to win, learning or salvation? If you can unite both, do so; but if not, choose the most precious." Here again the learning of the public schools is contrasted with the religion of the monks.

To clinch the argument we may cite the words of Gregory, when the Emperor Julian in 362 is said to have aimed a deadly blow at Christianity by closing the public schools to Christians. Gregory attacked the edict in unmeasured terms, insisting that he preferred learning to all earthly riches, and held nothing in the world dearer, next to the joys of heaven and the hopes of eternity. But why should Gregory have regarded the prohibition as a grievance if the Church had its own ecclesiastical schools in which it itself gave literary and philosophical instruction. What was the antithesis between education and salvation if the monasteries gave a liberal education?

No. The true models and source of the schools of England are not the schools of the Church but the schools of heathendom, the schools of Athens and Alexandria, of Rome, of Lyons, of Vienne. They were in fact the very same "heathen" or "pagan" or, in other words, Græco-Roman institutions, in which Horace and Juvenal, Jerome and St. Augustine had learnt the scansion of hexameters and the accredited methods of speech-making and argument. To understand the medieval and the modern school, we must therefore know what the Greek and Roman schools, both of classical times and of the so-called Dark Ages, from which they were descended, were like.

CHAPTER II

THE GREEK AND ROMAN MODELS

ANCIENT Greece, the Hellas of the golden age of Athenian ascendancy, knew no organized schools in our sense. There were private tutors in various subjects, music, reading, and gymnastics for boys; peripatetic and migratory lecturers *de omnibus rebus et quibusdam aliis*, physics, law, ethics, divinity, philosophy, not only for youths, but also for men who "in trim gardens took their pleasure," and there found "retired leisure," σχολή, whence *schola* and school, which they devoted to discussion. The organized school was developed in Macedonian Greater Greece, at Alexandria and Pergamus. A Mime of Herondas, called the Master (διδάσκαλος) is the earliest literary picture of a school, *c.* 250 B.C. A mother takes her boy to the grammar school (γραμματεῖον) and asks the schoolmaster to give him a good flogging. He has stripped the very roof off her house by his losses, gambling at odd-and-even and knucklebones, while his writing-tablet lies neglected in a corner, and he says his repetition at the rate of a word a minute. The master, nothing loth, brings out his leather strap. The boy is hoisted on the back of another, with two others to hold his hands and legs, and the strap is applied till the boy is "as mottled as a water-snake," while the mother still cries, "give it him, give it him," and threatens him with gag and fetters. We can hardly imagine the Athenian boy of the age of Pericles and Socrates being thus flogged into the service of the Muses and threatened with the treatment of a slave. But this method became the usual one. The only actual picture that remains to us of an ancient Roman school, a painting now at Naples, reproduces a similar scene.

At Rome, schools began, if not with the study of Greek, at all events as a result of Greek influence. When captive Greece captured Rome, it did so mainly by carrying schools

ATHENIAN GRAMMAR AND MUSIC SCHOOLS. SIXTH CENTURY B.C.

FROM A KULIX, BERLIN MUSEUM

into the conquering city. Plutarch attributes the first schools in Rome to an innovator in moral as in intellectual matters, Spurius Carvilius, and his Greek freedman, in the year 260 B.C. Suetonius, *c.* 121, 'attributes them to Livius Andronicus and Ennius, the first Roman poet, both of them Greek freedmen, in 204 B.C., and to Crates of Mallos, a Greek ambassador from Pergamus in 157 B.C., who, having broken his leg by falling into a hole in a drain, stayed in Rome, and set up a school. At first, says Suetonius, the grammar school masters were called *literati*, a translation of the Greek *grammatici*, which word superseded it. Oddly enough, the term *ludus literarius*, grammar school, is used by Plautus in one of his plays, which were of course translated from the Greek, a century or two before the word *schola grammatica*, of which it is a translation, is found, though probably in ordinary talk grammar school was always used then as it certainly was from the first to the nineteenth century. According to Suetonius, at first the same masters taught both grammar and rhetoric; but these subjects were afterwards taught in distinct schools. The grammar school's proper function was considered to be teaching and explaining the poets, while the historians and orators were left for the rhetoric school. But in Quintilian's day, *c.* A.D. 90, the grammar school had encroached on the rhetoric school, and had taken the exposition of the historians and orators as well as the poets into its curriculum.

We know very little about the Roman schools before Quintilian. But we gather from stray passages of Martial, Horace, and Juvenal that the schools were distinguished by early hours and much flogging. The edification or cult of character, which some modern " Educationists " seem to regard as a new idea for schools, was as much insisted on as the instruction in literature, and was effected by beginning school at dawn and shouting at and flogging the boys with the rod or cane (*ferula*), the tawse (*scutica*), and the birch (*flagellum*), very much as in the English schools down to 1850. In the Greek grammar schools, Homer, and in the Latin grammar schools, Virgil, were the supreme authors studied; but Horace and Claudian became classics and entered the schools while they were still alive. Quintilian's Institutes of Oratory or Rhetoric, written about A.D. 90, is a detailed treatise on educational

theory and practice.   Like all Latin literary efforts, it is
founded on Greek originals.   Eratosthenes, he says, maintained that boys should not be taught at all before seven
years old, but Quintilian decides with Chrysippus that they
should begin at three years old, if learning is made pleasant.
He recommends for teaching reading the ivory letter game.
Writing was to be learnt by going over with the stilus letters
ready engraved on the wax tablet.   A quick and good hand-
writing, which was apt to be despised and neglected by gentlemen (*honestis*), should be early cultivated.   Moral sentences
should be used as copies, that the boy may imbibe morals
insensibly.   When boys are set to serious learning, the question at once arises, " Are boys better taught at home or in
schools ? "   The objections to schools are chiefly on the score
of morals, but an immoral private tutor or bad parents are
worse.   " And boys take vice to school from home, they do
not bring it home from school."   Moreover, as the orator has
to live a public life, he must not be brought up alone, when he
would lose the " almost sacred friendships of school," and the
common sense learnt by mixing with his equals.   Quintilian
decides therefore in favour of the public schools.

The first was the grammar school under the *grammaticus*.
This school should be not too large and not too small.
How many boys were too few or too many we are not told.
Classes are mentioned, but as to how many classes there were
and how many in a class, no indication is given.   An usher is
contemplated, but other assistant masters seem unknown.   It
is certain that an Eton of 1000 boys never entered the dreams
of Greek or Roman.   We may safely fix 100 as the upward
limit of a school.

Grammar teaching Quintilian divides into two parts, the
science of correct speech and the explanation of the poets,
though it should not be confined to poets.   The former includes
also correct writing, and the latter correct editing of MSS.
A grammar schoolmaster must know music, since he has to
teach metre, besides philology and grammar; astronomy
and philosophy, as he has to explain Empedocles and Lucre-
tius; and must have no small knowledge of rhetoric since he
has to explain everything fully and clearly.   " Grammar," he
says, " is a necessity to boys, a pleasure to their elders, an

agreeable companion in retirement, and is the only branch of study which is of more use than show." Grammar schools, Quintilian complains, then encroached on the rhetoric schools. The rhetoricians would not teach anything but forensic or parliamentary speaking (*deliberativas judicialesve materias*), leaving to the grammarians speaking in fictitious characters (*prosopopoias*), as e.g. in that of Hannibal relating the passage of the Alps, and persuasive arguments (*suasorias*), as e.g. whether it is better to follow pleasure or virtue. " So that those old enough for more advanced studies remain at school and learn rhetoric of grammarians, with the absurd result that a boy is not thought fit to go to a master of speech before he has learnt how to speak." Quintilian fixes no age at which boys should leave the grammar school for the school of rhetoric ; except " when they are fit ". While, however, he complains that the grammar school overlaps the rhetoric school, he would have the rhetorician trench on the grammarian's province, and, restricting the latter to the explanation of the poets, begin with reading the historians and the orators. These recommendations, however, certainly did not prevail, and the historians and orators were read in grammar schools, and rhetoric and declamations practised in them at Rome and afterwards throughout Christendom till at least the eighteenth century. In another general practice, which Quintilian wished to change, he was equally unsuccessful. Though Chrysippus had approved, he strongly disapproves of corporal punishment, as fit only for slaves, and tending to harden, not to reform. " Besides," he asks, " after you have driven the boy by flogging, what will you do with him as a young man, when you cannot hold this over him, though his tasks are more difficult ? "—a question which our ancestors answered by the very simple method of extending the rule of the rod to the University as well as to the school.

The rhetoric school, except for the very select few, like Cicero or Quintilian himself, who went to what is sometimes called the University of Athens, seems to have performed for the upper classes the function of the Secondary School and University, as well as that of the Inns of Court and Theological Colleges. The one aim of Roman education was to fit a boy for public life, as advocate or

2

statesman, and generally both, and this was done by training him for public speaking.   Besides the foundation of
grammar, in its wide sense, Quintilian would have every bud-
ding orator learn mathematics, including geometry, from the
mathematician, music from the musician, and the art of
gesticulation from the actor.   For these last items he is only
repeating Greek formulæ and does not represent actual Roman
practice.

The rhetoric school itself laid down formal rules for the
construction of speeches, and an analysis of the figures of
speech, which strikes the modern as pedantic to the last
degree.   The over-subtle Greek mind, in its analysis of
oratory as of philosophy, ran into precisely the same sort of
excesses as the medieval mind did in the analysis of theology.
In fact, the Greek rhetorician was the intellectual father of
the Oxford schoolman.   In the rhetoric school, the boys at once
began to practise public speaking.   They began with narration,
i.e. stating a case in the best way and language possible ;
then proceeding to speeches in supporting or attacking the
statement (ἀνασκευή or κατασκευή).   The examples given
are of a puerile kind, e.g. whether the stories of the wolf of
Romulus and the Egeria of Numa are true.   Next followed
panegyrics or censures ; and contrasts, e.g. whether Alexander
or Cæsar were the greater man.   Plutarch's " Lives " is one
of the results of such exercises.   Then commonplaces (com-
munes loci), declamations against gaming or adultery, gener-
alities to be used in particular cases of attack against e.g.
Clodius or Milo.   Next, theses, e.g. is town or country life
better ? is a successful lawyer or a successful soldier the greater
man?   " Conjectural causes " followed.   " Why the Lacede-
monians represented Venus armed? "   " Why Cupid carried
arrows and a torch?"   Lastly, preparatory to the Senate, the
praise and blame of laws, i.e. speeches on the model of a
minister introducing a bill or moving to repeal an act; and
trying fictitious cases, preparatory for the Courts.

It is clear from Quintilian that in his time the schools of
rhetoric had got very far from life.   Declamations were still
modelled on Demosthenes and Cicero, though, from the loss
of constitutional liberty, such subjects as the praise of tyran-
nicides and the *laus et interpretatio legum* had become empty
verbiage.   As Seneca said, "We learn for the schools, not for

life ".   Rounded periods, far-fetched conceits and out-of-the-way expressions gained applause in the schools, but they tended to destroy real oratory and hastened rather than hindered the decadence of public life.

It is in the age of Quintilian that we first find private persons endowing schools and founding exhibitions.   The younger Pliny, A.D. 97-108, in a letter to a friend, sending him a copy of a speech he made to his fellow-citizens of Como on giving them a public library, incidentally mentions that, instead of a gladiatorial show, he had established exhibitions (*annuos sumptus in alimenta ingenuorum pollicebamur*), since to make any one willingly undergo the tedium and labour of education, not only premiums, but endowments were required.

The institution of both grammar and rhetoric schools becomes more organized and more widespread in every generation.   Vespasian, A.D. 69-79, was the author of a system of endowed schools, being, according to Suetonius, "the first to endow Latin and Greek rhetoricians with a stipend of 100,000 sesterces " [= £800, says Mr. A. S. Wilkins in his *Roman Education*].   Antoninus Pius, A.D. 140-162, extended the system beyond Italy and "bestowed honours and stipends on rhetoricians and philosophers in every province".   Hadrian, A.D. 117-138, had established an Athenæum including public grammar school buildings.   Alexander Severus, A.D. 195-212, "established (*instituit*) salaries for rhetoricians, provided school halls for them (*auditoria decrevit*), and a system of exhibitions for the sons of poor men, if free-born (*discipulos cum annonis pauperum filios modo ingenuos dari jussit*)," a limitation which, whether through conscious imitation or mere coincidence of circumstance, was reproduced as to the qualification for fellowships at All Souls and scholarships at Eton in the reign of Henry VI.   Constantius Chlorus, A.D. 305-306, with vicarious liberality, ordered the municipality of Augustodunum (*Autun*) to pay Eumenius, the master of the rhetoric school, from the public funds a salary of 600,000 sesterces (£4800 a year).   The Christian Emperor Constantine in A.D. 321 relieved grammar schoolmasters and other professors (*professores*) from military and municipal service, while leaving them open to accept municipal honours, "so that they may more readily enter numerous pupils in liberal studies ".

The anti-Christian Emperor Julian, in A.D. 362, forbade school-masters to teach except under decrees of the municipal councils, "and that higher honour may accrue to the city schools," directed that these decrees should be submitted for imperial confirmation.   This, it has been conjectured, was with a view to preventing the appointment of Christians.   According to Augustine and others, he also by edict prohibited Christians from teaching in the schools ; but as there is no record of any such edict forthcoming, this accusation must be received with the caution due to all the statements made by early Christian apologists about their opponents.   It is more probable that the centralizing edict was only to prevent town councils from appointing local favourites to the exclusion of better men from outside, and from cutting down salaries. For the Christian Emperor Gratian, in A.D. 376, went even further in extending the interference of the central authority, charging the Prætorian Prefect of Gaul that "in all towns which are called metropolis," equivalent in modern parlance to county boroughs, "notable professors should be elected," and paid according to a scale of salaries laid down, viz. masters of rhetoric schools, twenty-four annonæ, and masters of grammar schools, Greek and Latin, twelve annonæ.   An *annona* was the yearly pay of an ordinary soldier or day labourer, so that the grammar schoolmaster was reckoned as worth twelve times, and the rhetorician twenty-four times an ordinary man.   So that if £52 a year was the pay of a working man, the schoolmaster received £624 or £1248 a year.   In Trier, or Trèves, then the capital of the Western Empire, the rhetoric master was to draw 30 annonæ, the Latin grammar schoolmaster 20, and the Greek grammar schoolmaster, "if a fit one can be gotten," 12 annonæ ; a striking piece of evidence of the tendency to the disappearance of Greek from the schools of Northern and Western Europe, as the like words used by Colet in the statutes of his reformed St. Paul's School in 1518 are to its reappearance.   In A.D. 414 Honorius and Theodosius extended the privileges of grammar masters, rhetoric masters, and philosophy preceptors, to their wives and children, their sons even being exempt from military service.

In the later Roman Empire endowed grammar and rhetoric schools were ubiquitous.   The lives and writings of the

GREEK GRAMMAR SCHOOL MASTER OF CAPUA WITH WIFE AND SON
(NOT, AS COMMONLY SAID, BOY AND GIRL PUPILS)
IN NAPLES MUSEUM

chief and earliest Latin "doctor," whom the Middle Ages worshipped, St. Augustine of Hippo, and his contemporary the Christian poet Ausonius, may suffice by way of sample.

Augustine was born at Tagaste in Numidia, on the north coast of Africa, on 13 November, 354, of a Christian mother and a still heathen father. Though he was "seasoned with salt," i.e. made a catechumen, a ceremony practically equivalent to our infant baptism—baptism being delayed till at least the age of thirty—he attended the elementary school, the grammar school, and the school of rhetoric just in the same way, and learnt the same things, as the "heathen" Juvenal or Quintilian had done. He tells us (*Confessions*, I, ix. 14) what miseries he endured when obedience to teachers was set before him that he might flourish in the world and distinguish himself in eloquence and gain wealth and honours. "I was put to school to get learning of which I knew not what use there was ; and yet, if slow to learn I was flogged. For this was deemed praise-worthy by our forefathers. Many before us, passing through the same course, had appointed these troublesome ways, multiplying labour and sorrow upon the sons of Adam." His faith indeed was shaken, because he prayed to God to escape a flogging, yet flogged he was. He played too much at games of ball, loving the pride of winning, was eager for the shows and sports of his elders, and, as he did not want to learn, he learnt badly. "I have never," he says, "thoroughly under-stood why I hated Greek literature in which I was dipped as a little boy. For I liked Latin, not indeed that which the preparatory masters taught me (*quas primi magistri*), but that which those who are called grammarians (*grammatici*) teach. For as to the primary instruction, in which reading, writing, and arithmetic are learnt, I thought it no less of a burden and a punishment than the whole of Greek." Yet now he would rather forget the wanderings of Æneas or the death of Dido which he wept over than the more certain learning of reading and writing. "But though a veil hangs over the entrance of the grammar school (*gramaticarum scolarum*), yet it is rather a covering of error than the honour due to a mystery." But still "one and one are two and two and two are four was a hateful sing-song," while "the wooden horse, the burning Troy, and the shade of Creusa were a charming vision ". He

concludes with rather obvious good sense that he hated Homer
for the same reason as he supposes a Greek boy would have
hated Virgil.   Latin being his mother-tongue he had learnt it
naturally and without trouble, but Greek was dinned into him
with difficulty and with fierce threats and punishments.   Greek
he therefore never learnt properly, he could not understand
the Greek fathers on the Trinity, and falls into some strange
mistakes over the New Testament in consequence (*Sources
of the De Civitate Dei*, 1906).   Augustine abuses Homer, as
Plato did, for the immoral behaviour of his gods, and he comments on dropping the *h* in human as being considered a worse
crime than hating humans.   On leaving the elementary school
at Tagaste, Augustine went to Madaura to learn grammar and
rhetoric, and at sixteen had a year's holiday, while his father
was saving up to send him to what we may call Carthage
University.   Here he stayed three years ; was head of the
school of rhetoric (*major in schola rhetoris*) and a member of
a band of students called *Eversores*, upsetters, apparently as
turning everything upside down.   Reading Cicero's *Horten-
sius* converted him to philosophy and the love of God.   From
nineteen to twenty-eight he himself taught rhetoric and " sold
victorious eloquence for money," first at Tagaste, then at Carthage.   He wrote a book on *The Beautiful and the Fitting*, and
dedicated it to Hierius, an orator of Rome who, though a Greek,
had become a celebrated speaker in Latin.   Augustine left
Carthage for Rome, partly for better pay, partly because he
heard that the Roman students were kept in better order, and
did not break in on the lectures and insult the lecturer.   But
when he found that the Roman students used to combine together to evade payment of fees, he accepted an invitation from
the prefect of Milan to a public school of rhetoric there.   His
fellow-townsman and friend, Nebridius, while studying philosophy, acted as assistant-master in the Grammar School to
Verecundus, a citizen of Milan.   Augustine finally " found
salvation," partly under the influence of Simplicianus, who had
converted Ambrose himself, then bishop of Milan, partly because he developed a disease of the lungs which made continuous speaking painful.   Moreover, at this moment, Victorinus,
who was a famous rhetoric teacher at Rome, and had been
decreed a statue in the Forum, publicly professed himself a

Christian.   So in 387, at the age of thirty-three, Augustine
was baptized.   At the end of the next vintage vacation (*vin-
demiales ferias*) he gave up his school, or, as he puts it, "with-
drew the service of his tongue from the talk-market, that boys
might no longer buy, not God's law and God's peace, but lies
and tricks for the war in the courts, and arms for their fury,
from his mouth ".   He then betook himself to theological
controversy and shortly became a bishop.   But even as a
bishop, in his latest work written in 427, *On Christian Teaching*, Book iv. while repudiating any intention of "giving the
rules of rhetoric as he had learnt and taught them in secular
lecture rooms," he defends the art of rhetoric as one "to be
learnt at the right and proper time of life," i.e. boyhood.   " It
is enough that boys should give attention to it."   In the earlier
part of the same work, written, it is said, some twenty years
earlier (ii. 39-42), he says that dialectic, i.e. logic, is indispensable "because it runs like a system of nerves through the whole
body of scriptures," and "all branches of heathen learning,"
and, while containing much superstition, "contains also liberal
instruction adapted to the use of the truth ".   He cites Lactantius, Victorinus, Cyprian, and others who were "laden with
the spoils of the heathen, while Moses himself was learned in
all the wisdom of the Egyptians".   The reasoned defence of
learning in this book was one of the main influences which
prevented the monastic *furore* which attacked all learning, as
it attacked marriage and other institutions of civilization, from
converting the darkness of the Dark Ages into absolute black-
ness.

Of the same generation as Augustine, on the opposite
shore of the Mediterranean, lived Ausonius, another provincial
schoolmaster, who found his way to Rome in the higher sphere
of an imperial official.   Born near Bordeaux, with a patrimony
of 1050 acres, he was educated in the grammar and rhetoric
school at Toulouse, of which his uncle was master.   He himself became grammar schoolmaster at Bordeaux, and was public
orator of the city before becoming prefect, first of Illyria, then
of Gaul.   When he retired in his old age to his paternal inheritance, he addressed a poem to his grandson and namesake,
telling him not to be afraid of his schoolmaster and to like his
Virgil and Horace ; his Terence and Sallust ; Homer and

Menander ; and holds before his eyes " the rewards of learning, the seat in court, the purple-bordered robe, the consulship ". One of his poems is a commemoration of the Bordeaux masters. His own had been Tiberius Victor Minerius, who had taught at Constantinople and Rome before settling at Bordeaux, whence he had sent 1000 youths into the Forum, i.e. into business, and 2000 to the Senate, i.e. public life.   Ausonius mentions six successors, one of whom had been his fellow-pupil ; another was the scion of an ancient Druid family at Bayeux. He commemorates also Leontius and three other Greek grammar masters and six Latin grammar masters.   Of the former, Annaeus Sperchius had taught at Corinth and Menestheus at Athens, while Citharius, who had come from Syracuse and was "another Simonides," made a good marriage in Bordeaux, but died young.   Of the Latin grammar masters, Macrinus, Ausonius' own teacher, was a man of low family, place, and merit, but sober and useful for boys.   Phœbicius had come from Armorica (Brittany), while Sucuro, a Bordeaux boy, had taught a grammar school at Poitou ; and, though his learning was inferior and his manners unpleasing, Ausonius could not leave him out.   Besides these, Ausonius commemorates his uncle Arborius, who taught rhetoric at Toulouse, and while still young, had a noble and well-endowed wife, house, school, and the friendship of princes, the brothers of Constantine, with whom he went to Constantinople and died there rich, his body being sent by the Emperor for burial at Bordeaux.   Next, Ausonius celebrates Exuperius, whom Toulouse first venerated, then dismissed, who at Narbonne taught for large fees two future emperors, and was made by them prefect of Spain. Marcellus, another Burgundian grammar master at Narbonne, was making a fortune when his own misbehaviour robbed him of everything ; while a third who had fled, owing to a Don Juan exploit, from Bordeaux, married and made a fortune as a teacher of rhetoric at Lerida (Ilerda) in Spain.   Nor does Ausonius omit to mention his two elementary teachers, Crispus and Urbicus, who taught both Latin and Greek, or even the usher (*subdoctor sive proscholus*) Victorius, who was keener as an antiquary than as a *littérateur*, and knew ancient law and history better than his Virgil.

   It was while Augustine and Ausonius flourished that

Roman Britain was becoming England and the Roman schools and Christianity were disappearing. After the defeat in Italy of the last Roman Emperor " made in Britain," in 410, the Saxons or English poured over the land, and by the middle of the fifth century the Romanized Britons were exterminated or driven out of the whole of the east, south, and midlands, and their towns burnt or abandoned. So far as the Anglicized portion of the island was concerned, Roman civilization was swept away ; Christianity and the Latin language disappeared, and heathen English lived in their place. Attempts have been, and are still, made from time to time to prove that Roman institutions and even schools remained, but they invariably break down from lack of facts to support them. As the result of the latest scientific investigation of the history of the English conquest of England, Professor Oman, assisted by Professor Haverfield, the chief authority on Roman Britain, writes in *England before the Norman Conquest:* " The invaders . . . had well-nigh exterminated the earlier Christian inhabitants. . . . The English had from the first spared a certain number of the conquered Britons. . . . But it is certain that they were but a remnant and exercised no influence on their masters ; it is not even clear that they preserved their Christianity."

Meanwhile on the Continent in spite of barbarian invasions the schools continued.

In the succeeding age, born in 431, the year after St. Augustine's death, on the other side of the Mediterranean, St. Sidonius Apollinaris flourished as grammar schoolmaster, imperial official, writer of *vers de société* and bishop. He was educated in Lyons Grammar School (*Carmina*, xx. 1) with his fellow-poet Avitus, who became prefect of Arles, and for a short year Emperor of the West. Among his epistles are two addressed to the masters of the rhetoric schools of Vienne and Perigueux respectively (*Ep.* v. 10; viii. 11), the latter written in 483. A letter to his son at school at Lyons warns him, very much as a modern father might, against taking part in loose talk.

In the generation following Augustine, Sedulius, recognized as a Christian poet in a decree of Pope Gelasius in 496, and specially recommended by Colet for St. Paul's School in

1518, was a teacher of philosophy in Italy, before he wrote his Easter Song (*Carmen Paschale*), under Theodosius and Valentinian, 450-5. Dracontius, who calls himself pupil of the grammarian Felicianus, "who had restored letters to Carthage," wrote a sacred poem in good hexameters, "De laudibus Dei," in 484-96, which bear evident traces of the school of rhetoric (Teuffel, *Roman Literature*, 1900, ii. 508); while a MS. Codex Salmasianus preserves poems of a schoolmaster (*scholasticus*) named Coronatus, who wrote under the Vandal king Hilderic at the same place. Under Theodoric the Ostrogoth, King of Italy 493-526, there is abundant evidence that the study of classics continued, though Latin was dying out as a vernacular language and becoming more and more a merely literary vehicle. It is sufficient to mention Boethius, the dominant author of the Middle Ages, partly because of his *Consolations of Philosophy*, partly because of his school books on Aristotle. The special work on school training attributed to him during the Middle Ages, *De disciplina Scolarium*, is easily detected as the product of at least six centuries later, since it is full of stories about life in the University of Paris. Striking testimony to the continuance of education in grammar schools is found in the works of Ennodius, a native of Gaul, Bishop of Ticinum (Pavia), 513-21, in which are preserved twenty-eight speeches (*dictiones*), composed in and for the school of rhetoric. Some seven of them relate to actual episodes in the school of Deuterius at Milan; including one on the removal of the school into new quarters, which had been a law court in the Forum. A chance phrase, torn from the context, "I now detest the very name of liberal studies," has been misinterpreted by Dr. Sandys and others to mean that, as bishop, Ennodius repudiated the classics, and the inference has been drawn that the whole Church did so. But the phrase ends a letter to Arator, the future poet, who turned the Acts of the Apostles into hexameters, advising him not to give up without long consideration the life of a man of the world for that of learning. It only expresses that which all scholars have at times felt, like Faust, their own weariness of the literary life. That Ennodius did not as bishop repudiate the classics is obvious from one of his speeches made on the admission of this same Arator to the school, when in a

Incipit .i. inchoat t inıtıum sumıt · Instaratio .i.
Inuentio t infoꝑmatio · Statio inde componitur
instatıo · erudio · Transıt inparticipium instatu
cur instatura · doiecta · o · fit instatutio · hinc et insta
tutionum · liber uocatur · quı talıam ubi docet quomodo
prepı instituendi sunt · Prisciani ꝓꝓ nomē ductoris
isrius libelli · gramatici nomen est offıcıı · Caesariensis
dr acesarea capodocie regionis · Tres sunt cesaree ·
ex nomine cesaris dictę uidelicet una est · palestine
regionis altera philippi · quam edificauit ipse philip
pur · suo que nomine et imparatorıs · imponunt e inoī
ut cesarea philippi · Tertia capodocie · dequa ır teo dr
Cesariensis · Inde enim oriundus fuit et ibi multo
tempore docuit · posdea ut quidam essequnt pome
puro · uel secundum ıohannem scotu cesariensis dr·
.i. regalis · ꝓꝑter dignıtatē · Quattuor · inhoc loco peꝗ
penda sunt locus ꝑsona tempur et causa scribendi ·
Locus ꝓma per sona ꝑcianus · temꝑ sub iuliano
confule · Caura scribendi adinstituendos pueros · Nam·
ꝓꝑt magnum suum opus · hunc composuit libellum · ut
pueros erudiret · dehis tamen tribʒ partibʒ quia in his
difficalioꝑ inueniuntur questiones t quia ꝓcasus

＿Ƒ＿

somewhat similar spirit he contrasts the work of the school-master "who possesses and draws water from the Castalian spring itself," with his own dry work as a preacher, " shut into a corner of the Church". When Arator won a school prize, the learned Bishop delivered another speech in praise of classical literature, in which he indulges in the usual exaggeration, such as Cicero, imitating the Greeks, bestowed on it in his speech *Pro Archia*, and Richard of Bury in his *Polybiblion*, and modern plagiarists have bestowed on the "hundred best books". Ennodius testifies clearly enough that the Christian bishop of the sixth century was not necessarily opposed to classical learning nor the Christian Church to grammar schools.

It is perhaps no proof of the continuance of schools in Western Europe that the Eastern capital, Constantinople, in the first quarter of the sixth century saw the composition of the chief of all Latin grammars, that of Priscian, who, as Cassiodorus says, "was in our time a teacher at Constantinople". It is in fact mainly a translation of the Greek Apollonios and of the commentary of Dionysius Thrax. But its composition, and its subsequent ascendancy throughout the Middle Ages, testified by the existence of over 1000 MSS., sufficiently show that there were grammar schools creating a demand for Latin grammars, even on the largest scale.

At the opposite end of the Roman world, Virgilius Maro, a grammarian of Toulouse, who wrote, it must be admitted, in a fantastic and almost unintelligible style, introducing from Greek new words and misapplying old ones, like some of the word-torturing writers of our own day, is nevertheless a sufficient witness of the continuance of the public schools in the West at the beginning of the next, the sixth century. In an amusing discussion, which, according to him, lasted fourteen days and nights between Galbungus and Terentius as to whether the pronoun *Ego*, " I," can be used in the vocative case, he shows a keen wit, sharpened by dialectic ; nor is the point discussed more minute or trivial than some of those of our modern scientific grammarians. Virgilius mentions his own master Æneas and several other grammar masters, though it is probable that most of them and their discussions are mere *jeux d'esprit.*   He tells us that libraries were then divided into two parts, classical and Christian.

At Rome, between 526 and 534, we have striking evidence of the care with which the grammar schools were looked after by the State, even under the barbarian invaders, in a letter written by Cassiodorus (*Var.* ix. 20) in the name of Athalaric, son of Theodoric, " King of the Goths and Romans," to the Senate. After an eloquent exposition of the claims of the grammar school as " the fairest foundation of literature, the glorious mother of eloquence," and grammar as " the mistress of words, the tiring-maid of the human race . . . the special possession of the lords of Rome, unknown to barbarian kings," he requests the Senate to see that when one master succeeds another, there is no delay in the payment of his stipend to the new man, and that it is regularly paid half-yearly.   For " if," he says, " the royal wealth is bestowed on actors for the public enjoyment, and they, who are not necessary, obtain their pay with exact punctuality, how much more ought those to receive it without delay who produce good conduct, and nourish intelligence for the benefit of the empire ".

Venantius Fortunatus, born at Treviso, who settled at Tours under the protection of Gregory of Tours, its bishop, and wrote about 570 a life of St. Martin of Tours in three books of hexameters, tells us how he had been educated in the grammar and rhetoric schools ; " he had imbibed the rills of grammar and drunk from the deep pools of rhetoric ".   In a preface to Pope Gregory, quoting the Greek rhetorical terms in Greek letters, he prays pardon for any metrical blunders ; not without reason, as he makes the first syllables of *initium* and *adhuc* long.   Of Gregory the Great himself, Gregory of Tours says that he was " so well grounded in grammar, logic, and rhetoric that no one in Rome was considered even second to him," which must mean that he had attended a public grammar school and rhetoric school.   For whenever, as in the case of some of the bishops, whose lives Fortunatus wrote, one was brought up in a monastery it is specially recorded. For by this time the monasteries, which at first were peopled with those who had, like St. Augustine, fled from the world after having exhausted all its pleasures, were beginning to be recruited from boys brought up in them from infancy.   But the monasteries did not then, nor, as will be seen, except for a very few years in the Carlovingian period, keep public schools for general education.

The time was, however, one of transition. It was the era in which the schools were passing from secular to ecclesiastical control. Gregory of Tours himself is the first eminent literary man who is recorded as having received his education, not in a public school but from two bishops of Clermont, Galens and Avitus. His Latin was defective in consequence, and his knowledge of the classics confined to Virgil and Sallust. "St." Lubin, who became Bishop of Chartres in 544, was, according to a life nearly contemporary "an agreeable teacher," and taught and superintended the teaching of his successor Calétric ; while it is recorded in set terms of Béthaire that, though a Roman born in Italy, he came to Chartres to be taught by Bishop Pappol, who *c.* 573 proclaimed him "teacher of divinity and (school) master of that whole city". He became bishop himself in 594. So of Launomaurus, St. Lomer, afterwards Abbot of Courgeon, *c.* 550, it is stated that his parents "had handed him to a certain venerable priest, Chirmir, to be imbued with sacred literature and morals". In a letter written in 595 Pope Gregory rates Desiderius, "Bishop of Gaul" at Vienne (*Ep.* xi. 54), because "as we cannot relate without shame, it has come to our knowledge that your brotherhood teaches grammar to certain persons : which we take all the worse as it converts what we formerly said to lamentation and mourning, since the praise of Christ cannot lie in one mouth with the praise of Jupiter. Consider yourself what a crime it is for bishops to recite what would be improper for a religiously minded layman". If, he says, it afterwards appears that he has not been employed on trifles and secular literature, so much the better. Part of this sentence is an adaptation of Jerome at his worst, but it is valuable as showing that even in the Christian grammar schools the old curriculum was retained and boys were still brought up on Virgil's *Eclogues*. For the words are a distinct reference to the line *Ab Jove principium, Musae, Jovis omnia plena*, and the loves of Corydon and Alexis.

This letter has been sometimes interpreted as showing that Gregory was wholly opposed to learning. But this interpretation is inconsistent with his own writings and acts.   What he objected to was not the teaching of school generally, but its being taught by the bishop, whose business was prayer, psalm-singing, and preaching, not teaching.   Gregory always recognized the necessity of classical study for the young.   But he did not think it should be mixed with religious instruction in those charged with the care of the Church.   This letter is the more remarkable because, at the end, it becomes a letter of introduction for the second batch of missionaries to the English, clerks and monks, whom Gregory was sending with Laurence the priest and Mellitus the abbot to Augustine of Canterbury, thus bringing us into direct connexion with the conversion of the English and the foundation of the first English school, already recorded.

CHAPTER III

THEODORE OF TARSUS AND ALDHELM OF WINCHESTER

IT is an ill wind that blows nobody any good. By a curious chance, it is to the first great recorded outbreak in Europe of the bubonic plague that England owes the name most famous in the history of its early schools, that of the Greek Archbishop, Theodore of Tarsus; just as to the second and third great outbreaks, the Black Death and the Secunda Pestis of 1349 and 1361, it owes its most famous "Public" School, Winchester College. After the death of Archbishop Deusdedit, the first native English archbishop, in 664, Wighard, "a good man and a fit priest," was nominated by the Kings of Kent and Northumberland as his successor and sent to Rome for consecration. There the plague caught and carried off him and all his party. So the Pope first offered the vacant post to Hadrian, an African, a monk in the Niridane monastery near Naples, "brought up alike in monastic and ecclesiastical learning"—a distinction all important in the early history of schools—"and of the greatest skill in both the Greek and Latin tongues". Greek was no doubt still the vernacular of the towns of Southern Italy. Hadrian modestly declined the office, and suggested first a monk of a neighbouring monastery, who proved to be too fat, and then "a native of Tarsus in Cilicia, named Theodorus, a man instructed both in secular and divine literature, Greek and Latin, and of venerable age"—he was already sixty-six years old—who accepted the office. By an odd coincidence of name, this Greek Deusdedit, this foreigner, who would nowadays be superannuated from the Civil Service and from the mastership of any public school, proved one of the most active archbishops who ever sat on the throne of Canterbury. Theodore being a Greek, the Pope was rather suspicious of his orthodoxy and insisted on Hadrian's going to look after him "lest after the manner of Greeks he should introduce something against the true faith in the Church over which he was to preside". Theodore arrived at Canterbury on 27 May, 669, with the English Benedict Biscop, whom he made Abbot of St. Paul's, afterwards known as St. Augustine's monastery, close to the cathedral but outside the walls of the city. Hadrian arrived a year later and took over this abbey from Benedict, who became a monastic founder in the North. "Soon afterwards," runs one of the most famous passages in Bede's *History*, Theodore "travelled through the whole island wherever the English races were settled, and spread abroad the right rule of life, the canonical mode of celebrating Easter, Hadrian going with him and working with him in everything. And he was the first archbishop whom the whole English Church consented to obey. . . . And because both were abundantly learned in sacred and profane literature, they collected crowds of disciples, and streams of saving knowledge daily flowed from them to irrigate their hearts, as together with holy writ they gave to their hearers instruction both in the arts of metre and astronomy and ecclesiastical arithmetic. The proof is that even to this day," Bede wrote about 731, "some of their pupils survive, who know Latin and Greek as well as their own language in which they were born". Bede descants on the happiness of those times, when "Christian kings were a terror to barbarians," and "whoever wanted to be instructed in holy lessons had masters at hand to teach them". Further, "they spread the knowledge of the tones of musical singing in Church, which till then they had known only in Kent," a Kentish precentor Edsi being imported by Wilfrid to Northumbria to teach it. This is a lapse on Bede's part, as he had previously told us that Deacon James had taught it forty years before.

It is strange that this account of what, in later times, would have been called Theodore's metropolitical visitation of all England, should have been quoted as evidence of his founding of Canterbury School. Yet the passage, which has nothing to do with Canterbury at all, is absolutely the sole foundation on which the claim of Theodore to be its founder is based. In the course of their progress about the country the two not only preached theology but taught the art of metre, so that the theologians might not make false quantities in reading the lessons and chanting the psalms. By the ecclesiastical arithmetic which they taught was meant the way to construct and use a proper calendar, so that the English might not, like the British Church, be guilty of the heretical practice of celebrating Easter, and with it the other movable feasts, at the wrong time, according to the original Jewish and Greek instead of the later Roman reckoning; a matter which Bede, throughout his ecclesiastical history, treats as of the very first importance. But neither the calendar nor the Gregorian chant can be considered grammar school subjects, nor is a word said about the establishment of any school, except for singing.

As for Canterbury itself, there is indeed indirect evidence that both Theodore and Hadrian taught there. Albinus, who succeeded Hadrian as Abbot of St. Augustine's in 710, is cited as a proof of his (Hadrian's) and Theodore's learning. He was " so well taught in the study of grammar that he knew Greek to no small extent and Latin not less than English, his native tongue ". More specifically, Bede says in his preface that Albinus was his chief authority for all the information he gives about Augustine and Gregory, Albinus having collected all the materials, documentary and traditional, about them then existing in Kent. He " was the most learned man of his time in everything,. having been educated in the church of Canterbury " by Theodore and Hadrian. Similarly, Bede speaks of Tobias, Bishop of Rochester, who died in 726, as being " a most learned man, for he was a pupil of Theodore and Hadrian, and so together with a knowledge of literature, ecclesiastical and general, Greek and Latin were as familiar to him as his native tongue ". This may be accepted as proof that Theodore and Hadrian taught in the school at Canterbury. But to teach in a school is one thing, to found it is another. As Bede had already spoken of Canterbury School as the model and parent for Dunwich in 631, the passages cited can hardly be alleged as evidence of its foundation by Theodore more than forty years later. What they do show is the important fact that the Archbishop himself acted as a teacher in the school which formed then, as in the fourteenth

3

century, an integral part of the foundation of his cathedral church. At the latter date, the archbishop had delegated the actual teaching to others, though still himself appointing the master and acting as its governing body.

In view of the constant confusion between monastic and ecclesiastic learning, it is important to remember that Canterbury Cathedral at this time was not in the hands of the monks, but of the secular, or ordinary, clergy. Augustine himself was a monk, but so exceptional a thing was it at that time for a monk to be made a bishop, that he thought it necessary to send to the Pope for special instructions as to how he, a monk, was to live with his clergy, and his embassy consisted of a secular priest and a monk. The Pope answered that the usual rule was to divide the possessions of the Church into four ; one for the bishop and his household for hospitality and maintenance ; another for the clergy ; a third for the poor ; the fourth for repair of the fabric. But as Augustine was a monk, he should imitate the early Church and live with his clergy, having all things in common. But any clergy, not in holy orders, who married were to have separate incomes provided for them. In fact, the monks were settled by Augustine in the monastery of St. Paul, afterwards known by the founder's own name, outside the walls of Canterbury. Its primary object was to be a mausoleum for the burial of the kings and bishops ; the pernicious practice of burial within the walls of the cities and in the churches themselves not having been introduced, and being indeed expressly forbidden by canon law. Augustine's successor was not a monk but Laurence the priest, who had been one of the special messengers to Gregory. From this time to the eleventh century the cathedral seems to have been entirely served by clerks or secular clergy. Even the monastic historians admit that it was held by secular canons from the year 833 to 1005. When, however, Archbishop Elphege or Alphege was besieged and captured and eventually killed by the Danes in 1011, it is represented that there were monks who came out of the burning cathedral with him and were all murdered. But this seems only an invention of the post-Conquest monastic historian to cover and explain the fact that in 1020 the Church was under a Dean, and therefore secular. Bishop Stubbs maintained that the great favourer of monasticism, Dunstan, did not turn the secular clergy out of his own episcopal see as his contemporary Ethelwold did at Winchester. At what date the monks, who held Canterbury in the time of Lanfranc, were introduced is not known. Eadmer, a monk, who wrote c. 1100, gives an account of the Saxon Cathedral which he remembered as a boy at school before Lanfranc rebuilt it on an enlarged scale. It was on the model of the Roman basilicas, a long pillared hall, and was indeed " that very church which had been built by the Romans as Bede bears witness . . . in imitation of" St. Peter's. West of the middle of the nave were two towers projecting beyond the aisles. The south tower had on its south side the principal door "called by the English of old time and even now 'Suth dure' (South door) and often mentioned by this name in the law books of the ancient kings. For here the Supreme Court of Appeal for the kingdom was held." The North Tower contained the school. "And as in the other tower forensic contests and lay pleas were held, so in this one the youthful brethren were instructed in learning the offices of the Church day and night according to the times and seasons." In Eadmer's day, therefore, it was the monastic school, the school of the novices. But the Tower was not the natural place for a monastic school. The general rule was for the monastic school proper, the school of the novices, to be held in a corner of the cloister; and there are traces of the monastic school at Canterbury as at Westminster in the cloister to this day, in the solitaire boards carved in the seats where the boys used to sit. The school in the North Tower must have been a tradition from the days when the Church was secular and the Tower was used as a public school to which the public had access, not as the private school of the monks. The distinction between the private monastic school of the monasteries and the public clerical school is well marked, as we shall find when we renew the acquaintance of this school in the thirteenth century, outside the monastic precinct and in the town near the archiepiscopal palace.

Meanwhile, for information as to what a cathedral school in Saxon times was, and what it taught in detail, we must wait till we can pass from Canterbury to York, and we must go round by Winchester, Malmesbury, and Worcester on the way.   For in the generation after Theodore, the centre of educational interest is no longer in Kent but in Wessex.

Wessex had been converted to Christianity by a new mission from Rome, quite independent of that of Augustine.   Birinus, a " Roman bishop," as the *Chronicle* calls him, sent out by Pope Honorius and consecrated by the Archbishop of Milan at Genoa, converted King Cynegils and planted his see at the " city called Dorcic," the Oxfordshire Dorchester, in 634.   The usual relapse to Paganism, which appears to have taken place in all the Saxon kingdoms after their first conversion, followed. Wessex fell under the power of the heathen king of the Mercians, Penda.   In 643 Cenwalh became king.   The *Saxon Chronicle* records under that year that he " had (i.e. caused to be) built the church on Winchester," or, as the two early eleventh-century editions of the *Chronicle* put it, built " the old church ".   The later eleventh-century, Canterbury, edition under the year 648, has " here was built (*getimbrod*) the min- ster at Winchester that King Cenwalh had made and con- secrated (*gehalfod*) in St. Peter's name ".   As the original *Chronicle* records that Cenwalh was driven out of Wessex by Penda in 645, and only baptized in East Anglia in 646, and returned to Winchester in 648, the later edition gives probably a correct inference as to the date of the building, as Cenwalh, when he came to the throne, was not a Christian.   The con- version of the " church " of the ninth-century writer into " minster " in the eleventh shows how the word minster, which properly means a monastery, had come to mean any great church.

The Old Minster at Winchester remained a church of secular clergy until 964, when the priests or canons were driven out and replaced by monks.   The remembrance of this distinction is vital to the history of schools.   For it is partly under cover of the confusion caused by the term minster that the modern monastic writers have persistently misrepresented the early schools as held in monasteries, and monks as the chief educators.   The " auld kirk " or the Old Minster at Winchester was called old in later days to distinguish it from Alfred's foundation of the New Minster, consecrated in 903 two years after his death ; which also was a church of secular priests, and not of monks, till 964.   To the year 648 then, the foundation of Winchester Grammar School as part of the foundation of the Old Minster must be imputed.

The bishopric of Wessex was not restored till two years after the building of the Winchester church, and then at Dorchester under Angilbert, a "Gaul" who had "stayed no little time in Ireland to read the Scriptures "—a striking testimony to the continental reputation of that island for theological study. He retired in dudgeon to the bishopric of Paris in 663 when the King, being tired of a bishop who could not talk English, divided the Wessex bishopric and set up a native Englishman, Wini, at Winchester. Wini soon after went to London, and Wessex was left bishopless. When a Wessex bishop reappears in 670, under King Cenwalh, in the person of another " Gaul," Eleutherius or Llothair, nephew of Angilbert, it is at Winchester, not at Dorchester, which had then been permanently annexed to Mercia.

Meanwhile, the first West Saxon school of note has been claimed to have been not at Winchester, but Malmesbury ; in connexion with Aldhelm, equally famous as English singer and Latin poet, who died Bishop of Sherborne in 709. But an attitude of suspicion and scepticism is required as to the life of Aldhelm, especially as told in the unveracious volumes of William of Malmesbury, and the recent romance of Bishop Browne of Bristol, both under the bias of local patriotism. The latter claims Aldhelm as one in whom met the two streams from which English educational institutions and learning flowed, the Roman and the Irish ; as being a pupil both of Abbot Hadrian of Canterbury and of an Irish hermit named Maidulph at Malmesbury. The odd thing is that William of Malmesbury made Aldhelm a pupil of both at once, producing documentary evidence without perceiving the absolute inconsistency of his documents with each other and with his own dates of Aldhelm's life. He makes Aldhelm a pupil of Hadrian on the strength of the fragment of a letter credited to Aldhelm in which he addresses " Adrian" as "the venerated preceptor of my rude infancy ". Now according to William of Malmesbury, Aldhelm, who, as we learn from the unimpeachable evidence of Bede, died in 709, was seventy years old at his death. But Hadrian only arrived in England in 670, when, on Malmesbury's showing, Aldhelm was over thirty years old. Bishop Browne, to get over this difficulty, adopts a suggestion in Dr. Giles' edition of Aldhelm's letters in 1848, that Aldhelm did not refer to his infancy in age but in learning. This explanation savours too much of the theological harmonizer. There is no shadow of a hint in the letter itself that infancy is used metaphorically. Moreover, Bede's silence is absolutely fatal to Aldhelm's instruction by Hadrian. Bede is loud in praise of Aldhelm, who was by far the greatest literary figure of his age, as being a "master of style" and "of wonderful erudition both in the liberal and ecclesiastical writings," i.e. in the classics as well as in the Scriptures. Careful as Bede is in the case of comparatively obscure scholars like Tobias and Albinus of Kent, to record that they were pupils of Theodore and Hadrian, he could hardly have failed to mention it in the case of the far more famous Aldhelm.

Still less could Bede have failed to mention Aldhelm's education if it had been under an Irish hermit. William of Malmesbury's documentary evidence for this is a charter, by which Bishop "Leutherius" of Winchester purports to grant to Aldhelm the priest "land the name of which is Maidulphsbirig . . . in which place from the first flower of infancy and from the very beginning of the rudiments he was brought up in the liberal studies of letters and nourished in the bosom of holy mother Church"—the last words being a mere rhetorical amplification of Bede's words. Careful as Bede was to note the Irish studies of Bishop Angilbert and of Egbert and the Scottish (i.e. Irish) teacher who taught little English boys in Northumbria the monastic rule, it is not likely that he would have left unnoticed this wonderful Irish teacher who, living among the unconquered Britons, taught a scion of the royal house of their mortal enemies, the West Saxons.

The charter cited by William of Malmesbury has every mark of spuriousness, particularly in the excessive amount of information it contains as to the reason for the grant, the education of the grantee, and the exemption of the site granted from episcopal authority, which was no doubt the real object of the forgery: an exemption unknown in England in any genuine charter before the Conquest. Bath Abbey is the first instance of it. It is certain from this and other indications that William of Malmesbury had not the least idea that when

ADHELM AS BISHOP OF SHERBORNE

Aldhelm was an infant, i.e. under seven years old, a boy up to fourteen, and a young man, Malmesbury was in a hostile country.   It was not, accepting Malmesbury's dates, until Aldhelm was nineteen, that West Wiltshire became Saxon territory by the battles of Bradford-on-Avon in 651, and "at the Pens" (at Peonnum) in 658.   The story he tells of this Irish philosopher with a school of Saxon youths about him is therefore simply impossible.

In truth the Irish Maidulph is probably an invention of William of Malmesbury's own pure brain, an eponymous hero evolved out of the place-name of Aldhelm's monastery, as given in Bede, Maildufs town, which much later generations identified with Malmesbury for the sake of getting the famous Aldhelm as their patron saint and founder.

It is impossible to deduce Malmesbury out of Maildufs town.   According to Mr. Plummer it is a mixture of M[ailduf]-Ealdemesbury, so representing the names both of Aldhelm and his teacher; but these and intermediate forms are only found in late editions of the *Chronicle* and spurious charters. According to the episcopal authority of Dr. Browne the place-name reproduces the very terms in which the Irish teacher addressed his pupil, mispronouncing his name, Mo-allem, " my darling-Aldhelm ".   So Malmesbury is " my-darling-Aldhelm's-borough ".   William of Malmesbury tells us that Mailduf was also called Meldum, and so gets Meldumsbury.   The place-name Malmesbury is susceptible of a very obvious derivation : as being the bury or fortified hill of malm.   Malm is a soft friable rock consisting largely of chalky material; and mealm, the Anglo-Saxon spelling of it, appears in Alfred's Orosius with that meaning.   The Ordnance geological survey shows Malmes-bury as the northernmost and culminating point of a narrow streak of "cornbrash," or malm, which lies west of the chalk which forms the greater part of Wilts.   It is one of the class of place-names which are descriptive of the soil of which it is composed, like Claygate, Sandy, Broadchalk, and Marlborough in Wiltshire itself.

There is no more reason to identify Malmesbury with Bede's Maildufs town than there is to identify Boston with Bede's Icanho, Beverley with his Inderawald, or Southwell with his Tiovulfingaceaster.   They are all identifications by ecclesiastics in search of a patron saint several centuries after the Danish destruction of the places mentioned in Bede. We do not even know that Maildufs town was in Wiltshire. That Mailduf is a Celtic name is most probable, but there is nothing to tell us whether the particular Celt who gave his name to the place lived twenty or one hundred or two hundred years before Aldhelm.

Fabricius, who wrote a life of Aldhelm nearly a generation before William of Malmesbury, being a medical man, doctor indeed to Henry I before he became a monk, a less romantic historian, was significantly ignorant of either the African-Kentish or the Irish-Wiltshire teachers. He says that Aldhelm was put by his most Christian father to the holy studies of literature and astonished his teachers by the quickness of his apprehension and the retentiveness of his memory. He makes no attempt to say who the teachers were, though he credits Aldhelm with knowing not only Greek as well as Latin, but also "the Psalms, Solomon's three books, and the Law of Moses in Hebrew". As for the Hebrew *credat Judaeus Apella*. To Bede, Aldhelm's early life was known only in connexion with Winchester. For he says, on the authority of Pecthelm, a West Saxon, who became Bishop of Whithern in Galloway, and was one of Bede's principal informants as to Wessex history, that Aldhelm was with himself "a deacon or monk for a long time under Hedde" (for so he is spelt in the earliest version of the *Chronicle*), bishop of Winchester from 676 to 703, whose miracles Aldhelm and he witnessed. Mr. Plummer, by a very exceptional lapse from accuracy, has mistranslated Bede's *cum successore suo Aldhelmo* in his edition of Bede as meaning that Pecthelm was under Aldhelm as "deacon *and* monk". The "deacon or monk" of Bede was no doubt because Bede's notes were uncertain on the point, and as a monk he wanted to claim Aldhelm as such from his youth. The doubt is almost conclusive that in fact he was a secular. There is a fragment of a letter, which may or may not be genuine, purporting to be addressed to Aldhelm by a certain Scot (*quodam Scoto*), i.e. Irish monk, asking Aldhelm, when abbot, to take him in and teach him, and he bases the request on the ground that he is a foreigner, "because you too were a foreigner in Rome, and moreover were nurtured by a holy man of my race ". If the letter is genuine, it looks as if Aldhelm was taught by the holy Irishman at Rome, or he might well have come in the train of Bishop Angilbert, and have taught Aldhelm at Winchester. It is in connexion with Winchester that we find the long account of Aldhelm's studies, which is the *locus classicus* for English learning at the time. This occurs in a letter addressed to Bishop Hedde, guessed by the editors to be "about 680," though it might just as well belong to any year of Hedde's bishopric. In it Aldhelm pleads his studies as an excuse for not spending the coming Christmas at Winchester "dancing (*tripudians*) in the company of the brethren"—the earliest reference in England to the Christmas high jinks, descended from the Roman Saturnalia, which afterwards became connected with those curious medieval institutions, the Boy-bishop, the Feast of the Ass, and the Lord of Misrule. It has been suggested that the reference to his dancing shows that Aldhelm was still quite a young man. But old men and high dignitaries of the Church did not disdain to take part in these festivities. Though the more puritanical spirits, as early as the twelfth century, thought such customs, as that of the Archbishop of Rheims playing ball in the cathedral with his clerks, better honoured in the breach than in the observance, they lasted till the Reformation ; only to be superseded by interludes and plays presented by the schoolmasters and their scholars.

"For," is Aldhelm's excuse, "no small time must be spent in the pursuit of reading by one who . . . would at the same time explore Roman Law (the Code) to the marrow, and examine all the mysteries of the Roman Lawyers (the Digest) ; and at the same time, what is much more difficult, digest the hundred kinds of metres into prose rules, and explore the mixed modulations of song in the straight path of syllables " —by which he seems to have meant writing Latin verses which would scan. Prosody, with all its terrible Greek technical terms, acephalos, lagaros, catalectic and brachycatalectic and the like, he found especially difficult because there were so few teachers. Aldhelm was also studying mathematics, which oppressed him much as they do the ordinary classical scholar to-day. " The despair of doing sums oppressed my mind so that all the previous labour spent on learning, whose most secret chamber I before believed myself to know, seemed nothing, and to use St. Jerome's expression, I, who before thought myself a past master, began again to be a pupil.   At last an opportunity presented itself, and by the help of God's grace, I grasped, after incessant study, the most difficult content of things, that which lies at the base of reckoning ;—what they call fractions ". He went further than this, into Astronomy, no doubt as expounded by Boethius ; but of this "as to the Zodiac and its twelve signs which circle in the height of heaven I say nothing, lest . . . it should be made to seem cheap and worthless : especially as skill in astrology and the computation of horoscopes needs elaborate explanation from some one more learned than myself."   Bishop Hedde, whom Bede describes as " a good man who exercised the teaching function of a bishop more through his natural love of virtue than through a literary education," must have felt rather relieved at the absence of such a prodigy of learning.   One would like to know where Aldhelm was when he wrote.   The prominence given to Roman law and prosody almost looks as if he was at Rome.

Great student, however, as this letter sufficiently shows Aldhelm to have been, there is no evidence (beyond the doubtful fragment of the begging Irish monk) that he was ever a schoolmaster or teacher at Mailduphstown or anywhere else.   Certainly his works are not of a scholastic but of a theological and literary character.   It would be beyond the scope of this book to follow Aldhelm through his Latin verses on the Praise of Virginity addressed to the lady who rejoiced in the name of Bugge or Bug : or his theological animadversions on the proper time of keeping Easter directed to the Welsh prince Gerontius, whom Newman exploited ; or his clever and witty riddles in Latin verse, which we may read with admiration and pleasure even now.   It may be noted that there is no evidence whatever that he knew Greek—a fact which is almost conclusive against his being a pupil of Hadrian's—all the Greek words used by Aldhelm being taken second-hand from the grammarians or the Latin fathers and ecclesiastical Latin.   On the other hand, he knows his Virgil by heart, and quotes or adapts or imitates him a thousand times.   He also knew at first hand, Ovid, Horace, Juvenal,

A FIFTEENTH CENTURY MASTER OF SHERBORNE SCHOOL.

FROM A MISERICORD IN SHERBORNE CHURCH

Persius, Lucan, Claudian, Terence, and Seneca. He knew all the Christian Latin poets, Ausonius, Sidonius Apollonaris, Prudentius, affecting especially those curious authors who versified the Bible, Sedulius, Juvencus, Avitus, Arator, Proba. His acquaintance with the Latin grammarians, Priscian, Donatus, Servius, the Virgilian commentator, Sergius Pompeius Trogus, Phocas, was extensive, and he was intimate with Isidore of Seville. Cicero, Sallust, and Pliny were perhaps known only at second-hand through Priscian. He was thoroughly at home in the late Latin authors in prose, Sulpicius Severus, Augustine, Orosius, Cassian, and St. Cyprian.

Mr. Wildman in his *History of Sherborne* has claimed Aldhelm as the founder of Sherborne School. Since Aldhelm was, as Bede tells us, the first bishop of that see, established west of the forest of Selwood, by division of the Winchester diocese on Hedde's death in 705, the claim must be pronounced *prima facie* a good one. Sherborne was a college of secular clerks until it ceased to be a cathedral in 1075, when it was converted into an abbey. There is evidence in the fifteenth century of the grammar school being carried on, not in the abbey nor under a monk, but under a secular master, known to us by his munificent subscription to the rebuilding of St. John's Hospital there. The last master before the dissolution became the first master of the Free Grammar School of King Edward VI, which took its place, when, as at St. Albans, it occupied the Lady Chapel of the monastic church for its schoolroom. So a patriotic Sherbornian may well claim its creation by Aldhelm and continued existence from his day to our own, when it again finds itself under a Winchester-bred scholar, Mr. Nowell Smith.

Mercia and the Middle English, under the warlike King Penda, remained heathen long after the rest of England. Only after their conquest by the Northumbrian King Oswy in 665 did the Mercians become Christians, and shared a bishop whom the Middle English had set up two years before in the person of the Scot (Irish) Diuma. He and his successors, including even the English-born, though Scottish-bred, Trumhere, seem to have been wandering missionary monks with no fixed see. Not till 669 was a bishop's see settled at Lichfield under Ceadda, or St. Chad, who lived in a mansion there with a band of seven brethren and a lay-brother, an ex-Court official, who looked after their worldly wants and managed their property.   In 672, one of these brethren, Wynfrid, a clerk, and not a monk, succeeded St. Chad.   From his date we can postulate the establishment of a school in Mercia, and that at Lichfield.   A few years later two more Mercian bishoprics were established, one west of the Severn at Hereford, the first mention of which is the death of its bishop, Putta, in 688, and another about the same time at Worcester for the Huicci, originally a branch of the West Saxons, and part of Wessex. Hereford and Worcester no doubt date their schools from that time.

It is to Oftfor, a pupil of Archbishop Theodore at Canterbury, or his predecessor as bishop, Bosel, that we must assign the credit of establishing education and founding a school at Worcester.   Oftfor was himself a Northern Englishman, a Northumbrian.   Bede records that after he had worked hard in both monasteries of the Abbess Hilda (i.e. at Hartlepool and Streaneshalch, the latter rightly or wrongly afterwards identified with Whitby) in reading and practising the Scriptures, desiring higher work he went to Canterbury to Archbishop Theodore of blessed memory, and having spent some time on sacred reading there, took the pains even to go to Rome, which at that time was thought to require great courage. Returning thence, he went to the province of the Hwicci over which King Osric then presided, and stayed there a long time preaching the word of faith and setting an example of how to live.   Meanwhile, as the prelate of that province, Bosel, was so infirm as to be unable to perform the duties of a bishop, Oftfor was, in 691, unanimously elected bishop in his place. Tatfrid, who had been at the same monastery as Oftfor, and had been elected bishop a little while before Bosel, died before he was consecrated.   From the words " a little while before," Mr. Plummer, in his edition of Bede, argues that the frustrated election of Tatfrid and the erection of the see of Worcester in the person of Bosel could not have been earlier than 685.   As the erection of a bishop's see carried with it the erection of a school, we may therefore date the school from 685, or, if Bosel was already too infirm to start a school, at least from the accession of the travelled and learned pupil of Theodore in 691.

The Cathedral Chapter at Worcester was originally one of secular clergy, as it was everywhere in England as elsewhere, till the monastic movement connected with the names of Dunstan and Oswald at Worcester. The notion put forward by the late Bishop Stubbs in his early days, that there was a double establishment of clerks and monks, has no evidence to support it. It was founded on a general theory wrongly evolved from a misunderstanding of Bede's account of Canterbury, already discussed.

There are indications of considerable learning among this secular clergy in some scanty remnants of early MSS., which Canon J. Maurice Wilson has recently found in the bindings of later MSS. belonging to the later monastic library. They comprise a leaf of the end of St. Matthew's and beginning of St. Mark's gospel in the Vulgate, written in England in the later seventh or early eighth century, some leaves of Jerome's commentary on St. Matthew, written in Spain not later than the middle of the eighth century, a leaf of Gregory's *Pastoral Care* in English writing of the same period, and extracts from Paterius in Italian script, but corrected by an English hand.

CHAPTER IV

THE SCHOOLS OF NORTHUMBRIA: BEDE AND ALCUIN

IN the eighth century the centre of interest in English schools is to be found no longer in the south but in the north. As in the seventh century English learning was embodied in the names of Theodore and Aldhelm, so now it is connected with the names of Bede and Alcuin.

The beginning of education in Northumbria has been often attributed to Bede and of York School itself to Archbishop Egbert. But just as Canterbury School must be attributed to Augustine, and not to Archbishop Theodore, who taught it, so York School must be attributed, not to the later archbishop who taught it, but to Paulinus, the founder and first bishop of the church of York. The continuance of the song school under James the Deacon after Paulinus' flight is indirect testimony to the fact that Paulinus had established both grammar and song schools there, and to the revival also of the grammar school with the return of Christianity. The learned and Romanizing Wilfrid is not likely to have neglected the grammar school any more than the song school. In regard to the latter, we learn from Eddi, whose Christian name was Stephen, that on Wilfrid's return to Yorkshire from Canterbury, where he acted as bishop during the vacancy of the see before the Greek Theodore's arrival, he took back with him the singers (*cantatores*), Eddi and Eonan, and masons, and instructors in almost every craft (*artis*). Eddi was the biographer himself. Bede, rather inconsistently with what he had said before, says, " and from this time in all the English churches they began to learn the tones ·of the chants (*sonos cantandi*) which till then they had only known at Canterbury ; and the first song master in the Northumbrian churches, except James above-mentioned, was Æddi, surnamed Stephen, who was invited from

46

Kent by the most reverend Wilfrid ". Of Acca, who became Bishop of Hexham in 709, Bede, who knew him well, specifically tells us that he had been " brought up from boyhood and educated among the clerks (*eruditus in clero*) of Bosa, Bishop of York," who succeeded Wilfrid as bishop in 678. Bede's particularity in referring to the clerks of Bosa, who had himself been educated not by clerks but in Hilda's double monastery at Streoneshalch, founded in 657, shows that Bishop Bosa lived, not as a monk, but a clerk, and that his staff, the York Cathedral Chapter, canons, as they were later called, were not monks but seculars. So too, Bishop John, better known from the name given him in the tenth century, of St. John of Beverley, who had been also educated under Hilda, and became Bishop of Hexham in 687 and of York in 705, kept a school not only of clerks but of lay boys about him. Heribald, afterwards Abbot of Tynemouth, himself told Bede a story of his own schooldays. " During my early youth, while I was living among the bishop's clerks, having been sent to the grammar and song schools (*legendi quidem canendique studiis traditus*), one day, when we were riding on a great plain, the youths who were with him, especially the lay boys, began to ask the bishop to let them race their horses against each other." At first the bishop refused, but as they all kept on asking him, he gave them leave to race, except Heribald. Heribald, however, who had a very good horse given him by the bishop himself, could not keep his horse quiet, and against his orders soon joined them, with the result that he was pitched off his horse on to his head, and came into collision with a stone, miraculously the only stone there was in the whole plain. He remained unconscious till next morning when, thanks to the bishop's prayers, aided by a doctor who bound up his broken head, he recovered. While he was still half-unconscious, the bishop asked him who baptized him, and when he heard the name of the priest who had done it, said he had not been properly baptized, because the priest could never manage to learn the offices of catechism and baptism, and so had been inhibited from duty. The precise point of the anecdote is somewhat obscure. But it is interesting for the historian of education to find the bishop thus going for a ride with his tribe of schoolboys just as Dr. Burton at Winchester took his tribe of ten young noblemen-commoners out hunting on Saints' days in 1731. It is interesting too as showing that the English priesthood of the day was a learned priesthood, and that a priest who could not manage to learn the Latin services was sequestered from office.

Meanwhile, another strain of learning had been imported into Northumberland, not from Rome but from Ireland. King Oswald, who recovered the North from the Welsh in 634, had been in exile among the Scots, i.e. Irish, of Hii or Iona, and had there become a Christian, and, like Sigberct of East Anglia, when he became king, re-introduced Christianity under a bishop and other missionaries from the place of his conversion, Iona.   The see was placed at Lindisfarne or Holy Island, which, *more Scottorum*, was more of a hermitage than a cathedral town.   But Bede tells us that churches were built all over the place (*per loca*) and monasteries endowed by the King, "while little English boys were taught by Scottish teachers the observance of regular discipline together with higher learning (*cum majoribus studiis*), as they were mostly monks who came ".   The learning of the Irish was wholly in psalm-singing and theology, not in the classics, and the *majora studia* meant the Scriptures, not philosophy or literature.   At Lindisfarne itself, the school perished with the cathedral in the Danish invasion.

At Hexham, on the other hand, the school exists to-day. It was made a bishop's see in 678 under Eata, who had been brought up at Lindisfarne (Bede, III, 26), "one of the twelve English boys whom Aidan had taken at the beginning of his bishopric to be educated as a Christian".   The school was no doubt then founded.   When Acca succeeded Wilfrid as bishop there in 709, Bede tells us (V, 20) he built a very large and noble library.   He also sent for a celebrated singer named Maban, who had been thoroughly taught the tones of chants by the successors of the pupils of the blessed Pope Gregory in Kent, to teach him and his clerks, and kept him there for twelve years.   Acca himself was also " a very skil-ful singer as well as very learned in sound literature," and had been at Rome with Wilfrid.

Ripon was founded by Eata as a monastery shortly before 661, when it was taken from him and his Scottish monks and given to Wilfrid, who built a great church, of which the crypt still remains, in 671. Alcuin tells us that Wilbrord or Clement, the English "apostle of the Netherlands," born in 658, was educated there from babyhood till he was twenty years old. The monastery was probably destroyed by the Danes, as it disappears from history after 791, and only reappears, *circa* 925, as a new foundation of King Athelstan's, when he established the supremacy of the English in the North over the Danes. It was then a church of secular canons, with whom a grammar school was a matter of course. This school, which still flourishes, we shall meet later.

It is, however, the monasteries of Wearmouth and Jarrow, or rather monastery (for they were intended to be one house under one abbot), which have been commonly represented as the first northern schools, or school, with Bede as the master of it. These monasteries were due to direct intercourse with Rome and not in any way to the Irish tradition. For they were founded by Biscop Baducing, i.e. son of Badoc, better known as Benedict Biscop (the latter name not meaning that he was a bishop). He was one of the thanes of Oswi, King of Bernicia, or Northumberland, until at the age of twenty-five he gave up secular life, and went to Rome with Wilfrid, where he became a priest, and then returned to preach the charms of ecclesiastical life in Northumberland. On a second visit to Rome he became a monk. Some years after he returned to England with Archbishop Theodore. In 674 he founded and endowed the monastery at Wearmouth which was built by masons from Gaul, in the Roman style, with glass windows, then unknown in England. A fifth visit to Rome resulted in the importation of many books and a large collection of relics and pictures, and also of John, the Precentor (*archicantor*) of St. Peter's itself, and Abbot of St. Martin's, who taught, not only the brethren at Wearmouth but the other monasteries and the whole country round, "the Roman order" of singing and reading throughout the whole year, and wrote a treatise on it, which Bede had seen. In 682 Biscop founded Jarrow. Bede who was born in what was afterwards the monastery's property at Sunderland was, " at seven years old " (i.e. in 680), " by the care of his friends given to be brought up (*educandus*) by Abbot Benedict and afterwards by Ceolfrid," who became Abbot of

4

Jarrow in 682 and of Wearmouth as well in 688 or 689.   Bede
says (*c.* V. 24): "I passed the whole of my life living in that
monastery, and gave my whole work to the study of the Scriptures; and in the intervals of the observance of the regular discipline and daily singing service in church, I have always held it
a pleasure to learn or teach or write".   Besides Ceolfrid, "one
of those who instructed me in the Scriptures, and had been
brought up under Chad in his monastery (viz. Lindisfarne) and
under his mastership," named Trumbercht, is incidentally mentioned.   Others were brought up with Bede in the monastery,
notably Hwœtbert, Ceolfrid's successor as abbot in 716, who
had been "from his earliest boyhood educated in the same
monastery, not only in the observance of the regular discipline
but also exercised with no little industry in writing, singing,
reading, and teaching".   Among the "almost 600" monks
whom Ceolfrid left when he retired from the abbacy, there
must have been material for a considerable school, very different in size from the monastic schools of later days, when
the largest monasteries had only sixty monks all told, and
those "in school" were never more than ten in number, more
generally two or three, and not seldom, none.   On the other
hand, it is certain that the majority of the inhabitants of the
early monasteries came to them grown-up, like Biscop himself, and Eastorwine, the next abbot, a relation of Benedict's,
who was a king's thane, and only became a monk at the age of
nineteen, or like St. Guthlac of Croydon, who became a monk
at forty.   Moreover, by no means all monks were educated,
indeed the majority were not.   Thus, in the *Ecclesiastical History*, we hear of one, Ouuin, an East Anglian, who came to
Northumberland as chief thane and major-domo to Queen
Ethilthrith, and then became a monk at Lastingham under
Chad, and "not being good at the Scriptures" worked the
harder with his hands.   Bede, as Mr. Plummer points out, is
always warning the learned monks not to despise their
unlearned brethren, and prophesies how at the Day of
Judgment many learned will be found among the unlearned,
while those who were ignorant of the very elements will receive the reward of goodness among papal doctors.

In a famous letter to Archbishop Egbert, Bede insists that
the archbishop ought to make every one learn the Creed and

the Lord's Prayer by heart. "As to those who know Latin, there is no difficulty ". As to the illiterate (*idiotas*), that is those who know none but their own language, they should be made to "learn them in their own language and sedulously sing them ". "This," continues Bede, "ought to be done not only with the laity but also with clerks, and with monks, who do not know Latin," and for this reason he had himself issued a translation of both of them into English "for the many ignorant priests there are ". Bede himself was, according to Alcuin's poetical history (*l.* 1304) "because of his proficiency rightly made master," when quite a youth (*juvenis*), of the monastic school, and he often speaks of him as *Beda magister*, the schoolmaster.

Two of his books are perhaps school-books, the *Orthography* and *Prosody* (*de metrica arte*), to which is appended a treatise on Figures of Speech, not however of figures generally but of those found in the Scriptures. The dedication of the latter to a co-Levite, i.e. deacon, shows that it was written before he became a priest. This he did at the age of thirty, and it appears from his own statement that from this time till he was fifty-eight years old he devoted himself to commentaries on scripture, that is, he ceased to teach and became a writer. Alcuin distinguishes between his teaching as magister and his editing books as doctor. Most of the other books are commentaries on various books in the Bible and hagiographies. Even his great historical work, the *Ecclesiastical History of the English*, though it is the only sane and sensible history produced in Europe for nearly 300 years, is in inception only a collection of saints' lives. It must have taken many years to prepare, and was written in the last decade of his life. The account of his death, purporting to be given by Cuthbert, a fellow-pupil, to Cuthwin his fellow-lector, represents Bede as a schoolmaster even in his latest years. During his last illness he continued " to give lessons daily to us his pupils," though breathing with difficulty, and "was translating into our language St. John's Gospel and Isidore's Book of Notes," and singing in English, "for he was learned in our poems," some very obscure verses about the Day of Judgment. On his last day, when all the rest of his pupils had to go out in procession with the relics of the saints, as it was Wednesday in Rogation week, one boy named Wilbert remained, who began to take down from Bede's dictation the last chapter of St. John. In the evening when the boy said, " There is still one sentence not finished," he said, " Well, write it," and a little while afterwards the boy said, " Now it is finished," and he said, " Yes, you have spoken truly. It is finished," and so died singing the Gloria. It may seem unkind to throw doubt on this story over which much sentimental rhetoric has been expended. But there are several suspicious features about it. Imprimis, as regards external authority, it is derived only from a St. Gall manuscript of the ninth century. Secondly, as regards internal evidence, is it only a strange coincidence that Bede's *Prosody* is dedicated "*ad Wigbertum levitam*," and at the end contains an inscription by Bede to Cuthbert, his co-Levite? It looks as if some hagiographer had written up the story, casting it in the names of persons who really belonged to the beginning and not to the end of Bede's life. The tale of the translation of St. John down to chapter vi., verse 9, may well have been suggested by the mention of his translations into English in the letter to Archbishop Egbert. But it is strange that while nearly all Bede's other works, of which he gives a list in the *Ecclesiastical History*, are extant, no trace or other mention of this his last work, and therefore one would suppose peculiarly sacred, is to be found. Further, why Bede should have been so anxious to complete it down to a verse, which occurs in the beginning of the miracle of the loaves and fishes, remains unexplained. The equal anxiety to complete extracts from Isidore is inexplicable from Bede's point of view, but is explicable from the hagiographers knowledge of Bede's *Orthography*, which does consist of such extracts.

The inference to be drawn from Bede's own writings is that he taught the monastic school only when he was a young man, a deacon, which he became at nineteen years old. When he became an author he was so far from having a tribe of pupils ready to do the writing for him, that in the preface to his commentaries on St. Luke he says he was his own dictator, notary, and bookmaker, i.e. he wrote the whole with his own hand. The truth is that a very small proportion of the monks in these early monasteries was literate. The majority were engaged in manual labour, tilling the fields, milking the cows, baking—

Ceolfrid, the abbot, when at St. Botulph's Monastery, acted as baker—and performing domestic offices, such as cooking and washing. The school was a small and select affair. The notion of one of these great monasteries as simply a home of learning is a delusion. It neither professed to be, nor was intended to be, nor was in fact, a university college. It was much more like a voluntary workhouse or a penitentiary.

Some writers, beginning with Alcuin's biographer, have had visions of a long chain of monastic schoolmasters, from Hadrian to Bede, Bede to Egbert, Egbert to Alcuin, Alcuin to Rabanus Maurus, and so on. But the first three links of the chain are purely imaginary. As we have seen, there is no evidence whatever of Bede's being a pupil of Hadrian's. There is also no evidence whatever of Archbishop Egbert being a pupil of Bede's, any more than there is of Egbert's founding the school of York, though, unfortunately, following Bishop Stubbs, Mr. Plummer, in his generally careful and critical edition of Bede, stated both as proved facts. The argument from silence is not always conclusive. But it is conclusive in a writer like Bede, who was careful to give the names of eminent men's teachers. Bede never suggests such a relationship, though it is difficult to see how he could have avoided referring to it in the letter of advice to Egbert, already mentioned. In it Bede regrets that he had not been able to accept Egbert's invitation to stay with him at the Minster, as he had done the year before, to indulge their common taste for reading, as then he could have said viva voce what he writes, for the somewhat superior tone of which he now apologizes. Had Bede ever been Egbert's master, surely a reference to this fact would have been a much more effective apology. Bede speaks too of his "brotherly" devotion to Egbert in sending the letter, an expression which surely no master would use to his quondam pupil.

Equally significant is Alcuin's silence on the point. He gives a long account of Egbert, and speaks of him as an illustrious teacher (doctor), which may only refer to his theology and preaching, and what he specially records of him is his ordination of ministers for the various altars and his improving the singing of the psalms. His account of Bede follows immediately on that of Egbert, and begins with the remark that Bede died in the early days of Egbert's archbishopric. Though he says Bede was master in his monastery, he never suggests that Egbert was Bede's pupil there or elsewhere, which was almost a necessary observation if it had been the case.   It is intrinsically improbable that the very secular Egbert, a near relation of King Ceolwulf, in whose time he was made bishop, and brother of King Eadred, Ceolwulf's successor, and almost joint ruler with him of Northumbria,—their legends being found on the obverse and reverse of the same coins,—was brought up in the distant monastery of Jarrow.   The church of York itself was, as we have seen, not monastic, and Egbert was no doubt brought up among the clerks of Bishop Wilfrid II.   Alcuin is equally silent as to Egbert's being his own master.   It is clear he was not.   The Bede-Egbert-Alcuin succession, adopted in the Dictionaries of *Christian Biography* and *National Biography*, and thence by Stubbs and Plummer, is derived from an anonymous life of Alcuin, printed by Mabillon from a "very ancient MS. at Rheims," which has never been seen since 1617, and is said by Mabillon to have been written some twenty years after Alcuin's death.   This life professes to be derived from information supplied by Sigulf, one of Alcuin's pupils.   But the date assigned is quite problematical.   The life is highly superstitious and so clearly a piece of hagiography, written for reading in church or refectory, being full of miracles interspersed with pious reflections, as usual in the lessons for saints' days, that it cannot be accepted as a good historical authority.   However, the French legend-writer tells how Hechbert followed in Bede's steps as a teacher.   "For from dawn, if there was no obstacle and it was not a saint's day, to the sixth or very often till the ninth hour, sitting on his bed, he opened the secrets of Scripture to his pupils as was appropriate to each. Then he got up and said his prayers and Mass.   And then again towards Vespers, when, except in Lent, he took a spare but well-cooked meal with his pupils, he did not spare the tongue of the reader, so that he might be refreshed with bread in both kinds.   Afterwards you might see the boys in the father's presence, piercing each other with their sharpened weapons, discussing in private what afterwards they would in serried ranks fight in public."

This is a picture, not of a public school such as that which

a busy bishop might have held at York, and Alcuin in the
Palace school at Aachen, where grammar and literature and
logic were taught, but of an aged abbot in the retired leisure
of a monastery with a few of the ,younger brethren learning
theology.   The picture is inconsistent with a later passage,
seemingly taken from Alcuin's poem, but transferred from
Albert to Egbert, which depicts a real public boarding school.
" He had indeed a crowd of scholars, noblemen's sons, some
of whom were taught and instructed in the rudiments of
the art of grammar, others in the discipline of the liberal
arts, and some in holy Scripture."   That Egbert did indeed
teach at York school is not to be doubted, since Alcuin himself says so.   But neither Alcuin nor Alcuin's biographer
represents Egbert as creating or founding the school, any more
than Bede represents Theodore and Hadrian as founding
Canterbury School.

Of Egbert, Alcuin simply says that " Wilfrid (II) handed
over (in 732) to Egbert the rights of the venerable see when
he caused him to be his successor.   He was of royal blood and
was a most illustrious ruler of this Church and an admirable
teacher (*egregius doctor*) " and ruled for thirty-four years.
This matter-of-fact sort of way of speaking of Egbert's teaching entirely negatives any idea of his, having founded the
school or of Alcuin's being his pupil.

The seventh canon of the Council of Clovesho, held in 747
during Egbert's episcopate, postulates an adequate supply of
schools.   It ordered that bishops, abbots, and abbesses should
take care that Scripture reading should be continually practised
in their families, lamenting that there were then very few to
be found who were really ravished by the love of holy learning
or wished to work out anything thoroughly.   The canon then
proceeds : " Moreover let the boys at school be compelled and
exercised in the love of sacred learning, that so they may be
found well learned for all the needs of God's Church, and not
become rectors so greedy for earthly business that the house
of God is depraved for want of spiritual adornment ".   What
precisely this means it is difficult to say.   But it appears to
be aimed at the tendency already noticeable, which became
more and more pronounced as time went on, for the secular
clerks to be more devoted to law and legal and state business

than to theology and parochial work of a purely pastoral character. It is chiefly interesting as showing that there were sufficient schools to demand legislation, and that they were not then, any more than later, confined to teaching singing or the psalms or to other purely ecclesiastical instruction, but gave a general and liberal education.

It is not, however, till we come to the last half of the century that we get any detailed information about the schools and what they taught, and then it is of the school of York. The claim of this school to be "Our Oldest School," dated originally no farther back, and had no more established foundation than an article by the present writer under that title in the *Fortnightly Review* for November, 1892. When it was first put forward a reservation was made for the superior claim of Canterbury, if it found its *vates sacer* and proved its title to continuity as a public school, and not a mere internal monastic school. The present writer has himself had to play the *vates*, in the absence of any more sacred representative of that character, and, by investigations at Canterbury and Lambeth, the results of which have already been given, or will be given later, in this work, proved, or at all events give good ground for believing in its continuity as a public school from the days of Augustine to those of Henry VIII and of George V.

If, however, York School cannot claim the primacy in point of date, it can assert supremacy over Canterbury in the eighth century. Its famous master, Alcuin, noised its name abroad in Europe in his own age, and his description of it has made it a classic institution in the history of education for all time. The description is contained in a poem, *Of the bishops and saints of the church of York*, written when Alcuin was himself Schoolmaster and Librarian of York Minster. This poem is now only known from a transcript of the original MS. at Rheims, made by Mabillon. It was destroyed in the French Revolution, together with much English history, in manuscripts, which by exportation had escaped destruction at the English Reformation. The transcript is now at Trinity College, Cambridge, from which it has been printed several times, the best and latest edition being by James Raine, Chancellor of York Minster, in the Rolls Series. The greater part of the poem is a versification in very fair Latin hexameters of Bede's *Ecclesiastical History*.

When after 1350 lines, the poet reaches Archbishop Egbert, he becomes an original, and almost the sole, authority for what he relates. The passage referring to Egbert has been already quoted. Very different from the rather perfunctory way of speaking of Egbert is Alcuin's enthusiastic and almost adulatory expressions about his successor, Ethelbert, or, as he calls him for the sake of the metre, Albert. " My muse forbids more to be told [of Egbert] hastening to the end of my song and the deeds of my own master, who after Egbert received the insignia of the venerable see, called Albert the wise. A man good and just, generous, pious and kindly, defender, teacher, and lover of the catholic faith, rector of this church, teacher, advocate, pupil." Then after more lines of a tombstone kind of praise, he proceeds : " In speaking of whom, you the youth of York will gladly accompany me in my poetic excursion, since he often drenched your senses with nectar, pouring forth sweet juices from his honey-flowing bosom, he whom fair philosophy caught up out of his earliest cradle and carried to the top of the citadel of learning, opening to him the innermost recesses of wisdom ". Born of sufficiently noble parents " he was soon sent by their care to kindly studies and entered in the Minster in his boyish years ".

It is unfortunate for the history of education and of the Church in England that the word Minster should be only translatable into Latin by the word monastery, from which it is itself derived, which in old English meant any great church, just as *monasteriolum*, or little minster, meant any small church, even an ordinary parish church. In later medieval and modern times the word minster came to be used exclusively for cathedral or collegiate churches, not of monks, but of the secular clergy, like York, Ripon, Beverley, and Southwell Minsters in the North, Lincoln and Lichfield in East and Mid England, and Wimborne Minster in the South. The name survives in the Minster Pool close to the cathedral at Lichfield, and in Minster Street just outside the cathedral precinct at Winchester itself. The use of the term gives a totally erroneous impression of their constitution and the character of their inmates. So that the great colleges of secular canons have been claimed as monasteries ; and Mr. Loftie in his *History of London* was actually misled into speaking of St. Paul's as a monastery.   Albert was not, any more than Egbert, a monk.   "In his boyhood as he grew beautiful in body, so he became proficient in genius for books." He became a Levite, i.e. deacon, as a youth (*adolescens*) and a priest when still a quite young man (*juvenis*).   "Then pious and wise, teacher at once and priest, he was made a thane (*comes*) of Bishop Egbert to whom he was nearly allied by right of blood.   By him he is made advocate of the clergy and at the same time is preferred as master in the city of York."   This is a striking phrase, because it exactly describes the duties of that one of the four principal officers of every cathedral church of secular canons in post-Conquest times, who was called at first Schoolmaster and afterwards Chancellor.   The *defensor cleri* was the official and advocate of the clergy, the lawyer of the establishment, who drafted deeds and letters, as well as taught school.   It is noteworthy too, as an indication of the continuity of the institution from Alcuin's time to later years, that Alcuin speaks of "the school," not of the church, but "of the city," of York.   *Et simul Euborica praefertur in urbe magister.*   In later times we shall find the school called indiscriminately the grammar school of the church and of the city of York.   The school, in other words, was, in the eighth as in the fifteenth and twentieth centuries, a public school, for the benefit alike of the church and the city and diocese of York.

Alcuin was evidently a good deal more interested in the educational than in the legal work of the York schoolmaster. For he proceeds to give us, if not a curriculum, at least a conspectus of the subjects taught in the school.   And a very varied and extensive list of subjects it is.

"There he (Albert) moistened thirsty hearts with divers streams of teaching and varied dews of study ; busily giving to some the arts of the science of grammar (*grammaticae rationis artes*), pouring into others the streams of the tongues of orators ; these he polished on the whet-stone of law, those he taught to sing in Æonian chant, making others play on the flute of Castaly, and run with the lyre over the hills of Parnassus. But others, the said master made to know the harmony of heaven and the sun, the labours of the moon, the five belts of the sky, the seven planets, the laws of the fixed stars, their

rising and setting, the movements of the air and the sun, the
earth's quake, the nature of men, cattle, birds, and beasts, the
different kinds of number and various (geometrical) figures :
and he gave sure return to the festival of Easter ; above all,
revealing the mysteries of holy writ, for he opened the abysses
of the old and rude law."

In fact, the school was Encyclopædian.   The one master
taught all the subjects of learning, not only the trivium,
grammar, rhetoric, and logic ; and the quadrivium, arithmetic,
geometry, music, and astronomy ; but the subjects of the higher
faculties, law, and " above all " divinity.   He therefore performed the functions afterwards separated by division of labour
between the Grammar Schoolmaster, the Song Schoolmaster,
and the Chancellor at the cathedrals themselves ; and between
the boys' schools on the one hand and the universities and
colleges for men on the other.   Alcuin's poem is one of the earliest
and most weighty witnesses to the truth, sometimes, but vainly,
sought to be denied, that the universities grew out of the
schools, and particularly not out of monastic schools, if such in
any real sense there were, but as being purely the creation of the
secular clergy, out of the schools of the cathedral and collegiate
churches.   This is, however, to leap over some four centuries.
In the middle of the eighth century University and Grammar
School were one.

Under Albert York School was a boarding school.   " Whatever youths he saw of eminent intelligence, those he joined to
himself, he taught, he fed, he loved : and so the teacher had
many disciples in the sacred volumes, advanced in various
arts."   If we ask what kind of youth is referred to, the answer
is, much the same kind as in the public school to-day.   It was
no mere choristers' school or ecclesiastical seminary.

Albert travelled abroad and went to Rome, and was everywhere received as a prince of doctors, and kings and princes
tried to get him to stay and " irrigate their lands with learning ".
When he returned home, at the request of the people he became,
in 766, archbishop.   " But his old fervent industry for reading
the Scriptures diminished not for the weight of his cares, and
he was made both a wise doctor and a pious priest."   He built
a great altar where King Edwin had received baptism, covered
with silver, gold, and precious stones, and dedicated it to

" Paul the doctor of the world, whom as a doctor he especially
loved ".   He rebuilt the cathedral, " supported on lofty columns
standing on carved arches, and all glorious within with ceilings
and windows, and surrounded by thirty chapels (*porticibus*),
holding many upper chambers under divers roofs, and containing thirty altars with their various ornaments ".   This building was erected by his two pupils, Eanbald and Alcuin, under
Albert's directions, and was consecrated to the Holy Wisdom
ten days before he died.   In 776, two years and two months
before his death, Albert retired into private life, handing on
the archbishopric to Eanbald.   "But he gave the dearer
treasures of his books to the other son, who was always close
to his father's side, thirsting to drink the floods of learning.
His name, if you care to know it, these verses on the face of
them will at once betray.   Between them he divided his
wealth of differing kinds : to the one the rule of the Church,
the ornaments (*thesauros*), the lands, the money (*talenta*) ; to
the other the sphere of wisdom, the school (*studium*), the
master's chair (*sedem*), the books, which the illustrious master
had collected, piling up glorious treasures under one roof."   To
use later terms, while one pupil became Archbishop, Precentor,
and Treasurer, the other became Chancellor, i.e. Librarian,
Lawyer, and Schoolmaster.

Then follows the famous catalogue of the York Minster
Library.   " There you will find," says the Master, with pardonable exaggeration, "the footsteps of the old fathers, whatever
the Roman has of himself in the sphere of Latin, or which
famous Greece passed on to the Latins, or which the Hebrew
race drinks from the showers above, or Africa has spread abroad
with light-giving lamp."

Theology comes first : Jerome, Hilarius, i.e. probably Hilary
of Poitiers, an anti-Arian writer, contemporary with St. Jerome,
Bishop Ambrose (of Milan), Augustine, St. Athanasius, Orosius,
who wrote his *History* in 416; the chief Doctor Gregory (the
Great), Pope Leo (II ? 683), Basil (Bishop of Cæsarea, 331-379),
Chrysostom, who was schoolmaster at Antioch from 381 to 397
and was then Patriarch of Constantinople.   Among the less-
known theologians are Fulgentius, a rhetorician, *c.* 395, and Victorinus (Marius), who combated the Arians in 350.   Boethius,
470-525, presumably for his *De consolatione*, figures rather

oddly among the theologians. Cassiodorus (Magnus Aurelius Senator), a little later than Boethius, 468-575, was probably mentioned largely because of his *Reckoning of Easter*, a most important point in the controversy between the Eastern and the Western Church, and in England between Celt and Saxon. England brings up the rear with Aldhelm and " Bede the Master ".

Next mentioned are " the ancient historians," perhaps as opposed to the modern Bede ; Pompeius Trogus, meaning probably the author of a *Universal History* finished in the year 9, which only survives now in a fifth-century abridgment ; and Pliny the elder's (23-79) encyclopædic *Natural History*. Then come rhetoricians, " the keen Aristotle himself and the great rhetorician Tully," Cicero being prized chiefly for his un-original treatise on rhetoric, the *De Oratore*.   Four lines full of the names of poets follow.   Among them appear, but only at the bottom of the list, three classical authors, Maro Virgilius, Statius, and Lucan.   In the van, the Miltons no doubt to Alcuin, and both of them, like Alcuin and Milton, schoolmasters as well as poets, were Sedulius, who wrote an Easter song, *Carmen Paschale*, *c.* 460, and Juvencus, who turned the Gospels into verse in his *Historia Evangelica* rather more than a century earlier, *c.* 330. Next are mentioned Alcimus, whose name of Avitus Alcuin for some reason transferred to Orosius, in 523 ; Prosper of Aqui-taine, 379-455 ; Paulinus of Nola, who was consul and governor in 380, became a Christian in 390, and as Bishop of Nola in 409 wrote Christian Sapphics and Horatian stanzas ; Arator who in the middle of the sixth century versified, of all curious books to versify, the Acts of the Apostles ; Venantius Fortuna-tus, educated at Ravenna and settled at Tours, and later, bishop of Poitiers, 535-600.   Last comes (L. Cecilius) Lactantius (Firmianus), tutor to the son of Constantine in Gaul in 313, whose *Institutions* certainly contributed to inspire Milton, as shown in a paper for the British Academy at the Milton Ter-centenary.

The grammarians naturally appeared in force.   They are headed by (M. Valerius) Probus of Beyrut, who from soldier turned scholar, *circa* A.D. 56, and wrote a treatise on Nouns and Verbs, called " Catholica," a name which from this work became the regular term in medieval times for a word-book or dic-

tionary.   Next came Focas, i.e. Phocas, who wrote on genders
in the fifth century.   Then follow Donatus and Priscian, the
two great names in grammar for a thousand years.   Ælius
Donatus was a schoolmaster at Rome about the middle of the
fourth century.   He is perhaps best known now as having
had St. Jerome under him as a boy.   Expounding the remark
in Ecclesiastes that there is nothing new under the sun, Jerome
quotes Terence's " every good thing has been said before," on
which he says, " my Master Donatus used to say, ' Perish those
who have said our good things before us ' ".   *Pereant qui ante
nos nostra dixerunt.*   He wrote two grammars, a " greater " and
a " lesser ".   A study of the " Ars Major " in three books was
required for the B.A. degree at Oxford in 1264.   But it was
the " Ars Minor " or the " Lesser Catechism in the Parts of
Speech," which was the primer in use throughout Europe, and
made his name a household word.   A " Donat " or " Donet "
came to be used for an elementary work in any subject from
theology to haberdashery; Piers Plowman, in speaking of
learning the art of fraudulent shopkeeping as " going among
drapers my donet to learn ".   There is a ninth-century Donat
in Anglo-Saxon characters in the British Museum.   William
of Wykeham in 1400 required that the candidates for scholarships at Winchester should know " reading, singing, and old
Donatus ".   Even in 1535, Tindal's parallel to Macaulay's
" fifth-form boy " is to say, " I had nede go lerne my Donate
and accidence again ".   Priscian was the great Constantinople
compiler or translator, a knowledge of whose " Ars Major "
was required of every B.A. at Oxford in the thirteenth century,
and who lived between 450 and 515.   Servius was the great
Virgilian commentator of the fourth century, who is even now
quoted.   Eutychius, or Eutyches, who wrote on the Aspirate,
was a pupil of Priscian's and wrote *circa* 526.   Pompeius
(Maurus) was an African, of Mauretania, who wrote a commentary on Donatus in the sixth century, which is quoted by
Theodulf, Bishop of Orleans, in 798.

Alcuin concludes his list : " You will find, reader, many
other masters eminent in the schools, in art, in oratory, who
have written many a volume of sound sense, but whose names
it seemed longer to write in song than the usage of the bow
allows ".   This is tantalizing indeed, as we should like to

AN ANGLO-SAXON SCHOOL-BOOK SHOWING CAR-DRIVING AND
SKIRT-DANCING

FROM PRUDENTIUS' "VICES AND VIRTUES"
BRIT. MUS. MS. 24199, f. 18.   TENTH CENTURY

know who the other authors were. It is idle to speculate, though one cannot help wondering whether on the one hand Ovid, so often quoted in the twelfth century, was not omitted because his name was impossible for hexameters (though Naso presented a way round) ; and whether, on the other, Caedmon, or Aldhelm's Saxon poems, found a place in this school and minster library.

Alcuin reigned as schoolmaster at York from 776 till he was persuaded by Charlemagne, with whom he stayed in 781 on returning from Rome with the pallium for his fellow-pupil, Eanbald, to transfer his doctor's throne to the Frankish Court. This he did in 782 and remained master of the Palace School till he retired in old age to be Abbot of Tours. He always retained, however, a keen interest in England and things English, especially in York and its minster, and above all its school. In a letter to the canons of York, written about 793, he refers with affection to his school time both as boy and master. " You," he says to the seniors, " nourished my tender years of childhood with a mother's love, you endured with pious patience the frolics of my boyhood, and with the discipline of fatherly chastisements educated me till I was grown up, and strengthened me with the learning of the holy rules." Then addressing the juniors he adds : " You who in age are my sons, but by the holiness of your lives my fathers, never, I beseech you by God's mercy, forget the master of your learning. For He who sees my heart is witness how devotedly it always desired your profit in ecclesiastical study and spiritual learning. Remember me. I am yours in life and death, and perhaps God in His pity will grant that you will bury in old age him whose infancy you nourished." He concludes with some good advice "to avoid fine clothes like the laity," and " to tread the holy threshold of the church instead of gadding about the muddy streets of a dirty town ". Three years later Alcuin wrote to congratulate the then Archbishop of York, Eanbald II (not his fellow-pupil, Eanbald I), on his accession. He congratulates himself, " the lowest slave of the Church, that I have educated one of my sons to labour in my stead in the church, where I was nurtured and educated, and to preside over those treasures of wisdom to which my beloved master, Archbishop Albert, left me heir". In a passage, which is unfortunately corrupt, Alcuin then urges Eanbald to "provide masters for the boys and the clerks, and to separate the spheres of those who read books, who serve the chanting, and who are assigned to the writing school, having for each class their own masters, so that they may not make a business of pleasure and wander about the place, practising useless games, or becoming addicted to other futilities". The division of labour, thus recommended, was destined to become permanent. The writing became afterwards a separate and inferior study. It was relegated to monks or to a professional class of scribes, clerics of course, but of an inferior order. The twin masters of grammar and song continued to provide for public education throughout the Middle Ages. But though the Precentor, as a minster officer in later times and in most cathedrals, though not at St. Paul's, took precedence of the Chancellor, the Chancellor's deputy, the Grammar Schoolmaster occupied everywhere a much superior position to that of the Precentor's deputy, the Song School-master. The latter tended to sink into an elementary or preparatory schoolmaster, "to teach the petties" reading and singing. One of Alcuin's last letters, written after he had re-tired on the abbacy of Tours, was a request for some books from the library at York to be sent him "that he might spread the sweet savours of England on the banks of the Loire".

We have evidence that York School continued to flourish after Alcuin's day in a letter written between 849 and 854 by Lupus, Abbot of Ferrières, an abbey Alcuin at one time held, in which he writes to Abbot Altsig at York asking for some books of Jerome's and Bede's, and also for the twelve books of Quintilian's *Institutes of Rhetoric* to be copied and returned. This is curious as Quintilian afterwards survived only in fragments, and the re-discovery of a complete copy at St. Gall by Poggio in 1416 was one of the great events of the early Renaissance.

We have seen that Hexham School dated probably from 678. Apparently the school had not been maintained with such vigour as under Acca. For in 797 Alcuin writes to Ethelbert, Bishop of Hexham, "and all the congregation in the church," not, be it noted, a monastery "of St. Andrew," urging him to teach the boys and youth there the knowledge of books, to lead them to God, for "he who does not sow, neither shall he reap, and he who does not learn cannot teach, and such a place without teachers shall not, or hardly, be saved. It is a great work of charity to feed the poor with food for the body; but a greater to fill the hungry soul with spiritual learning. . . . The increase of the flock is the glory of the shepherd and the multiplication of learned men is the salvation of the world"—a sentiment which sounds more like the middle of the fifteenth or sixteenth than the end of the eighth century. This letter is of itself sufficient to show that when a Council at Rome in the year 826, held by Pope Eugenius II, ordered that all bishops should take "care that masters and teachers should be established for their subjects, and in other places, where need was, to teach grammar and the liberal arts", they were only crystallizing into positive statute what was already the customary law of the Church.

There is another letter of Alcuin's which reveals to us another field of educational interest in the kingdom of Mercia. Very little is known of the internal history of Mercia until the days of King Offa, who came to the throne in 755, and so established Mercian ascendancy in England that he procured in 788 the erection of Lichfield into an independent archbishopric with seven bishoprics under it. Offa, who was in close communication with Charlemagne, seems to have desired to emulate him both as a promoter of education and as an imperial ruler, and to have tried to get Alcuin to desert the Frankish for the Mercian Court. For a letter from Alcuin to Offa written about 792 begins by saying that, desiring as always faithfully to carry out Offa's wishes, Alcuin has sent him his most illustrious son, as he had asked, praying him to receive him honourably until Alcuin himself, D.V., comes to him. Meanwhile, however, Alcuin rather takes away his illustrious son's character, as he goes on: "Do not let him wander about with nothing to do, nor become the slave of drink, but provide him with pupils, and order him to teach them diligently. I know that he is a good speaker (if *bene dicit* is the right reading—it is more probably *docet*), and I trust he will prove proficient, for the proficiency of my pupils is my profit with God." Alcuin concludes with expressing the great

5

pleasure he had in hearing of Offa's projects for learning, so that the light of wisdom may shine in his kingdom, as it was being extinguished in many places.   It looked at that time as if a United Kingdom of England was being definitely established by Mercia's becoming England.   If so, the chief schools of England would have had to be sought in the Midlands and the North, not in the South.   But the Danish invasions, which began in Offa's last years, changed the balance of power.   Sea-power became the dominant factor, and Wessex, which at first suffered most, saved itself by organizing its naval as well as its military forces and thereby obtained the supremacy of England.

CHAPTER V

ALFRED THE GREAT AND THE SCHOOL OF WINCHESTER

IN the history of education it will be found that, almost invariably, the development of schools has followed on the development of power. Power breeds wealth, and wealth creates a demand for literature and learning. So in Saxon England schools followed the standard of the Bretwalda. A gloomy interval in the history of English education ensued after the death of Offa and the widespread devastation caused by the Viking invasions. When the curtain rises again, the scene has shifted from the North and the Midlands to the South, and centres in the great figure of Alfred.

It has been said that Alfred's father, Ethelwulf, and Alfred himself had been educated by St. Swithun, who became Bishop of Winchester in 852, and that Ethelwulf had even taken deacon's or subdeacon's orders. There is not the smallest real authority for either statement. The story as to Ethelwulf is derived from William of Malmesbury, and he derived it from a professional hagiographer, Goscelin, of the eleventh century, who probably invented it. For a writer of a century earlier, Lanfert, a priest and monk, whose contemporary account of the translation of St. Swithun and of the miracles afterwards wrought at his tomb is extant, states plainly that the life of St. Swithun was unknown because no materials existed for it. So says also Ælfric in his *Lives of the Saints*, written in English in 996: "His life is not known to us, but that he was buried at his bishop's stool west of the church". Needless to say, the account of the translation of St. Swithun contains no hint of the rain legend, the affair going off without a hitch, the only thing mentioned as flowing freely being wine, not water, two butlers being employed the whole time of the feast in going up and down to the cellar.

There is even less probable foundation for the story that Swithun educated Alfred.   Dean Kitchin, in his history of Winchester in *Historic Towns*, says unqualifiedly: "The kindly saint had gifts of influence and teaching; the youth of Alfred was spent at Winchester under his eye".   The Dean himself stated that he knew of no contemporary or early authority for this at all, and was merely repeating other authors.   Another writer, Mr. W. B. Wildman, a master at Sherborne School, in his *History of Sherborne* claims Alfred for a pupil of that school.   He argues that as Winchester was all "to-broken" by the Danes in 856, and Hampshire was abandoned to them, and as both Alfred's brothers, Ethelbald and Ethelbert, were buried at Sherborne, that Sherborne, not Winchester, was then the West Saxon capital, and there Alfred received his education, "and was once a boy at Sherborne School".   This may be conceded as probable, from 856, when Alfred was eight years old.

Now, the *Saxon Chronicle* was undoubtedly compiled at Winchester in Alfred's time,—not indeed, as Dean Kitchin (followed even by Sir William Maunde Thompson, who in his *Palaeography* prints a facsimile of a piece of it as "monastic" writing), says, "with the help of the brethren of St. Swithun's convent"—which did not come into existence till half a century afterwards,—but by some of the cathedral clergy, the secular clerks of the Old Minster, who preceded the monks.   It may therefore be taken as a first-hand authority for Alfred's life.

It tells us, under the year 853, that King Ethelwulf sent his son Alfred to Rome.   At Rome, "Sir Leo, Pope, hallowed him to king", for so the Pope's action in taking him "as a spiritual son and decorating him with the belt, office, and vestments of a consul" (as related in what is said to be a genuine letter from the Pope to Ethelwulf) was regarded.   Asser's *Life of Alfred*, a romance written a hundred years later than Alfred's time, asserts that Alfred was again taken to Rome by his father in 855, and then stayed a whole year.   The *Chronicle* says only that the father went to Rome in 855, and stayed there a year, implying that, as Freeman inferred, Alfred remained at Rome till his father came to fetch him.   Besides the inherent improbability of a small boy going to Rome and back twice in three years, there is the improbability of the silence in Alfred's own *Chronicle* as to such remarkable journeys if they had occurred. The latest editor of what we may be pardoned for calling " Asser " in inverted commas, to remind the reader that it is not a real biography but a romance, Mr. W. H. Stevenson, does indeed attempt to controvert Freeman's inference on the strength of a Rochester charter purporting to be witnessed by Alfred in 855. But as he admits in a note that the date of the charter is wrong and may be 853, Freeman's inference holds the field. If then Alfred was at Rome from 853 to 856, we may presume that he began to learn his Latin there, and at all events was not being educated by Bishop Swithun at Winchester. On the way back Ethelwulf married Judith, the daughter of Charles the Bald, King of the Franks, a girl of thirteen, on 1 October, 856, and took her home with him. Hereby hangs a tale of great importance in the history of early English education. For if " Asser " is to be believed, Alfred never had any education in his youthful days in the ordinary sense, that is, he never learnt Latin, nor even to be able to read. For that romancer interpolates into his extracts from the *Chronicle*, under the year 866, in which year Alfred's second brother, Ethelred, became king, Alfred being then eighteen, a long account of the infancy and boyhood of Alfred. After asserting that he, being better-looking and better-behaved than his brothers, was the favourite child of his father (apparently a mere inference from the fact that he alone went to Rome), " Asser " says that " through the carelessness of his parents and tutors (*nutritorum*) " Alfred remained illiterate until his twelfth year, " or later ". But he diligently learned " Saxon poems by day and night, often listening to them when recited by others and, being easily teachable, retaining them in his memory ". After a divagation about Alfred's skill in hunting, comes the " Tale of the Pretty Picture Book ", second only in fame to the " Tale of the Burnt Cakes ", and of about the same historical authenticity. " It happened then once upon a time that his mother showed him and his brothers a book of Saxon poetry which she held in her hand, and said, ' I will give this book to the one of you who can learn it quickest '. At which, Alfred, inspired by God and at-

tracted by the beauty of the initial letter of the book, answering
before his brothers, who were older in years but not in grace,
said to his mother, 'Will you really give this book to the one
who can understand and read it to you first?' and she, smiling
with pleasure, repeating her promise said, ' Yes, I will '.   Then
he at once took the book from her hand, went to a master and
read it.   Then he went back and read it aloud to his mother.
After this he learnt the daily course, that is the hours and
psalms and prayers, which he collected in a book and carried
about in his bosom day and night.   But, alas! his great desire,
the liberal art [i.e. Latin] he could not satisfy, as at that time,
it was said, there were no good teachers in the whole of
the West Saxon kingdom."   This last remark of course is
merely taken from Alfred's own preface to his translation of
Pope Gregory's *Pastoral Care*, and exaggerated in the taking.
For the preface does not say this at all, but something quite
different, namely, that there were very few (*swithe feawa*)
priests south of Humber who could understand their service
books in English or translate a Latin writing into English.
Alfred was speaking of the ordinary Mass priests and can hardly
have meant to include bishops, judges, canons, and other learned
persons, who would act as teachers.   "Asser," however, goes on
to say that Alfred "used frequently to complain with deep sighs
that it was the greatest of the trials of this mortal life of his,
that, while he was of an age and of leisure and opportunity to
learn, he had no masters, and when he was older and had
something in the way of masters and writers, he was so assailed
by diseases unknown to all the doctors in the island and by
the home and foreign anxieties . . . of a king, and by pagan
attacks by land and sea, that he could not learn (*legere*).   But
yet, among the hindrances of this present life from infancy to
the present day, and, as I believe, to the day of his death, as
he never ceased, so he still never ceases from his insatiable
longing for learning."

    This story of itself convicts the writer of not being a
contemporary, or having any first-hand knowledge of the
life of his subject.   For if he had, he could not have represented Alfred and his elder brothers as children gathered
round their mother's knee, pleased with a pretty picture book,
but unable to read it in 860, in which year, according to him,

MOTHER TEACHING SON WITH PRETTY PICTURE-BOOK

BRIT. MUS. MS. HARL. 4431, f. 261. THIRTEENTH CENTURY

Alfred was twelve years old. The expressions used in the story, particularly *mater sua*, make it clear that "Asser" never realized that by the time Alfred had come to his twelfth year, and indeed by the time he had come to his sixth year, there was no mother, but only a young stepmother, a mere girl, a foreigner to boot, to show the young princes pictures in the Saxon tongue. Nor was there even a stepmother available. For in 858 Alfred's eldest brother, Ethelbald, had succeeded not only to his father's throne but, according to "Asser", to his father's wife also "against all Christian and pagan custom". So that Alfred's brother, instead of being of an age to hang round a young stepmother's knee with Alfred, was old enough to be, and was, her husband. In this very year, 860, "Asser" says Ethelbald in his turn died, and Judith, a second time a widow at the age of seventeen, returned home; and by the time Alfred was thirteen, "his twelfth year and more", had gone off with yet a third admirer, Baldwin, Earl of Flanders.

In a romance written a century after the hero's death, this slip is pardonable enough: in a contemporary so intimate as "Asser" was alleged to have been with Alfred, it would have been impossible. All therefore that the passage shows is, that to a writer in England at the beginning of the eleventh century, there was nothing strange in boys learning to read at their mother's knee any more than in the twentieth century, and that he thought that the same thing was probable in the middle of the ninth century. This in itself is sufficiently startling to those who regard the English before the Conquest as unlettered barbarians.

"Asser's" account of Alfred's learning is in other respects absolutely self-contradictory and unintelligible. After describing the education of Alfred's children (of which anon), he says that Alfred was always complaining to his intimates that "God Almighty had made him ignorant of divine wisdom and the liberal arts", i.e. of theology and Latin. But at length "God . . . unable to bear this longer . . . sent Werfrith, Bishop of Worcester", and Plegmund, Archbishop of Canterbury, and others, all Mercians, and the king made the former translate Gregory's "Dialogues" into Saxon, and made them read aloud (*recitare*) to him night and day, so that he had knowledge of nearly every book, but could not understand a (Latin) word.

But all this was changed after the arrival of " Asser ".   For in the year 887, when Alfred was thirty-nine years old, " the often-mentioned Alfred, King of the Anglo-Saxons, by Divine inspiration first began to read and translate (*interpretari*) on one and the same day ".   For one day when " Asser " read a passage from a book to prove some point, Alfred suddenly produced a book which he carried about with him, in which he had written " in his youth " the daily services, psalms, and prayers, and asked " Asser " to write the passage down.   Finding no vacant place in the book, " Asser " wrote it on a loose " quartern " (as the Westminster boys still call them), and so from this and two other scraps of Latin, Alfred " at once began to read and construe into English, and so, like the thief who learnt the rudiments of Christianity on the Cross "—a somewhat unflattering comparison perhaps—" on St. Martin's Day ", 11 November, 887, " Alfred learnt in one day to read Latin and holy writ for himself ".   So that, having at the age of three learnt to read Saxon in a few minutes, at the age of thirty-nine he learnt Latin in one day.

Such childish miracle-mongering is explicable enough in a hagiography put forth a hundred years after the event.   It is incredible that it should be written, even by a British-born bishop, as " Asser " is represented to have been, of the ninth century, of his own contemporary.   The miracles merely cover the fact that Alfred was, unlike Charlemagne, able to write as well as read and talk Latin.   This is strikingly evinced by his translation of Pope Gregory the Great's *Pastoral Care* from Latin into English.   It is the preface to this book, written about 893, a copy of which he sent to every cathedral in his kingdom, that contains the famous lament over the decadence of learning in England.   He recalled how in the " good old days "—" for some men throw the golden ages back "—" what wise men there were throughout the English race both of the sacred and secular orders " of the clergy and laity, " and how zealous the former were in learning and teaching, and how foreigners came to England in search of wisdom and learning, and how now we should have to get them from abroad.   So general was the decay of learning among the English that there were very few on this side of the Humber who could understand their services in English or translate a letter from Latin into

English; and I believe there were not many beyond Humber.
There were so few of them that I cannot remember a single one
south of the Thames when I came to the throne," i.e. in 871,
not, be it observed, when he was young.   This he puts down
to the Danish invasion in which the churches "filled with
treasures and books" had been "all ravaged and burnt".
Alfred rather stultifies himself, however, as a *laudator temporis
acti* by going on to say that even when the churches were full
of books, most of "God's servants had very little knowledge of
them because they were not written in their own language".
But as they could read English, to prevent such a catastrophe
again, he began to translate the Pastoral or Shepherd's Book,
"sometimes word for word and sometimes meaning for meaning".   He further expresses the hope that "if we have peace"
all the free-born youth of England who are rich enough shall
be set to learning, but with the naïve qualification, "as long
as they are not fit for any other occupation, until they are well
able to read English, and further let those afterwards who will
continue in learning, learn Latin and go to a higher rank".
It was this passage no doubt which inspired "Asser" to de-
pict the King as establishing, like Charlemagne, a kind of
Palace School, and assigning to it an eighth of his total income,
"a school which he had with great zeal collected from many
noble boys and also boys who were not noble, of his own
nation".   In another passage "Asser", after giving a very in-
accurate account of Alfred's family, depicts him as bringing
up his two eldest children, a boy and a girl, at Court and on
English literature, while the youngest was sent to school to
learn Latin.   "Ethelward the youngest of all . . . was sent to
the grammar school (*ludis literariae disciplinae*) with nearly all
the children of noble birth and many also not noble, under the
diligent care of masters.   In that school (*scola*) books in both
languages, Latin and Saxon, were read continually.   They also
had leisure for writing, so that before they had strength for
manly arts, namely, hunting and other pursuits proper to gentlemen, they were seen to be studious and clever in the liberal
arts.   Edward and Elfthryth were brought up in the King's
Court with great care on the part of their male and female
tutors and governesses.   But even they were not allowed to
pass their time in the worldly pursuits proper to those of noble

birth without a liberal education. For they diligently learnt the psalms and Saxon books, and especially Saxon poems, and very often use books [now]." Mr. Stevenson comments on the school to which Ethelward was sent. "It is evident that this was not a school in the modern sense, but that it resulted from Alfred's causing the young nobles who were brought up, according to custom, in the Court, to be educated with his own children, and that he had added a sprinkling of promising youths of lowly origin." But this is a mere *parti pris* assertion. The words used are the appropriate words used long before and long after this time for sending a boy to a grammar school. The very words *traditus litteris*, or *scolae*, are the stock phrase, used of Augustine of Hippo, of Ordericus Vitalis, of William of Wykeham, and of scores of medieval saints and bishops. The words *ludi litterariae disciplinae* can only be construed as grammar school. The very point of the passage is the contrast between the elder children who were brought up at Court and only learnt English and studied English literature, and the youngest son who was sent to school to learn Latin. The passage cannot of course be claimed as evidence that there was a grammar school at Winchester in Alfred's time, nor that Alfred did in fact send his youngest son to it, to mix with young nobles and ordinary freemen's sons there. "Asser" probably supposed that the Ethelward, who became Bishop of Sherborne in succession to the real "Asser" somewhere about the year 910, was Alfred's son; and, as bishop, he was presumed to know Latin and to have got his Latin in the ordinary way in a grammar school. The passage is, however, evidence that there was such a grammar school at Winchester in the year 1001—the alleged date of the only MS. of "Asser"—to which young noblemen and others resorted to learn Latin, and in which English literature was not, as in after days, neglected.

The evidence as to the character of the school and the scholars so exactly coincides with that given by Alcuin of those at York, which it is not likely that "Asser" saw or consciously copied, that we may safely infer that it was the common character of the English pre-Conquest schools. We have ample evidence that it was the same in France and Germany. We hear of King Chilperic, in Gregory of Tours' history of the Franks, who flourished about the time of Augustine, *c.* 584, that he wrote books of verse in imitation of Sedulius, though the verses mostly would not scan. In the life of St. Paul of Verdun we are told that he was sent to a grammar school, (literally, " to the studies of liberal letters "), " as was formerly the custom among nobles ". A similar phrase is used of St. Waleric about the year 622, " he heard in the neighbourhood that it is the custom for teachers to instruct schools of little boys of noble birth " ; and in 696 of St. Chlodulf, " a boy of ability was sent to school as is usual for the sons of nobles ".

" Asser ", in his curiously involved and very unconvincing style, goes on to assert that Alfred also reviewed all the judgments of his judges, given when he was away, and if they were wrong and the judges said they decided as they had because they knew no better, he told them either to give up their places or learn better. " So that in a marvellous manner nearly all the earls, provosts, and thanes who had been illiterate from infancy began to learn grammar, preferring to undergo an unaccustomed discipline, however laboriously, than to give up their offices and power. If through age or through their intellects being rusty from disuse, they could not get on, he ordered his son if he had one, or other near relation, or failing him, his (Alfred's) own man, free or slave, whom he had long before promoted to learning, to read English books to them, day and night, whenever they had any leave." A learned Court indeed ! Under such rigorous rules these poor old gentlemen " used to sigh and lament in the recesses of their minds that they had not stuck to their studies when young, while they thought the young men of the day happy in being educated in the liberal arts ". " But ", adds " Asser ", " this eagerness of old and young for learning Latin we have already unfolded to the King's knowledge ".

CHAPTER VI

THE SCHOOLS FROM EDWARD THE ELDER TO EDWARD THE CONFESSOR

THE influence and the example of Alfred in his insistence on the importance of education continued to be felt and followed in the reigns of his son and grandson, Edward the Elder and Athelstan.

In the *History of Warwick School and College*, it has been shown that the existence of the school attached to the collegiate church of All Saints at Warwick in pre-Conquest days was vouched for by a royal writ of Henry I in 1123, confirming to the church "all its customs and the ordeals of iron and water as it enjoyed them in the time of King Edward and my father and brother, and the school in like manner". In all probability the church and school dated from the year 914, when Æthelflæd, the lady of the Mercians "with all the Mercians built the burh . . . towards the end of harvest at Warwick ". The building of the borough, the arx (citadel, castle, or walls) of Warwick, was only one of a series of like buildings by Edward the Elder, Alfred's son, in concert with his sister, Ethelfled, the lady of the Mercians. Whether the building of a "burg ", as the Winchester *Chronicle*, a "burh ", as the Mercian *Chronicle* calls them, was the erection of citadels on a hill, or the planting of new towns, or merely the walling, sometimes, as at Towcester, expressly stated to be of stone, of old towns, is a matter of controversy foreign to this book. It is certain that these boroughs formed a series of fortresses, which held the Danes in check, and ended in the complete re-conquest of all that part of England, which Alfred's treaty with Guthrum had handed over to them, or rather left in their possession. Almost every place where this burg-building took place is afterwards found as a royal borough

76

with a collegiate church, generally reckoned as a "royal free chapel" of secular clerks or canons with, wherever there are early documents forthcoming, its grammar school attached. Some of the boroughs were afterwards places of no importance. But the bulk of them remained among the chief towns of England up to the Reformation, and, with their schools, many of them so remain to this day. Professor Oman has shown cause for attributing the invention of these boroughs to Alfred and not, as has hitherto been done, to his son and daughter. He points out that when Winchester and Southampton, London, Oxford, and Chichester had been recovered from the Danes by Alfred, they were put into such a state of defence and with such an arrangement for their garrisoning, not only by the people of the town, but by the neighbouring landowners, the burh-ware, that thencefore there is no record of the burning and devastation of the towns by Viking raids.

In the case of Winchester, London, and Chichester, it was only a matter of re-peopling the city and restoring their Roman walls. What amount of rebuilding and restoration of cathedral and school was required, we do not know. We do know that it was restoration and not creation. In the case of Oxford, however, given by Alfred in charge to his son-in-law the Ealdorman of Mercia, which then first appears in English history, it is most probable that there was a new foundation. For it can hardly be mere coincidence that Oxford, like Warwick, was a royal borough and had its castle on a mound and its two collegiate churches, St. George's in the castle and St. Frideswide's, which afterwards became a Priory, in the town, and its school which appears as a flourishing concern as early as 1118; and that similar mounds, castles, collegiate churches, and early schools are found in Bridgenorth, Tamworth, Stafford, Bedford, Leicester, and other boroughs which Ethelfled is recorded as establishing in Northern and Western Mercia, while Edward did the same in Southern Mercia and Essex.

This borough-building movement is somewhat doubtful in detail, because the chronology of the Wessex *Chronicle*, which records Edward's achievements in that line and takes no notice of Ethelfled's, does not coincide with that of the Mercian *Chronicle*, which records Ethelfled's boroughs and takes no notice of Edward's. But that it was a concerted movement between the two and was carried on continuously for some ten or twenty years, there is no doubt.   Apparently it began with the year 907, when the Mercian *Chronicle* says "Here was Ligceaster (Chester, not Leicester) renewed". This entry points to restoration not creation, the Roman walls still standing.   Here, too, we find the collegiate church of St. John the Baptist, a building far older than the present cathedral, which is a much later monastery converted, standing on its fortified mound by the river with its ancient school in connexion with it.   After a great battle at Tettenhall in 910, in which Edward, with a mixed force of Mercians and West Saxons, defeated the Danes; and the death soon after of Ethelfled's husband, her new borough-building movement started. The first works of the lady of the Mercians, as she was called after her husband's death, were the boroughs of Bridgenorth and Scargeat, which is with some probability guessed to be Shrewsbury.   At Shrewsbury was the school in which Ordericus Vitalis learnt grammar, while his father was still a secular priest, before he exported his son to Normandy to become a monk.   The abbey swallowed up the church of St. Peter, but another collegiate church, that of St. Mary, survived to the Reformation, and Shrewsbury Grammar School appears incidentally in the thirteenth century.

Next year, 912, the lady built the burh at Tamworth in the beginning of summer, and that at Stafford before Lammas, loaf mass or harvest mass, on 1 August.   At Tamworth was the ancient collegiate church of St. Edith and an ancient school.   At Stafford there were two collegiate churches, one in the castle, now a mile outside the town, and St. Mary's in the town, to which the school was attached.   In 913 followed Stamford, also with its borough south of the river as well as north, and its very ancient churches and early school.   In 914 Edward built Bedford, where the collegiate church of St. Paul with its school was converted under Henry I into a monastery, while Ethelfled built Warwick.   She took Derley, one of the Danish Five Boroughs, by storm in 917, and there the collegiate church of St. Mary had its school, handed over to the regular canons afterwards, and moved out to Derley in Henry II's time. We need not go through the whole list.   But at Leicester we find the church of St. Mary *de castro* (in the castle) robbed of

ETHELFLED'S MOUND, WARWICK CASTLE, AD. 914

its endowments, and transferred to the Augustinian Priory of Leicester in the meadows outside the town, and the school appearing as a going concern in the early thirteenth century, and re-founded in connexion with the later collegiate church of St. Mary in the Newark, or new work of the castle, which became the mausoleum of the Dukes of Lancaster in the fourteenth century. So at Nottingham we find the school appearing among the earliest town records in close connexion with the church.

It is evident that a definite policy was pursued of establishing the garrison system, the burh-ware, in these newly fortified places where also markets were set up, and churches, for the purpose of consolidating the conquest with all the spiritual as well as the material advantages of civilization. Just as Alfred ensured his treaty with the Danes by the baptism of Guthrum, so did Edward and Ethelfled by providing means for the Christianization of the newly founded or newly recovered towns. They " aimed at consolidating by arts what they had achieved by arms ; educating the heathen when they had subdued them ". It is not perhaps insignificant in this regard to find that the later coins of Edward " develop an interesting and variegated series of new devices—a church tower with elaborate arcading, another quite different sort of church represented from a side view—a flying dove bearing an olive branch "— as if to give public notice of his policy of peaceful penetration.

This view of the origin of the schools in these places is strengthened by the pursuance of this same policy by Edward's son, Athelstan, who carried the arms and the arts of Wessex to Northumbria, including, as it then did, the Lowlands of Scotland. While in the case of Tamworth, Stafford, and Warwick the founding of the collegiate churches and schools by Ethelfled are, it must be admitted, only matters of inference, in the case of Beverley, Ripon, and Chester-le-Street by Athelstan there is some positive testimony.

The next great figure in English education is that of Dunstan, born in 925. He has been credited as a pupil to the monastic school of Glastonbury. But, as Bishop Stubbs has pointed out, the original biographer of the saint, a certain " Old Saxon " B., writing within twenty-five years of his death, speaks of Glastonbury, not as a monastery, but as a church, so

ancient that it was regarded "as not built by any human art".
Here his parents sent him as a student in the sacred leisure of
letters (*sacris litterarum otiis*), a characteristic translation of
grammar school, which shows that the writer knew that the
original meaning of school (σχολή) was leisure.   " In which
God deigned to give him such grace that he excelled all his
contemporaries, and easily out-stripped them in the easy
course of his studies.   Then seeing the excellence of their son
his parents imposed on him the tonsure", not of the monks
but " of the clerkship or clerical order, and made him a fellow
in the famous college of Glastonbury Church (*inque famoso
Glastoniensis ecclesiae sociaverunt coenobio*) ".   That he was not
then a monk, or an oblate with a view to becoming a monk,
is clear from the fact that some years afterwards he contemplated matrimony.   In the interval he carried on his studies
at Glastonbury, extending them even to the "books of Irish
pilgrims, who visited it as the burial-place of Patrick, junior,
which books philosophizing on the path of the true faith he
diligently studied, as also those of other wise men ".   It
seems to have been some years after that he yielded, and then
only after a severe illness, the description of which suggests
some indiscretion, to the persuasion of his kinsman Ælfeah,
Bishop of Winchester, to become a monk.   In 943 Dunstan
went to Glastonbury as its head.   The *Chronicle* puts it
that King Edmund gave Dunstan Glastonbury, where he
was afterwards the first abbot, but B.'s life represents the
King as leading him to the priestly, not the monkish chair.
It is true that B. uses the word abbot, but Bishop Stubbs
points out that abbot seems to have been loosely used for the
head of a collegiate church as well as of a monastery, and as it
only means father, was as appropriate to the one as to the other.
In the same way, as we have already shown, the word minster,
now used indiscriminately for any great church, is a corruption
of monastery.   Moreover, it is probable that the church remained
secular, and had not become monastic, as we hear of Dunstan's
pupils and clerks, and not of monks.   Conspicuous among
them was Ethelwold, the future Bishop of Winchester, who,
after some years in the King's Court, was tonsured and went
to Glastonbury as a clerk, and there, according to Ælfric's
life of him, learnt grammar and music and theology.   " Most

of them were sought for as pastors of churches, as provosts, deans, abbots, bishops, and archbishops, and were most illustrious in each order." It was only after Dunstan's exile in 955, when he fled to Flanders, that he imported on his return the Benedictine rule and built monastic buildings at Glastonbury.

Dunstan's reputation as a teacher must have been one of comparative mildness in those harsh days, for it procured him among his miracles the honour of protecting the boy monks at Canterbury from excessive chastisement. Osbern, who, when Precentor of Canterbury Cathedral monastery, wrote a life of Dunstan towards the end of the eleventh century, in the interval between Lanfranc's and Anselm's archbishoprics, relates an incident which happened when he was himself a boy there. A girl, blind from her birth, attended the service on the Eve of St. Bartholomew, when all the relics of Christ's Church were exhibited, and was allowed to stay all night in the church by Dunstan's tomb. While " we ", says Osbern, " were singing at Lauds the words ' Let your loins be girded ', her eyes began to itch, and by the time we had finished the Gloria she could see; which the boys, winking at each other, put down to Dunstan himself. When it was fully light, we went in to our masters, to be beaten for the faults we had committed. But behold the good Godric rushed up in a rage saying, ' Do ye stupid men behave cruelly to these innocents when our kindly father Dunstan has just shown his sweet mercy for us sinners? Go. You see the miracle performed by Christ on the blind son performed again and yet dare to be guilty of cruelty. Go.' And so we escaped their impious hands and went to church." The bells were rung and the whole city flocked in to rejoice at the miracle.

This very simple tale has been worked up by succeeding writers into an absurdly exaggerated story; which is worth quoting as it shows the extraordinarily rapid growth of legend in the monasteries of the eleventh and twelfth centuries, and how little credit is to be given to stories about saints, which are not absolutely contemporary. This later version has even been inserted in some of the MSS. of Osbern himself, as though it were his own composition. " One day ", runs this version, " when the fury of the masters raged more than usual against

6

the boys, and there was no hope of intercession, they believed that one remedy only remained, to fly to the memory of the oldest father Dunstan, and to show him not so much an interceder as a defender against ministers of iniquity.   So they betake themselves at dawn to him asking his clemency with many tears, while the masters were sitting in divers places where the boys would have to pass and with manifold diligence waiting for them to come out of church.   And behold while they were crying, the pitiful father Dunstan appeared, and touching with a rod he carried in his hand one of them who saw with his eyes open but was incapable of moving, thus addressed him : ' Stop crying, boys, as I allow no molestation of you to-day.   For I came called by your tears.   Now I will go and throw the masters who are waiting for your coming out into deep sleep.   But you, my boy, who see and hear me speaking, when you know that you are free through my bounty, do me the favour to tell the Provost of the Church in my name to turn out of doors the infant son of Earl Harold who was recently buried near me.   For it is indecent that the bodies of pagans should be buried where the divine mysteries are daily celebrated. ' " Dunstan went on to threaten that the Church would never prosper if this was not done.   " So saying he was taken back into his tomb.   The boy who had seen this, now a reverend senior, earnestly asked me to write this without mentioning his name [this is a commonplace in saints' legends, borrowed from Christ in the Transfiguration] immediately winked at his companions saying : ' Did you see father Dunstan ?   Did you hear what he said ? ' and told them all saying, Thus he said and thus.   The boys therefore got up to enter the house of martyrdom.   They passed before the first masters.   They were asleep.   They passed before the second. They were asleep.   They passed before the third and fourth. They were asleep.   But when they woke up a little while afterwards, they were in a state of fury at the derision they had incurred and determined to take revenge on the boys at Tierce, as they could not touch them in the morning through Dunstan's protection.   For there was a custom in the church then that those whom Prime preserved from punishment, Tierce should punish more severely.   But Dunstan, always and everywhere faithful, so separated the masters from them at that hour, that he gave them cause not so much to think about hurting the boys as to discuss their own confusion. So the boys that day avoided the danger and next day joyfully saw the Eve of Christmas. The one who acted as the father's messenger faithfully gave his message to the Provost, but he disbelieving it paid no attention ", with the result that the saint in disgust left the church, and it was burnt " not long afterwards ", in 1067, with the whole of the monastery, except the refectory and dormitory and so much of the cloister as enabled the monks to go from one to the other without being rained upon.

Eadmer, also a Precentor of Canterbury, who wrote a more superstitious life of St. Dunstan in the second decade of the twelfth century, instead of ascribing the final escape of the boys from their flogging to the advent of the Christmas holidays, represents it as a custom in the evil Saxon days for the boys to be "tortured with stripes on the fifth day before Christmas, not for anything they had done but merely for custom (*pro usu*)". He converts the appeal at Dunstan's tomb into a vision of the night before, and adds horror to the flogging by describing the instruments as " whips of bull hide with knotted thongs ", making consciously, no doubt, the discipline in the Saxon school resemble that of the old legend of the flogging of the Spartan boys at the altar of Artemis of Ortygia. Eadmer also adds to the miracle an appearance of Dunstan to the Churchwardens, instead of a message to the Provost, with a definite prophecy of the burning of the church if the stinking carcase of the pagan boy, pagan merely because unbaptized, is not removed.

The whole tale, and especially crediting the burning of the church to the fact of poor Harold's son being buried in it, is a curious instance of the way the Normans slandered the conquered Saxons, and could not even abstain from libelling the schoolmasters. In a recent history of the King's School, Canterbury, the Rev. C. E. Woodruff has taken the latest and absurdest version of the story and told it as if it applied to the Grammar School. But it is evident from the reference to the number of masters that the story is told not of the public grammar school, but of the few boys in the monastery in training for monks. For while a master and usher and some-

times a vice-monitor formed the whole staff of the ordinary
public grammar school, the monastic discipline assigned one
older monk as a master to every two boys, who was between
them wherever they went during the day, slept between them
at night, and in general spied out all their ways.   Only in
choir did they escape the masters' surveillance and fall under
the milder rule of the Precentor.   The fact that these boys
sang in choir is itself conclusive proof that they were young
monks, not ordinary schoolboys, as the outside choir-boy was
unknown in monastic churches before the fourteenth century.
By the fact that four masters are spoken of, we may infer that
the boy monks of the time numbered either eight or sixteen,
according as the use of the term second or third masters
in the plural is taken to be rhetorical embellishment, as is
probable, or sober fact.

Bishop Stubbs attributes to Dunstan certain educational
institutes included among the so-called " Canons of King
Edgar ", of uncertain date.   They are attributed in Johnston's
translation of them, published in 1720, to the year 960, but
may be later.   They imply a general practice for parish
priests to keep schools and engage in education, including
technical education.   Thus canon 10 is: " We enjoin that
no priest receive another's scholar without the leave of him
whom he formerly followed " ; canon 11 : " and that every
priest in addition to lore (or learning, i.e. Latin) do diligently learn a handicraft " ; canon 51 : " and that priests
diligently teach youth and educate them in craft that they
may have ecclesiastical support ".   But the value of these
canons, as evidence of the state of English education at the
time, is questionable.   They read like scraps of ancient canon
law.   Thus the requirement as to learning a handicraft, which
was noted as to St. Paul, was required of Jewish rabbis, and
savours of Eastern and settled city life.   However, Dunstan
himself is depicted as being a skilful goldsmith, and therefore
adopted as the patron saint of the Goldsmiths' Company of
London, and the opportunity of taking the devil by the nose
by his red-hot pincers was given by his being engaged in the
practice of that craft.   So we may perhaps believe that he
furbished up these old canons in the hope of reviving that
wholesome discipline.   There is no evidence that the law ever
accorded with fact.

In the same way, we must discount as being too good to be true the Ecclesiastical Laws, imputed by the editors to *c.* 994, which follow the Edgar canons in the great Anglo-Saxon MS. at Corpus Christi College, Cambridge, which contains also the earliest copy of the *Chronicle*. The nineteenth of these laws runs: "Of schools in churches. If any priest wishes to send his nephew or other kinsman to be taught at the churches which are entrusted to us to govern, we willingly grant him this". The next heading is: "That priests shall keep schools in the villages and teach small boys freely (*gratis*). Priests ought always to keep schools of schoolmasters [as opposed perhaps to schools of religious merely] in their houses, and if any of the faithful is willing to give his little ones to be educated he ought to receive them willingly and teach them kindly. For it has been written 'The learned shall shine as the brightness of the firmament' and 'those who have educated and taught many righteousness shall shine as the stars for ever'. But they ought not to expect anything for their instruction except what they wish to do of their own accord." These laws, however, are nothing more than a slightly varied version of the canons of Theodulph, Bishop of Orleans, promulgated at a diocesan synod, *c.* 797, which are themselves merely repetitions of the fourth and fifth canons of the Sixth Council of Constantinople, held about a century earlier, in 682, and propounded in a place and among people not yet subject to barbarian conquest. Applied either to France in the days of Charlemagne or England in the days of Ethelred, they can have been little more than a pious aspiration.

We come to firmer ground in the school books of Ælfric, who was a pupil both of Dunstan and Ethelwold. There can be no more convincing proof of the widespread extent of schools in the post-Alfredian age than the three educational works of Ælfric, the Anglo-Latin Grammar, Glossary and Colloquy. Our Ælfric, who was at one time identified first with an Archbishop of Canterbury and then with an Archbishop of York of the same name, has now been definitely shown to have risen no higher than to the abbacy of Eynsham, a monastery newly founded, which he accepted about the year 1005, very much as Alcuin before him did that of Tours, and

Alexander Neckham, after him, that of Cirencester, by way of a retiring pension. Ælfric was, as the introduction to his *Grammar* tells us, brought up under Bishop Ethelwold, "in whose school he spent many years", and whose method of translation "following the simplest meaning" he was content "to practice as he learnt it in the school of Adelwold, the venerable prelate who taught many to good purpose", and was Bishop of Winchester. The writer of Ælfric's life in the *Dictionary of National Biography* places this school of Ethelwold at Abingdon. But this writer (the Rev. W. Hunt) is also responsible for St. Swithun's imaginary tutorship of Alfred the Great, and for inventing an imaginary college at Winchester to which to send Archbishop Chicheley, through making a mistake as to the date of the foundation of Winchester College. The translation of Ethelwold's school from Winchester to Abingdon is quite unwarrantable in face of Ælfric's own description of himself as a scholar of Winchester (*Wintoniensis alumnus*) in the dedication of his life of Ethelwold to the then Bishop of Winchester, Kenulf. There is not the smallest reason to suppose that Ælfric ever had anything to do with Abingdon. He never suggests any such connexion himself, nor has anyone before Mr. Hunt ever suggested it. Abingdon was only founded with clerks from Glastonbury, who became monks there about 955. Ælfric, who, as he tells us, wrote Ethelwold's life twenty years after his death, which took place in 984, and outlived King Ethelred who died in 1016, could hardly have been more than a boy in 964 when Ethelwold turned out the clerks from the old minster at Winchester and put in monks. Ælfric was no doubt one of the "youths and young men" whom he describes Ethelwold as being "fond of teaching and translating books into English (*libros Anglice eis solvere*) and exhorting to better things, so that a great many of them became abbots and bishops of England". Ælfric shared his master's taste for translation, and, following Alfred the Great's example, spent nearly his whole literary life, which began when he was a monk at Cerne in Dorset, in giving Latin works an English dress. The first of these works, the *Homilies* or Sermons, is fixed to the year 994. For he tells us that his English-Latin grammar was composed shortly afterwards, and we know it was before the *Lives of the Saints*, which can be fixed to 996.   The *Grammar* may therefore be safely assigned to the year 995.   The fact of the *Grammar*, and glossary which accompanied it, and the *Colloquy* or Dialogue, on which the boys were to practise as a First Latin Book, being written with an English translation, is a very remarkable testimony to the good sense as well as the learning of our Old English forefathers.

The grammar is a translation of Priscian.   " I Ælfric ", as the author informs us, " as not very learned, have been zealous to translate these excerpts from the smaller and larger Priscian into your tongue, my little boys, so that when you have read through the eight parts of Donatus, by this book you can implant both tongues, Latin and English, in your tender years till you come to more advanced studies.   I know many will blame me for having occupied my mind with such studies, as turning the art of grammar into English, but I intend them for lessons (*lectionem*) for ignorant small boys, not for their elders."   Many, he proceeds, will blame his simple translation, as there are many ways of construing the same passage, " but let anyone say what he likes about it, I am content to do it as I learnt it in the school of Ethelwold, the venerable prelate, who taught many for their good ".   He then expresses his wonder that some pronounce words like *pater* and *malus* short in prose, because they are counted short in verse.   " To me it seems better to invoke God the father honourably with a long syllable than to make it short like the Britons, as God is not subject to the art of grammar."   This is a very ancient jest, first told by Suetonius, in the opposite way, of a grammar schoolmaster who, when the Emperor Tiberius made a mistake in grammar and a courtier said, if it was not Latin it soon would be, replied, " Not so, for, Cæsar, you can give laws to men, not to words ".   Gregory the Great in the preface to his *Moralia* apologizes in advance for any bad grammar by saying that he considers it below the dignity of the subject " to keep the language of the divine oracles in subjection to the rules of Donatus ".

Ælfric's story is a curious testimony to the antiquity of the English mode of pronouncing Latin, which prevailed in our schools at least from the days of Edward VI till in the days of

George V boys are being taught to patter their *pater*, even in prose, in some foreign fashion. Indeed the existence of this English grammar shows how much under Alfred's example the Winchester School of those days, and English schools in general, were in advance of later ones, in which no English-Latin grammar was used till the eighteenth century.   It was reserved for the days of the Commonwealth and its apologist, Milton, to make the first attempt at an English grammar.   Yet even in 1863 the boys at Winchester learnt their Greek grammar in Wordsworth's Latin.

Except philologically, the *Grammar* has, however, little interest.   The *Colloquy*, on the other hand, gives us a vivid picture of the Saxon School at work.   A Latin heading calls the book " Dialogue to exercise boys in talking the Latin tongue, first compiled by Ælfric and afterwards added to by Ælfric Bata, his pupil, in Latin and English".   Who Bata, or the Bat, was, is unknown, except that in the life of Dunstan by Osbern, he is casually mentioned as having "tried to dispossess the Church of Christ ", but in what way does not appear. It is supposed, however, that it was by the Protestant view he took of the Sacrament, in editing Ælfric's *Homilies* in strong opposition to the Real Presence doctrine, which Lanfranc and Anselm afterwards combined to make the orthodox view of the Roman Church.   The *Colloquy* begins by the pupil D., for *discipulus*, saying, " We boys ask you, master, to teach us to speak Latin correctly, as we are unlearned (*idiote ; ungelaerede*) and speak corruptly ".   The object is characteristic of the whole of medieval grammar school education.   It was not as nowadays only to read or write Latin but to speak it, to use it as a living language.   If we could call up some of those medieval school boys, of whom our historians of education in their ignorance have spoken so disrespectfully, we should find that if it came to a Latin conversation, they would put our best scholars to shame with the readiness of their discourse and the copiousness of their vocabulary.   It may be observed, by the way, that the word for boys (*pueri*) is already translated *cildra* or children, which remained the word in common use for boys at school for many centuries, especially at Winchester.   Some women writers, and some male supporters with more gallantry than historical accuracy, have tried to make out that the word

BOY BEING HANDED AT GRAMMAR LESSON

BRIT. MUS. MS. BURNEY, 270 f. 94, C. 1350

children in use at Winchester College, and appearing in the English Statutes of many schools, shows that girls as well as boys were intended to be included in the grammar schools. Ælfric lends no colour to the suggestion, but when he speaks of girls calls them *puellae* and translates it *maeden cildum*, or maiden children. After asking what the boys want to learn to talk about, to which the boys reply that they do not care, the next question of the master is highly characteristic, "Are you willing to be flogged (*flagellari, beswungen* or *swinged*) while learning"; at which the boys at once express their preference for flogging to ignorance, though they craftily profess to think that he will be kind and not "swinge" them unless obliged. So inseparable was the connexion of education and corporal chastisement! It may be remembered that when Heloise's uncle entrusted her to Abelard's tuition, he particularly enjoined him to flog her well, if she did not pursue her studies diligently.

This necessary preliminary being satisfactorily settled, the master proceeds to interrogate the boys as to what they do. The first boy says he is a young monk and sings the seven hours with his brethren and meanwhile wants to learn Latin. The rest are described as ploughboy, shepherd, cowherd, hunter, fisherman, hawker, merchant, seaman, shoemaker, salter, cook, baker. Beginning with the ploughboy, they are then taken each through his day so as to bring in all the variety of words possible, and provide an extensive vocabulary, including beasts, birds, and fishes and all the implements and technical terms connected with the various crafts.

It may be noted that the school was not restricted to freemen, as the master, after hearing the ploughboy's account, exclaims, "Hi, hi, great toil is it", and the boy answers, "Great indeed, because I am not free". The school seems to have been a Sunday School. For the huntsman is asked, "Were you hunting to-day?" and answers, "No, for it's Sunday, but yesterday I was", and took two stags and a wild boar, the former in nets, but the boar he followed up with hounds, and standing straight in front of him stabbed him in the throat; on which the master says as our modern "pig-stickers" well might, "Truly brave were you then". The fisher boy calls his salmon "lax", as our Norwegian neigh-

bours do still.   The merchant (*mercator*)—in English "chapman" and "monger"—describes how he fares over sea and
brings back purple and silk and gems and gold, wine and
oil, and ivory, brass and tin, and sulphur and glass ; no petty
tradesman he.   After they have all told their tales, including a cook, the "wise counsellor" of the monks' monastery
is called in and asked which craft is the first.   He determines formally in favour of the monk, on the authority of the
dictum, "seek first the kingdom of God".   But he decides
really in favour of the ploughman, who provides food, the *sine
qua non* of society.   At this all the rest cry out that their
work is equally necessary and an interesting debate follows
in which they all give reasons.   The debate is wound up in
scholastic style by the counsellor, who determines by a sort
of compromise that every one does good who does his own
work well.   "Oh, all you good fellows and good workers, let
us end this dispute and have peace and harmony among us,
and let each help the other by his craft, and let us all meet
at the ploughman's, where we find food for ourselves and fodder
for our horses.   And this is the advice I give all workmen,
that each of them should do his work as well as he can, as
the man who neglects his work is dismissed from his work.
Whether you are a priest or a monk, a layman or a soldier,
apply yourself to that, and be what you are, as it is a great
loss and shame for a man not to be what he is and what he
ought to be."   What is probably one of Ælfric Bata's addi-,
tions, which is in fact a criticism on his master, then follows.
The children are asked how they like the speech, and say,
"Very much, but what you say is too deep for us and beyond
our age".   The youthful monk is then interrogated as to his
life.   He relates how he gets up at night to sing nocturns,
sometimes of himself if he hears the bell, but often he is woken
up by the master with his "yard": how he eats meat and has
good dinners, and drinks beer, or water, but not wine, because
he is too poor to buy it, and wine is "not for children but
their elders and 'wisers'".   Asked if he was flogged to-day,
he says, "No, for I held me warily"; asked whether his fellows
were flogged, says, "Why ask me that?   I cannot open our
secrets.   Each one knows whether he was flogged or not."
Finally, the master advises the young monks to behave dis-

creetly, to sing in tune " and go out without disorder to cloister or school (*gimnasium*) which is translated ' *leorninge* ' ".

The importance of this work for the light that it throws on old English schools can hardly be over-estimated, if it is really a picture of an actual school of the time. *Prima facie* as all Ælfric's other writings are translations, this is one also. But as no Latin dialogue from which it is translated has yet been produced, it must be accepted as original. It may be noted that, though the principal boy is made to be an "oblate ", or young monk, the master himself is obviously a secular, and from his eagerness to interrogate the boy-monk, not acquainted with the secrets of monastic life, while the school is clearly not in the monastery, and the boys are lay folk drawn from all ranks and occupations. It is an important school which is depicted, with its merchants' and seamen's sons, and evidently was written for, or in reproduction of, not the school of a monastery, with its scanty band of oblates, not the school of a village like Eynsham, but of a great city like Winchester, which though surrounded with wheat fields and forests was also, with its St. Giles' Fair, one of the chief resorts of merchants and, as a great port, of seamen also.

It was at the very time when the *Colloquy* was being written that the Vikings' raids were being renewed which ended twenty years later on the death of Edmund Ironsides in the supersession of the house of Egbert and Alfred the Great by that of the Danish Canute, in 1016. Canute had previously become a Christian, and married his predecessor Ethelred the Unready's widow, and ruled as an English king under the laws of Edgar. So it is not so surprising as it might have been to learn from Herman, the historian of Bury St. Edmunds, writing towards the end of the eleventh century, that Canute founded exhibitions for poor boys. Relating Canute's expulsion of the hereditary priests, the secular canons of Bury, and conversion of their collegiate church into a monastery, about 1020 (1032 according to Florence of Worcester), he says, " Nor must we pass over in silence what this good king did by way of charity, namely, whenever he went to any famous monastery or borough he sent there at his own expense boys to be taught for the clerical or monastic order, not only those whom he found among freemen but also the cleverer of the poor, and with his own hand in

kingly munificence he also in his progress made some free."
The local historian of a century later, Abbot Sampson, with
the usual "heightening" characteristic of legends of heroes
as they recede into the past, goes further and depicts Canute as
"establishing public schools throughout the cities and boroughs
and appointing masters to them, and sending to them to be
taught grammar not only noble boys of good promise, but also
the freed sons of slaves, charging the cost on the royal purse".

The curious document called "the Ranks" (Be gething-
thum), the work of some unknown hand between 1020 and
1060, shows that the Danish dynasty had at all events made
no difference in the regard paid to learning. "If a scholar
became so proficient in learning that he had been ordained
and served Christ, he was then thought worthy of such honour
and peace as belonged and appertained to his order, if he be-
haved as he should."

We hear nothing of the half-Norman-born and wholly
Norman-bred Edward the Confessor in connexion with
schools, except in the tale told in the fifteenth-century historical romance of the mythical Ingulf of Croyland in connexion with Westminster. Ingulf is made to say of Queen
Edith: "I often saw her when as a boy I visited my father
who lived in the King's Court, and when I met her as I was
coming from school she often used to pose me in grammar
and verses, and passing readily from the solidities of grammar
to the etherealities of logic in which she excelled, used to shut
me up in the subtle threads of her arguments, and then she
made her maid count me out three or four coins, and send me
to the royal larder to refresh myself, and so dismissed me".
Alas! there is even less foundation for this tale of Ingulf and
Queen Edith than for that of Alfred and the pretty picture
book. Another tale Ingulf tells of himself is quite enough to
condemn his work as a forgery. "I," he says, "the humble
servant of St. Guthlac, was sent in my tender age first to learn
grammar at Westminster and afterwards to Oxford University
(*studio*)". A pre-Conquest monkling studying at Oxford
University would indeed be a prodigy. Ingulf's chronicle has,
however, been definitely shown to be a product of the last
quarter of the fifteenth century, its earliest MS. being not
earlier than 1486. There is no trace of any school at Westminster before 1354, when, as will be seen, we first hear of boys

in the Almonry. No doubt there, as elsewhere, the boy novices in training for monks were taught in the cloister, but there was no school to which an outside boy visiting his father would go, or in coming from which he would meet the learned and argumentative queen, perhaps evolved from the Lady Margaret Tudor.

We have, however, an authentic account of the foundation on 3 May, 1060, by Queen Edith's brother, the last English, and he was half Danish, king, Harold, when he was Earl, of a school at Waltham, Essex, attached to and forming part of the collegiate Church of the Holy Cross. The church had been founded by Tovi the Proud, at whose wedding-breakfast King Harthacnut drank and died, with endowments for two clerks or secular priests. To them Earl Harold added eleven others, " wise, learned, selected from the commons or carefully chosen from the highest in the land. Among them was a certain Dutchman (*Teutonicum*), Master Athelard, born at Liége, brought up in the school of Utrecht, who came to him by a divine and unexpected gift, that he might establish in Waltham church the laws, statutes, and customs, both in ecclesiastical and in secular matters, of the churches in which he had been educated, since he [Harold] had heard from many people that the Dutch churches were governed by most carefully devised rules. So if anything needing punishment or rebuke arose among the clerks it was punished by the Dean or Master Athelard himself, mere excess by a sharp word, breaches of order by the birch, and serious offences even by deprivation of the prebend." The school is depicted by one of the canons, who was driven out of his canonry in 1177, when Henry II converted the house into a Priory of Augustinian canons by a cheap and vicarious atonement, fulfilling his vow to found monasteries in expiation of the murder of Thomas à Becket. The historian relates how Harold, on his way back from his victory over the Norsemen at Stamford Bridge, to meet the Normans at Hastings, stopped at Waltham and prayed before the Rood and met with the dismal portent of the Christ bowing His head. Two of the senior brethren of the Church, Osgood Cnoppe and Ailric the schoolmaster (*childemaister*), were sent with Harold to Hastings, and brought back his body after the battle. The expelled canon had been nominated a canon at the age of five by Queen Adaliza, in whose gift the prebends were, and was fostered in the Church for fifty-three years, till the expulsion in 1177. So that he knew it from 1123. He says he had no doubt that what had been customary in the times of his predecessors had lasted down to his own day. "For the first rudiments of learning he was sent to Master Peter, the son of Master Athelard, the organizer of the Church". The fact that Master Peter was the son of Master Athelard is one of the many instances which show that, as in many other of the great churches, marriage, which the monks chose to call *luxuria* or *lechery*, was the real crime for which the secular canons were superseded in the twelfth century by regular canons, as under Dunstan they had been superseded in the tenth century by monks. The canon gives a striking picture of the school under Master Peter. "A most copious spring of learning and instruction flowed from that Peter, after the Dutch fashion, for besides reading and the composition of letters and verses, singing was no less learnt and practised in the church; and a well-devised difference from the usual habit of boys was, that they walked, stood, read, and chanted, like brethren in religion [i.e. monks], and whatever had to be sung at the steps of the choir or in the choir itself they sang and chanted by heart, one or two or more together, without the help of a book. One boy never looked at another, when they were in their places in choir, except sideways, and that very seldom, and they never spoke a word to one another; they never walked about the choir to carry copes or books or for any other reason, always remaining in the choir unless sent on an errand by the master. As if walking in procession, from school they go to choir, and on leaving the choir go to school, like canons getting up in the night [for service]." Such good little boys were surely never seen before or since.

The Dutch practice of combining the grammar and the song school was in fact old-fashioned and retrograde compared to the English or Frankish method, which, as we saw, separated the grammar from the song school; and fortunately for learning, the Dutch method did not prevail.

The selection of a Teutonic model by Harold was, however, probably due, not to any reactionary tendencies in his educational views, but by way of deliberate counterbalance to the Frenchification and monasticism which Edward the Confessor favoured and endeavoured to force on the English people.

An interesting piece of evidence of what was actually taught in the English schools, may be seen in the list of school books entered on a fly-leaf of one of them, Isidore's *De natura rerum*, which in the fifteenth century belonged to St. Augustine's, Canterbury, and is now in the British Museum. " These are the books that were Athestane's : Of the nature of things : Persius : On the art of metre : The small Donatus : Extracts on the art of metre : The Apocalypse : The large Donatus : Alcuin : A Gloss on Cato [the pseudo-Cato's *Moralia*]: a little book on the art of grammar, which begins 'The earth which part': Sedulius: And one arithmetic [or, computation book, gerim] [which] was Alfwold the priest's. A Gloss on Donatus. Dialogues."

Tenth Century Schoolmaster's Books. Cott. Dom., I. f., 55 b.

The Provost of King's, Mr. M. R. James, in his catalogue of the libraries of Canterbury and Dover, attributed these books to a gift of King Athelstan's. Even assuming that Athestan is equivalent, as is probable, to Athelstan, the attribution is not very likely. Several of that king's gifts to Canterbury are extant, all large tomes with grandiloquent inscriptions as to the royal donor. This humble little octavo book is by no means royal in appearance. If it had been the king's school book, the writer of the list would surely have given the king his title. It is far more probable that the books, all school books, belonged to a schoolmaster of the name of Athestan, who when he retired or died left them to the monastery. Alfwold the priest, who by the epithet was probably not a monk, was probably just another master. The casual sort of way the list is entered affords a convincing proof of the commonness of school books, and therefore of schools, among the English at the time it was made, which Mr. Gilson, the Keeper of the Manuscripts, places about the middle of the tenth century.

CHAPTER VII

THE SCHOOLS FROM LANFRANC TO BECKET

ONE of the worst effects of the Conquest was the foisting of the Italian adventurer Lanfranc into the See of Canterbury. *Prima facie*, as an ex-schoolmaster himself, he might have been supposed to be the best person possible for the schools. But it is a strange thing that, as in these later days so in those days, some of the occupants of episcopal sees, particularly reactionary in their attitude to the schools of the nation, have been ex-schoolmasters. Lanfranc's scholastic career has been misrepresented as that of a monk keeping a school in a monastery, as if it was a normal thing for a school to be kept in a monastery. A little care in reading the historians shows, however, that in keeping a school as a monk he was doing a most exceptional and unheard-of thing, and that he did not keep it in a monastery. Lanfranc had the good fortune to have his biography written by one of his own pupils, Gilbert, who became Abbot of Westminster in 1082. He tells us that Lanfranc was born at Pavia, where his father held municipal office, but being early left an orphan, he left that city and went to a grammar school (*ad studia litterarum perrexit*); where we are not told, but presumably at Rome. A later biographer, a monk of Bec, heightens of course the original story. Lanfranc's parents, instead of being middle-class citizens, were now turned into nobles. In his boyhood he is represented as having been brought up not only in the school of the liberal arts, but also in the secular laws of the country : while when he was a young man (*adolescens*) as a speaker he overcame veteran opponents in actions at law through the torrent of his eloquence ; and his wisdom was such that he gave legal opinions which were gratefully accepted by counsel and judges or mayors of the city. But when he was philosophizing in exile—where or why is not vouchsafed—then the love of true learning illuminated his heart and he became a monk at Bec. Pavia, he says, remembers all this. But it is on the face of it a ridiculous exaggeration, with about as much historical truth in it as there is in Dr. Portia's triumphal appearance in the Supreme Court of Venice.

To return to the more authentic writer. According to Gilbert, Lanfranc, having stayed at his unspecified grammar school some time, returned home "perfectly imbued with all secular learning". Then he went to France in the time of King Henry, and afterwards taking with him many scholars of great fame, went to Normandy, and settled at Avranches, where he taught for some time. A tale is then told of his falling among thieves on his way to Rouen, who, after taking everything he had, tied him to a tree with his hood over his head. At night, to keep up his courage, he tried to say Lauds and could not, as he did not know them by heart. Whereupon he vowed, if set free, to give up the classics for the Church services. In the morning some passing wayfarers heard his cries and set him free, and he at once asked for the worst and vilest monastery they knew. He was shown the way to Bec, just being founded by Herluin, a Norman lord and warrior, who at the age of thirty-seven, desiring to become a monk, learnt grammar and became an excellent exponent of the Scriptures. Here Lanfranc found Herluin building an oven with his own hands, and became a monk. Such was his humility in his new life that when he was reading in the refectory and was corrected by an illiterate prior in what the prior thought was a false quantity, he quietly repeated the word with the false quantity, " for to make a syllable long instead of short, or short instead of long was, he knew, not a deadly sin, but not to obey his superior was no small fault ". After some years the monastic buildings, having been erected on a swampy subsoil, fell down, and to provide funds for their re-erection on a larger scale and another site, " Lanfranc by the licence of the abbot again kept a school, and gave his receipts from the scholars to the abbot, who gave them to the workmen ". This is a striking, because a casual and incidental indication, first, that keeping a public school was not a monk's business, and required special leave from the abbot because it was a breach of the rule; secondly, that keep-

7

ing school was even then "a gainful profession" and was not done gratuitously ; lastly, that the monks did not, as is often absurdly represented, act as architects themselves any more than they acted as schoolmasters themselves, but employed, as they could hardly help doing, professional architects and builders.

The school thus set up outside the monastery grew, we are told, to a total of a hundred, sons of noblemen, clerks, and laity flocking there from all round.   Chief among them was Anselm, who eventually followed his leader in becoming first a monk at Bec, then prior, and afterwards Archbishop of Canterbury.   Others were Henry, Dean of Canterbury, Hernost, Bishop of Rochester, and his successor Gundulf; William, Abbot of Cormeilles, William, Archbishop of Rouen, and Gilbert Crispin, the writer, Abbot of Westminster.   William of Malmesbury, himself a monk, writing in 1125, shows very clearly what sort of school he thought Lanfranc kept.   "After he had been made a monk at Bec, this man, not knowing how to earn a living by agricultural work, kept a public school of logic, in order to temper the poverty of the monastery by the liberality of scholars.   His fame went out into the remotest parts of the Latin world, and Bec became a great and famous school of literature."   He, like Crispin, makes it clear that the school was set up as a public school outside the monastery as an exceptional measure to raise funds for its support.

It was a misfortune for the school at Canterbury and elsewhere that this late converted monk became archbishop.   For a determined effort to expel the monks from Canterbury and the other monastic cathedrals in England and to reinstate the seculars was frustrated by the now monkish Lanfranc.   So the school, instead of being restored to its position as a part of the cathedral foundation, as at York and St. Paul's, where it was taught and governed by a resident member of the Chapter, was left to the care, necessarily intermittent, of the generally non-resident and roving archbishop, who was more often than not a busy statesman.

William of Malmesbury indeed imputes to Lanfranc a continued interest in scholars.   "He was not ashamed when archbishop to gird up his clothes and set food before the poor, and to make scholars of slender means engage in the battle of disputation. The wordy warfare over, both parties went away pleased, the victor receiving a prize for his learning, and the vanquished a consolation for his disgrace." The first part of the sentence refers to the Maundy, a custom still observed in Austria, where on Maundy Thursday the Emperor washes the feet of twelve poor men, as the Johannine Christ did those of the disciples, and gave them the *mandatum novum*, "Love one another". In the Middle Ages it was usual in many places to include in the Maundy a certain number of poor scholars. Thus, at Worcester, as we learn from a customary of the end of the thirteenth century, the prior of the cathedral monastery maintained in Lent thirteen poor, of whom three were clerks appointed by the schoolmaster, "and the Schoolmaster further had this grace, that every week when he was teaching school, he received a Maundy (*mandatum*) from the Almoner, which he could give to whichever of his clerks he liked". This custom was said in 1535, to have been instituted by St. Oswald, who expelled the cathedral canons for monks, and St. Wolstan, the last English bishop. So if Lanfranc's Maundy included some scholars, it was through no exceptional encouragement of learning on his part. But in Lanfranc's own Acts we have no record of anything done for the benefit of schools or scholars. He and his pupil and successor Anselm were too busy in promoting monasticism and the Papal power and in riveting on the necks of the Latin West the doctrine of Transubstantiation, in opposition to Berengarius, and the rational doctrine of the Sacrament, which Ælfric's works show to have prevailed in England before the Conquest, to have time or inclination for improving the schools.

It has been already pointed out that a monastery was not mainly recruited from boys brought up in it. The lives of Lanfranc himself, as of Herluin and of Anselm, of Alexander Neckham, of Abbot Matthew of St. Alban's and Abbot Sampson of Bury in the succeeding generations, show that they were mainly recruited from grown men who for some reason felt a "call" for the monastic life, either in a fit of remorse for crimes committed, or under the spell of religious revivalism, or simply as seeking a quiet and well-fed life. How unimportant a part the "school" in the monastery

played may be judged from the fact that in Lanfranc's famous
" Constitutions " or Rules for monasteries, out of twenty-four
chapters, only one, and that one of the shortest, the twenty-
first, occupying two and a half pages out of one hundred and
seven, is concerned with the boys, and out of those two and a
half pages about the boys not a word suggests any instruction
in anything but reading and singing.   For these and these
alone were the necessary preparation for acting as a choir-
monk, whose whole duty was to sing psalms, read the lessons,
and say long prayers, all by heart, seven times a day.

   These " Constitutions ", though addressed only to the Prior
of Christchurch itself, were apparently accepted as a Rule for
the whole order of Benedictine monks in England.   The regulations as to the boys, whether the oblates, boys vowed to
monkery in their earliest infancy, the *infantes* or children, or
the *juvenes* or youths from fourteen to twenty-one, who
came in as *pulsantes* or postulants, knocking for admission are
very minute, very stringent, and very monastic, but not at
all scholastic.   They imply no learning whatever beyond
knowing the psalms and services by heart.   Their framer
evidently regarded boys as quite as dangerous elements in
the cloister as women.   The only mention of their learning
is in the direction that the prior shall wake the brethren up in
the morning as soon as it is light enough for the boys to see
to read in the cloister; when they have said their prayers
they are then to read aloud for some time.   They are
not allowed to touch each other, or even speak to each
other, much less to any senior monk.   When reading even,
they are to sit " separate from each other, so that one cannot
touch another with his hands or clothes.   No child shall
dare to make a sign or say a word to another except in
the sight and hearing of the master ; nor get up from the
place in which he sits unless told or given leave to do so.
Wherever the children go there shall be a master between
every two of them.   They shall not put anything into
anyone's hand or take anything from anyone's hand, except in
the case of the abbot, the senior prior, or their own master ",
and that not everywhere but only " in proper places, where it
cannot or ought not to be otherwise ".   The precentor, too,
when he is in their school, may give or take from them a book

47534

from which to sing or read, and if they are serving at the
altar, they can give or take things as their orders require.
They shall be flogged in a chapter of their own, as their elders
are in the great chapter.   When they go to confession they
shall go to the abbot or prior or those specially assigned for
the purpose by the abbot.   While one confesses another shall
sit on the steps, and the master shall sit close by, outside
the chapter-house.   Wherever they are, no one except the
persons above mentioned may make signs to them, no one
may smile at them.   "No one shall go into their school, no
one shall speak to them anywhere, unless leave to go in or
to talk to them has been given by the abbot or prior.   A
monk of more than ordinary gravity and discretion shall be
master over the other masters, one who knows how, when he
has heard any charge against them, to inflict punishment in
moderation on those who are at fault or to let them off."
This master was called not the schoolmaster but the order
master (*magister ordinis*).

Similarly stringent regulations apply to " the young men
coming in from the outside world ".   They are given in
charge to masters, to be looked after in most things as is
before provided with regard to the boys.   They shall, as is
above said, sit separate from each other ; shall never leave the
place in which they are kept, except with the monk who has
charge of them ; shall carry lanterns in pairs ; and shall make
confession to no one but the abbot or prior, unless by special
arrangement.   No one shall be allowed to sit in the place
assigned to them except the abbot, the prior, and their
masters ; nor make any communication to them by words or
signs, except with the leave of the abbot or prior ; and when
leave is given the master ought to sit between the youth and
the one who is talking to him.   Even as to these older boys,
it is enjoined that " No youth is to talk to another, except so
that the master may hear and understand what is said by
both of them.   The masters ought to sit between them or in
front of them, so as to be able to see them, if they want to.
When they go to bed the masters ought to stand in front of
them with lighted candles until they lie down and are covered
over."   They were treated, in fact, not as boys at school or
young men at a university, but like rogues in a reformatory.

The Novices' School was of course very small in point of
numbers. Though Lanfranc increased the number of monks
and fixed it at 140 to 150, this number was not in fact maintained. After 1220, before which there are no records, it is
certain there were never more than sixty monks. At the
Dissolution there were only fifty-three, of whom nine were appointed to be scholars and two to be choristers on the new
foundation, and were presumably therefore still novices and in
the Novices' School. There is no means of ascertaining the
number of the Novices' School at any given time at Canterbury. But at Winchester, where sixty monks was the regular
number, there were never more than eight at once in the
Novices' School, generally only two or three and sometimes
none. The Novices' School inferentially appears in the
accounts as early as 1312, when the Almoner accounts for
"beer sent to the youths' bishop"—the boy-bishop of the
secular schools—"on Innocents' Day, 3½d.". But we get no
mention of the number of the youths till 1352 when the
Almoner's account includes "in a courtesy made to the Lord
Prior, the Sub-prior, the Third Prior and five youths at Fair
time (1 September, the famous St. Giles' fair), 20s. 6d.". The
object of this "courtesy" or present appears in 1386—"a
courtesy made to the Lord Prior at Fair time for his knives,
13s. 6d., the Sub-prior, 3s. 4d., the Third Prior, 2s., and for
seven youths in school for their knives, 5s. 10d.".

That the youths in question were the young monks being
taught the order is made clear by the roll of the Almoner (who,
by the way, was himself, with one other monk, a student at
Oxford) for 1390, in which the entry appears as "for two
youths in school for their knives, 2s.", while the Hordarian's
roll for 1495-6 distinguishes the payment "for 28 brethren
being out of school, each 12d., 28s.", and "for 4 youths in
school, each 12d., 4s." By means of these knives, provided
by various officers in different years, we know the number of
these youths in school in thirty-six years between 1352 and
1537. The highest number was 9 in 1397 and 1472. There
were 8 in 1399, 7 in 1387, 1423, and 1483; 6 in 1433, 1438,
and 1477; 5 in 1401, 1405, and 1409. In five years there
were 4, in nine years there were 3, in six years 2, and in one
year, 1533, there was only one youth in school. Lastly, in two

years, 1485 and 1516, there were absolutely none in school, the Hordarian entering in 1485, " Of any payment made to youths in the school this year nothing, because none ", and the Almoner paying in 1516, "For knives this year nothing, because no one in the school this year ".

These brethren in school were not the boys (*pueri*) of Lanfranc's " Constitutions ", i.e. under fourteen years old, but the youths " coming in from the outside world ". The practice of oblates or boys devoted in babyhood or childhood to be brought up in the monastery had apparently ceased long before the fourteenth century.

Even if we double the Winchester figures of the fourteenth century for Canterbury in the Norman period, though it is very doubtful whether 150 monks were ever there, a possible average of eight boys or youths in the school is reached. This is hardly a sufficient number to justify the talk of the monastery being a school.

Nor from what we know of the instruction given and its results was the monastic school more worthy of regard for the quality of its teaching than for the quantity of the taught.

Very different was it with the secular schools.

The flood of the Norman Conquest had hardly abated before we find the schools emerging into the light of history. The main difference caused by the Conquest was the gradual substitution of Norman for English schoolmasters and the translation by the schoolboys of Latin no longer into English but into Norman-French, which, till the reign of Edward III, was the vernacular of the upper classes in the country, of the middle classes in the towns, and of the whole cultured and clerkly class. That the schools did not disappear and that they were frequented by the same class as before appears in the Conqueror's own family history. Henry " his youngest son in the course of nature, but the first-born in the purple and on English soil ", claimed the kingdom of England against the eldest son, Robert Duke of Normandy, on that account. Being a younger son, he seems to have been at first destined for the Church. At all events he was brought up as a clerk and has descended even to nursery history as Beauclerc, the good scholar. The Rev. William Hunt, in the *Dictionary of Na-*

tional Biography, with the curious *penchant* which he displays
for sending people to imaginary schools, has sent this young
Henry, as he sent the grammarian Ælfric, to school at Abingdon Abbey, and made him there receive "under Grimbald,
that education which in after years gave him the title of
Beauclerc". It is strange to find that for all its pretence of
exact detail there is not a tittle of evidence for this statement.
Its sole foundation appears to be a passage in the "Abingdon
Chronicle" which, so far from showing that Henry was at
school in the abbey, is direct evidence that he was not. The
chronicler says that in 1084, when Henry was fifteen years old
(*jam adolescens*), while his brothers were abroad in Normandy,
he, by his father's orders, spent Easter at Abingdon, with
Osmund, Bishop of Salisbury, and Miles Crispin, knight, of
Wallingford, provisions being supplied by Robert d'Oilli, Constable of Oxford Castle, not only for the royal party but for the
monastery. *Expressio unius, exclusio alterius.* The fact that
the chronicler expressly recorded that Henry spent this particular Easter holiday at Abingdon, not under the tutelage of the
abbot or any monk, but under a bishop and a knight, is as
good proof as there could be that he was not there at other
times, and was not at school there. Besides there is positive
proof that Henry was not in any monastic school. William of
Malmesbury, who knew him personally, says of him : "Henry
senior was born in England in the third year after his father's
coming there. As a child (*infans*) he was excellently educated
by the unanimous desire of all, because, being the only one of
all William's sons born in the purple, the kingdom seemed to
be his right. And so he received his first instruction in the
rudiments in a grammar school (*tyrocinium rudimentorum in
scolis egit litteralibus*), and so eagerly did he imbibe the honey
of learning into his very marrow that afterwards no confusions
of war, no political shocks could shake it out of his noble mind.
Though he never read much in public, nor chanted except in a
low voice, yet his learning was, as I can truly affirm, although
confused (*tumultuarie*) of great assistance to his science of reign-
ing, according to that saying of Plato's, 'Blessed is the state
in which philosophers are kings or kings philosophers'. And
so in hopes of being king he fortified his boyhood with learning, and, even in his father's hearing, frequently quoted the

proverb, 'An illiterate king is a crowned ass', *Rex illiteratus asinus coronatus.*"

The mention of the grammar school shows that Henry was not educated in a monastery at all. If he had been, the monk Malmesbury, who lost no opportunity of lauding the monks, would not have lost the opportunity of saying so. By using the technical terms for grammar school, precisely the same, except for the word *scolis* for *ludos*, as that used by the pseudo-Asser in describing the education of the children of Alfred the Great, he clearly shows that he was referring to some public school and not to any monastic one.

If we may guess what particular grammar school it was to which Henry went, we must guess it to have been the same Winchester grammar or high school to which the pseudo-Asser sent Alfred's younger sons. The only possible competitor with Winchester for the honour of educating Henry I is St. Paul's School, London. But London was not the Conqueror's capital. To William as to Alfred his capital and chief residence was Winchester. There his treasury was, and there we may be sure his heart was also. There Domesday Book was compiled and kept. There the Conqueror kept his Court, except on two of the great feasts when he "wore his crown" at London and Gloucester.

Whatever the school may have been which Henry attended in school terms, it is interesting to find him under a private tutor, Osmund, Bishop of Salisbury, in the holidays. For it is in connexion with Osmund that we have what, if we could be sure that we had it in its original form, would be the earliest post-Conquest document relating to a public school. This is the famous "Institution of St. Osmund", the foundation statutes of Salisbury Cathedral, when first established, not where it now is in the city of the plain, New Salisbury, but in the city on the hill, in the castle of Old Sarum : a name chiefly famous in modern times as the typical example of a decayed and rotten borough, but in the eleventh century the Acropolis of Mid-Wessex. It was then a city so populous and thriving that, under the decree of the Council of London of 1075, which directed the transference of bishops' sees from decayed villages to large towns, the Mid-Wessex see was moved there from Sherborne. Osmund, the Conqueror's chancellor, was made bishop in 1078. He built a new cathedral and established in it a chapter of secular canons under the *Institution* or foundation statutes dated 1091. Unfortunately the *Institution* is only known to us by an entry in a fourteenth-century hand, interpolated in the earliest extant episcopal register of Salisbury, written about 1250. This document begins, " These are the dignities and customs of the church of Sarum which I, Osmund, bishop of the same church, have instituted in the name of the Holy Trinity in the year 1091 and granted to the canons and persons of the same church, with the advice of the lord archbishop and of other my co-bishops whose names are underwritten, and the assent of the Lord King William ". It then proceeds to set out the duties of the various " persons " or dignitaries. The Dean and Chanter (*Cantor*, i.e. Precentor), Chancellor and Treasurer shall be continuously resident in the church of Sarum without any kind of excuse. The archdeacons are so to arrange that two of them are always to reside, while " the canons nothing can excuse from being personally resident in the church of Sarum unless for the sake of schools or the service of the Lord King (*causa scolarum vel servitium Regis*), who is able to have one in his chapel, the archbishop one, and the bishop three ".

There are points in this sentence which strongly suggest that the document as it stands is not in its original state. The first is the use of the word Sarum. This was a twelfth or thirteenth-century quasi-classical innovation for Saresburia, like Oxonia for Oxeneford, and was due perhaps, as Dr. Poole thinks, to a misreading of the abbreviation Sar'. Its use may, however, be explained away as the mistake of the copyist, who substituted for the original the word commonly used in his own time.

A similar explanation may perhaps be put forward of the evident blunder in grammar in the sentence as to attendance at school and the royal service excusing from residence at Salisbury, in which *servitium regis* is left as an *accusativus pendens*. But the first excuse for non-residence *causa scolarum*, " attendance at the schools ", meaning the Universities, is an absolute anachronism : there having been no Universities to attend in 1091, while the power of authorizing non-residence of canons for the sake of education was the

peculiar prerogative of the Popes until 1163, when it was conferred on bishops in general. It is a grievous pity that the
Institution, as it stands, is thus of doubtful date. For in de-
fining the duties of the four " persons" in detail, it brings out
the relative importance and precise status of the two distinct
cathedral schools, the Grammar School and the Song School.
" The Dean presides over all canons and all vicars as to ruling
(*regimen*) souls and correction of morals; The Chanter ought
to rule the choir as to chanting and can raise or lower the
chants; The Treasurer is pre-eminent in keeping the treasures
and ornaments and keeping the lights; In like manner the
Chancellor in ruling the school and correcting books." After
dealing with the division of the common fund in which the
four "persons" take two shares to one taken by the simple
canon, and certain minor perquisites of the canons, which have
all the air of an interpolation or interpretation, not of original
legislation, the *Institution* passes on to the deputies, the
" devils" or understudies of the four "persons". " The Sub-
dean holds from the Dean the archdeaconry of the town and
suburbs, the Subchanter (*Succentor*) from the Chanter, what
relates to chanting. If the Dean fails the church the Subdean
fills his place, so the Succentor that of the Precentor. The
Head of the school (*archiscola*) ought to hear and determine
the lessons (*lectiones*) and carry the seal of the church, compose letters and charters and note the readers in the table,
and the Chanter likewise [ought to note] the chanters." It
seems from the context that the *archiscola* or head of the
school is here regarded as a distinct person from, and as being
the deputy of and subordinate to the chancellor. This alone
is fatal to the authenticity of the *Institution* as it stands. A
concatenation of evidence from other and older cathedrals,
York, London, and Lincoln, shows that the term chancellor
was not applied to this officer in England until the end of the
twelfth century. What is more, at Salisbury itself in 1139
the term schoolmaster is used for the person afterwards
known as the chancellor. By a deed of that year King
Stephen gave " Henry, Bishop of Winchester, and all his justices
and barons and faithful subjects, French and English, in Wiltshire" to know that he had " granted for the use of the schoolmaster of Salisbury (*ad opus magistri scolarum Sarisberie*)"

Odiham and other churches in Hampshire. Further, the list
of bishops who witness the *Institution* is not only inconsistent with facts, as for instance, in giving Martin as Bishop of
London instead of Maurice; John as Bishop of Bath, when
there was no Bishopric of Bath; but is also in conflict with the
order and names of the bishops who signed William Rufus'
Confirmation Charter of Lincoln Cathedral, dated the year
before, 1090; and this charter is of superior authority being
known from a copy in *Registrum Antiquissimum* at Lincoln,
which is of the late twelfth century, two centuries earlier than
the earliest copy of the *Institution*. Indeed, the *Institution*
does not profess to be taken from the original charter, but
only from a copy in what is described as "a dirty little old
book".

In view, however, of the *Explanation* of the *Institution*
given in a document executed on the removal of the cathedral
establishment and the city of old Salisbury to the present
cathedral and city of new Salisbury founded by Bishop
Poore in 1227, coupled with the evidence adducible from
York, London, and Lincoln, we may conclude that a school
was an integral part of the foundation of the new cathedrals
of Norman times, as it had been of earlier cathedrals, and
that the keeping of the school was the duty of one of its
principal officers, thence called schoolmaster and afterwards
chancellor.

Thus at York, when the cathedral statutes were written
down in a codified form in 1307, the date of the earliest
extant *Chapter Act-Book*, or minutes of proceedings or acts
of the chapter, it is stated that "The Chancellor," then the
third person in the minster, ranking after the dean and
precentor, "was anciently called schoolmaster". This statement was not founded on mere "tradition", which generally
means guessing or inventing, but has written authority in the
authentic history of York by Hugh the Precentor, which ends
in 1127. Describing the work of Thomas, the first Norman
archbishop, appointed in 1070, after the harrying of the North
by the Conqueror, Hugh describes how the archbishop found
only three out of the then whole number of seven canons "in
the burnt and destroyed church and city", the rest were either
dead or in exile. He recalled the exiles and added others and

established a provost. The canons then lived all together. A few years afterwards he divided the possessions of the Church into separate prebends or estates and established a dean, treasurer, and precentor, "the schoolmaster (*magister scolarum*) he had established before". In fact, as we have seen, the schoolmastership dated from the separation of that office from the archbishopric in the days of Alcuin, and the provostry, which was an external rather than an internal office, the provost's chief duty being to manage the property of the church, probably dated from Saxon days in the tenth century. The increasing importance of the singing and music in cathedral establishments now reduced the schoolmaster from the second to the third position in the church. When Hugh records, under the year 1120, that the schoolmaster accompanied Thurstan the Archbishop Elect to Blois, he calls him by the name *scholasticus*, a title which never seems to have come much into use in England, though it was the regular title of the schoolmaster in many, indeed in most, cathedrals in Normandy, France, Italy, and Germany. Between 1154 and 1181 Archbishop Roger granted to the dean and chapter "to the fee of your school" 100s. a year, charged on the synodals, or payments made at the Easter assembly at the mother church of the four archdeaconries of the diocese, and in 1189, when the archbishopric was vacant, the King's receivers accounted on the Pipe Roll for half a year's payment of this to the schoolmaster. It is not till 1191 that the chancellorship is mentioned, and the chancellor declared in a solemn judgment by Papal delegates to be the third person in the minster and to take precedence of archdeacons, who had apparently tried to take precedence of him. In 1271 we find the chancellor under that name demanding payment from the archbishop of the stipend of five pounds due to the "chancery" from the synodals, being the sum payable to the schoolmaster.

At St. Paul's we find even earlier than at York a positive mention of the schoolmaster, and proof of his afterwards changing his title to that of chancellor, while there is no mention of a precentor till then, and at St. Paul's the chancellor always continued to take precedence of the precentor. It is fortunate that the chief city of the world has preserved the evidence of the antiquity of its chief school better than most towns. A copy, made in 1241, is preserved of a grant to the schoolmaster about the year 1111. Bishop Richard de Belmeis (*de bels mains*), of the fine hands, or the fair house (*de bello manso*)—for opinions differ as to the origin and meaning of the name—or as he calls himself, "Richard by the grace of God, minister of the church of London", addressing William the dean and the whole assembly (*conventui*) of brethren, says, "Know ye my dearest sons that I have confirmed to our beloved Hugh, schoolmaster (*magistro scolarum*), in virtue of the dignity of his mastership and to his successors in the same dignity the place of Master Durand in the angle of the tower, viz. where Dean William by my command placed him between Robert of Eu and Odo. I grant to him also and to the privilege of the school the custody of all books of our church", and he orders the dean to give them him with a duplicate catalogue, getting back any books, whether secular or theological, which had been lent out to anyone, and to place them in presses by the altar which he had made for the purpose. Here then is Master Hugh in Norman London performing himself the same joint function of schoolmaster and librarian as Alcuin performed at English York 400 years before.

This document marks, not the foundation of the school as misinterpreted by Bishop Stubbs, nor the gift of a new house to the master of it, but, the confirmation to the schoolmaster *ex officio* of the house which Master Durand, the immediate predecessor of Master Hugh, had been given, apparently as a personal, not as an official residence. The date of this document is between 1111, when William became dean, and 1128, when the bishop died. Durand had been master some time, since his name appears among the witnesses to chapter documents from 1104. No doubt the school had existed from the foundation of the church in 604, or at least from the days of Alfred's recovery of London from the Danes. On the retirement or death of Master Hugh a few years later, probably about 1125, the same Bishop Richard informs the same dean and the chapter, and William of Oschenden, the bishop's steward, and all the bishop's men, that he has granted to "Henry, my canon, pupil (*nutrito*) of Master Hugh, St. Paul's School (*scolas*

APPOINTMENT OF MASTER OF ST. PAUL'S SCHOOL. c. 1125

Sancti Pavli), as honourably as the church ever held it at its best and most honourable wise; and the land of the court which the aforesaid Hugh inclosed for his house there; and the meadow which I gave the said Hugh in Fulham, viz. four acres, from the ditch to Thames, at 12d. a year; and in alms (i.e. in perpetuity, rent free) the tithes of Ealing and the tithes of Madeley ".

Bishop Stubbs was misled into thinking that this and the previous document witnessed to the foundation of St. Paul's School, chiefly by the word for school being *scolas* and *scolarum* in the plural. But a school was nearly always spoken of in the plural, and the schoolmaster of a single school was called *scolarum magister* in Latin — and of course nearly all the documents relating to schools are in Latin—from the beginning of the twelfth century to the middle of the reign of Henry VI, and in most official documents to Henry VIII's reign. At Oxford a man still talks of being " in the schools ", when he is undergoing an examination in some single school, of classics, or law, or history.

The third recorded master of St. Paul's School became, some fifteen years later, the hero of a document, which has been often quoted and generally misinterpreted by historians of London and of education. The actual document, and not merely a copy in the chartulary, is still to be seen in the Library of St. Paul's Cathedral. It is a writ written at Winchester by " Henry, by the grace of God, minister of the Church of Winchester ", to the Chapter of St. Paul's, William, Archdeacon, and their ministers. " I command you ", it runs, " by your obedience that, after three summonses, you pronounce sentence of excommunication against those who without the licence of Henry the Schoolmaster, presume to lecture in the whole city of London, except those who teach the schools of St. Mary-le-Bow and St. Martin-le-Grand." Dugdale's comment on this in his *History of St. Paul's* was, " which Henry was so respected by Henry of Blois that he commanded ", etc. ; and this comment was repeated in Knight's *Life of Colet*, which until quite recently was regarded as the chief authority for the history of St. Paul's School, and one of the chief authorities in the history of schools in general. It never occurred to them to ask why or how a Bishop of Win-

chester could issue mandates to the Chapter of St. Paul's, and
the Archdeacon of London, or that such a decree was a somewhat remarkable way of showing respect to a schoolmaster.
The simple fact is, that Henry of Blois was holding the see
of London *in commendam*, that is, in charge, as acting-bishop
during a vacancy of the see which followed on the death of
Robert de Sigillo in 1138. The writ was issued in the ordinary course of episcopal business, to protect the schoolmaster
of St. Paul's in the monopoly which he in common with all
other masters of cathedral schools enjoyed in the liberty or
area of jurisdiction of the bishop or chapter. The exemption
of St. Mary-le-Bow (*de arcubus*) church was due to its being the
seat of the Court of Arches, the supreme ecclesiastical court of
the Archbishop of Canterbury, and as his " peculiar " church
exempt from the jurisdiction of his suffragan, the Bishop
of London. St. Martin's-le-Grand being a collegiate church
of Saxon creation and a royal free chapel, was exempt by
the royal prerogative, and probably also by special Papal
privilege, and the exemption must havé dated from Saxon
times. Henry of Blois himself had been dean of it before he
became bishop. Schoolmaster Henry is found signing documents as *magister scolarum* down to the year 1170, when he
was succeeded by Ralph of Highbank, *de alta ripa* or *Haute
rive*, who held till 1181, when Master Richard of Stortford
came in. He generally signs his title at full length " Schoolmaster of the School of London (*magister scolarum London*)
[*iensium*] ". The schoolmaster's endowment was largely increased by Bishop Richard Fitzneal, probably in consequence
of a decree of the Lateran Council in 1179. " Finding ", he
says in a deed of 1198, that when he was first called to the
bishopric, i.e. in 1189, "the Schoolmaster of St. Paul's enjoyed
only the name of master and derived little or no emolument
from the mastership ", he had assigned to it the tithes of the
episcopal manor of Fulham, of 11 acres of land at Barnes
and of some 210 acres scattered about in other places, and
now confirmed the gift. A later thirteenth-century hand has
written in the margin of this deed, " Note of tithes granted to
the Schoolmaster, now the Chancellor ". When Stortford
vacated office, his successor, John of Kent, was no longer
called schoolmaster but chancellor, signing a deed of the

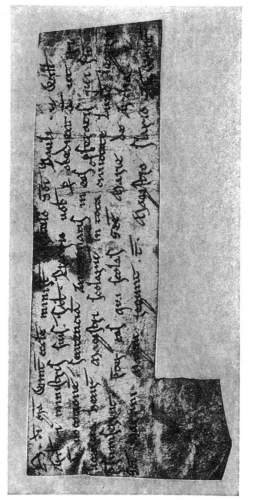

WRIT BY ACTING-BISHOP TO ENFORCE MONOPOLY OF ST. PAUL'S SCHOOL, 1139

bishop's as such in 1205. In the earliest chartulary of St. Paul's, where the deeds quoted above, with some other later ones referring to the Chancellor as such, are collected, they are headed " Of the Schoolmaster and Chancellor seven deeds ". So that at St. Paul's, as at York, there is positive evidence that the dignitary called chancellor had at first been called schoolmaster, and was so called because he actually taught the cathedral school.

It would be a very strange thing if the statutes of Salisbury had really anticipated by a century the development of London and York, and, it may be added, of Lincoln and Wells, especially when the Archbishop of York and the Bishops of London and Lincoln are represented as being witnesses to the *Institution*. Indeed, Henry Bradshaw inferred a sort of committee of bishops headed by Thomas of York, to give a new constitution to the old cathedral of York, and settle the constitutions of the new cathedrals of Lincoln and Salisbury. While rejecting the copy *Institution* as an exact reproduction of the original, we may feel sure from it that, at the end of the eleventh and the beginning of the twelfth century, the normal state of things in the cathedrals was that the bishop had delegated to the dean and chapter the supervision of the schools, and that one of the chief canons, the second or third in rank, was called schoolmaster, and personally taught the cathedral school himself; and, if he allowed other schools in his district, himself issued the licence without which no one was allowed to teach school.

A similar state of things prevailed in the collegiate churches, which were almost subordinate bishop's sees and the constitution of which reproduced that of the cathedrals. We have already seen that the schoolmaster of the collegiate church of St. Martin's-le-Grand was by custom, already ancient, exempt from the jurisdiction of the schoolmaster of St. Paul's.

There was a school at Shrewsbury at least as early as 1080, for Ordericus Vitalis, the Anglo-Norman historian, tells us how at five years old he was put by his father to be instructed there in grammar by Siward, and he was no monk but " a noble priest ", or, as he puts it elsewhere, " I was put to school (*traditus scole*) at Shrewsbury and performed the first

8

duties of clerkship in the basilica of Saints Peter and Paul. Then Siward for five years taught me grammar (*litteras*) and also put me to psalms and hymns and other necessary instruction." But meanwhile the *basilica*, which was his father's, his father being one of the married clergy, was converted into a monastery. So then his father, who presumably had to forswear matrimony and become a monk, sent Orderic abroad to Normandy, where at eleven years old he received the clerical tonsure, and at sixteen became a monk. Shrewsbury School went on after the transfer of the church to the regulars. For on 10 October, 1232, we find King Henry III appointing Master Roger of Abboteslee, schoolmaster (*rector scolarum*) of Shrewsbury, to appear for the Crown in a suit to be tried by Papal delegates in St. Mary's, Shrewsbury, which, with St. Chad's, is mentioned as a collegiate church in Domesday, and remained a collegiate church of secular canons till 1547. This school was beyond doubt not merely the precursor, but the immediate predecessor of the present Grammar School, refounded under a charter of Edward VI, dated 10 February, 1551-2, and endowed with tithes formerly belonging to these two collegiate churches.

At Beverley Minster, the East Riding Cathedral, as it practically was, of the Archbishop of York, we find a tale told by a miracle-writer of the first half of the twelfth century about the schoolmaster of an incident which happened certainly not later than the first quarter of that century. A certain schoolmaster (*scholasticus quidam*) came to Beverley wishing to teach school there, as the place was full of clerks, and was received by the prelates of the church with whole-hearted zeal. Here, as he excelled in literary knowledge and was notable for his moral excellence, his manners, free and affable, pleased everybody; so did his skill in the exercise of his profession, which showed a judicious mixture of mild persuasion and good-tempered severity. Outside the church he was assiduous in teaching a crowded school, inside it he exercised the care of the choir in a kindly spirit, not as a lazy prebendary but as an active officer. This paragon, however, saw a pretty girl and fell in love with her. Though he never told his love, the discipline of the school began to be relaxed and the fervour of learning to grow cold; and you would think the man was suffering from some dreadful disease, so much were his youthful good looks disfigured by pallor and emaciation. In our day he would presumably have married the girl and lived happily ever afterwards, with a boarding-school, the more successful through the attractive wife. As it was, he wasted away, till one night, when the poor man had lain weeping before the altar from midnight matins till lauds, St. John of Beverley came to the rescue, and he got up cured of his disease to the astonishment of all beholders.

At Pontefract, in the West Riding of Yorkshire, where Ilbert of Lacy founded the collegiate Church of St. Mary and All Saints in the castle in the lifetime of the Conqueror, Thomas, Archbishop of York, when he consecrated the church at the same time confirmed to it the school of Kirkby and Pontefract, that is, of the old Anglo-Danish town of Kirkby and the new Norman Castle of Pontefract.

At the south-east end of England, Robert, Count of Eu in Normandy, before 1090 founded (or did he only augment and reconstitute a Saxon ?) collegiate church in the castle at Hastings, and assigned separate properties to the various canons or prebendaries, including Aucher and Gymming or Wymming, each of whom besides lands and a church in the country had a mansion house in the castle. His grandson, in a recital of the foundation, said that " to Aucher's prebend belongs the teaching of the Grammar School and to Wymming's the teaching of the Song School ".

In the West about 1100 Henry I confirmed to the (collegiate) Church of St. Oswald at Gloucester, a royal chapel, the school of the whole of Gloucester, as Bishop Samson and his predecessors, Bishops of Worcester, had given and confirmed it.

There can be no manner of doubt then that all the cathedral and collegiate churches kept schools, and that the schoolmaster was one of the most important of their officers, and school teaching one of the most important of their functions.

Though the cathedral and collegiate churches were the chief, they were not the only source of schools in the eleventh and early twelfth, any more than in later, centuries. On the contrary, in every town of considerable population there was a demand for, and consequently a supply of schools.

Thus at St. Albans, which was an important royal borough

before it became the site of the abbey to which the borough was afterwards granted, there was an important school. A story is told of Geoffrey of Maine, who became abbot in 1119, which has become celebrated because it enshrines the earliest mention of the performance of a play in England. Geoffrey, says the chronicler, came from Maine where he was born, being summoned while still a secular by Abbot Richard (who became abbot in 1097) to keep the school at St. Albans. "But when he arrived the school had been granted to another master, as he did not come in time. He taught school (*legit*) therefore at Dunstable, while waiting for St. Albans school, which was again promised him. There he made a play of St. Katharine which we call, in the vulgar (i.e. French) tongue, a miracle play (*miraculum*). To present it more gorgeously, he borrowed some choir copes from the sacrist of St. Albans. The following night Master Geoffrey's house was burnt down with all his books and the borrowed copes. So not knowing how to repair the loss to God and St. Alban, he offered up himself as a burnt-offering to God and took the religious habit in the house of St. Alban. And this was the reason why after he was promoted to be abbot he was so diligent in making precious choir copes for it." Here then we have incidental evidence, not only of a school at St. Albans, kept, of course, by a secular, and as there is ample evidence in later times to show, not in the abbey but in the town, but also of a school at Dunstable in Bedfordshire, another royal borough, which was afterwards granted to a monastery. That the school at Dunstable was of a permanent and public character, and not a mere private adventure of Master Geoffrey's, appears from a deed mentioned later.

The school of St. Albans appears again in about 1164 as the school in which its most famous master, Master Alexander Neckam, punningly Latinized as Nequam, had been taught as a boy and himself taught as a man. A whole volume of the Rolls Series is filled with some of his works, in which both his prose "On the Nature of Things" (*De Naturis Rerum*) and his poem in "Praise of Divine Wisdom" (*De Laudibus Divine Sapiencie*) amply justify his fame, while a school-book of his, *De Utensilibus*, a Latin-French word-book, written no doubt for the boys of St. Albans, has also been printed. Neckam was born at St.

Albans in September, 1157, on the same night as Richard I was born at Windsor, his mother being wet-nurse to the king, and went to St. Albans School.

> Hic locus etatis nostre primordia novit,
> Annos felices leticieque dies.
> Hic locus ingenuis pueriles imbuit annos
> Artibus, et nostre laudis origo fuit.

> St. Albans knew me when I was a boy,
> Those years of happiness and days of joy.
> The liberal arts St. Albans taught me then,
> The first beginning of my fame 'mongst men.

Thence he went to Paris, though he tells us he did not like the rough sea, and he knew his Paris well, where he was a slender pillar of the school of Little Bridge, i.e. Adam du Petit-Pont, also an Englishman :

> Scarce any place is better known than that,
> Where as an arch of Petit-pont I sat.

In the encyclopædic fashion of the day,

> There faithfully I learnt and taught the arts,
> While reading Scripture added to my parts ;
> Lectures on canon law and medicine,
> On civil law, too, I did not decline.

Neckam's coming somewhere about 1185 to be school-master of St. Albans school is the subject of a rather untranslatable anecdote. For Alexander Nequam having taught school for a year at Dunstable, asked urgently for the school of St. Albans, and Abbot Warren (1183-95) invited him in this terse and witty letter : "If you are good, you may come ; if bad, by no means come " (*si bonus es, venias, si nequam nequaquam*). To which Alexander wrote back equally tersely and wittily : " If you wish it I will come, but if not, pardon " (*si velis, veniam, sin autem, veniam*) as if he had said, "I don't much care ".

Neckam was master till about 1195. He became Abbot of Cirencester in 1213 and died 31 January, 1216-17, and his effigy in stone lies in the cloister of Worcester Cathedral, where he was buried.

The next master was Warren, nephew of Abbot Warren, who is recorded as having been himself, before taking the habit, a secular well known both for his literary attainments and his good looks. Warren sen. with his brother Master Matthew, who had been well trained in medicine at (the University of) Salerno, and their nephew Master Warren and two of their pupils and companions, Fabian and Robert of Salerno —a curious instance of the cosmopolitan character of the Universities of those days—" warned by a special and spiritual vision, vowed to take the habit of religion of St. Albans ". All did except the nephew, Master Warren, and " he fulfilled by an honourable life what he lost in the habit ", and died a secular at St. Albans, having " taught the school in the borough of St. Albans for many years, than which there could scarcely be found in England any school better or more fruitful, or more useful to or fuller of scholars, and this, Master Nequam, who had preceded Warren in teaching it, saw and bore witness of ". The mention of the school as being in the borough, and of Warren as remaining a secular and keeping the school, shows that, here as elsewhere, the school was not a monastic school in the sense of being in the monastery or taught by monks.

Under the next abbot, John, 1195-1214, who was "in his young days M.A. of Paris, where he was thought a Priscian in grammar, an Ovid in verse, and a Galen in medicine ", we again get a glimpse of the school in a strange tale told about William Pigun, " a traitor monk " of St. Albans, who had conceived a great hatred against the abbot. The seed of this enmity was that this Pigun had a nephew Robert, whom he brought up at his own expense, being a boy of good ability, at school in the town of St. Albans. This William then asked Abbot John to take Robert when still very young to be a monk; but as he was not yet arrived at the age of puberty, or of such an age as to be fit and acceptable, the abbot, though not refusing altogether, put him off. William, impatient and proud, immediately procured the reception of his nephew as a monk at Peterborough, where he became prior.

This passage emphasizes the fact that the school was not supported by the monastery as a free school, but that it was frequented by outsiders, who paid tuition fees, and that it was not even a necessary avenue of admission to the monastery.

Quite different is the later development of a kind of parlour boarders, or private pupils, kept by another Abbot John, more than a generation later, 1235-60, of whom we are told: "this abbot was among all the prelates of the realm, the mirror of religion, the model of wisdom, famous for his wit, and above all, generous and open-handed; so that many of the nobles of the kingdom entrusted their children to his custody to be educated". It may be noticed the words are *educandi gratia*, to be brought up, not to be taught. We may suppose that if they were taught as well, they were sent to the public school for the purpose, like the boarders in the conclave or boarding-house at St. Mary's Abbey, York.

At the latter end of the twelfth century Bury St. Edmund's School which, we have seen reason to believe, existed when there was a collegiate church before Canute's time, was given an endowment which converted it into a free or partially free grammar school. When Samson, the hero of Carlyle's *Past and Present*, became abbot about 1180, one of his first acts was to tell Master Walter, son of Master William of Dice (Diss), who asked him for the vicarage of Chevington, that when his late father was schoolmaster (i.e. about 1150), "and when I was a poor clerk he granted me admission to his school and the benefit of learning in it without any payment and by way of charity, so I for God's sake grant you what you ask". Soon after Samson bought a stone house, apparently the house of one of the Jews expelled from Bury by him, and gave it for a schoolhouse on condition that poor clerks should for ever be free of the rent, to which every scholar whether able or not was compelled to pay 1d. or ½d. twice a year, and in 1198 he endowed "the schoolmaster who for the time being taught in the town of St. Edmund's" with half the revenues of a rectory, "that forty poor clerks might be free of all payment to the master for their instruction". At Bury the site of the school, sometimes called the High School, in School Hall Street, can be identified; it was outside the abbey precinct, in Raingate Street. In later days the abbot's jurisdiction over the school was exercised by him only as a court of appeal, the immediate patron being the sacrist. The Song School (*scole cantus*), which taught reading as well as singing, we find later (1267-1426) quite a distinct institution in connexion with the Douze gild of twelve clerks in the town, though also under the patronage and protection of the abbey.

In the twelfth century the movement was renewed, by which not only schools but churches and hospitals, boroughs and markets were brought under the dominion of the "religious", the monks and the regular canons. A wave of monastic *furore* swept over Europe, and threatened to annihilate the secular clergy altogether, as in the Buddhist regions of Thibet and China, or reduce them to the merely subordinate position as "poor parsons of a town," which they hold in the Greek Church, while all the lucrative and governing posts are held by monks. Impelled by the doctrine of vicarious atonement, the secular lords, who spent their time in robbing and murdering the peaceful inhabitants and each other and ravishing virgins and wives, founded monasteries out of their ill-gotten gains in which monks and regular canons might, on their behalf, carry prayer, fasting, and abstinence from sexual intercourse to as great an excess as they carried self-indulgence. The Cluniacs, a new order of reformed Benedictines, with its centre at Cluny, and the Augustinian canons, who followed the monastic rule without wholly immuring themselves in their monasteries like the monks proper, spread over the country. Henry I in his anxiety to gain and retain the support of the Church for his very dubious and uncertain title to the throne, won, as was alleged, by conspiracy against William Rufus and upheld against his elder brother Robert, threw himself into the movement with vigour.

Reading Abbey was founded by him in 1125, chiefly, according to William of Malmesbury, to serve as a convenient hotel at the first or second stage of the journey from London or Windsor to Gloucester. Apparently the patronage and government of the school of Reading had been transferred, or was intended to be transferred, together with the churches of Reading which were all granted to the abbey. But either the grant was not clear or the secular clergy had disregarded it and continued to keep the schools in their hands. For in the abbey chartulary is the copy of a writ by which, between

1125 and 1139, Roger, Bishop of Salisbury, in which diocese Berkshire was until after the Reformation, informed the archdeacon of Berkshire and all the deans (presumably rural deans, unless it may include the Dean of Windsor and the Dean of Salisbury, to whose office divers churches in Berkshire were annexed) and the whole clergy of Berkshire that he prohibited any one from keeping school at Reading except with the consent and good-will of the abbot and convent. The abbot and convent were thus given the same monopoly of school-keeping and of granting licence to teach, which was enjoyed in the diocese at large by the bishop, or in London by the schoolmaster of the cathedral. Bishop Hubert, in 1189, confirmed to the abbey the school of Reading (*scolas Rading*) with the churches of Reading, as it held them in the days of Bishops Roger and Jocelyn. He gave archiepiscopal confirmation in the same words when he became Archbishop of Canterbury in 1193. The school, like the churches, had existed before the abbey in the hands of the secular clergy, and probably in the hands of the canons of a collegiate church of secular canons, which there is reason to think existed there before the abbey was founded. The writ of Bishop Roger, addressed to the secular clergy, represents the decision of a contest about the school in the abbey's favour.

So at Dunstable, another royal borough, when Henry I founded the priory of Austin canons about 1130, he gave to it the whole manor and borough and its market " and the school of the same town ", previously existing, as we saw, *circa* 1100.

At Huntingdon before the Conquest there was a collegiate church of secular canons at St. Mary's Church. Henry I, in a foundation or confirmation deed of the priory of Augustinian canons there, between 1124 and 1135, originally in the town and afterwards moved outside " because of the noise of the town," gave it five churches in Huntingdon, " and the chapel of the castle and the school of the same town ", and the gift was confirmed by the Pope in 1147.

The clearest evidence of contest over such a transfer is at Bedford, where St. Paul's Church appears in Domesday as a collegiate church of secular canons. A few years before 1160, the Norman lord, Simon Beauchamp, founded in Bedford an Augustinian priory, and provided that, as the secular canons of St. Paul's died off, they were to be replaced by regular canons, and granted the church to them. One of the secular canons was Nicholas, also Archdeacon of Bedford and Canon of Lincoln. About 1155 he executed a deed, clearly under compulsion, addressed to " all the sons of holy mother church ". " Know ye all that St. Mary's chapel, with the tithes of Hordelhide and Bedford school (*scolas Bed*) which I have held for some time with the consent of my fellow-canons, I confess to be of the right of and appurtenant to St. Paul's church, and therefore I have voluntarily resigned them to Auger the Prior, and the convent of canons regular of that church." The priory having acquired the church and school, was afterwards moved outside the town, down the river to Newenham, and became known as Newnham Priory. Not till after the dissolution of monasteries did the school escape from the control of the regulars, when it was refounded by the corporation under a charter of Edward VI, and re-endowed by William Harper, ex-Lord Mayor of London, under Queen Elizabeth.

At Christchurch, Hants, the ancient collegiate church of twelve secular canons, known as Twyneham, had been given by Henry I to Richard of Redvers. His son Baldwin at first confirmed it to the dean, Hyllarius, and the secular canons, " with all its free customs, as they anciently held the same, namely, the school of the same town, its free courts " and so on. But in 1150 regular canons were introduced and as the secular canons died off, their places were not filled, and it was expressly provided that " none of their families should be brought in as by inheritance ". A formal deed of confirmation of all the rights of the seculars to the regulars was executed in 1161. The school then passed to the priory and the master was appointed by it. The school does not appear again in history till the dissolution of the priory was impending in 1538, when a vehement petition for its continuance was presented by the prior, John Draper, one of the chief reasons alleged being that the canons and their predecessors " have used contynually hitherto to kepe a maister to teache grammer to children and schollers there, and certeyn of them havyng meate drynke and clothe ". Like the school

HUNTINGDON GRAMMAR SCHOOL, TWELFTH CENTURY

at Dunstable, it perished with the priory at the dissolution of monasteries.

At Thetford, on the other hand, is an exceptional instance of a resumption of this right of school government from a Cluniac priory. Bishop Herbert, known by the surname or nickname of Lozinga, who had been made Bishop of the East Anglian See when it was at Thetford, in 1094 removed the see to Norwich. By his advice the ex-cathedral church of St. Mary was converted into a Cluniac priory by Roger Bigod in 1107. But seven years later the priory was moved outside the town, the monks preferring rural solitude to town life; and having quarrelled with the monks over the possession of the body of Bigod, the bishop restored the town church of St. Mary to secular hands, and with the church, the school. So in, approximately, the year 1114 we find him addressing the brethren (the monks) and his sons (the secular clergy): "know ye that I have given back to Dean Bund his school at Thetford as he best and most fully held it, and I order that no school shall be held there except his own or any which he shall allow". The restored Dean of Thetford remained an independent ecclesiastical potentate with power of probate of wills and other ecclesiastical rights belonging to "peculiar" jurisdiction, exempt from the archdeacon, until the Reformation. The school appears at intervals in the Norwich episcopal registers from 1328 to 1496, the bishop appointing or licensing the master, but whether in the vacancy of the deanery or in resumption of the jurisdiction over the school from the dean does not appear. Refounded or re-endowed in the reign of Queen Elizabeth by Sir Robert Fulmerston's will of 23 January, 1566, this school became the subject of a leading case in the law of charities, was refounded by Act of Parliament in 1610, and still continues.

Cluniac foundations were comparatively rare in England— there were only twenty-five—because, owing to their subjection to the foreign house at Cluny and their exemption from epis- copal control, they were not popular with the bishops. But the Augustinians were spread over the land, many of the secular collegiate churches being converted into their stricter and therefore, theoretically, more holy houses, while many of the hospitals were taken out of secular hands and placed under some branch or other of their order. In the borough of Derby Domesday Book tells us there was in the time of King Edward, in the king's demesne one church with seven clerks, namely, All Saints' Church, which remained collegiate till the dissolution of collegiate churches under Edward VI, and "another royal church in like manner of six clerks". In 1137, a body of Augustinian canons was introduced and placed in the "oratory" or chapel of St. Helen's, by an ancient sacred well, called St. Helen's well, the property of one Towyns, which was rebuilt and endowed at the request, as we are told, of many lords and knights holding fees in Derby. A few years later, the secular canons were turned out of the second collegiate church which was, as appears from the Domesday description of its property, St. Mary's, and not, as Dr. Cox in the *Victoria County History of Derby* suggests, St. Alkmund's, since the latter was a dependency of All Saints and so remained to the dissolution. But dwelling in the noise and bustle of towns did not suit the canons, who liked the life of country gentlemen, so, somewhere about 1148, they moved out a mile down the river Derwent to a place called Darley, the meadow by the Derwent, as Derby is the town by the Derwent, given them by one Hugh the dean, dean probably of the dissolved collegiate church of St. Mary, not merely rural dean. Thus they became known as the Abbot and Canons of St. Mary of Darley. In the Darley chartulary, the first two or three pages are unfortunately missing, so that we cannot ascertain the exact date and character of the first plantation in Derby and removal to Darley. The earliest extant document is an undated confirmation by Bishop Walter Durdent, consecrated 2 October, 1149, of the possessions of the abbot and canons, "whatsoever has been reasonably given them," including "of the gift of William of the April-beard and mine, the school of Derby" with three churches in Derby, as to which it is provided that "the abbot shall be dean of all the churches given to the church (the abbey) in Derbyshire and especially of those in Derby, and that he may hold a chapter of the secular clergy that with them and through them he may judge whatever, according to the canons, Deans can judge". This confirmation was wrongly taken as the foundation deed of the school in Lysons' *Britannia*, a mistake repeated in Carlisle's *Endowed Grammar Schools* in 1818, and thence transferred to the *Endowed Schools Commission Report* in 1867, with the result of Derby's being misplaced as the second earliest school in England, Carlisle, of which anon, being put first. It is obvious that a confirmation implies a previously existing foundation in the case of the school as in the case of the three churches.

William of the April-beard was a member of a family of that remarkable name, given in French as *barbe d'Averil*, who were clerks in the service of the Earls of Chester. This one was perhaps the master of the school, and one of the secular canons, when it was thus transferred from the secular to the regular canons. The school remained in Derby. Very shortly after, it was endowed by Walchelin, the moneyer or minter of Derby and Goda his wife. They gave the house in which they lived and some other property to the abbey "on this disposition, that the hall shall be a school for clerks and the chambers shall be for the house (*hospicium*) of a master and clerks for ever, so that neither the abbot nor the master may take anything for leasing the house". The school was thus to be a boarding school. Several of its later masters are known, and after the dissolution of the abbey it returned from the dead hand to the Town Council of Derby, as a foundation of Philip and Mary.

At Gloucester the school which we saw was kept by St. Oswald's collegiate church was in 1137 transferred to the government of Llanthony Abbey, a house of Augustinian canons about a mile outside the town. This appears from a charter of 30 July, 1199, addressed to the Church of St. Mary and St. John the Baptist and the regular canons of Llanthony, witnessing that King John has "granted and confirmed to the said church the donations which have been reasonably made to them of the gift of Henry our father; the chapel in the castle of Gloucester and a school in the same town (*et unam scolam in eadem villa*)." The grant was not really by Henry II or John himself, for a deed of Milo, constable of Gloucester, states that his father Roger had given the chapel in the castle to the Church of St. Owen, and he himself had given this church and its belongings to Llanthony when its church was dedicated in 1137.

The right of patronage of the priory was apparently much resented in Gloucester and was continually being contested. On 31 January, 1286-7, Bishop Godfrey Giffard issued a commission to his Official Principal, to inquire as to the right of collation to the school in the borough of Gloucester and the possession or quasi-possession of this right, also how the collation has been hitherto accustomed to be made and by whom, and to do further thereon and concerning the premises as the course of law demands, giving notice to those who are interested to be present at the inquiry. The result of the inquiry is seen in letters patent of the bishop of 21 November, 1287, addressed to the Archdeacon of Gloucester. " The collation of the school in the borough of Gloucester to which scholars flock, for the sake of learning, some from our diocese and others from divers parts, clearly belongs, as we have been informed by the evidence of trustworthy witnesses, and as clearly appears by inspection of the muniments and charters which they have concerning the same school, to the religious men, the Prior and Convent of Llanthony by Gloucester, and is recognized as belonging to them of old time ; and they from the time during which they have held the collation, as we are informed by trustworthy witnesses, have held possession of the right of collation to the same, though others indeed may, though not without incurring the guilt of usurpation, perhaps claim the right." The bishop therefore, " to put an end to all controversy and prevent fierce disputes arising hereafter ", commands the Archdeacon to cause public notice to be given on three Sundays during high mass, in all the parish churches in the municipality and others in the neighbourhood, of an inhibition "against anyone calling himself a scholar keeping any school for the sake of teaching in the said borough, except that one the teaching (*regimen*) of which has been granted to a fit master (*doctori ydoneo*) by the collation of the Prior and Convent of Llanthony, who have been and are notoriously in possession or quasi-possession of the right of collation to such school from time whereof the memory of man runneth not to the contrary." "Other schools, if there are any to which anyone has been collated to the prejudice of the said religious " the bishop directed to be " wholly suspended ". The troubles of the priory did not end then, as in

1341 they found it necessary to get a royal charter confirming their right to the school.   In 1380 Bishop Henry Wakefield issued a mandate to the Archdeacon of Gloucester to observe Giffard's decree.   In 1410 this school became the subject of a " leading case" in the Court of Common Pleas (*Year Book*, 11 Hen. IV, 47, Case 21, *De Banco* Roll, 11 Hen. IV, Mich, m. 484, Hamlyn & Darcy *v.* More), which confirmed the law that schools were subject to the ecclesiastical not the lay courts ; the claim of the Prior of Llanthony to put down rival schools not being enforced by the secular arm.   Once again in 1513 the rights of Llanthony Abbey had to be reasserted ; the bishop's Official directing the archdeacon to " publish an inhibition against anyone calling himself a scholar keeping any school for learning or sending any one not of mature age to such schools, except those schools or that school the teaching of which has been freely granted by the Prior and Convent of Llanthony to a fit master ".   The bishop, however, " reserving to himself in the person of his Official the examination and approval of the master appointed by the convent."   The school building itself always remained in the middle of the town in Old Smith Street or the Schoolhouse Lane, now Long Smith Street, as appears from two priory rentals of 1455 and 1535.

So at Bristol.   An inquisition was held in 1318 by order of the bishop as to the rights and privileges of the Gild of Kalendars, established in All Saints', the town church, apparently as against the regular canons of St. Augustine's Abbey (now the cathedral).   The jury found that the beginning of the gild passed the memory of man, and that it used to be called "the Gild or Brotherhood of the Community of the clergy and people of Bristol, and that the place of assembly . . . of the same used to be at the church of the Holy Trinity, Bristol, in the time of Aylward Mean and Bristoic his son, lords of the said town before the last conquest of England ". It must be admitted that Bristoic looks remarkably like an eponymous hero evolved out of the name of the town.   But there is no doubt that the gild existed before the Conquest. They found further that in the time of " Henry Fitz-Empress," one Robert Hardyng, Mayor of Bristol, ancestor of the Earls of Berkeley and Lord Fitzhardinge, "translated the gild from

Holy Trinity Church to the church of All Saints, and established the school of Bristol for teaching Jews and other little ones under the government of the said gild and the protection of the mayor of Bristol for the time being ; and founded the monastery of St. Augustine in the suburb of the said town, and appropriated the church of All Saints to it". The gild was confirmed by the Cardinal-legate Gualo in 1216. Unfortunately the report breaks off without telling what was done. The somewhat astonishing fact that Robert Hardyng established or maintained a school for Jews may be accounted for by the necessity of making provision for the orphans of those who were killed or who fled from the outbreak against the Jews in 1146. If this school was the city grammar school, it was transferred from the governance of the seculars to the regulars on the foundation of Keynsham Abbey, six miles from Bristol, in 1171. For although the foundation charter of the abbey does not mention the school, Leland says positively that "William Erle of Gloucester, founder of the monasterye of Cainesham, gave the prefecture and mastershippe of the Schole in Brightstow to Cainesham and took it from the Calenderies". Leland's statement is supported by a Rent-roll of Bristol, made about 1295, which includes an item of "12d. of Roger Pert for Walter, parson of the church of St. Philip, for the old school opposite St. Peter's", and St. Peter's belonged to Keynsham Abbey. The new school, wherever it was—from about 1495 till 1535 it was held in Frome Gate—would not have paid rent and therefore was not included in the roll. In 1259, an ordinance of "the Hospital of St. Mark of Billeswick, otherwise Gaunt's", provided that out of 27 poor, 12 were to be "scholars, ministering, in the choir only, in black copes and surplices, admitted and removed at will of the master and to sing at the disposition of the Precentor, and to be more plentifully provided for than the other poor . . . according to the means of the house, and one of the twelve scholars of ability to be elected to keep in order and teach the others, and he to be provided for even more plenteously and competently than the others".

In 1177, as we have seen, the school of Waltham fell under the dominion of the regulars on the conversion of the College into a Priory. The school continued, of course, under a secular master, as in 1423 we find John Olyver of Waltham Holy Cross, "scolemayster", being charged with having assisted in obstructing the Sheriff of Essex.

The transfer of the school of Waltham to the regulars must be one of the latest. For by the end of the twelfth century an entire change had come over the educational and religious situation. Silently and without authority of Pope or King, by the spontaneous action of the much-abused secular clergy themselves, new institutions had sprung up just in time to save the Western Church, and England in particular, from falling entirely under the dominion of the monks, as the Eastern Church had done. About 1150 even in England the clergy at length yielded to the monastic craze and abandoned the struggle against enforced celibacy, with such results as are revealed in the famous tales of Abelard and Heloise, of Absolon and the carpenter's wife at Oxford, and the miller's daughter of Trumpington at Cambridge. Meanwhile, there had sprung up, first in Italy, next in France, and then in England, those assemblies and unions or gilds of clerks for the sake of study and advancement of learning, which, known at first as *Studia generalia*, public or general schools, eventually acquired for themselves the exclusive use of one of the many terms for a corporation, the Universities. Almost at the same time as the medical schools in the salubrious climate of Salerno, *circa* 1090, and the legal schools at Bologna, there blossomed out an international institute in theology at Paris at the end of the eleventh century, and a national institute primarily in law, then in theology, but eventually, predominantly in logic and canon law, at Oxford at the beginning of the twelfth century. We cannot here enter into the vexed question of when the *studium* of Oxford could first be termed a University, a term which first appears at Paris in 1219 and at Oxford in 1245. But a *caveat* must be entered against the theory of Dr. Rashdall (*Universities of Europe in the Middle Ages*) that it arose from a migration *en masse* of English clerks from Paris in 1165 to 1167, in response to an edict of Henry II. This edict has been shown conclusively elsewhere not to be capable of such a construction or of originating such a movement, while the author of the theory admits that no single instance can be produced of any clerk who left

Paris in consequence of the edict, still less of any clerk going from Paris to Oxford. Oxford University was in full bloom when Giraldus Cambrensis lectured on Ireland to the masters and scholars there in 1189, and there is evidence of a teacher there, Theobald Stampensis (of Etampes), eminent in canon law and rhetoric between 1119 and 1135, of a teacher eminent in canon law, Robert of Cricklade, teaching clerks at Oxford coming from divers places in England, c. 1135, of a teacher eminent in theology in the person of Robert Pullen (the chicken) from 1133 to 1138, and of one eminent in civil law in the person of Master Vacarius between 1145 and 1150.

The written history of St. Frideswide's is now admitted to be a concoction of inconsistent fictions. All we really know is that there was an ancient collegiate church of secular canons, called St. Frideswide's, of pre-Conquest origin, which, of course, had its school, and which in 1122 was converted into a priory of regular canons. Another collegiate church called St. George's was founded in 1074 in the castle by the constable, Robert d'Oilli. This was not converted into, but annexed to an abbey of regular canons founded at Oseney just outside Oxford, in 1129. An early sixteenth century copy of its statutes is preserved in a Bodleian MS. They show that it consisted of twelve secular priests and as many scholars. Their oath on admission included a promise not to climb over the castle walls at night or procure any one to do so, and to report to the warden, who was a canon of Oseney, all who did. After taking the oath and inscribing his name on the register, the scholar gave a feast to his master and fellow-scholars at a cost of 1s. 6d. The scholars maintained a light at the high altar of St. George's called the Scholars' Light. They were fined a farthing for swearing and a halfpenny if they shirked services on feast days. The small amount of the fine shows that the statutes were of great antiquity, dating from times when a penny a day was substantial pay. It is therefore practically certain that the College of St. George's, being in the castle and outside the city, maintained its school as well as St. Frideswide's, just as at Paris the suburban college of Ste. Geneviève maintained its school as well as the central Cathedral church of Notre Dame. At Paris, the rivalry of these two schools and the fact that the master, driven out by the Chancellor of Notre Dame for theological heterodoxy, found shelter in the other, was one of the main contributing causes to the development of the University, which ultimately shook itself free to a large extent of the Chancellor.

We can but guess that when Theobald of Etampes dubbed himself Master of Oxford in a letter to Thurstan, Archbishop of York, in answer to a question, he was the Master of the School of St. Frideswide's, which, St. George's being outside Oxford, would be *par excellence* the school of Oxford. The question was whether monks could legally impropriate churches and tithes. Theobald answered by an exposition of the canon law, citing from Jerome, Ambrose, and Pope Gregory the same passages which afterwards appeared in the first part of the *Corpus Juris Canonici*, the Decree as edited by Gratian, to show that monks being dead to the world had no right to the possessions of the clergy, or clerks, which had been given to them for doing duty for the world. A monastery, he says, is a place and prison of the damned, monks having damned themselves here to avoid eternal damnation hereafter. If monks have been allowed to become clerks and bishops, that was not by ecclesiastical law but by a privilege, by special dispensation "for want of clerks". A monk, answering this, derides the "want of clerks". He asks whether there is want of clerks at Rome, Milan, Paris, Rouen, Bayeux, York, London, Salisbury, Lincoln? "Are there not monasteries inhabited by clerks at Milan, Turin, Lyons, Rome, Rouen, London, Salisbury, Lincoln, York?"—meaning apparently the cathedrals called minsters at those places—a mere juggle with words, though it is an ambiguity which has misled historians from that time to this. Lastly he exclaims, "want of clerks when everywhere in the world are liberal masters, who are also called clerks? You even, a nobody, are you not said to teach (*regere*) 60 or 100 clerks, more or less, in the guise of a master, to whom you have made yourself a grasping word-monger, wickedly deceiving them as you are yourself deceived? For, to say nothing of other parts of the empire, are there not throughout France and Germany, Normandy and England, not only in cities and walled towns, but even in villages as many learned schoolmasters as there are tax-gatherers and magistrates? where then is your want of clerks?"

Nothing could more strikingly prove the ubiquity of schools than this passage; while its grudging testimony to the success of Theobald himself as a teacher of classes of 60 to 100 is a convincing proof that the Oxford school was flourishing. One swallow does not make a summer, but it is a proof that summer is nigh. After all, the number of schools which went to make a University was not very large. A bull of Innocent III in 1207 fixed the *maximum* number of masters in theology (D.D.'s) at Paris at eight, including the members of the chapter of Notre Dame. So if Oxford boasted four doctors, whose names have come down to us, in as many different faculties between 1120 and 1150, she was not very far behind.

The rise of the University schools had great influence on the schools everywhere else. It caused a distinction to be drawn between the theological school, the law school and the schools of other faculties, and the grammar school, whereas hitherto all the sciences were, or might be, taught in one school. Incidentally it differentiated the Chancellor of the cathedral and collegiate churches from the schoolmaster, and tended to limit the local schools generally to grammar and elementary logic and rhetoric. It also seems to have raised the question of free schools. Between 1170 and 1173 Pope Alexander III wrote to the French bishops to rebuke the practice of those who "assume the name and dignity of Schoolmaster in the churches" refusing to give ecclesiastical licence to teach without payment of fees, and orders them to extirpate it at once. He ordered the schoolmasters that whenever fit and well-bred men wished to teach grammar schools (*studia litterarum*) they should allow them to do so without any charge, lest learning, which ought to be given gratis to all, should seem to have a price set on its head. A writer of the early thirteenth century asserts positively that this was aimed at the Chancellor of Paris, who used to exact a mark, 13s. 4d., a huge sum for those days, as a fee. At the Lateran Council of 1179 this provision was made general. The decree of Pope Eugenius of 826 had ordered all bishops to provide schools. These schools were now to be made free, at least for the poor. In order that the poor, who cannot be helped by their parents' means, may not be deprived of the opportunity of learning and becoming proficient, in every cathedral, a competent benefice was directed to be bestowed on a master to teach gratis the clerks of the church and poor scholars. For licence to teach nothing was to be charged. Innocent III at the next Lateran Council in 1215 complained that this decree was not observed, so it was repeated with an extension. In all churches of sufficient means a master was to be established to teach the clerks of the church gratis in the faculty of grammar and other things, while every metropolitan church was to have a theologian, endowed with a prebend, to instruct priests and others in holy writ. If the maintenance of two masters proved too onerous, the grammar master might be provided for in some other church in the diocese. This decree made statutory what had apparently already become customary. At St. Paul's, "Master Ralph the theologian," signed deeds in 1183. In 1205 the schoolmaster, become Chancellor, took over the theological teaching.

A majority, however, of the cathedrals, especially in the south of England, remained in the hands of the monks, and in these there were no secular canons and schoolmaster or chancellor to whom the bishop could entrust the government and teaching of the schools. In these cases, Canterbury, Winchester, Rochester, Worcester, Norwich, the bishop retained the schools under his immediate control and himself appointed the master. At Winchester, for example, we find Henry of Blois, Bishop of Winchester, appealed from in the case, to adopt modern terminology, of Phantom v. Jekyll, reported in John of Salisbury's Letters.

The plaintiff, Jordanus Fantasma in Latin, and in Anglo-Norman Jordan Fantosme, "the Ghost," was afterwards the author of a poem on the war between Henry II and his son in 1174. The case seems to have been heard some time between 1154 and 1158, when John of Salisbury was acting as Official Principal of the Prerogative Court of the Archbishop of Canterbury.

"The case of master Jordan Fantosme, and master John Joichel, clerks of the lord bishop of Winchester, has been carried before me. Having heard the case and inspected the documents, we inhibited the said John against teaching school in the same city against Jordan's will." The parties alleged mutual breach of faith, and Joichel appealed to the Pope; but

John of Salisbury, while reserving this question, says that he
" being clear on the right of master Jordan to the school, after
consulting the bishops of Chichester, Hereford and Worcester,
charged the lord of Winchester not to suffer the said Jordan
to be further vexed by the said John on the matter of the
school, on pain of excommunication.   A few days afterwards
however the parties came before us again, Jordan alleging
that John had usurped the school again and incurred excommunication.   He denied it and was prepared to swear that he
had desisted from the mastership after the injunction." Jordan
was ready to produce witnesses, but the other " refused a day "
on the ground that he was " starting for Rome ".   " Pray ",
says the harassed judge to the Pope, " by the help of the Lord
put an end to their litigation ".

The school over which Jordan and Jekyll quarrelled in 1155
was in Minster Street, outside the precinct, though on land
belonging to the cathedral monastery.   In a grant to the Priory
of St. Denis at Southampton some land in Minster Street is
described as being " between the house which was Jordan
Fantasma's and the house of Aimer the squire ", and in
another deed as being held at a rent of 2s. in lieu of all
services to Mr. John Judicialis, the Joichel or Jekyll of the
trial.   This house must have been the school house which
in 1367 is described as being " where the school is now held ".
In 1392 an assessment for the maintenance of the city walls
was paid for it in the name of the " High School " (*alta scola*),
called in 1450 and 1483 "le scole-hows " and in 1544 the
" High Schole House ".

There is evidence at Durham towards the end of the
twelfth century of the existence of the cathedral school owing
to its receiving a kind of exhibition endowment, probably
copied from one which Winchester School already enjoyed.
It was of a kind which proved to be the embryo from which
the collegiate system of Oxford and Cambridge, of Winchester
and Eton, was evolved.

At Winchester, about a mile out of the town, in or about
the year 1130, bishop Henry of Blois had founded the
Hospital of St. Cross (Holyrood as the similar place was
called at Edinburgh) for the infirm poor.   Besides the 13
brethren lodged and boarded in the hospital, 100 poor from

the city were every day entertained in a hall built by the Hospital gate, called the Hundred-menne-hall, at a dinner cooked by the Hundred-men-coke, the pottage or porridge of which it largely consisted being ladled out of the "Hundred-men-pot" by the "Hundred-men-ladel". Besides "sufficient pottage" the dinner consisted of a loaf of coarse bread weighing 5 marks, 3 quarts of weak beer, a herring and two pilchards, or, if not a fish day, two eggs and a farthing's worth of cheese. The poor men were allowed to take away the relics of their portion with them. Among the 100 men were 13 poor scholars of the city school "sent there by the Master of the High Grammar School of the city of Winchester". There are no extant documents to show that this substantial exhibition of a good meal a day for thirteen of the High School boys was provided for in the original charter, but it was stated by witnesses in 1373 to have been so and to have prevailed at all events beyond the memory of witnesses who carried it back to 1313. Further, Simon of Farlington in Hampshire, close to Winchester, who was Archdeacon of Durham, gave the manor of Kyhou (Kyo) to the Almoner of Durham Cathedral Priory in 1180 "for the maintenance of 3 scholars of Durham School, whom the master shall choose by way of charity and send with a platter or tally with the images of the Virgin and St. Cuthbert on it, to the Almoner, who shall provide them with food, drink, and lodging in the Almonry". There can hardly be a doubt that this Hampshire man knew St. Cross and deliberately imitated what he had seen well done there, on a smaller scale as became an archdeacon compared with a bishop, in connexion with Durham Grammar School, which has flourished continuously to this day.

It is a remarkable thing that the two earliest exhibition foundations known in France also owed their origin to Englishmen, the first of them in the same year, 1180, when Jocius or Jossy of London, on his way home from a pilgrimage to Palestine, founded what was later called the Eighteen College (*Collège de Dix-huit*). Finding that St. Mary's Hospital at Paris by ancient custom provided for payment a room for poor clerks attending the schools to live in, he converted this into an endowment by buying the room for £52, on condition that the

Governors of the hospital should always find eighteen beds for as many scholars-clerks and give them 12s. a month for maintenance, in return for which they were to carry the cross in the burial processions before the bodies of those who died in the hospital. Seven years later this was imitated in the Hospital of St. Thomas the Martyr (Becket) at the Louvre, which became the House of the Poor Scholars of the Louvre. The College of St. Honoré grew from a similar provision by a Bishop of Paris at St. Honoré's. Others followed, and later these Houses of Poor Scholars attached to hospitals blossomed into independent colleges.

A still earlier instance of a hospital affording exhibitions to scholars was said to be found at St. Katharine's Hospital by the Tower of London, founded by Queen Matilda, the wife of King Stephen, and reported to be for a master, three brothers chaplains, three sisters and six poor scholars. But the scholars were not part of the original foundation in 1147, which consisted of a grant of a newly built hospital to the Priory of Holy Trinity as governors with the endowment of a mill and £20 rent to maintain thirteen poor. The six scholars were not introduced till 1277. Then Queen Eleanor, the dowager of Henry III, who had wrested the hospital from the priory, added considerable endowments with three priests and twenty-four poor, among whom were to be "6 poor scholars who should assist the chaplains in the church in aid of divine service when they can conveniently take holiday from their studies (*cum hii pro suo studio commode potuerint vacare*) so that they may by their merits and diligent help be more bountifully considered in the alms of the Hospital".

But it may be said that all these schools of the eleventh and twelfth centuries, and indeed up to the sixteenth century, were no schools of any moment, and gave no education fit to be called a liberal education. Mr. Bass Mullinger, the historian of Cambridge University, wrote in *Social England* in 1895: "We hear but little concerning schoolboy life in medieval times, but that little is generally unfavourable. . . . The average attainments were limited to reading and writing, to which in the cathedral schools there were added chanting and an elementary knowledge of Latin." Sir Richard Jebb made, in the *Cambridge Modern History* in 1902, the amazing state-

ment that the "schools of the monasteries and those attached
to the cathedrals, alone tempered the reign of ignorance.   The
level of the monastic schools was the higher.   In the cathedral
schools the training was usually restricted to such rudiments of
knowledge as were indispensable for the secular clergy, viz.
reading, writing, arithmetic and elementary music."   The Rev.
T. A. Walker, M.A., LL.D., Fellow of Peterhouse, in the
Cambridge History of English Literature in 1908, repeats the
same idea: "The early education of the generality of English
youths in the Middle Ages was found in a school attached to
some cathedral or convent.   In the old grammar schools,
reading, writing and elementary Latin constituted, with singing, the subjects of instruction.   The 'litel clergeon, seven
yeer of age', of *The Prioress's Tale* learned in school 'to
singen and to rede, as smale children doon in hir childhede'.
He had his primer.   A schoolfellow translated and expounded
for the enquiring child the *Alma redemptoris* from the anti-
phoner of an older class.   The prioress, doubtless, here indi-
cates the teaching of the conventual schools of her day."

This is really lamentable.   The whole of the schools of the
Middle Ages, that is, from 450 to 1550, are judged and condemned by the standard of a small song-school described in a
fifteenth century work of fiction.   The smallest attention to
what Chaucer wrote makes it perfectly clear that the "litel
schole" on the borders of the Jewry, which, though said to be
"in Asie", is manifestly drawn from London or Lincoln, was
not a grammar school, but a song, or elementary school.
There were "children an heep"

> That leréd in that scolé yer by yere
> Such maner doctrine as men uséd there,
> This is to say, to synge and to rede,
> As smalé childer doon in her childhede.

The "litel clergeon", *clericulus*, seven years old, sat "in the
scole at his prymer", i.e. learning his A B C, learning to spell
and read, and heard his elders singing the *Alma redemptoris*.
He asks the elder to "expounden this song in his langage,
and preyde him to construe it".   The elder boy says he has
"heard" that it meant to invoke the aid of Our Lady, but he
could not tell him any more.

> I can no more expounde in this matère ;
> I lernè song, I can but smal grammère,

which means that he learnt singing, but no grammar, and simply learnt the music and the words, without understanding them, as the little clergeon himself then proceeded to do,

> ". . . til he coude it by rote
> And then he sang it wel and boldély
> Fro word to word, according with the note."

How can these misrepresentations be repeated by one writer after another, when the smallest consideration must show their impossible absurdity ? For if the schools were nothing but choristers' schools to teach psalm-singing, where did people like John of Salisbury or Alexander Neckham, get the education which enabled them to write the books which still remain to show us, not only their skill in writing Latin prose and Latin verse, their literary powers, their ability and wit, but their knowledge, both of the Scriptures, and of classical authors, especially in philosophy. It may be said they got them, not at school, but at the university. But a university, that is a school of the higher faculties for grown-up or growing men, could not flourish if it was fed only by schools in which boys had learnt nothing more than to stumble through a few psalms.

We need not, however, press the general argument. It is enough to quote one single passage descriptive of the schools in the capital of England, in print in English for at least 300 years in one of the best known and most quoted of Elizabethan books, John Stow's *Survey of London*, published in 1596, which alone should have saved Mr. Mullinger and his congeners from the absurdities current on this subject. This is the famous *Description of London* with which William Fitzstephen, cleric and judge, prefaces his biography of his former master, Thomas à Becket.

"In London", says Fitzstephen, "the three principal churches have famous schools privileged and of ancient dignity, though sometimes through personal favour to some one noted as a philosopher more schools are allowed. On feast days the Masters celebrate assemblies at the churches, arrayed in festive garb. The scholars hold disputations, some

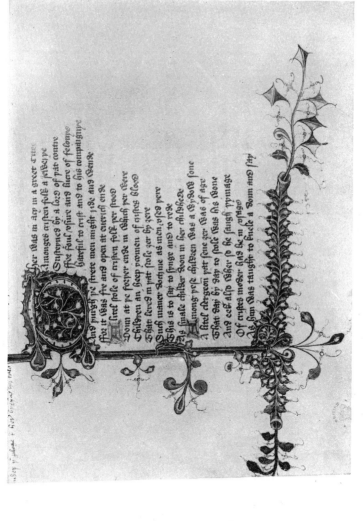

A SONG SCHOOL DESCRIBED IN CHAUCER'S PRIORESS' TALE

BRIT. MUS. MS. HARL. 7334. f. 200, b

argumentatively, others by way of question and answer.
These roll out enthymemes, those use the forms of perfect syl-
logisms. Some dispute merely for show, as they do at collections ; others for the truth which is the grace of perfection.
The sophists and those in training in sophistry are pronounced happy because of the mass and volume of their
words ; others play upon words. Those learning rhetoric
with rhetorical speeches speak to the point with a view to persuasion, being careful to observe the precepts of their art, and
to leave out nothing that belongs to it."

So much for the elder scholars. Their feats in logic and
rhetoric have been thought to show that the schools of
London at this time were really a teaching university, eight
centuries in advance of our new one. The mention of " collections ", the term still in use at Oxford for the college exa-
minations at the end of term, might be supposed to point the
same way. The medieval school term ended, as church
services end now, with a collection, for the benefit of the pre-
siding genius, the schoolmaster. School fees, like barristers'
fees, were *honoraria* and supposed to be voluntary offerings,
and collections came to be a sort of Speech Day, at which the
pupils showed off their accomplishments ; and they, or their
parents, bestowed their bounty on the master.

Rhetoric and logic, however, were not then university
subjects, but school subjects, and were begun at a much
earlier age than now. With grammar, rhetoric and logic
formed the *trivium*, which was the domain of the grammar
school, while the *quadrivium* and theology became the
domain of the university. A London university might,
however, well have been developed from these three schools,
as one had just been developed at Paris from the two schools of
the Cathedral of Notre Dame and collegiate Church of Ste.
Geneviève. If London had been the political capital only, as
Paris was, and the courts of law had settled there and not
outside it at Westminster, and if it had not been the chief
port and commercial emporium of the country, its schools
might have run the same course as those of Paris, and Oxford
would never have been the seat of a university. As it was,
commerce proved more lucrative and attractive than learning.
Though the mention of philosophy shows that there were

scholars of the University age and type at the London schools in 1118, they were probably in the minority.   The stress laid on rhetoric suggests that the elder scholars were no older than the boys in the top forms of St. Paul's School now.

At all events, besides the votaries of philosophy and logic, there were the younger pupils, those under fourteen, who only, in the strict language of the time, were called "boys", whose studies were purely grammatical.   They "hold contests in verse, or pose each other on the principles of grammar or the rules of preterites and supines.   Others in epigrams, rhymes and metres use the old street eloquence, with Fescennine licence scourging their schoolfellows, without mentioning names; hurling abusive epithets and scoffs at them : with Socratic salt girding at the failings of their fellows, or perhaps of their elders ; and in bold dithyrambics biting them with the tooth of Theon."   "The audience ready to laugh with crinkled noses redouble their shrill guffaws." The last words are a quotation from Persius by this twelfth-century author who, according to the theory we are demolishing, had only learnt at a choir-school to stumble through the Psalms.   But the whole passage is a satire on that sort of notion of our ancient schools.   It demonstrates, in a way the more effective that it is incidental, and not written for the purpose of telling us what the schools did, that they were giving precisely the same kind of classical education as the great public schools gave in the sixteenth to the nineteenth centuries, and perhaps even more effectively.

Nor were athletics and games neglected in these schools. Every year on Shrove Tuesday, the Carnival, "to begin with the boys' games, for we were all boys once", says the learned judge, "all the boys in the schools bring their game cocks to their masters, and the holiday is devoted to looking on at the cock-fights in the morning, after which in the afternoon the whole youth of the city goes into the suburban level", as he calls Smithfield, for "a solemn game of ball", presumably football.   "Each school has its own ball"; and nearly all the holders of civic offices each provide one.   "The grown-up people, the fathers and rich men of the city come on horseback to see the struggles of the young, and grow young with them ; and get hot with excitement, by looking on at so much exer-

A GAME OF BALL, STRIPES v. PLAIN. c. 1310

BRIT. MUS. MS. ROYAL 10 E IV., f. 94, b.

cise, and share the enjoyments of the free-born youth". We are also told how, when it freezes, the boys and the whole population go out and skate on Smithfield marshes, on those bone skates of which many specimens may be seen in the British Museum and at York. "On summer evenings", on the other hand, "the schoolboys and other young men of the city go out to take the air at the three principal suburban springs, where the transparent stream goes bubbling over the bright pebbles, namely Holywell, Clerkenwell and St. Clement's Well", just as the modern youth resorts to the river at Richmond or Hampton Court. Clerkenwell, in particular, took its name from this resort of the clerks or scholars, just as did the Pré aux clercs at Paris, the Smithfield of that city.

Nor was the inclination of boys to succulent food neglected. When in 1142, the canons of St. Paul's were called on to meet a claim for alleged unpaid purchase money of certain lands in the city, and executed a solemn deed before the Sheriff, the Alderman and beadle of the ward, to whom various fees were paid, to prevent such a claim being made again, the schoolboys, who were called in as witnesses to the purchase, were given " 3d. to buy cherries".

Stow in his *Survey* (p. 73) unfortunately threw the history of London schools into hopeless confusion by guessing that the other two schools of London besides St. Paul's were those of Westminster and Bermondsey. He was of course followed by other writers. Stow guessed the first, because of the tale of Ingulphus as a Westminster schoolboy and Queen Edith in the forged Croyland Chronicle, and the second, because, as he says, Bermondsey was the only other monastery in or near London then founded. But if he had stuck to his text he would have seen that both were impossible, as neither of them were in the then London but far outside it ; while there is no trace at any time of a school at Bermondsey, which was well outside even the borough of Southwark, and none at Westminster before the fourteenth century, of which hereafter. Stow had not access as we have to the statutes of St. Paul's made in 1243-54 by Dean Henry of Cornhill, and in 1294-1304 by Dean Ralph Baldock, or he would have found the two other privileged schools mentioned by name. In the earlier statutes it is said of the Chancellor, " All scholars living in the

city are under him, except those of a school of the Arches and
of a school in the Basilica of St. Martin's-le-Grand, who claim
that they are privileged in those and other matters". In the
later statutes the same words are repeated with the illuminating
difference that instead of the schools being in the singular they
are in the plural "except the scholars of the schools of the
Arches and of St. Martin-le-Grand".

We find the latter school appearing on 24 August, 1298,
in the city records when John the cap-maker of Fleet Street
entered into a recognizance to Master Hugh of Wytington,
schoolmaster (*magistro scolarum*) of St. Martin's-le-Grand for
payment of £8 at Michaelmas year. This recognizance was
cancelled at some unspecified date when Master John, brother
and executor of Master Hugh, acknowledged that he had been
satisfied of the debt. It would appear from the words of the
earlier statute that the school was held actually in the church.
But by 1368 we find it outside the church in the precinct.
For the church, we are told in letters patent of William of
Mulsho, Dean, 23 January, 1367, confirmed by King Edward
III, 25 November, 1368, had been with its bell-tower, cloister,
and other necessary buildings blown down and totally ruined
by tempest, pestilence, and other misfortunes, so that its
canons, vicars, and other ministers intended to abandon it, as
the endowment was not enough to enable it to be rebuilt,
when William of Wykeham, then dean, came to the rescue,
"moved by its sanctity as being among the other (royal)
chapels of the realm, the most devout and ancient, founded
and endowed by kings of England, and placed in the most
commanding part of the city of London, and rebuilt it of his
own substance, and erected it into a new form of wondrous
beauty, adorned with carvings of stone and laid the foundations deep in the bosom of the earth and intended to consum-
mate the same in wondrous wise at immense expense". Stirred
by Wykeham's example, Joan of Hemenhale, rich widow of a
mercer, founded and endowed a chantry in the college, and
the chantry priest was assigned for his lodging "the seler
situated above the school within the close of the chapel on the
East side". At the same time an order was made for another
benefaction, given by Thomas of Ousefleet, a former dean,
under which a mark was distributed at his Obit among the

canons, vicars, and other ministers of the church, including the schoolmaster. The school was still flourishing in 1394 and in 1446, when its privileges were attacked along with those of the other two privileged schools. Presumably it went on till the college, having been annexed to Westminster Abbey by Henry VII, fell with the abbey in 1540.

The school of the Arches, or St. Mary-le-Bow, appears several times in the Archiepiscopal Registers at Lambeth. Archbishop Winchelsea interfered on 25 September, 1309, in a dispute as to the appointment of the master. Master John, rector of the grammar school (*scolarum gramaticalium*) of the Church of the Blessed Mary-le-Bow, said that he had been appointed master by the dean of the church, the Dean of Arches, "to whom by ancient and hitherto peacefully observed custom" the appointment was well known to belong. But after he had quietly ruled the school, the Official Principal, the superior of the dean and supreme judge of the ecclesiastical court, "wishing to change the custom" had removed Master John and appointed Master Robert Cotoun. The archbishop told his Official to replace Master John. On 23 March, 1383, we find Archbishop Courtney himself, probably because the deanery was vacant at the time, appointing his beloved son, William Poklynton, clerk, "to the teaching and governance of the grammar school of the deanery of the Arches". But the record is cancelled in the manuscript. Archbishop Arundel, however, on 4 October, 1399, also committed the teaching and governance of the grammar school of the Arches to Master Thomas Barym, master in grammar;—the earliest evidence it is believed of the existence of a degree in grammar, as distinct from that in arts. It is curious that Stow misinterpreted a subsequent confirmation of the privilege of this school by Henry VI in 1446, which expressly mentions it as a school in the Church of St. Mary-le-Bow, as being its foundation: "In this parish", he says, "a grammar school was kept by commandment of Henry VI, in a house for that purpose prepared in the church-yard. But that school being decayed the schoolhouse was let out for a rent in the reign of King Henry VIII for 4s. a year, a cellar for 2s. a year and two vaults underneath the church for 15s. the two." Perhaps it had then been superseded by the better-endowed school of St. Anthony's Hospital founded in 1446.

It is rather remarkable that Fitzstephen does not mention among the schoolboys' amusements the ceremony of the boy-bishop or St. Nicholas; probably because they had not in Becket's boyhood obtained the vogue they enjoyed from the middle of the twelfth century. The feast of St. Nicholas was a most important day in the school life of the Middle Ages, mixed up as it came to be with the earlier celebration, handed down from Roman times, of the Saturnalia in December and of the Kalends on New Year's Day, in Christian circles known as the Feast of Innocents. This feast was only one and the last but, as it turned out, by no means the least, especially in England, of a series of feasts which lasted from 16 December to 6 January, and took on their maddest, merriest mood on Christmas Day and the three days following it, and became known as the Feast of Fools, the Feast of Asses and the Boy-bishop.

In the festivities, which centred round the boy-bishop, the medieval schoolboy found the relaxation and reaction which were to compensate him for the restraint and repression of the year. Santa Claus and Father Christmas and the pantomime which delights the modern schoolboy are direct descendants from the performances of the boy-bishop. Yet the very existence of that functionary, though he existed in England down to 1557, came to be quite forgotten.

The whole of Christmas time from the day of O Sapientia, 16 December, was given up to festivity. In the monasteries the various officers of the convents celebrated their " O's " on successive days by a series of feasts. These feasts were called O's because at vespers on these days the anthems all began with O. Thus on the 18th at Winchester Cathedral the Gardener appropriately celebrated his O with the anthem, " O root of Jesse ". Though commonly supposed to be peculiar to monasteries, the same practice was observed, and had no doubt been originated by the clergy of the cathedral and college churches. Thus a special statute was made at St. Paul's in 1263 that the " OOO against Christmas should no longer be kept ". The bursars' dinner at All Souls' College, formerly held on 19 December, and the New College dinner on 23 December, are the lingering survivals of these " O's ".

Christmas of course was kept with much feasting, and the

fun was fast and furious. The next three days were given up to the three orders in the church. Boxing Day, the day of St. Stephen, the proto-martyr, who was a deacon, was the deacons' day. On Christmas Day after vespers a procession was formed, in which the deacons appeared in silk copes, like priests, carrying lighted tapers, and the procession, after going round the church, went to the altar of St. Stephen, if there was one, a deacon taking the staff of the ruler of the choir, and acting as precentor, and three deacons chanting the "verse" and "prose". On St. Stephen's Day itself the deacons performed the priests' parts in the service. At vespers on 27 December a lord of fools was elected by the deacons. The *Te Deum* was sung, and he was then "chaired", or carried on the shoulders of his companions, to the common room, where the rest of the staff of the church were drinking. "At his entry all rise, even the Lord Bishop, if there, and with due reverence fruit, spices, and wines are given him. When the drinking is done they proceed to perform divine service". In the course of it, the two sides of the choir gradually sang higher and higher, trying to shout each other down. Service done, they "make a rush" into the streets, and "process" through the town, "visiting" the people and levying contributions. In 1236 Bishop Grosseteste of Lincoln, though we have evidence that he had himself when an undergraduate at Oxford performed the part of "lord of misrule," thundered against the vicars of the choir of the Minster for their Feast of Fools, with its plays and maskings. He thundered in vain. For in 1390 Archbishop Courtney after an archiepiscopal visitation there objected that on 1 January, "the vicars and clerks, dressed like laymen, laughed, shouted and acted plays which they commonly and fitly call *The Feast of Fools*", and he ordered them to stop it together with their public drinkings in the church. A sarcastic person has written in the margin of the Chapter Act Book, in which the order appears, "Harrow barrow. Here goes the Feast of Fools (*Hic subducitur festum stultorum*)."

The subdeacons gave even a rowdier turn to their celebration. The ruling idea of the Roman Saturnalia and Kalends of January feasts was imported with its inversion of status, the subversion of society, the slave becoming the master and the

10

master the slave.   The subordinate members of the choir sat
in the seats and performed the functions of their superiors,
and burlesqued them.   We know what they did chiefly from
the denunciations with which the more puritanical authorities
from time to time tried, mostly in vain, to put down their
performances.   They rang the bells jangled, sang out of
tune, the two sides of the choir trying to howl each other
down, said a burlesque mass, preached a sham sermon, put on
their vestments inside out, censed the altar and the choir with
incense made of black puddings and sausages or out of old
shoes, even sang ribald and indecent songs, played dice on the
altar, ran and danced indecently in the streets, sometimes
dressed as women or with monstrous masks, and wound up
with an uproarious supper.

On St. John the Evangelist's Day the priests had their
turn; gave a mock blessing, and proclaimed a ribald form of
indulgence.

On the Eve of Innocents' Day the priests gave way to
" the children," that is, the schoolboys and the choir boys,
whence its name of Childermas.   In *The Medieval Stage* Mr.
E. K. Chambers quotes as the earliest mention of the boys'
celebration, the *Festum puerorum*, one from Switzerland in
991, when King Conrad was spending Christmas with Solomon, Bishop of Constance, and went over to the monastery
of St. Gall hard by, to see the sports with which the monks
passed the three days and nights of Christmas, especially the
procession of the children (*infantum*), not as Mr. Chambers
supposes the boys of a public song school, but the oblates
or boy novices.   The King was much impressed by their
discipline, for when a heap of apples had been placed in
the middle of the church in front of them, not one even of the
smallest went up to it or even paid any attention to it.
However, a much earlier notice of these celebrations occurs
in England at the end of the seventh century when, as we
have seen, Aldhelm wrote to Hæddi, the Bishop of Winchester, to express his regret that he could not get there for
Christmas and dance with the brethren (*Natalis Domini
solemnitatem . . . tripudians celebrare*).   A Winchester Tropar
written before 980 gives the songs sung by the three orders
of deacons, priests, and boys, the former on the day of St.

Stephen the protomartyr, 26th, the priests on the day of the protopriest, St. John the Evangelist, 27th, and the boys on Holy Innocents' Day, the 28th. The latter began with an excellent hexameter, "*Psallite nunc Christo pueri dicente propheta,*" "Hymn ye now Christ, ye boys, in the well-known words of the prophet".

At first the boys' service was a solemn celebration of the Slaughter of the Innocents by Herod. At some time towards the end of the eleventh or beginning of the twelfth century the cult of St. Nicholas of Myra was introduced from the East and antedated the Boys' Feast by transferring the beginning of it from Innocents' Day to his day, 6 December.

This probably imaginary saint, from various episodes in his career, had a varied *clientèle*, being patron of seamen, thieves, marriageable maidens, children, more particularly schoolboys, clerks and scholars. He was *par excellence* "Bishop" Nicholas, because when the Bishop of Myra died, and the canons were assembled in the church to elect his successor, and could not agree, some one had the happy inspiration of taking the first "man in the street," and going to the church door found the pious and early-rising Nicholas, then a layman, coming to the church to hear matins; whereon he was made bishop. His patronage of children, which has given him the honour of Protestant celebrity as Santa Claus and Father Christmas, is attributed to the ascetic sanctity of his babyhood, which led him, as the service on his day is never tired of repeating, while still a long-clothes baby, to abstain from more than one meal on Wednesdays and Fridays, *O nova res, quarta feria et sexta tantum semel in die papillas bibebat.* His connexion with schoolboys and scholars is due to the story of his resurrection of three boys or youths who on their way to Athens University had been murdered in a hotel in Myra by the host. The bishop saw in a vision their dismembered bodies, cut up and hidden in a pickle-tub. He went to the inn, charged the host, who confessed, and called on the boys to come out of the tub, which they did. As related by Wace, the twelfth-century poet of the Norman Conquest, the story runs in modern spelling :—

Trois clercs allaient à l'école
(N'en ferai mie grande parole)
Leur hôte par unit les oscit [1]
Leurs corps meussa,[2] l'avoir en prit.
St. Nicholas par Dieu le sait,
S'empresse, fut là si comme Dieu plait.
Les clercs à l'hôte demanda, si la mostra
Ne peut musser, St. Nicholas fait sa prière :
Les âmes [re]mit aux corps arrière.
Parceque aux clercs[il] fit tel honneur,
Font les clercs fête en ce jour,
De bien lire, de bien chanter,
Et de miracles reciter.

Hence St. Nicholas is often shown with three boys in a tub, the tub having no connexion with washing (with which the medieval schoolboy had but little to do), but being the pickle-tub in which the saint found the boys' bodies.   The seal of Pocklington Grammar School—still a flourishing institution —founded in the fifteenth century in connexion with a gild of St. Nicholas, represents one of the boys just getting his first leg out of the tub, at the fortunate appearance of the bishop in full pontificals.   There was a " boom " in St. Nicholases in the eleventh century, owing to some Italian merchants having stolen his bones and "translated" them to Bari in South Italy, where divers miracles were performed.   In the first part of the twelfth century it was so great that Dean Kitchin has been able to show that the so-called " Norman" font in Winchester Cathedral, on which his story is carved, was only one of a dozen others all representing the same story, and all turned out from the same factory near Tournay.   Some of the earliest plays, written in the twelfth century, are founded on the incidents in his career.   He came in handy for the boys' holidays, while the plays instituted under his auspices outlasted his own memory.

Though elected on St. Nicholas' Eve, the boy-bishop did not officiate, after St. Nicholas' Day, till after Christmas.   On the evening of St. John's Day at vespers at the words in the *Magnificat*, " He hath put down the mighty from their seat, and hath exalted the humble and meek "—*Deposuit potentes*, as it was shortly called—the bishop or dean (at Winchester College no doubt the warden) descended from his stall, which was at once occupied by the boy-bishop in full pontificals, while his dean, archdeacons, and other dignitaries, and canons,

[1] Killed (?)   [2] Hid.

SEAL OF ST. NICHOLAS GILD AND GRAMMAR
SCHOOL, POCKLINGTON, 1514

all boys, attired in the characters of those they represented, were exalted to the upper stalls. In the procession, the usual order was reversed. The canons went first, the boys, with the boy-bishop last, brought up the rear. At St. Paul's it had been the custom for the boy-bishop to appoint the real dignitaries and canons as candle-holders and incense-bearers, and to perform the other tasks usually done by choristers, acolytes or clerks. In 1263 this was forbidden, and those of the second or third form, i.e. real acolytes or clerks, were to be selected for these offices. But at Salisbury the Processional, even up to the sixteenth century, prescribed that, for the procession, the boys were to write on the table of the day the names of the canons to minister, the greater to be incense-bearers and book-bearers, and the lesser to carry the candles.

The copes and vestments of the boy-bishop and his canons were no mere stage properties. In an inventory of the treasures of St. Paul's in 1295 are " a mitre embroidered with flowers for the use of the Bishop of the little ones ; a pastoral staff, whose curve and pommel is of copper gilt, with many vines and images, assigned for the use of the Bishop of the little ones ". In a later inventory, there was " a new white mitre with an orphrey " or golden fringe, and twenty-eight copes and mantles for the boys, but these were getting worn out. At York, in 1321, the Master of the Works gave " a gold ring with a great stone for the Bishop of the Innocents ". In 1491 the boy-bishop's pontifical was mended with silver-gilt. At Winchester College the inventory contained " a mitre of cloth of gold of the gift of the Lord Founder, with trappings of silver gilt of the gift of one of the fellows, for the Boys' Bishop, and a pastoral staff of copper gilt for the same ". At Wykeham's Oxford College, where the boy-bishop, was probably a chorister, and not a scholar, the mitre was of bawde-kin only. In the household of the Earl of Northumberland, who had his own chapel staff and grammar school in his household, there was for the boy-bishop a mitre well garnished with gold and precious stones, a cross with staff of copper gilt with image of St. Nicholas in the midst, a stained cloth of the image of St. Nicholas, and a gorgeous set of vestments in red with lions of silver and birds of gold on the orphreys. When Archbishop Rotherham made his will in 1481 he gave to the

College of Jesus, which he had founded at Rotherham in imitation of Eton and Winchester, for the " barnes' bishop "— i.e. " bairns' bishop "—a mitre of cloth of gold, with two silver enamelled knoppes.

To return to the ceremonies of Childermas Eve.   The boy-bishop being arrayed, he and his procession marched to the altar of St. Nicholas, when there was one, or, if not, some other saint, e.g. at Salisbury that of the Trinity and All Saints, the boy-bishop beginning the chant, taken from Revelations, " 144,000 who were bought from earth, the first-fruits of God and the Lamb "—an odd adaptation implying that 144,000 babies were killed by Herod in a small village near Bethlehem. Then three boys sang a " verse ", a continuation of the same passage from Revelations : " These were bought of all, *quia non inquinati sunt cum mulieribus, virgines enim permanserunt.* Therefore they reign with God and the Lamb with them. They follow the Lamb wherever he goes."   The boy-bishop, like a real bishop, " censed " the altar and the image of the saint.   The boy-precentor began the anthem of St. Mary. Then the boy-bishop took his seat, and said the verse : " Thou art beautiful in form beyond the sons of men ", a verse repeated by the choir to him, words which called for the requirement, in the York Minster Statutes, that the boy-bishop was to be the senior boy " so long as he was sufficiently good-looking ".   " Afterwards ", the rubric runs, " let the boy-bishop bless the people in this form : the cross-bearer takes the boy-bishop's staff, and turning to him, begins this anthem : ' Prince of the Church, Shepherd of the sheepfold, vouchsafe to bless thy people '; then turning to the people, says : ' With gentleness and charity humble yourselves for the blessing '. Then he hands the boy-bishop his staff, and he, first crossing himself on the forehead, says : ' Our help is in the name of the Lord '; then turning to the clergy he lifts his staff, and says : ' I sign you with the sign of the cross '.   Then turning to the people : ' Our help be ' (turning to the altar) ' in Him who has bought us and redeemed us ' (placing his hand on his breast ' with the price of His flesh '."   Afterwards the boy-bishop began compline like the priest, and after compline delivered the blessing : " Almighty God bless you, Father, Son, and Holy Ghost ".

Supper followed. At St. Paul's the boy-bishop might choose whichever of the canons he pleased to sup with, but by the statute of 1263 if he went to the dean's he was only to go with a staff of fifteen, namely, two chaplains, two taper-bearers, five clerks, two vergers and four residentiary canons; if to any lesser dignitary with fourteen only, and if to a simple canon with thirteen only. The boy-dean was to go with three companions; the boy-residentiary-canon with two only. As there were suppers also on Innocents' Day and the next day, it was provided that the same company was not to sup more than once with the same person. The earliest mention in England of the boy-bishop is in connexion with this supper. A statute made between 1189 and 1199 enumerates among the duties of a new residentiary canon that after the supper he is to conduct the boy who supped with him back to the Almonry with dancing and singing and torches, and there hand round drink and spices and a livery of wine and candles, and two servants are to wait there till another boy comes from a senior canon's. He is to give a second supper on the Octave of the Innocents, entertaining the [boy]-bishop and his boys and their companions, and giving them presents when they leave. It is somewhat comically provided that if he has to wait till very late for their arrival that evening he need not attend matins next morning.

In the thirteenth century a reaction set in against the too popular ceremony. While the men of old, says a statute of St. Paul's in 1263, had provided that in commemoration of the Holy Innocents, who had shed their blood for the Innocent Christ, an Innocent boy should discharge the office of prelate, and a boy preside over boys and an Innocent rule innocents, now an unruly crowd converted the ceremony to the dishonour and derision of the house of God. So they ordered the service to be conducted with due decorum and made various provisions, some of which have been already mentioned, for cutting down the numbers and expenses and preventing crowding. So at Salisbury in 1319, an edict was issued against the people crowding in on the procession and the boy-bishop was forbidden to have a supper, or visit anyone, inside or outside the precinct, except in the boys' common-room, and as soon as Innocents' Day was over he and the other boys were to go to school as usual. This was however *brutum fulmen*. There is evidence at Salisbury of a feast in 1413 and of visitations and collections amounting to £3 15s. to £4 9s. 11d. from 1440 to 1459. At Wells in 1331 the chapter condemned the theatrical plays performed in the cathedral and the monstrous masks worn at them, and ordered the service on Innocents' Day to be performed quietly and without tumult or burlesque ; but this had to be repeated seven years later. Bishop Grandison of Exeter, who was very much of a Puritan, complained in 1360 to the chapter of his cathedral and also of his collegiate churches of Crediton, Ottery St. Mary, and Glasney that on Christmas and the four following days not only during Hours, but, what was worse, even during the solemnities of the mass, the vicar and boys performed unfitting and noxious plays, indecent for decent clerks, by which the vestments and other ornaments of the church were spoilt. At Ottery in 1339 he had ordered that the boy-bishop should not go about outside the parish with "dissoluteness and insolence" collecting money and neglecting his duty.

Yet at Worcester the first extant mention of the Grammar School occurs in 1291 on a dispute between the rector of St. Nicholas' Church and the master and scholars of the school as to the right to the wax of the candles used on St. Nicholas' Day by the boys, and it required the personal intervention of the bishop to give solemn judgment in the boys' favour. At York in 1396 the boy-bishop spent a whole month after Innocents' Day in tours round his diocese with a mounted staff consisting of a tenor singer, who led his horse, a middle voice singer or baritone, a steward and preacher, and two others whose duties are not specified in the account-roll. Only once in the whole month of January is it recorded that he went to school, and on that day they "went out of town" directly after breakfast. The party levied half a mark each from the heads of the greater monasteries, and half that, 3s. 4d., from four of the lesser ones, with 2s. from five others.

The Countess of Northumberland contributed no less than £1 and a gold ring ; Lady Marmion half a mark, a ring and a silk purse ; Lady de Rous, and Sir Stephen Scrope each half a mark. The oblations on the day amounted to no less than £1 4s. 1d. with a silver spoon, a silver ring and a silk purse, while the chapter gave over £1 10s. more. The total receipts were £8 15s. 5d. Of this, the supper on Innocents' Eve cost 15s. 6½d. and that on Innocents' Day 16s. which included twenty-two fieldfares, eight woodcocks, a plover, 3d. worth of small birds, and sixty warden-pears. The tenor singer was paid a whole mark, 13s. 4d., the preaching steward only 4s. 8d. Twenty-eight pairs of gloves at 1½d. each were distributed among the vicars choral and the two schoolmasters of grammar and song, and the lucky youth who played the boy-bishop pocketed no less than £3 17s. 11½d.—a year's income of most grammar school ushers or chantry priests.

The ceremony was solemnly allowed by the statutes of Winchester College made in 1400 : "We allow that on the Feast of Innocents the boys may say and perform vespers, matins and other divine service to be read or sung, according to the use and custom of the church of Sarum". The allowance was acted on. In 1400 the college paid 2d. for two Founders'-kin's contributions to St. Nicholas Light. In 1404 the City minstrels were paid 2s. for their services on Innocents' Day. In 1462 the warden made the college pay 4d. which he had given to Bishop Nicholas (*Episcopo Nicolatensi*), visiting him in his lodgings on St. Nicholas' night. Though the Council of Basle had in 1435 thundered against the disgraceful abuse of the Feasts of Fools, Innocents and Boys, in which they dressed up as bishops and gave the episcopal blessing, yet an Eton statute in 1443, cap. 31, said of St. Nicholas' Day, which was the founder Henry VI's own birthday, "on which day and by no means on the feast of the Holy Innocents we allow divine service, except the sacred portions of the mass, to be performed and said by a boy-bishop of the scholars chosen yearly". Accordingly the accounts for 1446-7 show a payment of 1s. 6d. for making a rochet for a Bishop Nicholas (*Nicolacensi*). According to the Elizabethan schoolmaster Malim the election had been held on St. Hugh's Day, 17 November, the accounts for 1536-7 showing a payment of 4d. for a parchment roll on which to write the names of the bishop's officers on St. Hugh's Day. Eton being in Lincoln diocese the martyr boy-bishop St. Hugh had apparently superseded or been added to the boy-bishop.

Colet as a Reformer was an enemy of old superstitions, yet

his statutes for the refounded St. Paul's School in 1518, though not providing for his boys having a boy-bishop themselves, recognized the old custom by ordering that "all these children shall euery Childermasse day come to Paulis church and here the chylde bisshopis sermon, and after be at the hye masse, and eche of them offre a jd. to the child bisshope, and with them the maisters and surveyors of the scole". Erasmus indeed composed a sermon for the boy-bishop. One such sermon written about 1490 is preserved. It is a sober-sided performance enough; the chief joke in it being that the boy is made to wish that all his masters which taught him cunning in his youth were promoted to be perpetual fellows of that famous college of the King's foundation in Southwark called the King's Bench, and end their life in the holy way called in Latin *Via Tiburtina* and in English the highway to Tyburn. Colet's view of the boy-bishop was probably very much that of the German schoolmaster Schade, known as Mosellanus, whose school books were read at Eton and other English schools. In his *Paedalogia* or *School Dialogues*, published in 1521, dedicated to the headmaster of St. Thomas's School, Leipzig, he makes two boys discuss the boy-bishop. One of them sneers at the celebration, but the other, asked what is the good of it, says, "I don't know, but you get an extra good dinner".

At length on 22 July, 1541, the King's Majesty, minding nothing so much as to advance the true glory of God without vain superstition, commanded that the superstitious and childish observations, whereby upon St. Nicholas, St. Katharine, St. Clement, the Holy Innocents and such like, children be strangely decked and apparelled to counterfeit priests, bishops and women, and so led with songs and dances from house to house blessing the people and gathering of money, and boys do sing mass and preach in the pulpit, with other unfitting and inconvenient usages, be lost and clearly extinguished. Revived under Mary they finally disappeared under Elizabeth. Even in Catholic France and Germany the boy-bishop died at the same time in nearly every place, though at Noyau he survived till 1721 and an Ass-Archbishop lived at Sens till the nineteenth century. The truth is that in the sixteenth century the boy-bishop was no longer required. Regular holidays had then been instituted.

The dramatic instinct in children and their elders was satisfied by the performance of regular stage plays at schools, of
which the Winchester and Eton accounts furnish more or less
continuous evidence from the end of the fifteenth century, and
the Westminster Play is the surviving classical specimen.

CHAPTER VIII

UNIVERSITY COLLEGES, COLLEGIATE CHURCHES, AND SCHOOLS

THE twelfth century closed with a repetition by the Council of London in 1200 of the decree of the Lateran Council of 1179, "Let nothing be exacted from masters for licence to teach", and a revival once more, following the English canons of 994, of the canon of the Sixth Council of Constantinople in 692, that priests might send their nephews or other relations to be taught in cathedrals, and that they in their turn should keep schools in the towns or manors (*villas*) and teach little boys gratis, and have schoolmasters in their houses to teach boys, without expecting anything beyond what their relations were willing to give. A decree of the Lateran Council of 1215 complained that the former decree had not been observed, and ordered that not only in every cathedral church but in all others of sufficient means a fit master should be elected to instruct the clerks of the church and others in the faculty of grammar gratis ; while every metropolitical church was to keep a theological teacher to teach the priests and others in the sacred page and matters concerning the cure of souls. Both grammar and theology teachers were to be given the revenue of a prebend, though they were not necessarily to be canons. Four years later, Honorius III ordered this decree to be strictly observed, and that, if there was any difficulty in finding masters, canons should be sent to theological schools for five years to study theology, while retaining their prebends. In accordance with these directions we find in the Lincoln Episcopal Register, the earliest extant in England, frequent directions to rectors and vicars on institution to attend schools. Thus in 1219 the Vicar of Barton-on-Humber was directed to attend the Lincoln school for two years to learn theology, and in 1225 the Rector of Potter Hanworth,

SEAL OF CAMBRIDGE UNIVERSITY,
SHOWING CHANCELLOR AND PROCTORS, 1260

not yet even a subdeacon, was ordered, on account of his insufficiency in grammar, to attend a grammar school, no doubt that
at Lincoln.   So in 1230 the vicar of a Northampton church was
ordered to attend Northampton school for a year and then return to the archdeacon to show what progress he had made.

The educational activity evinced by these papal and episcopal mandates found its chief embodiment in the establishment
of new universities, headed by that of Cambridge.   Cambridge
first appears educationally in 1209 as a place to which a large
number of Oxford scholars seceded after one of the many bloody
town and gown riots there.   By 1231 it had blossomed into a full-
grown university with a chancellor of its own.   The existence
of a grammar school there before the university, and the effect
of the rise of universities in lowering the status of grammar
schools, are markedly shown in an entry in the Archdeacon of
Ely's book, preserved at Gonville and Caius College.   Hugh
Balsham, Bishop of Ely, in the octave of Michaelmas 1276,
made an ordinance settling questions which had arisen between
the archdeacon, the chancellor of the university, and the master
of the grammar school as to their respective jurisdiction over
clerks and scholars and the dependents of scholars.   As
between the archdeacon and the chancellor the points in dispute as to the jurisdiction over tradesmen and servants of
scholars were settled in favour of the chancellor, except for
moral offences, like adultery, of which the archdeacons took
cognizance, while the jurisdiction over priests who held chantries
and livings in the town, and yet were attending the university schools, was to turn on whether they were principally
scholars or principally priests or whether the matter in question
concerned university acts.   As between the grammar school
master and the chancellor and archdeacon, the decision was
that the master of glomery, as—by a curious corruption of
the word grammar he was called—had the jurisdiction in all
suits in which the glomericules (*glomerelli*), or grammar-school
boys, were defendants.   Whether the plaintiff were cleric or
lay, the grammar master alone should try and decide the case,
unless it related to the rent of a house, a matter which was
settled by a joint committee of M.A.'s and burgesses, or was
one of some serious crime which entailed imprisonment or loss
of university privileges, when the case was to go before the

chancellor of the university.   If, however, a university scholar were plaintiff in a case against a grammar scholar, an appeal was to lie to the chancellor.

The master's authority was shown by a beadle of grammar carrying a mace before him.   The right to have this mace carried everywhere else was confirmed, but, as the university statutes provided for two university beadles carrying maces at all university convocations and assemblies, including burial services, and forbade anyone else to carry them there, the grammar master was forbidden to have his mace carried at such meetings.   It is rather surprising to find that, with this important jurisdiction, the grammar master was required to swear obedience to the archdeacon on appointment to the school, and never to attempt anything against his jurisdiction.

After another secession from Oxford in 1238 universities appeared at Salisbury and Northampton.   The latter was suppressed by the Crown in 1265.   The former after producing two of the earliest university colleges in England was sufficiently flourishing in 1279 to produce a quarrel between the chancellor and the subdean of the cathedral on much the same points as were determined at Cambridge in 1276.   It had died out by 1325.

All this theological and scholastic activity was no doubt one of the causes of the codification into written statutes of the body of customary law which had been developed in the cathedral and collegiate churches.   These bear witness to the change in the status of the schoolmaster caused by the development of universities, and of theological schools at the cathedrals.

We now find three schools attached to the great churches, the theological school under the chancellor, who is generally required to be a master in theology, a doctor of divinity ; the grammar school under the grammar schoolmaster, generally required to be an M.A., appointed by the chancellor, whose deputy he was ; and the song or music school under the song schoolmaster, appointed by the precentor, whose deputy he was, for whom no special qualification was laid down. Oddly enough, the earliest extant edition of any English cathedral statutes comes, not from an English source, but from Scotland.   When the Bishop of Moray was establishing a cathedral at Elgin, he bestowed on the chapter the liberties and privileges of Lincoln, and accordingly Lincoln was asked to send a statement of its customs and constitutions.   The statements sent in response in 1212 and 1236 are earlier than any statutes at Lincoln.   In those sent in 1236 we find the first mention of choristers or a choristers' school.   The chanter (cantor) is the second person in the church.   The chanter's office is to rule the choir in raising and lowering the chant ; and to place the singers on " the table "—the orders for the week.   " To him also belongs the instruction and discipline of the boys and their admission and placing in choir."   On certain days he must himself lead the chant, and start the bishop when he is present.   He is bound to correct the chant-books and rebind them after the first binding, and if new ones are wanted, to get them written at the chapter's expense.   The chancellor is the third person.   " The office of the chancellor is to rule the School of Theology, to preach by himself or deputy", on certain days.   " To correct the reading books and rebind them after the first binding—if any new ones are wanted to get them written at the chapter's expense.   To place the readers and ministers of the altar on the table ; to hear the readers and determine the lessons.   To keep the chapter seal, to compose the lessons and deeds of the chapter and read whatever has to be read in chapter ; to keep the theological books of the church and the others in an aumbrey.   ' His dignity is that no one can teach (lecture, *legere*) in the city of Lincoln except by his license, and that he collates to all the schools in the county of Lincoln at his pleasure, except to those which are on prebends ' ", which fell under the jurisdiction of the other canons.

Statutes made at St. Paul's, London, about 1250, during the deanery of Henry of Cornhill, who had himself been chancellor for twenty-four years before becoming dean in 1241, are perhaps the next earliest.   Here the chancellor took precedence of the chanter, who was of later creation.   The chancellor, we are told, when present makes the table for lessons, masses, epistles, gospels, acolytes and hebdomadaries (the priests, who were in turn responsible for the services " in course ", as they still say at Winchester School, for a week) ; he hears the lessons, including that of the lord bishop on

solemn days, and carries him the book for the lesson at matins ;
and in a silk cope ministers to the bishop when he reads the
last lesson.   He introduces the clerks of the lower grade of the
church who are to be ordained, and presents them to the bishop
for ordination after having examined them in school ; and does
justice for their excesses to any who complains of them.
Under him are all the scholars who live in the city, except
those of a school of the Arches, and of a school of the basilica
of St. Martin's-le-Grand, who contend that they are privileged
in this and other things.   The same chancellor keeps an aumbry with the school books of the church.   He also prefers
a master of arts to the grammar school (*scolis gramaticis*) and
is bound to repair the school.   He composes the letters and
deeds of the chapter, and reads what has to be read in chapter.
He is the chief keeper of the seal, and receives a pound of
pepper for every deed sealed, and the chapter receives 3s.
The precentor's duty is laid down in much the same terms as
at Lincoln.   He is to rule the choir in raising and lowering
the chant and in psalmody ; to order the singers on the table
through the master of the song school, to goad the negligent
to sing, to chide and keep quiet those who make a noise or
rush about the choir in a disorderly manner.   On the greater
feast he begins the *Benedictus* and *Magnificat*, the processional
chants and the sequences, and examines the boys for admission
to the choir and for being placed on the table to sing.   But it
is specially noted that all power of punishing delinquents in
choir belongs to the dean and chapter as it did before the
creation of a precentor.

At Chichester Cathedral the ancient and approved customs
were ordered to be written down on 23 July, 1247.   They
were, as to the cantor, that " he ought to rule the choir as regards singing, and can raise or lower the chant, place readers
and singers both for night and day on the table, admit the
clerks to the choir; when orders are to be conferred read out
the names of those admitted ".   It will be noticed that in
tabling the readers the precentor here performed duties elsewhere done by the chancellor.   The chancellor, however,
" ought to rule [*regere, idem quod, legere*] school or present to
it, to hear the lessons and determine them ; to keep with the
help of a faithful brother the chapter seal and compose letters

and deeds". In 1232 a dispute with the treasurer had caused a statute to be made which enlarged on the chancellor's duties. It was added that he must hear the night lessons himself, immediately after vespers, or by a fit person "well learned in the method of pronunciation customary in the church"—a curious provision which looks as if some English pronunciation of Latin was already in vogue. Some insistence was exhibited on the point. The statute proceeds: "He can, however, if he wishes to lighten his labours, call the juniors of the second form and the boys of the third form and hear their lessons before that office. But whoever is going to read must present himself to be heard at a convenient time, otherwise if through mispronunciation or absurdity or otherwise he offend against the rule of the church, let him incur the penalty decreed below against those who commit default in duties assigned to them by the daily table, which in the church are commonly called *marances*." These penalties were, for a vicar, the loss of 1d. or 2d. ; if not a vicar, chastisement by the precentor or his deputy ; "but if of the third form," i.e. a boy, "let him be turned out of the choir, or receive from his master or the precentor's deputy seven strokes, or if he has committed a grave offence, fourteen". The chancellor's duties also included the maintenance of a notary and letter writer and other fit person sworn not to reveal the secrets of the chapter, to write the letters of the Dean and chapter. "He shall without grudging or waste of time supply him with all things necessary for writing. Also he shall himself, or through some other fit corrector, correct the books of the Church which need correction."

The earliest known appearance of the school at Wells is in a deed between 1175 and 1185, witnessed by Peter of Winchester, *magister scolarum*. An early grant in 1229 of a separate endowment of the school remains, when Roger, a canon, gave a house to be enjoyed by the schoolmaster for the time being for the use of the school at Wells, in consideration of which the master and scholars were bound to pray daily for the soul of the donor and other Christian souls. The statutes written down about the middle of the century are almost identical with the Institution of St. Osmund, the same distinction being drawn apparently between the duties of the chancellor and

the "archiscola" on the one side for the grammar school, and
the chanter and his Official for the song school on the other.
In 1298 the vicar choralship of the prebend of Biddenham,
which as it was assigned to the fabric fund, was not represented
by any canon, was given to the schoolmaster, whose stipend
from the common fund was £1 10s. 4d. in 1327, £1 6s. 8d. in
1343 and £1 10s. 5d. in 1536 ; but he generally held a chantry
as well, and as chantry priest shared with seventeen others in
the endowment, £11 18s. 8d. a year, of the New College of
Mountroy or Mounterey, founded for the chantry priests in 1401.

At York the statutes were not written as we now have
them till 1308.   The written statutes are then stated to be derived from inquiry as to the ancient customs, the earliest recorded statutory codification of them being dated 1250.   The
chanter has now become precentor, a distinction which marks
the development of the choir.   He now only begins the chant
and does not personally perform the chief part in the singing.
Most of his duties devolve on the subchanter or succentor.
His office is to instal any one raised to any dignity, or canonry,
or office.   To him belongs the rule of the choir as to singing
and psalmody.   When the archbishop celebrates, the precentor
presents the Antiphon to him or the *Magnificat.*   On solemn
days he is bound to begin the mass.   " Also to him it belongs
to collate to the song school (*scolas de cantu*) and cases concerning the school ought to be heard and determined before him :
though execution belongs to the Chapter.   The succentor
of the vicars writes the table of the chants ; hears what the
boys ought to sing and chastises them when necessary ; and
receives by way of emolument 20s. a year from the Song
School."   The statute as to the chancellor says that he was
" anciently called schoolmaster, he ought to be a master in
theology and actually lecture near the church.   To him belongs
the collation to grammar schools, but to the School of York
(*scolas Eboracenses*) he ought to present a regent in arts (i.e.
an M.A. who is actually teaching school, as he was bound to
do for two years after taking his degree) of whose proficiency
there is hope, who according to ancient custom of the church
will hold it for 3 years and not beyond unless by grace
for one year."   The chancellor has to preach on certain
days.   He keeps the seal.   " To him and his subchancellor in

his name it belongs to place those who ought to read on the table and licence them to read and hear them in the vestry before service. To him belongs the keeping of a chronicle of notable events and assigning of lessons for those who read on double feasts." The subchancellor ought to receive 20s. a year from the grammar school.

Some statutes of Southwell Minster, the quasi-cathedral church of Nottinghamshire, not a complete code, but touching only on certain points, made at the end of March, 1248, provided that schools of grammar or logic shall not be held in the prebends of the canons, except according to the custom of York; while in 1238 the prebendary of Normanton in Southwell Minster, who was ex-officio Chancellor of that church, is recorded as having asserted his jurisdiction over Newark Grammar School against the priory of St. Catharine by Lincoln who were impropriators of Newark church, but had to admit the supremacy of the chancellor by presenting the schoolmaster of Newark to him for admission.

The statutes of Hereford Cathedral do not appear to exist in any form earlier than a recension of the first quarter of the fourteenth century, now in the British Museum. They are to much the same effect as the rest, but the later date is seen in a further development of delegation. The office of the precentor, a word indicating the fourteenth-century date, is to begin the first chant in solemn processions, and the sequences at mass or vespers, to give the bishop the antiphons he has to begin, to take charge of the whole singing and psalmody, to find a succentor, and keep and repair the chant and psalm books. The succentor's office is to write the table for singers and rule the choir and the rulers of the choir; to find five clerks of his school in the first form to begin the antiphons on weekdays and at the office of the dead and to carry crosses, candles and incense-burners. He can chastise with blows any of the other clerks of the first form, but not turn them out of the choir without the canon's consent. Here the first form was the lowest, canons and priests sat in the first form; deacons and subdeacons in the second; clerks of inferior order in the third. The reference to the clerks of the third form in the succentor's school, who in another place are called " boys of his school of singing in boys' voices " was necessary to distinguish the choir-boys in the song school from the boys in the grammar school.   This was as usual under the chancellor not the precentor.   "To the office of the chancellor it pertains to keep the books of the church and repair them when necessary ; to order everything relating to reading, to hear the lessons ; to compose and write deeds and writs to be sealed with the chapter seal; to find a regent master in arts [the words to teach the grammar school appear to have dropped out of the copy] who on feast-days ought to attend choir in choir habit, and to table those who are to read, and hear the lessons in his master's place."   A separate statute directs that no one placed on the table to read should presume to read without having the lesson heard by the person deputed to do so, unless he is one who by learning and long use does not require hearing ; and if he does so presume, and makes any bad mistake in quantity or accent, if he is a clerk of the first or second form he shall be punished by discipline, i.e. flogged, for it is expressly ordered that even a deacon or subdeacon of the second form shall bare his back to receive discipline from the hebdomadary.   A priest-vicar who makes any such mistake was to be even more heavily punished.   Lest it should be said that it is only a guess that the words "to teach the grammar school" have dropped out of the statute cited, it may be noted that in 1385, when the chancellor was a non-resident Italian, the Bishop of Hereford complained that although he had often required the chancellor, to whom by custom the grant and appointment of the master of the grammar school of the city of Hereford belongs, to provide a fit master to teach the same school, he has expressly refused to provide one and so relieve holy church and the scholars wishing to learn from no small loss and burden.   The bishop therefore proceeded to appoint one himself to teach and govern the school with birch and rod, as custom is, for one year.   With the usual insouciance of the local and educational historian this has actually been quoted as the foundation of Hereford Cathedral Grammar School, whereas it witnesses to its being even then ancient.

The second half of the century saw the beginnings of the collegiate system at the universities, and a revival and development of it among the secular clergy throughout the country in

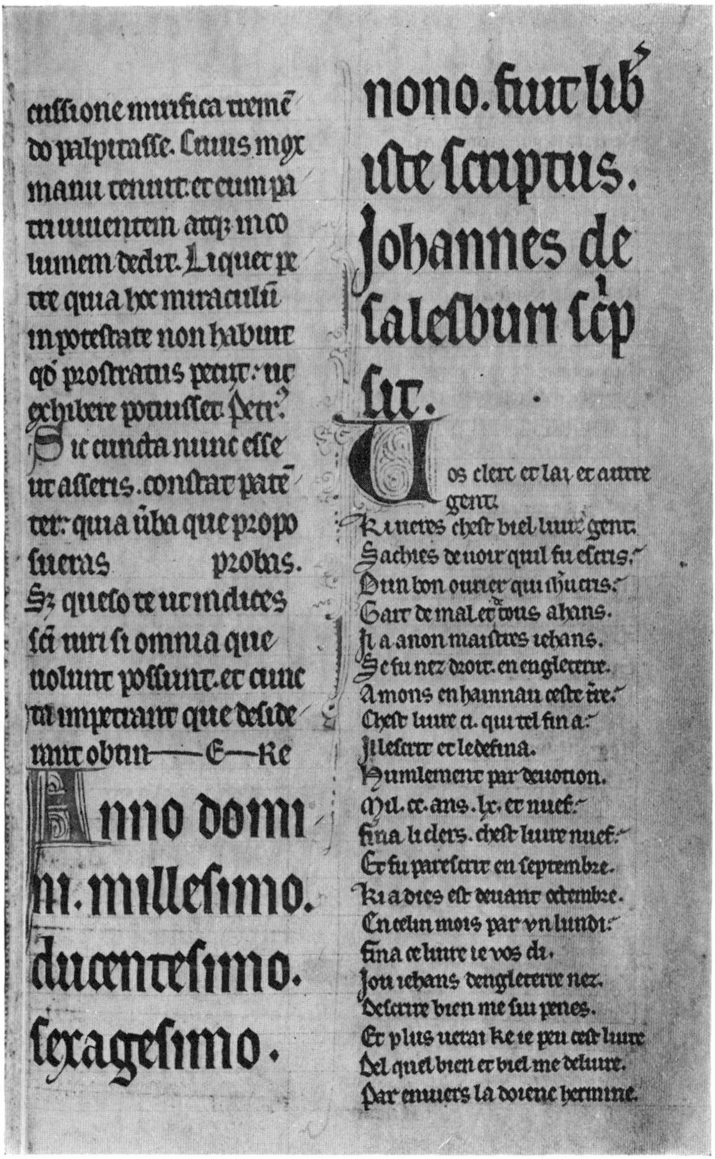

JOHN OF SALISBURY'S HOLOGRAPH LESSON-BOOK, 1269

BRIT. MUS. MS. EGERTON, 2569, f. 58

the collegiate churches.   It began with the universities.   We saw the embryo of it in the attachment of scholars to hospitals. Its development was marked by independent houses established *de novo* for scholars alone.

Paris set the fashion.   The Oriental College founded by direction of Pope Innocent IV in 1248, for boys to be trained up in Oriental languages and to become missionaries, and the theological college of the Sorbonne in 1257, were the two chief models.   The earliest English university college was at Salisbury, where there had been a university since 1209, the House of the Valley Scholars of St. Nicholas.   It was founded in 1262 by Bishop Giles of Bridport for two chaplains and twenty poor, honest, and teachable scholars in a house by St. Nicholas' Hospital, under the wardenship of a canon of the cathedral.   The Valley Scholars were a French religious order which had been founded by an English master of Paris University.   The English college had nothing to do with the order. In 1264, Walter of Merton, Chancellor of England, founded " the House of the Scholars of Merton ", first established at Maldon in Surrey to support twenty scholars living "at Oxford or wherever else a university may chance to flourish".   It was moved in 1270 to Oxford.   Merton, because he took away from his heirs by founding this college the right of succession that was theirs by the custom of the realm, gave a preference for the scholarships, that is fellowships, in the college, to his next of kin, and also attached a grammar school to it by the provision "also if there are any little ones of the heirs aforesaid, orphans, or otherwise through poverty wanting due sustenance while they are being instructed in the boyish rudiments, the Warden is to cause them to be instructed in the house aforesaid, until they can profit in the schools, if found of ability ", when they were to be elected scholars.   The same provision was repeated in the more elaborate code of 1274, when the house was moved to Oxford and the scholars lived in it ; but the number of the boys was limited to thirteen.   A grammar master, apparently to be one of the scholars, was to be appointed to devote his whole time to grammar and look after them ; though the scholars also were to resort to him " without blushing " in any difficulties in his "faculty", and he was to see that they talked Latin or the vulgar tongue (French), and instructed the seniors.

At Cambridge the first college was founded on 24 December, 1280, by Bishop Balsham of Ely, who placed some poor scholars in the Hospital of St. John " to live together and study in the university of Cambridge according to the rule of the scholars of Oxford who are called Merton's ". As the regular canons, who managed the hospital, quarrelled with them, on 28 May, 1285, he moved the scholars outside the town by St. Peter's Church, which he appropriated to them, and thus gave the college the name by which it is still known, Peterhouse.

The establishment of these university colleges was quickly followed, or accompanied by a new crop of colleges or collegiate churches of secular canons all over the country, each with its schools of grammar and song. Among the earliest appears to be that of Howden in Yorkshire, the rectory of which, belonging to Durham Cathedral Priory, was in 1266 divided into five prebends to support as many canons living together and serving parishes round about. There are next to no records of this collegiate church. But in a Durham Register we find in 1393 the Prior of Durham, as " Ordinary of the spiritualities of St. Cuthbert in Howdenshire," appointing masters of the song school (*scolas cantuales*) and grammar school (*scolas gramaticales*) there, " as they have been accustomed to be conferred ". In 1394 he appointed to the combined reading and song school (*tam lectuales quam cantuales*), while on a fresh appointment to the same school in 1401, he reserved to another person, no doubt the parish clerk, the right to teach eighteen boys reading. A new appointment to the grammar school in 1403 expressly directed the master to make his boys attend and sing at the Lady Mass in the collegiate church as anciently used. It is odd to find in 1409, and again in 1456, the reading school combined, not with the song school as usual, but with the grammar school. A fine Tudor building, built on to the south-west corner of the church, still used as the grammar school, now in a very small way, testifies to the continued interest of this earliest collegiate church of the second crop in its school until its dissolution.

The Collegiate Church of St. Thomas the Martyr at Glasney, now part of the town of Penryn in Cornwall, was founded by Bishop Bronescomb of Exeter in 1267. It was for thirteen clerks, one of whom was provost, the most usual number for such establishments, after " Christ and his apostles twelve ". They were especially directed to be called secular canons and to enjoy the same customs and liberties as those of Exeter Cathedral. A grammar school was a part of these customs, and we find Edward VI in 1548 on the dissolution of the college continuing the master with £6 18s. for his wages yearly.

In 1283 a collegiate church of a dean and seven canons was founded by Anthony Bek, Bishop of Durham, at Lanchester ; who also refounded and re-endowed the collegiate churches of Chester-le-Street in 1286, and St. Andrew Auckland in 1292, with an ex-fellow of Merton as dean, and a grammar school which still flourishes.

In 1283 the Bishop of St. David's in Wales " considering that health and solidarity arises from the unanimous and united company of an established college " made Llangadock church collegiate for twenty-one secular canons and as many vicars.

From this time to the dissolution of colleges in 1548 scarcely a year passed without witnessing the foundation of a college at the university, or a collegiate church with its grammar school attached, generally in the native place of its founder. The only difference between the university college, with its church attached, and the collegiate church, with its schools of grammar and song attached, was that the latter were primarily for religious services and secondarily for education, and the former were primarily for education and secondarily for religious services. The collegiate church was *ad orandum et studendum*, the house of scholars at the university *ad studendum et orandum*. Both were indifferently spoken of as colleges.

As the extant episcopal and other registers, like the Chapter Act Books of the cathedrals, mostly begin in this century, we get incidentally a good many notices of schools, especially where, the cathedrals being in monastic hands, the schools remained under episcopal control.

Thus the earliest notice yet discovered of the grammar school at Norwich is in the Coxford Priory Chartulary. On Thursday before the Conversion of St. Paul, 1240, the Official, the judge of the bishop's court, gave judgment in a case in

which Master Vincent of Skerning (Scarning)—the title shows
that he was an M.A.—then schoolmaster of Norwich (*rector
scolarum Norwicensium*), asserted that the school of Rudham
by Coxford was tributary to the school of Norwich, and that
no master could keep a school (*regere scolas*) there without
licence of the schoolmaster of Norwich.   The Priory of Coxford defended as patrons of Rudham School.   An inquiry
was held, both of masters who had taught school there, and of
scholars who had been at school there (*vacabant studio*) for
a long time.   The result was that it clearly appeared that
Rudham School was free of all subjection or payment of
tribute to Norwich School, and that the appointment to it belonged entirely to the prior and convent; judgment was given
accordingly.   Norwich School appears again in the statutes of
St. Giles's or the Great Hospital in 1256, Bishop Suffield the
founder ordaining that, like St. Cross Hospital, Winchester,
the hospital should provide dinner for poor scholars to be
named from time to time by the master of the Grammar
School.   After the dissolution the so-called King Edward VI.
School entered bodily into this hospital in virtue of an arrangement made by the city with Henry VIII.   The earliest
register of the Archbishops of Canterbury shows Peckham
visiting Norwich in 1288 when the See was vacant and appointing a master to the Grammar School of the city and
Diocese of Norwich in the person of Godfrey of Norton; a
precedent followed by Archbishop Whittlesey in 1369 appointing Master William Bunting clerk.   It is not till 1338
that a collation by the Bishop of Norwich himself has been
preserved ; but from that time to the Reformation there is a
continual stream of appointments by the bishop to the Grammar School and the Song School.   The Grammar School was
not in the monastic precinct but in the parish of St. Matthew,
nor were the masters monks, but clerks and masters of arts, or,
as in the case of John Spirlyng in 1434, of grammar.   For
lack of a secular chapter, the Bishop of Norwich appointed to
the Grammar Schools not only of Norwich but throughout the
county, a number of appointments by him to Thetford from
1329 to 1434 being recorded, while from such appointments
we hear of grammar schools, not otherwise known of, at
Fincham in 1432, Harleston by Redenhall in 1433, Shipdham

(Shipden) in 1455, Shouldham in 1462, and Thoney (Saham Toney) in 1474.

At Worcester on 26 May, 1291, Bishop Godfrey Giffard solemnly settled an action between Walter, rector of St. Nicholas Church, and Master Stephen of London, rector of the Worcester School, on behalf of himself and his scholars, as to the celebration of the feast of St. Nicholas by the company of scholars, as to the making of the wax candles used, for which the scholars made a collection, and as to the disposal or custody of the candles at the end of the solemnity. The Consistory Court had failed to decide this weighty question. So the bishop himself summoned the parties before him at Hartlebury Castle and decreed that as the feast had been formerly celebrated in St. Nicholas Church by the devotion of the scholars, so it should for ever continue to be celebrated, and that the rector of the church should have no claim on the wax or candles unless the masters and scholars chose to give part of it to him out of mere devotion. The remainder wax after the ceremony should be delivered by the master and three scholars to some trustworthy citizen or merchant who would undertake to restore it with due increase by way of interest to them when next they celebrated the feast ; and the rector if he wished could be present as a witness at the delivery of the wax and its redelivery. Any dispute was to be referred to the Archdeacon of Worcester or the Official, the judge of the bishop's court. This school too, therefore, was not in the monastic precinct or taught by monks but in St. Nicholas parish, a considerable distance from the cathedral, where it still was maintained by the city gild of the Trinity at its dissolution in 1548. An appointment of Master Hugh of Northampton, clerk, as master, by Bishop Reynolds on 28 May, 1312, is expressed to be made "whether the appointment belongs to us by episcopal or by archidiaconal authority", there being apparently some question whether the collation had not been delegated to the archdeacon. At all events the prior and monks had no hand in it.

Similarly at Carlisle, Pope Nicholas' taxation in 1291 shows that the schoolmaster of Carlisle (*rector scolarum*) received the large income of £20 6s. 8d. from the churches of Stanway and Dalston. He was described as "one of the monks" by Mr. C. Elton to the Schools Inquiry Commission in 1867, though Carlisle Cathedral was inhabited not by monks but regular canons, and in point of fact the schoolmaster here as elsewhere was always a secular clerk, not a regular at all.   Thus we find in the episcopal registers, Master Nicholas of Surreton *rector scolarum Karlioli*, being ordained successively subdeacon, deacon, and priest on 18 December, 1316, 26 February, 1317, and 22 September, 1319, on the title of probity, which apparently means good repute as master, and licences to Master William Salkeld, clerk, "to hold the grammar school in our city of Carlisle" by Bishop Halton in 1333, and to Master John Burdon, clerk, by Bishop Welton in 1362.

At Canterbury the archbishop retained control of the school, as is shown by a document of 21 March, 1291, by which, addressing his beloved son the master of the school of the city of Canterbury, Archbishop Peckham granted him special licence to take cognizance of and exercise jurisdiction freely in all cases of his school and scholars with power of canonical inhibition as has been anciently accustomed.   The first actual appointment of a master of Canterbury School now preserved appears in the register of Peckham's successor, Archbishop Winchelsea, who on 11 April, 1306, conferred by way of charity on Master Richard of Maidstone, clerk, the regimen of the school of the city of Canterbury and the same school, which belonged to his mere collation, and instituted him rector in the same with all its rights and appurtenances and invested him with it by his ring.   There is ample evidence that the school was in the parish and perhaps at one time in the church of St. Alphege, outside the monastery, opposite the bishop's palace.

The register of Archbishop Romanus of York in the year 1289 shows us the existence of two schools, one of which, Kinoulton, we know nothing of otherwise, while the other, Nottingham, used to be credited to the year 1512 until the publication of the Nottingham Borough Records exhibited it as a going concern in 1382.   It would appear that the master of Nottingham School had been objecting to a rival school being set up at Kinoulton.   Addressing the schoolmaster of Nottingham and the vicar of Kinoulton, the Archbishop informs them that, as he wishes his own rights to be kept in their integrity, so he did not wish to derogate from the rights of others, and he decreed therefore that only the clerks of the parish might attend the school which had from ancient times been customarily kept in that parish, all other clerks and foreigners being excluded and by no means admitted to it. Thus, he says, we both have regard to the rights of our free chapel, the church aforesaid, and the right of the master as regards stranger clerks is preserved in its integrity.

We get some light on the internal economy of schools from the accounts of the Merton College Grammar School beginning in the year 1277. There were apparently eleven boys, four of them in college (*in domo*), and seven others "in the town," under the care of Thomas of Wallingford. The cost of the commons of these last is given week by week, the numbers of the weeks being given, remarkably enough, not in Roman but in Arabic numerals. Commons for the eight of them, including the Custos, came to 5s. 4d. a week, or 8d. a head. This was precisely the sum allowed by Archbishop Giffard of York when he sent John Aucher and two companions to Beverley Grammar School the year before this, 7 March, 1276. The elder scholars, or fellows, were allowed 50s. a year, or a shilling a week. The "necessaries" of the boys included "a sheet for William of Portsmouth" at 15¼d., showing that schoolboys did not sleep on straw, as has been sometimes asserted. This was no special provision for a nominee of the still living Founder, for in 1304-5 we find a quantity of linen cloth bought at Winchester for 17s. 10d. and 2d. paid to a seamstress for making the linen into sheets.

In the summer term all the boys were in the town under Thomas of Wallingford. Hire of an inn (*hospicium*) for twelve boys and their master for the summer term cost 2s. 8d. ; their servants, a washerwoman, and boy (*garcioni*) were paid 20d., while to the Master of Grammar (*magistro glomerie*) for five boys was paid 20d. for the term, or 4d. a term each. This entry is of considerable antiquarian interest. It shows that instead of the term *Magister Glomeria* being, as stated by Dr. Rashdall in his *History of Universities*, a "wholly peculiar Cambridge institution", it was in use at Oxford. The fact is that the word Glomery is merely a familiar corruption of the word grammar, and was in use not only at Oxford and

Cambridge, but at Orleans and Salisbury and no doubt else-where ; the word *glomerelli*, for small grammar boys, being found at Bury St. Edmunds. Master Henri d'Andely, who wrote *circa* 1259 at Rouen in Norman-French a *Battle of the Seven Arts*, representing in mock-heroic verse the victory of logic studied at Paris over grammar cultivated at Orleans, mentions *les clers d'Orleans glomerians*. About 1290 at Bury St. Edmunds we find a common form for the use of the Sacrist of the Abbey, who exercised the powers of archdeacon in Bury. It ran " A. of B. official of C. hearing that certain pedagogues, wrongly usurping the title of master, with sacrilegious daring usurping the jurisdiction of Sir C., rashly presume to teach school without his authority in the liberty of St. Edmund and keep adulterine schools, pretending to teach dialecticians, gram-marians (*glomerellos*) and pupils of all kinds against the head-master (*magister scolarum*) of St. Edmunds " directs the clergy throughout the liberty to excommunicate the offending peda-gogues. A year or two later, one John Harrison (*filius Henrici*) was directed to desist within eight days from keeping an adulterine school for grammarians (*glomerellos*) and other *discipulos* against the privileges of the abbey and school of St. Edmunds. At Salisbury, the same building is described in 1308 as a school of glomery (*scole glomerie*) and in 1328 as a grammar school (*scole gramaticales*), thus establishing the identity of the term beyond dispute.

The second point of interest in this earliest account of the Merton schoolboys is the amount of the tuition fee paid to the Master of Glomery, 4d. a quarter, which is exactly half the sum settled by undated, but apparently fifteenth-century, statutes of the University for the fees in Grammar Schools at Oxford, unless a special agreement had been made for more, and also at Ipswich in 1477 ; while, at the Grammar School founded at Newland in Gloucestershire about 1480, it was provided that it should be half-free, grammarians paying 8d. a quarter and those learning to read 4d.

Merton school was apparently regarded as rather a grievance and a burden by the elder scholars, fellows as they came to be called, the governing body of the college, and it had come to an end altogether two years later. Friar John Peckham, Archbishop of Canterbury, as a result of a visitation of the

College on 31 August, 1284, issued an amended "rule" in seventeen chapters. In Chapter iii. he says : " Moreover the institutor of your college "—the earliest use of that word in relation to the house—" seeing that the clerks of England for the most part stutter and stammer in talking Latin" ordered that grammar pupils should be maintained under a grammar master, to be encouraged by a storehouse of grammar books ; and commanded "you to talk Latin (*loqui litteraliter*) which hitherto has been neglected". The Visitor therefore orders this to be amended as soon as possible and the books of Papias and Hugucio and Brito's *Summa* to be bought and chained on a proper desk. After reprobating other breaches of the Rule, the Visitor returned again to the grammar boys in Chapter xii. In many ways, he says, the Fellows have departed from the holy purpose of the founder. In the first place, they were only to admit the poor and not those who had sufficient means of their own or their parents' or who could by industry or favour provide for their own needs. In view of the founder's kin provisions, it is probable that the ex-mendicant friar was straining the word " poor ", as it has often been strained since in popular argument, out of all relation to the founder's real intention. The second breach is, says the Visitor, that against the intention of the rule, the Fellows were not willing to admit youths (*adolescentes*) able to become proficient, but only those already advanced in learning, whereas they ought, as above said, to admit those learning the rudiments of grammar, and he blames them for not admitting boys of the family of the founder.

That the Visitor's strictures were effective is shown by the accounts for 1290. There were then thirteen boys of founder's kin besides Roger, nephew or grandson (*nepos*) of Mr. Richard of Worplesdon, a former Warden, and their pedagogue (*petagogo*). Their cost was £7 10s. 8d., or a little over 1s. 6d. each, for half a year. In 1299 they were not boarded in college but in a separate house, for which 4s. rent was paid. A book, of which the name unhappily is not given, bought from Mr. Thomas of Wilton, cost no less than 2s. 6d., at least £3 of our money.

In 1300-1 there is a highly interesting account for one Bereford, who appears to have been a young aristocrat, as he had a

separate chamber.   Between St. James's day (25 July) and St.
Andrew's day (30 Nov.) he had five pairs of shoes for 2s. 1d.
His school fee (*scolagium*) for the winter term was 4d. in addition
to 1½d. as a tip (*dica*) for the usher (*hostiarii*), who is also
called vice-monitor.   A payment of 2d. for a cock for his use
against the carnival (*carniprivium*), shows that at Oxford in
the thirteenth as in London in the twelfth and Yorkshire in the
seventeenth century the custom of a cock-fight in the school on
Shrove Tuesday prevailed.   A halfpenny was paid for a hoop
(*troco*) for him, while on the day before Whitsunday some un-
decipherable sum was paid for his gloves (were they fives-gloves ?)
and balls.   In the same year among the " expenses of the
Founder's nephews " we find 2d. paid for two dozen of parch-
ments for them, 2d. for a pound of candles.   The *dica* of their
usher was ½d. each, and their scolage also was 4d. a term.
Their *dica* or offering on the feasts of the two patron saints of
schoolboys St. Katharine (of Egypt) and St. Nicholas (of Myra)
was a penny each, except for " little Peter Clive ", who only
paid a halfpenny.   In 1304-5 their scolage was at the rate of
6d. a term, or rather perhaps 1d. a week.   For it varied from
term to term, seven boys in the winter term costing 3s. 4d.,
and in Lent term 2s. 11d., while six boys in the summer
term cost 3s.   Seemingly there were only three terms in the
year.   In 1308 there were ten boys whose scolage in
summer was 3s. 4d. or only 4d. each.   We get a glimpse of
what they learnt in the purchase of "a Cato"—the pseudo-
Cato's *Moralia*—for 2d. and ivory tablets for 1½d., while in
the following year a Donatus, or accidence, cost 3d. and
parchment 5½d.

The small Merton Grammar School was by no means
the only Oxford Grammar School, nor the oldest, as may be
gathered from the existence in the Southern Proctor's and
the Chancellor's books of a copy of " Ancient Ordinances for
Masters in Grammar, but they are not in modern use ", which
must be of the first half of the thirteenth century.   The first
of them, providing that Inceptors in grammar are to be
bound by pledges (*fide media*) to observe the statutes and
customs ordained by the Chancellor, seems to show that the
Faculty of Grammar was organized on the same basis as that
of Arts, and that the licence to teach was only granted to

those who had already shown their capacity by actual teaching under supervision.   Inception in fact corresponded pretty nearly to the theoretical instruction accompanied by practice-schools of the most recent educational training.   The other grammar school statutes are of the ordinary gild type. All grammar masters were to attend the funeral of any of their number or of any grammar scholar.   They were to hold two stated meetings at the beginning and end of each term and other meetings when necessary.   They were all to have the same holidays, or, as it is expressed, to keep the same feasts.   On Fridays they were bound to dispute grammatical questions only, and not, presumably, questions of rhetoric or logic.   The longest and apparently most important statute is that "On making a roll".   "The names of all grammar scholars known and unknown shall be inscribed on the roll of the master regent in grammar", that is actually teaching grammar in the first two years after his licence, a provision curiously qualified by the condition "when there is any such in this University".   This roll every regent master of the faculty is bound at the beginning of each term, and twice a term afterwards, to read aloud in his school, "so as to exclude false brethren".   Every master is bound, on pain of perjury, not to enter anyone's name on his roll nor to defend anyone in life or death as his scholar, unless he knows or has good reason to believe that he attends the grammar school of some one licensed by the Chancellor to teach grammar in the accustomed way.   Every master is bound to give public notice in his school of this constitution, and that every one whose name is not found on the roll, or whose name is on the roll, but does not regularly attend school, is outside the protection and privileges of the University.   The grammar schools were not, however, like the schools of other faculties, confined to masters.   For the next statute directs that each public teacher of grammar, who has not been adorned with the estate of a master, is bound to tell the regent master or regent masters, if more than one, the names of his scholars as well boarders (*commensalium*) as others, and see that they are duly entered on the roll for the protection of the scholars.   On the other hand, every regent master in grammar is bound to the best of his ability to make all those publicly teaching grammar in the University, who had not obtained the honour of the mastership, observe the foregoing rules.

There are many other schools which appear in the thirteenth century in towns where there were monasteries, which were clearly not kept by the monasteries or monks, and remained under the control of secular clergy. They are mostly known only from casual entries in records. Among them is Colchester School. On 28 May, 1206, a grant was made by the Bishop of London of a soke in St. Mary's, Colchester, extending from the town wall to Head Street, which soke with the school of Colchester belonged to the barony of the see of London.

On 9 May, 1229, the schoolmaster of Leicester was appointed by Pope Gregory with the Abbot and the Dean of Christianity,—the rural dean so to speak, of the city of Leicester,—as judge to determine a case on appeal to the Pope between the prior and convent of Thurgarton and the rector of Banston as to a payment due from the latter. He with the Dean of Christianity as principal judges, with a subdelegate of the abbot, tried the case and decreed judgment against the rector on 9 April, 1230.

In July, 1242, the schoolmaster of Cirencester (*magister scolarum Cirencestrie*) was one of three judges who heard an appeal to the Pope in a case in which Gloucester Abbey was concerned.

The school at Lewes appears in 1248. The alien prior of the Cluniac priory there, Guigardus, and the convent contested the claim of the mother abbey to the tithes of Lewes, and the case was referred to the cardinal priest of St. Laurence in Lucina to hear as Papal delegate. On Whit-Monday, 1248, the priory appointed their beloved clerk Lucas, master of Lewes school, as their proctor, steward, or syndic. As 860 marks and costs estimated at 100 more were involved this was no small case. On 8 July Lucas duly appeared at Rome, and after various sittings and adjournments admitted the claim of the Abbot of Cluny. Archbishop Peckham was probably at this school as he declared that Lewes Priory was dearer to him than any other in England because he had been brought up close by it (not, be it noted, in it,) from a boy. In December, 1285, John of Hampton, master of Lewes School (*scole Lewensis*), was ordained acolyte by Peckham at South Malling church.   Another master appears in a will in 1405 as being owed "6d. for half a quarter" tuition fees.

Henry, schoolmaster of Battle, in Sussex, born in Cornwall, appears in a deed of 1 April, 1251, and another after 1261 ; he was a married man, for his daughter Alice appears as a grantor of land in 1277 and 1299.

At Arundel, about the same time, the prior covenanted with Master William of Wedon in consideration of a grant of land by him, to find him in eatables and drinkables at the monks' table and to provide him a fit house (*hospicium*) in which to keep his school decently, and a chamber in the priory, and a mark of silver so long as he was able to teach the school efficiently.

The schoolmaster of Marlborough (*Merleberge*) was one of three Papal delegates to try a case between a canon of Salisbury and the Archdeacon of Surrey.

Thomas of Kyrkeham, schoolmaster of Lancaster, appears as witness to a deed in the priory chartulary early in Henry III's reign. On 17 April, 1284, Emma, wife of Master Thomas of Lancaster brought an assize of *mort d'ancestor* and a few weeks later "Thomas le scholemaster of Lancastre" and Emma his wife successfully defended a counter action brought by the defendant in the former action.

At Chesterfield in the reign of Henry III, Sir Henry, clerk, of Ashbourne, thanked Simon, rector of Chesterfield, for having obtained for him from the Dean of Lincoln "the mastership of your (i.e. Chesterfield) school", especially as the rector had pressed his appointment before he had asked for it. It is notable that in 1337 Sir Henry of Sutton, schoolmaster of Chesterfield, appears with a wife Agnes holding land there.

At Malmesbury, the Priory Register written "at the end of the 13th or beginning of the 14th century" shows us Master Reginald, schoolmaster, and afterwards vicar of St. Peter's church, holding property in the town, and his school building later vested in the Pitancer.

At the following places where no monasteries existed, secular or lay records furnish notices of schools at this time. Included in the property of Baldwin de Insula, Earl of Devon, in 1263, was the township of Plymton with the advowson of the school.

At Louth when a new vicar was appointed on 23 October,

12

1276, a letter was sent to the schoolmaster of Louth to induct him.

In 1283, Robert Burnell, Bishop of Bath and Wells, appropriated to St. John the Baptist's Hospital, Bridgewater, the rectory of Wembdon, and in 1290 that of Morwinstow, in consideration of which, Geoffrey, Prior of the Hospital, covenanted in 1298 with Burnell's successor William of Marsh, to maintain within the walls of the Hospital, thirteen poor, able scholars, for instruction in grammar, and also to provide daily dinners from the Hospital kitchen for seven of the poorest scholars sent by the schoolmaster (*rector scolarum*) of the town of Bridgewater. The Valor Ecclesiasticus of 1535 shows fourteen scholars still being maintained out of the revenues of the two rectories.

The coming of age of Hugh de la Tour in 1309 was proved by a witness who knew it because his own son had been at Taunton School with him (*ad Scolas Taunton in societate predicti*) in 1293.

At Wakefield a court roll of the manor for 1298 shows Alice Sampson being indicted for breaking into the barn of Master John, rector of the school of Wakefield, at Topcliff, and stealing therefrom sixteen fleeces.

In a thirteenth-century feoffment among the Belvoir Castle MSS., Christiana, wife of the late schoolmaster of Helmsley, Yorkshire, was grantor.

It is difficult to decide whether the endowment of a house in High Street, Salisbury, given by Bishop Robert Bingham about 1270 for the use of masters who should instruct in arts on condition that poor scholars should be taught free was for the Grammar School or for the masters of the incipient University. As a little before in 1267 his predecessor had founded the college of St. Edmund for theologians, it is on the whole more probable that this was intended as a University not as a school foundation.

As local records come to be examined by more than the single pair of eyes which have lit on these notices, with as much attention to the evidence as to living educational institutions as has hitherto been paid to dead monasteries and chantries, the number of schools which can be traced to the thirteenth century or earlier will be indefinitely increased.

CHAPTER IX

THE ERA OF SCHOOL STATUTES

A T some time unknown before 1306 a new departure was taken in organizing the Grammar Schools at Oxford which appears to point to a considerable increase in their number, accompanied perhaps by a falling off or failure in the supply of regent masters, to whom, under the "Ancient Statutes no longer in modern use", their management was till then entrusted. For at a specially solemn congregation held at the beginning of Michaelmas term 1306, at which the Archdeacon of Oxford and the Bishop of Lincoln's Official Principal were present, representing the special episcopal control over grammar schools, perhaps in the absence of the Chancellor (for otherwise that control was exercised by him), it was provided that two M.A.'s should be yearly elected to superintend the grammar schools. If it had not been for the addition of the words "as has been the custom", we might have supposed this to be an entirely new arrangement, whereas apparently it was only the statutable and episcopal recognition of what had already been the practice. The superintending masters were to be paid a salary, as to which it is somewhat mystically stated "that saving the proper seat of the vice-monitor, the whole residue should be divided into two equal parts, to be applied one to the M.A.'s and the other to the vice-monitor"; and, to prevent fraud, the two M.A.'s were to collect this salary together. Who was the vice-monitor? In the Merton School documents the vice-monitor seems to be the same as the Hostiarius or usher. He appears also at this time in the Grammar School of Canterbury and in that of St. Alban's, and he is probably the usher or second master, who is also mentioned. But why the usher should have half the salary collected besides his own special fees as usher, and where the schoolmaster himself comes in, is most obscure.   Nearly half a century later we find that the University, having spent a large sum on the repairs of the Inn called "le Bufohall", or Toad-hall, the regent masters agreed in December, 1352, that the University should have two-thirds and the visitors of grammar schools one-third of the rent received for the hall until the sum spent was repaid.   This appears to be explained by another undated but probably late fourteenth-century statute to mean that in fact the whole sums called collections (*collecta*) paid to the grammar schools were divided into three parts, one to the superintendent masters, one to the teaching masters and the other to the vice-monitor.   It is then stated that to encourage the grammar schoolmasters to teach their boys with greater diligence the superintending Masters of Arts should take two marks only from them, whether there was only one master or more, and four marks from the University revenues, two marks in each term, the superintending masters at the same time being absolved from the obligation of ordinary lectures on Priscian's *De constructionibus* to which they had been obliged, though they are still to lecture in two terms cursorily, and to visit the grammar schools once a week.   If, however, the University rents assigned for the purpose proved deficient, 40s. a year for each superintendent master was to be made up out of the collections in the grammar school, i.e. the fees received by the grammar school masters.   These superintending masters correspond to the Master of Glomery at Cambridge, a term in use there as late as 1540.   There being only one at Cambridge, instead of two as at Oxford, points to a less number of grammar schools and schoolmasters.

It shows how erroneous is the usual view about the scanty instruction given in the grammar schools at this time, that the code of the faculty of grammar, in which this statute is embedded, provides that no one shall teach (*legat*) in it without the Chancellor's licence, nor get that licence without being first examined and found fit in verse making and writing prose (*de modo versificandi et dictandi*) and in books (*auctoribus*), "lest the saying of Isaiah might apply, 'thou hast multiplied the people but hast not increased joy'". On being licensed the masters were to swear to be diligent in teaching their scholars, and not let them for greater gain run about outside the school or play in school, and to teach them good conduct as well as learning. Every fortnight the boys were to be set verses to make, and letters to compose " in fitting terms, not in six-feet-long words and swelling phrases, but in succinct clauses, apt metaphors, clear sentences, and as far as may be full of good sense ". These verses and letters the boys were to write on parchment on the next holiday, and on the next school-day to recite them by heart to the master and give him what they have written. The masters were also to make them observe the rule in Latin or in French according to their statutes, i.e. to talk either in Latin or in French according to their age and advancement. This is an apt illustration of the passage in Higden's *Polychronicon*, written in 1327, a copy of which was one of William of Wykeham's gifts to his new college, commenting on the corruption of the English language. It "comes to-day", he says, "chiefly from two things, viz. that boys in school, contrary to the custom of all other nations, since the first coming of the Normans, abandoning their own tongue are compelled to construe in French; and also that noblemen's sons from their very cradles are taught the French idiom; and country men, wishing to be like them, that so they may appear more respectable, endeavour to Frenchify themselves with all their might". A remarkable proof of the extent to which it was carried is that there are three extant letters of William of Wykeham's to Englishmen and all are written in French. It is clear from the insistence on composition both in prose and verse that the medieval grammar school differed not at all in subject or method from the Renaissance school or the school of the so-called New Learning, the post-Reformation school, except that boys translated their Latin not into English but French. That difference disappeared, as will be seen, before the end of the century with which we are now concerned.

Nor was it only at Oxford, the centre of intellectual activity, that the schools were thus highly organized. On the contrary, the schoolmaster, the grammar school master, occupied a relatively lower position at Oxford, where he was overshadowed by the teachers in the higher faculties, than in places where he was the chief representative of learning, and required or kept a position corresponding to that of the Chancellors of Oxford and Cambridge themselves, especially when they were not overshadowed by the Chancellors of cathedral or great collegiate churches. A wealth of documents in the first part of the fourteenth century has been fortunately preserved which enable us to compare the position occupied by the schoolmasters at Canterbury and St. Alban's with that occupied by those at St. Paul's, London, and Beverley.

At Beverley on 27 October, 1304, the chapter of the Minster or collegiate church of St. John, on the complaint of Master Thomas of Brompton, rector of their school, that one Robert of Dalton, clerk, unmindful of his [soul's] health and not fearing the sentence of greater ex-communication healthfully promulgated four times a year in the minster against all those audaciously infringing the liberties of St. John of Beverley, kept a school in the town of Dalton to the prejudice of the liberty of the minster, directed Walter of Kelsay, their clerk, to warn the said Robert that within nine days, of which the first three should be taken for one warning, the next three should be taken for a second, and the third three for a third and peremptory warning, he should totally desist from keeping such school there or elsewhere within the liberty, and not attempt any such things thereafter. If he disobeyed, he was then and there excommunicated in writing by the chapter, and Kelsay was to proclaim or cause him to be proclaimed excommunicate every Sunday and feast day with bells ringing, candles lighted and extinguished, during mass in the parish church of Dalton. Some three months later, 20 January 1304-5, another rival schoolmaster appeared in Stephen of Garton, clerk, who equally unmindful of his soul ruled an adulterine, i.e. unlicensed, school (the word is commonly used of gilds established without the royal licence) in the town of Kelks, also within the liberty of Beverley. Walter of Kelsay was to warn him in the same way, but he was allowed only three days' grace if disobedient, and was to be excommunicated in his school, with a crowd of people standing round, as opportunity offered. Yet another rival schoolmaster appeared in Geoffrey of Sancton who kept a notoriously adulterine school in the territory of Beverley itself, and when summoned before the chapter induced the Provost to summon Master Thomas of Brumpton (*sic*), the rector of Beverley School, before him in a personal action about 12 March 1304-5. Later

in the year Geoffrey of Sancton, being warned to desist from
keeping the school, refused and was excommunicated, and
when he sought to bring an action against the schoolmaster
as such was refused a hearing.   The Official Principal of the
Court of the Archbishop (who happened also to be a canon of
Beverley) was therefore asked on 13 December to cause him
to be boycotted, "to avoid him and cause others to avoid him,
until, excluded from common intercourse, suffused with shame
he may be inclined to the grace of humility and the issue of
reconciliation ".   This seems to have been effective as, on 22
January, 1305-6, the chapter told one of their vicars that they
had given Geoffrey absolution and directed him to give solemn
notice of the fact in the processions held in the minster.   But
on 9 March, 1305-6, Robert of Dalton was again directed to
be warned against keeping school at Dalton to the loss and
grievance of the rector of the school and against the most
ancient and immemorial custom of that church.   It was not
till 6 November following that he was absolved.   Meanwhile
the master of Beverley School had changed, the Chancellor of
the minster having on 30 September, 1306, solemnly collated
Master Robert of Bolton to the Grammar School of Beverley (*scolas Beverlacenses gramaticales*) then vacant, and to his
collation belonging, to hold for three years.   Master Robert,
having presented a testimonial from the Vice-Chancellor,
Master Richard of Aston, and the University of Cambridge
under their seal, that he had duly acted as a regent Master of
Arts and been of good behaviour, was then admitted and sworn
to be obedient to the chapter and faithfully rule the school
and do all else which the laudable and approved customs of the
school and church required, and was inducted into the corporal
possession of the school.   Two years later the chapter decided that the schoolmaster was bound to keep the school
in repair himself, but the chapter was to rebuild it if it was
destroyed in any way.   On 5 May, 1312, a dispute between
the master of the Grammar School, then Master Roger of
Sutton, and the Succentor of the minster came before the
chapter.   The master refused to admit more than seven choristers
to the school and wished to make all choristers beyond that,
the ancient statutable number of choristers as it had been of
canons, pay fees (*salarium*).   The chapter, after having made

full inquiry of the seniors of the church, having regard to the ancient customs of the church and school, decreed that the number of choristers in the school was not to be restricted, but that all of them should be admitted quit and free (*liberi*) as regards the master, who should not exact any pay from them; but they granted an injunction to restrain the Succentor from admitting boys to wear the habit of choristers in choir in fraud of the schoolmaster.

At St. Alban's at this time, probably in consequence of some similar competition, we find some highly illuminating statutes. About 1286 Master Richard of Nantes gave a new school and master's house on Hokerhill in the town of St. Alban's to the scholars and their successors (as if they were a corporate body) for the use of poor scholars for a grammar school there to be held and kept freely and quietly for ever; in trust that " whoever shall be master of the scholars of the said school for the time being shall take no fees (*contribucionem*) from the sixteen poorest scholars of the said school, but the same sixteen poorest scholars shall, as regards the master aforesaid, be wholly quit of all fees; but the rest of the scholars shall pay fees to the aforesaid master according to ancient custom." The fees were probably 4d. a term, if the payments for the Merton College Grammar School boys may be cited as evidence.

On 16 September, 1309, new statutes were made for the school, in consequence, no doubt, of some dispute. They were " issued with the unanimous consent of the Master and all the Bachelors ", and were confirmed with the seal of the Official (i.e. the official principal or chief ecclesiastical judge of the liberty) of St. Alban's, and reduced to a " Public Instrument " by " William Henrison of St. Alban's, Public Notary ". The statutes run in the name of the master himself, who is described as " by lawful prescription competent judge of the rights of the Grammar School of St. Alban's ".

" In the name of God. Amen. The master forbids anyone hereafter to enter the school, unless his name has been placed on the Master's Register (*matricula*). If he does, he shall be turned out and not enjoy the privileges of the school."

The next two clauses forbid any assault on or annoyance

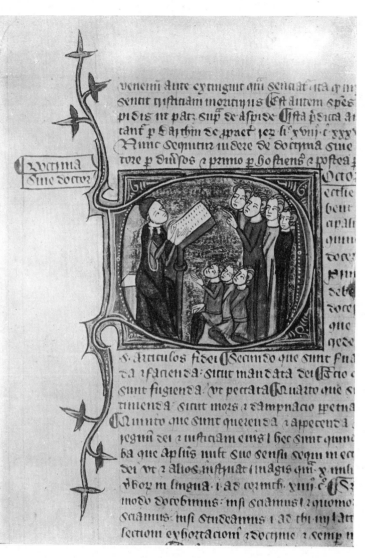

AN ENGLISH FOURTEENTH CENTURY SCHOOL

by a scholar to another scholar in school or out, or to a layman or other licentiate, or running about the streets or squares without reasonable cause, on pain of punishment in the one case at the will of the master, and in the other " by the master as Ordinary (*a magistro ex ordinario*) ".

" Also if a scholar, on account of any fault however contracted, is rebellious or otherwise absents himself maliciously, he ought to be summoned in due form of law and canonically corrected by the master ; and if he do not appear, his goods may be sequestered by the master, the secular arm being specially called in for this if necessary."

The next article forbids carrying arms in school or out " on pain of excommunication, which we hereby pronounce (*quam hiis scriptis proferimus*) ".

" Also the master forbids on pain of excommunication, which we hereby pronounce, any one hereafter, clerk or layman or other or bachelor of whatever condition or estate or by whatever name or dignity he may be called, laying violent hands on the scholars of the said master in any way, or defaming them, on pain above noted."   " Also if a scholar strike his fellow in school or out, or get in a rage or make a noise, his hood shall be taken by the hostiarius and he shall be brought before the Vice-monitor and chastised by him.   Also it is decreed (*statutum*) that the usher or his under-usher (*subhostiarius*) shall always sit by the door, and not let two or three scholars go out at once, unless for lawful and necessary cause ; and if after three warnings to do their office they do it not, the fourth time they shall be deprived by the master."

It is probable that the under-usher was a prefect and not a master.   For at Winchester, besides the second master who was currently called Hostiarius as late as 1863, there was a prefect also called *Ostiarius*, whose *scob* or seat (*scabellum*) was by the door, and on it a boy going out used to put up a roll or slip of paper with his name and *veniam exeundi petit* on it.

" Also the master forbids on pain of excommunication the bachelors to rage in school or make a noise ; and if after three warnings they will not stop, they shall be deprived."

The next articles of the statutes also concern the bachelors, and very interesting they are :—

"The master, on pain of excommunication hereby pronounced, forbids anyone henceforth to take or attempt to take a bachelor's place, except such as have studied in a University or can prove their status by legal proof.   Also if anyone wishes to ascend to the degree of bachelor he must take a proverb from the master and make verses, letters, and a rhyme (*versus, litteras, rithmum*) on it and read them publicly in school (*in scolis*) unless the master shall graciously relax any of these requirements, and must offer 6d. or more according to his means on the Sunday of St. Nicholas (i.e. the Sunday after 6 December); otherwise they shall not enjoy the privileges of bachelors.   Potations and other customs of this sort are to remain in full strength.   Also the master prohibits anyone, bachelor or other, whoever he may be, to keep a seat in school, without license, on pain of excommunication, unless he has first been examined by those whom the master [has deputed] to examine him in grammar rules, and he shall have been ready publicly to answer in school on them and other matters brought forward against him, and have done it."

It is perfectly obvious, therefore, that the bachelors are not (as suggested by the Rolls editor) ushers or masters but pupils, schoolboys of a larger growth, who had either taken the degree of bachelor in a university or were ready to take it in the school on due examination.   At Lincoln not only did the poor clerks, young men of from eighteen to twenty, attend the Grammar School, but even the vicars-choral, already deacons and priests.   There is therefore nothing surprising in finding bachelors attending the school at St. Alban's.   At Beverley, a far more important town than St. Alban's, as a great seaport occupying the position that Hull occupies now, and the minster of which was in effect the cathedral church of the East Riding, degrees of bachelors in grammar were conferred, for in 1338 we find a declaratory statute settling how many pairs of gloves the "bachelor newly created in the Grammar School" had to give and to whom, and this was made after due inquiry into what the "ancient custom" was, and confirmed by the promulgation of sentence of excommunication against all who infringed it.

At St. Alban's the bachelors performed recognized functions in the school much like those of the modern prefect or monitor. "The master inhibits on pain of excommunication that any person or persons shall lay rash hands or attempt any evil against the masters of the said school; and, if they do, while still under sentence of excommunication, they shall receive salutary chastisement (*disciplinam*) in the school from all the bachelors, unless satisfaction shall have been first made to God and the Church."

It is highly probable that it is from the "tunding" or "tanning", the power of the stick, thus exercised by them that they derived their name of bachelors. The old explanation of bacca-laureat, adorned with the berry of the laurel wreath, has nothing to recommend it.

Lastly, the master "if he wishes to avoid condign vengeance" is to choose two discreet bachelors and commit to them the administration of St. Nicholas' chest, they taking an oath to administer it for the use of the school and to render true accounts. "And if any scholar, even though a beggar, if his status duly appears, stands before the master, he may take the twelve candles from St. Nicholas' chest for a funeral or obit" if he return them safely. When St. Nicholas' chest was opened in 1325, we are told that it contained *inter alia* besides the statutes, "two mitres and an episcopal staff (*baculus episcopalis*) and two wax candles weighing less than two pounds". So that here as elsewhere the boy-bishop's ceremonies were duly performed.

On June 17 the statutes made by the schoolmaster were inspected and confirmed by Hugh [of Eversdone] the abbot. He added another very important statute :—

"We will and grant that the master for the time being may control, unnerve [*eneruat*], destroy, and root out all adulterine schools within our territory or jurisdiction; inhibiting on pain of excommunication, which we hereby promulgate, any one from attempting or rashly presuming to keep any schools within our aforesaid jurisdiction, without the will and assent of the master of our grammar school; and to the master we, by these presents, commit and grant the inquisition, summoning, examination or production of witnesses, absolution and execution of his sentences in all causes affecting all and every the said statutes and privileges granted him as aforesaid, and all contracts with and defamations of any of his scholars, with the

power of canonical coercion.   And all and singular contradict-
ing or resisting the said statutes and privileges or contravening
them or our confirmation, if they have been first warned by
the master, we excommunicate by our present authority."

"Brother John Passevant, archdeacon of the monastery of
St. Alban", also confirmed the statutes, and "seeing the burdens
imposed on the master of our Grammar School of St. Alban's,
and that their (*sic*) privileges and functions are thin and weak,
that he may among new grievances feel that a new remedy has
been found, grants the jurisdiction of the master over the causes
and actions of his scholars and bachelors, and also of laymen
and of all others who injure the scholars and bachelors of the
said master or make contracts with them or defame them
or lay rashly violent hands upon them ".   He adds a rather
quaint power to "compel all the tenants in our jurisdiction
to attend his own school, inhibiting also on pain of excommunication every one from attempting, or presuming to set up
or keep any school within our aforesaid jurisdiction, without the
will and assent of the master of the said school".

At Warwick about 1316 a somewhat similar contest took
place which the dean and chapter of the collegiate church
settled by directing that the grammar master should have the
Donatists—those learning the rudiments of grammar in Donatus' *Ars Minor* or primer—as well as scholars in grammar
or dialectics, while the music or song school master might keep
those learning their first letters, the psalter, music, and song.

In a document at Bury St. Edmunds the "adulterine"
school keeper is called "a seductor rather than a doctor" of
the misguided pupils.   It shows the superior position occupied
by the grammar master that while the grammar master enforced his own monopoly, in the case of the song schools and
their masters the sacrist was left to assert his jurisdiction over
those who "dared to teach boys their psalters and singing", or
as it was phrased in the fifteenth century, in 1426, "reading
or singing" without the licence of the Douze gild or gild of
twelve parish clerks or priests, in the liberty; while in 1370
the phrase used was "without the licence of the song school
master".

At Canterbury, as we saw, the schoolmaster occupied a
position quite independent of the monastery, being appointed

by the archbishop himself and exercising jurisdiction, with power of excommunication, just as the Chancellor of Oxford did, at first under the Bishop of Lincoln, and afterwards independently of the bishop directly from the Pope.

On 11 March, 1310-11 Archbishop Winchelsey " collated " Master John Everard to the school and invested him *presentialiter* in person. A series of documents, preserved among the monastic archives of Canterbury, show him the hero of a large number of fights to establish his jurisdiction.

The first case was against Richard Atte Halle or de Aula, as he is alternatively called. Hall was alleged to have assaulted John Plummer or " Le Plomer ", who is described as usher (*ostiarii*) and scholar. He was either a pupil-teacher, acting as usher or second master, or perhaps more probably a prefect in the school, who performed the duties of doorkeeper. The assault is said in one of the documents to have been committed in St. Elphege's or Alphage's church, perhaps then itself the school. Hall, being cited by Everard to appear in the school and answer to the charge, did not appear and was excommunicated. Everard, as rector of the school of the city of Canterbury, addressed on 17 December, 1311, a writ to the Dean of Canterbury (i.e. the Dean of Christianity or city dean, corresponding to the rural dean in the county, for the Chapter of Canterbury being the monks of the cathedral priory, there was then no Dean of Canterbury in our sense) to request him to publish the excommunication in all churches in the deanery and to summon Hall to appear on Wednesday after St. Hilary, 15 January. The Dean of Canterbury, however, demurred to publishing the sentence on the ground that he was not satisfied that the master had jurisdiction to pass it. Thereupon Everard went to the commissary-general of the Court of Canterbury at Canterbury, who sent a mandate on 13 January, 1311-12 to the dean, stating that Everard had shown him the register of the proceedings and ordered the dean to proclaim the excommunication and summon Hall to appear before himself in Christ Church, the cathedral, on the first law day after the Purification of the Virgin, which was 2 February. But the dean still refused to move, though he had been shown the commission of Archbishop Peckham of 21 March, 1291, before quoted, arguing that the words as had been of old accustomed "were of doubtful import". The commissary therefore held an inquiry with a jury of clerics and laymen, who found that for forty years and upwards the masters of the school and scholars of Canterbury had been in the habit of summoning by their usher to appear in the school all in the city of Canterbury who in any way offended against their scholars; punishing those who appeared and suspending and excommunicating those who did not appear, and committing the execution of the sentence to the dean. After this finding, on 8 February, 1312, the dean published the sentence. On 5 December, 1312, the Archbishop issued his writ to certify that Hall had been duly excommunicated, but "in contempt of the Keys of the Church" remained obdurate. This was the prelude to a writ for the committal of the excommunicate to prison. Next day, however, Hall procured a writ from the Crown, addressed to the Sheriff of Kent, to attach the commissary, Everard and Plummer, for proceeding in Court Christian, after a writ of prohibition had been issued from the Court of King's Bench, and directing the sheriff not to execute the writ for the arrest of Hall.

Next year Everard complained to the archbishop that Hall was still defiant, and though excommunicated had received the Sacrament and had intercourse with both clerks and laymen. This brought matters to a head. On 8 May, 1313, two years and a half after the proceedings commenced, an official of the Archdeacon of Canterbury informs the Dean of Canterbury that he had heard from the rector of St. Elphege, William of O[a]re, that he had absolved Hall, now described as a clerk, in form of law from the excommunication, and asked the dean to publish the absolution. Hall must therefore have submitted. The records of two other cases tied up with this show that Everard thenceforward exercised his jurisdiction unquestioned. On Saturday after All Souls' Day (2 Nov.), 1314, Thomas of Birchwood, a scholar of the school, was summoned for hindering the vice-monitor and scholars in their common learning, and assaulting Master Walter the vice-monitor a week before when he wished to teach him and duly correct him. Birchwood admitted the assault. The master took the evidence of the bachelors and others in the school, who swore to the facts. The case was adjourned for satisfaction to be made.

Again on Monday after 3 May, 1315, Roger the lime burner (*le lym burner*) was summoned for assaulting a scholar named William Bor.   He was suspended from going to church and the case adjourned for him to make his peace.   On Monday after St. Mildred's Day in the same year a woman, Jane Modi, was summoned for assaulting a scholar, Stephen of Borsted, and the case was adjourned to Saturday for sentence, in the hope of peace being made between the parties.

Some six years afterwards, the next master, Ralph of Waltham, asserted his jurisdiction to inspect the school of St. Martin's, said to be the oldest church in England, a peculiar of the archbishop's outside the city of Canterbury, chiefly with a view of seeing whether it admitted grammar scholars to the prejudice of his own described as the city school.

The rector of St. Martin's, who had the appointment of the schoolmaster, and John of Bucwell, the schoolmaster, appealed to the archbishop.   Under a commission from him dated 3 January, 1321-22, the commissary of the Court of Canterbury held an inquiry by a jury of sixteen, nine rectors and vicars of Canterbury and seven laymen.   They found on their own knowledge and on the evidence of witnesses as to ancient custom, that the school of St. Martin's ought only to have thirteen grammar scholars, and that the Canterbury master was accustomed to visit St. Martin's school in person or by deputy, and that when the usher or submonitor of the school visited St. Martin's to see what the number was, all the scholars above the number of thirteen hid themselves.   But they said that there was no limit in the number in St. Martin's school learning the alphabet, psalter, or singing.   The commissary gave judgment in accordance with this finding.   An appeal to the Pope was lodged, and on 26 October, 1323, the case was stayed and the Canterbury master was summoned to appear before the Official of the Court of Canterbury in St. Mary Aldermary's Church, London.   The examiner-general, however, of the Court found that the appellants had not proved their case, and on 20 March, 1323-24, the commissary of Canterbury was informed that he could proceed to execute his sentence.   St. Martin's was therefore in fact permitted only as an elementary school, with an Upper Division of a single class of thirteen grammar scholars.

A striking proof of the ubiquity of grammar schools at this time is seen in the appointment by the Dean and Chapter of Lincoln on one day, 15 June, 1327, of masters to no less than six schools in the county. The appointment only appears by accident. The dean and two canons sitting "in a certain low room (*bassa camera*) below the dean's chapel in his house, discussing the collation of the Grammar Schools in the County of Lincoln which were vacant, through the vacancy of the Chancellorship of the said Church of Lincoln thereby in their hands, and as to the persons to be admitted to such schools; Finally they conferred the Grammar School of Barton on William of Gurney, the School of Partenay (Partney) on John of Upton, the School of Grimsby on William of Coleston, the School of Horncastle on John of Beverley, the School of St. Botolph (i.e. Boston) on Robert of Muston, and the School of Graham (Grantham) on Walter Pigot, clerks, from Michaelmas, 1329, to the same feast next year, in such name as above and by way of charity; expressly granting that they and each of them should be inducted into the bodily possession of the said schools in accordance with their respective collations".

In the following year the dean and one of the canons met in the dean's drawing-room (*solario*) on 29 May, and called the six masters before them and continued them for another year, and did the same in 1331, on which occasion it was noted that the master of yet another school, Stamford, was absent without sending any excuse. Nevertheless, all were reappointed and so continued to 1335, when a new Chancellor having come into office, the notices of the schools cease. As we have already seen, there was also a school at Louth, but Louth, being a prebend, the prebendary of Louth himself appointed and the Chancellor and chapter had no jurisdiction except during a vacancy.

In 1309 and again in 1334 we find the chapter appointing during such a vacancy to the Grammar School of Strubby, which was also in a prebend. Stamford School is further known owing to the preservation at Exeter College, Oxford, of a MS. book, a commentary on the pseudo-Boethius' *De disciplina scolarium* by Master William Wetelay (Wheatley) " compiled by a master who taught school (*rexit scolas*) at Stamford A.D. 1309 ". He was afterwards master of Lincoln Grammar School where he composed another book preserved at New College, Oxford, on Boethius' *Consolation of Philosophy*, with two hymns to St. Hugh of Lincoln, which he tells us he composed for a play produced at Christmas, 1316, in which year there was great scarcity and mortality, to comfort himself and others in their misery.

Here then are ten grammar schools in this single county all appearing in the course of the years 1276 to 1329, and there were no doubt others in various prebends which remained unnoticed. To these ten at least one other school, Wainfleet, was added by William Waynflete, founder of Magdalen College, Oxford, in 1459; its present building being erected in 1484.

An interesting development of a boarding-house in a hospital in connexion with a cathedral school took place at this time at Exeter. Bishop Stapledon, in 1314, founded at Oxford Stapledon Hall, now Exeter College. Having seen that those "who had not drunk a foundation of grammar are rendered useless or at least less useful for higher learning", after founding his college at Oxford for scholars in logic, he had set to work to provide for the "maintenance of boys studying grammar, and receiving instruction in morals and life", in connexion with St. John the Baptist's Hospital by the East gate of Exeter. His head and career being cut off by a London mob in a rising against Edward II in 1326, the completion of his design was effected by his successor, Bishop Grandison, by an ordinance of 18 November, 1332. Under this the master and brethren of the hospital, in consideration of the appropriation to them of the church of Yarnescombe, were to provide an "inn" (*hospicium*) and all necessaries for a grammar master, and eight or ten grammar boys, to be elected, two, if possible, from the parish of Yarnescombe, and two or one from the Archdeaconries of Totnes and Cornwall, while the dean and chapter were to send three choristers, whose voices had broken, and the De Columbers, patrons of Yarnescombe, were to name one. The election was to be by the High (*Summus*) Master of the School of the City of Exeter, and the boys were to know their psalter and plain song. They were only to board in the hospital, and were to attend the City Grammar School for a period of five years, unless they got no

13

very quickly. Though not in terms connected with it, this house was plainly intended as a nursery for Stapledon Hall.

The same Bishop Grandison set a fruitful precedent for the treatment of property belonging to foreign houses in connexion with a new college and school founded by him at Ottery St. Mary's, Devon. On 2 January, 1337-38, he purchased from the Dean and Chapter of Rouen the manor and church of Ottery St. Mary, which had been appropriated to them in 1061 by Edward the Confessor, and founded a collegiate church therewith. The college consisted of eight canons, eight vicars-choral, eight clerks, and eight choristers, with a parish priest, a matins priest, and a chapel and chaplain of the Blessed Virgin. There was also a grammar schoolmaster (*Magister scolis gramaticalibus*) to teach the boys, and it is notable that it was expressly provided that he was not to be a married man. The pay of the schoolmaster was not extensive, being two marks (£1 6s. 8d.) a year, but the canons residentiary had only £2, and the warden £3, and this was " besides the profits of his school ", showing that the school was intended to be frequented by outsiders who would pay fees. The chaplain of the Blessed Virgin was to teach the Song School and playing on the organs—this word, like schools being commonly used in the plural for the singular. On 9 December, 1339, the founder expressed his displeasure at hearing that the choristers had not taken up their residence in the house he had provided for them, and that on Innocents' Day, not content with their dissolute and insolent behaviour in the parish—by which this Puritanical bishop meant the usual boy-bishop's celebration—they had wandered about outside it for many days leaving the church unserved. He ordered them therefore to go into their house and that the schoolmasters should sleep in their chamber, and that, as the flogging authorized by the statutes did not keep them in order, they should be fined as well the enormous sum of 3s. 4d. for every day's absence from choir " except when attending school ". The school continued to flourish till the dissolution by Henry VIII in 1545 when the master, Sir John Chubbs, received £10, a maximum salary. Henry VIII refounded the school as the King's " Newe Scole ", when he gave back the church to the parishioners in 1547.

OTTERY ST. MARY COLLEGIATE CHURCH AND GRAMMAR SCHOOL, 1338

When Queen's College, Oxford, was founded in 1340 by
Robert of Eglesfield, in honour of Queen Philippa, to whom
he was chaplain, and whom he undoubtedly wished to put in
the same position in regard to Oxford as Queen Joan of
Navarre held in regard to Paris University, through her mag-
nificent foundation of the College of Navarre, he provided for
a school of poor youths to double the number of the largest
number of scholars of the college for the time being, so long
as they did not exceed the number of the seventy-two disciples of Christ.   As the scholars actually provided never
exceeded the number of the twelve apostles, so the school
contemplated was in fact limited to twenty-four, and does
not appear to have numbered more than twelve.   These
youths were to serve as choristers in the chapel, whereas at
Winchester there were sixteen choristers in addition to the
scholars, to prevent the boys wasting their time in services
instead of learning.   The Queen's boys were, however, meant
to form a real school.   They were to have informators in
grammar while learning grammar, in logic while learning
logic, and that "not only in sophisms but in the texts"; a
"well-instructed" grammarian and a learned artist being appointed informators, and directed to teach them good manners
as well as learning, and see that they always spoke either
Latin or French.   Even at meals they were to learn, being
"posed" by the M.A. fellows at the high table, until the cloth
was taken away, when the boys had their meals at the lower
side tables, the junior M.A. opposing the junior boy, and so
upwards to the senior M.A. and the senior boy.   After a
solid foundation in grammar and competent instruction in
plain song, they were to spend eight full years in studying
philosophy, or four terms after taking their B.A. degree.
They were in fact partly schoolboys, partly like the undergraduate scholars of the present day.

This was the last school founded before the Black Death,
and probably the last English school in which the boys were
enjoined to speak French.

The accounts of Merton College School at this time bring
home to us the great change which now took place of the substitution of the English language for French, as the language
of the educated and upper classes.

In 1330-31 and for several years afterwards the boys were under the charge of John Eylesbury, "grammarian". In 1338 they were divided into artists (*arcistarum*) and grammarians (*gramaticorum*). In 1339 there were eleven boys studying grammar, who paid 5d. each for Lent and 4d. each for the summer term, and an usher was paid 8d. for the year. In 1347, when there were six boys, they seem to have been sent out to school, 10d. being paid to Master John Cornwall (*Cornubiensis*) for his school (*salario scole*) in Lent term and 2½d. to his usher, and the same for the summer term : while what was apparently an extra sum of 2d. per week was paid for the fees (*salario*) of the six grammar boys in the method of writing. In the autumn 4½d. a term was paid for the salary of six grammarians. In 1349 there were fourteen boys, the highest number ever reached. They were not all grammar boys as " candles bought at various times as well for the artists as the grammarians " cost 4s. 8¾d. Parchment (*membranis*) for the same cost 3s. 2¾d., while ink for the boys cost 2½d. A steel " so as to have fire at nights " with sulphur and tinder cost 1½d. The interesting educational items occur of " a broken Horace (*in debili libro oracii*) for the boys, ½d. ; divers pairs of tablets, for the grammarians to report the arguments, 2½d.", so that grammatical disputations were in vogue. Mr. John Cornwayle was paid for the salary of his house in the winter and summer terms, 12d. a term, and in the Lent term 10d., while his usher was paid 3d. and 2½d.

This John Cornwall is the master who is credited with effecting the substitution of English for French in the schools. John Trevisa, translator of Higden's *Polychronicon* in 1385, says : " Thys manere (of translating Latin into French) was moche y-used tofore the furste moreyn, and ys sethe somdel ychaunged. For Johan Cornwal, a mayster of gramere, chayngede the lore in gramer-scole, and construccion of Freynsch into Englysch; and Richard Pencrych lurnede that manere techyng of hym, and other men of Pencrych, so that now, the yere of oure Lord a thousond three hondred foure score and fyve, of the seconde kyng Richard after the conquest nyne, in al the gramer-scoles of Engelond childern leveth Frensch and construeth and lurneth an Englysch, and habbeth thereby avanntage in on syde and desavauntage yn another. Ther avauntage ys

that they lurneth ther gramer in lesse tyme than childern
were i-woned to doo; desavauntage ys that now childern of
gramer-scole conneth na more Frensche than can thir lift heele,
and that is harme for them an they schulle passe the see and
travaille in straunge landes and in many other places."
Pencrych has been guessed to be the master of Penkridge
Collegiate Church School in Staffordshire. His name may
be derived thence, but in point of fact the Merton College accounts show that there was a Pencrych Hall opposite Merton
in 1380, which in 1367 was occupied by Penkrissh, who was
then alive. He was probably therefore a grammar school
master who succeeded Cornwall in his school at Oxford.

Among schools, the first known evidence of which occurs
in the first half of the fourteenth century, are two schools in
Sussex; Richard le Scolemaister of New Shoreham in an
Assize Roll of 1302, and Master William, schoolmaster of
Seaford (Safford) in a deed of 1320.

The chantry commissioners of 1548 found that the Free
Scole of Crewkerne, Somerset, was "sometyme callyd the
chauntrie of the Trynitie". This school is reputed to have
been founded by John Combe—there is a place called Comb
St. Reine in the parish—canon of Exeter, in 1499. He undoubtedly gave it an endowment, but, if the chantry commissioners were right, the school had existed and was previously
endowed, as the Trinity chantry was founded under licence of
Edward II in 1310.

Ashburton Grammar School, Devon, is attributed by the
same commissioners to St. Laurence gild, the beautiful little
chapel at which, with its graceful tower is now the schoolhouse.
The gild was founded for the continual finding of a priest to
pray for the donors of lands to it, as also "to kepe a scole for
the erudycyon of children frely". The deed of endowment of a
chantry priest in the chapel of St. Laurence by Bishop Stapledon, the founder of Exeter College, originally Stapledon Hall
at Oxford, to whom, as bishop, Ashburton belonged, is dated
Monday before St. Laurence's Day, 1314. Though the deed
does not mention a school it would appear that this priest kept
the school. The chapel of St. Laurence itself was earlier, as
a visitation of it in 1301 is extant.

At Northallerton, in Yorkshire, is a grammar school, which

the present writer assisted to raise from a decadent state to its present flourishing condition as a mixed grammar school for boys and girls with not far short of 200 pupils. The appointment of its master in 1321 is preserved, and was clearly not that of the master of a new school. Northallerton and the district round it, known as Northallertonshire, had been given by William Rufus to the bishopric of Durham. The bishops subsequently divided the possessions and duties of the see between themselves and the monks of the cathedral priory. In this division the right and duty of exercising spiritual jurisdiction in Northallertonshire fell to the prior, on whom, accordingly, and not on the bishop, as in the case of Durham itself, devolved the appointment of the schoolmaster. Accordingly, in the second of the existing Prior's Registers at Durham, we find on 20 March, 1322, William, Prior, addressing his beloved in Christ, Robert Colstan of Alverton, clerk, being favourably inclined to him by the prayers made on his behalf, conferring by way of alms (*intuitu caritatis*, the usual formula in the thirteenth and fourteenth centuries for the collation to livings and other ecclesiastical offices), "the rectorship (*regimen*) of our school of Alverton; on condition (*ita*) that you exhibit effective diligence about the instruction of boys as due under the oath made to us". This appointment was rather exceptionally made, for what is now the regular term for schoolmasters "to last only for our pleasure" or at pleasure. In a subsequent appointment of John Podesay, as master, the Prior describes himself as "Ordinary of the spirituality of the Liberty of the Blessed Cuthbert"—the patron saint of Durham —"in Yorkshire", and the appointment was for five years during good behaviour, and was to teach both grammar and song schools—a result no doubt of the scarcity of educated clerics caused by the Black Death and subsequent plagues. For in 1426 a separate appointment to the song and reading school (*scolarum lectualem et cantualium*) is noted. In 1443, however, the two schools of song and grammar are again combined under Sir John Leuesham, chaplain, who is to teach reading, song, and grammar. This appointment was again only at pleasure. At the dissolution of chantries in 1548 this "gramer scole" was found to be endowed with lands "gyven by certen wele-disposed persones" worth £8 8s. a year and applied accordingly.   Another certificate describes " landes of the guylde there ", out of which John Foster, clerke, scholemaster, received £5 1s. 4d. only.   So the lands were confiscated to the Crown, and the master continued with a fixed stipend of £5 1s. 4d. only, subsequently reduced by office fees to even less.   Foster was still schoolmaster when the Exchequer held an inquiry as to the schools charged on the Crown revenues in 1571.

It is strange to find the Prior of Durham in the same capacity of Ordinary of Howdenshire appointing in 1393 to the separate grammar school and song school of Howden in " Howdenshire " since Howden had been made a collegiate church a century before, and the bishop himself lived within a stone's throw of it, in a great manor-house, part of which still exists. Here, too, the grammar and song schools were joined under one master in 1409.   They were separated again in 1412 and 1426, but in 1456 the grammar and reading schools (*scolas tam lectuales quam gramaticales*) were so united.

At Harlow in Essex, a new chantry school was founded at the altar of St. Petronilla, commonly abbreviated to Purnell or Parnell, a favourite female name, under licence of 17 July, 1324, by the rector, John of Staunton, King's clerk and Cantabrigian.   The endowment was worth, in 1548, £8 8s. 10½d. a year, and a rasin or bunch (*racemus*) of ginger.

In Lincolnshire, the Grammar School of Bourne, still existing ten years ago but now in abeyance, appears in 1330, when on Saturday after Christmas Day the cathedral chapter, in the vacancy of the chancellorship, admitted Sir John, son of Edward Faber, or Smith (Fabri) of Brune to the mastership, on the presentation of the Abbot of Bourne.   In view of this we may fairly claim as a scholar of this school, Roberd of Brunne, who, in 1303, began to "turn" "an Englyssh tunge out of frankys", the "Handlyng synne" as he mistranslated "*Manuel des pechies*", for the benefit of the "godë men of Brune and speciali the feloushape of Symprynghame" six miles off.

At Farburn in Yorkshire, near Huddersfield, a schoolmaster appears in 1348, being convicted at the assizes of murdering a man for the purpose of robbing him of £4, and, under the benefit of clergy, handed over by the King's Court as a clerk convict to a chaplain of the Archbishop of York; so that a mild imprisonment, followed by purgation would be all the punishment he would get.

The first actual evidence of Ripon Grammar School is the appearance in similarly unfortunate circumstances of Richard the chamberlain, clerk, formerly master of the schoolhouse (*scole hous*) of Ripon, in Michaelmas term, 1348. The sheriff was ordered, as he had been ordered many times before, to arrest him, with some 139 others; priests, clerks, men and women on a charge of felony, probably a riot, and, on the sheriff returning that he could not be found to proclaim them outlawed. In 1354 a tenement " formerly in the tenure of the schoolmaster " at 10d. rent was let to a chaplain for 2s. 1d., and this tenement on the south side of the churchyard is described as "formerly in the tenure of Master Richard, rector of the grammar school ", in rent-rolls of 1392 and 1397. Meanwhile a new schoolhouse had been provided, as the Fabric roll for 1380 contains an item of 6s. for rent of a messuage in Annesgate in the tenure of " Master Thomas, skolemayster ". The treatment of this school on the dissolution of the minster in 1548 curiously illustrates the reputation of Edward VI as a school-founder, but must be reserved for a subsequent volume. Statutes were made for the school in 1380, chiefly to enforce the master's attendance at the Lady Mass and his reading of the sixth lesson in church on Sundays and high days.

At Tickhill in the same county, formerly a considerable place as one of the chief seats in Yorkshire of the duchy of Lancaster, the chantry of St. Helen was founded by the wife of Adam Hertehill on 14 January, 1349. The main purpose of this chantry was a school. For a grammar school had according to a certificate of the chantry commissioners in 1548, been heretofore continually kept out of its revenues, amounting to £4 13s. 11¾d. a year. This must have been one of the latest school foundations before the Black Death.

CHAPTER X

THE BLACK DEATH AND WINCHESTER COLLEGE

THE Black Death of 1349, followed as it was by the *Secunda Pestis* of 1361 and a third plague in 1367, profoundly affected the universities and schools. The foundation of new colleges was absolutely stopped. None were created at Cambridge between 1352, when Corpus Christi College was founded expressly to repair the ravages created by the plague of 1349, and 1439, when God's House (now Christ's College) was founded to restore the supply of grammar masters, to the failure of which was attributed the fact that scores of grammar schools had fallen into abeyance. At Oxford none were founded between Queen's in 1340 and New College in 1379. The flow of scholars was seriously diminished. Perhaps the most striking testimony to this are two appointments of masters of Lincoln and York Grammar Schools respectively. At Michaelmas, 1351, the Lincoln Chapter granted their Grammar School to John Muscham "on this wise, that if an M.A. should come and ask for the school he should be admitted, since by custom the keeping of the school belongs to an M.A." On 9 June, 1368, the Chapter of York departed from the "ancient custom" of at least 150 years, of appointing for a term of three to five years only, and "because since the time of the past Death through the shortness of the time and on account of the rarity of M.A.'s, no master in arts has cared to teach the school", they appointed John of York M.A. "until he obtains an ecclesiastical benefice". The person appointed was still master in 1380, when he was admitted a freeman of the city.

Again on 19 May, 1351, the chapter of York Minster, during a vacancy in the office of the chancellor of the minster, caused by the death in the plague of William of Abberwick, ex-fellow of Merton College and Dean of the collegiate church of Auckland, deputed Sir William of Staunton of Alverton, chaplain, to be keeper of the Grammar School (*custos scolarum gramaticalium*) of Doncaster.   The use of the word "deputed" and the appointment not as master or rector, but as custos or guardian, show that the chapter thought themselves entitled only to appoint *ad interim*, a temporary master, until there was a new chancellor, whose duty and right it was to make a permanent appointment of a master of arts.

To the Black Death seems to be due the earliest reference to Ludlow Grammar School.   Though it was most probably maintained by the Palmers' Gild from its beginning in 1284, it is not till 1349 we get certain evidence of it.   John of Lyndessye (Lindsay in Lincolnshire) received orders at the hands of the Bishop of Hereford as sub-deacon on 19 September, deacon on 19 December, 1349, and priest on 20 February, 1349-50, on the title of "the School in the town of Ludlow".   It is difficult not to think that he thus took all the orders in rapid succession to enable him to qualify for the numerous preferments vacated by the plague.

William of Wykeham, the founder of New College, himself owed his own rapid rise and remarkable accumulation of preferments, surpassing even those of Henry III's Chancellor John Mansel, the proverbial pluralist of previous ages, largely to the plague.   Born in 1324, he was at the time of the Black Death merely a law clerk, who after receiving at Winchester, no doubt in the High School, the usual grammar school education in "the primitive sciences", but not proceeding to the University, had become an under-notary to the constable of Winchester Castle.   At the age of forty-two, he had risen to be clerk of the King's works at two royal manors, and overseer of the workmen at Windsor Castle, with wages of a shilling a day, and another shilling till he could be preferred to some benefice worth £20 a year.   It was not till after the great outbreak of bubonic plague in 1360-61, called by the chroniclers the *Secunda Pestis*, as second only to the Black Death of 1349, that no less than sixteen preferments—deaneries, archdeaconries, canonries, rectories—were, within eighteen months, heaped upon the servant whom the King delighted to honour, who then took inferior orders as an

acolyte, and in 1362 holy orders.   It is noteworthy that this
year saw the erection of the first collegiate church founded since
the Black Death.   This was Cobham College, Kent, founded
by John Lord Cobham for a master and five chaplains, one
of whom was to teach the six choristers singing for an addition to his salary of 6s. 8d., and another was to teach the
clerks and boys grammar at £4 a year, raised in 1405 to £5.
Is it merely a coincidence that of three letters now extant, all in
French, written by William of Wykeham one is to this very Lord
Cobham?   Wykeham having also the secular offices of
clerk of the exchequer, keeper of the forests and Privy Seal,
speedily accumulated the fortune which, when the bishopric
of Winchester, richest in England, and the chancellorship were
substituted for lower preferments in 1366-67, made him the
millionaire of his age.

It was therefore no rhetorical phrase repeating an obsolete
formula, but sober fact, which made William of Wykeham
give as a reason for his great foundations of Winchester College and its sister at Oxford, New College, "the cure of the
common disease of the clerical army, which we have seen
grievously wounded by lack of clerks, due to plagues, wars, and
other miseries".

He must have planned the twin colleges, which have
enshrined his name, very soon after his preferment.   For
already in February, 1369, his agents, fellows of Merton College, were acquiring the site of New College at Oxford.   On
1 September, 1373, he was already maintaining a school at Winchester.   He then made an agreement with Mr. Richard of
Herton, grammarian (*gramaticus*), that for ten years he should
teach and instruct in the art of grammar the poor scholars
whom the bishop maintains and will maintain at his own cost,
the bishop undertaking to find another fit person to help him;
in other words, an usher or assistant master.   Herton was not
to take any other boys to be taught without leave of the
bishop.   If ill, or during a single visit to the Court of Rome,
he was allowed leave of absence, finding, however, a substitute.   In 1376, when Wykeham had been convicted (wrongfully) of misfeasance in the chancellorship, and deprived of the
temporalities of the bishopric, he "brake up" his household,
"sending also to Oxford, where upon alms and for God's sake

he found seventy scholars, that they should depart and remove every one to their friends, for he could no longer help or find them ". Having been restored, he obtained a bull of Pope Urban VI, dated 1 June, 1378—the erection of colleges being a matter of papal prerogative—for the foundation of " a college of seventy poor scholars, clerks, to live college-wise and study grammar (*gramaticalibus*) near the city of Winchester ", words which suggest that the site had already been selected. Wykeham having " for several (*pluribus*) years of his life, from the goods given him by God, supplied the necessaries of life to scholars studying grammar in the same city ", for their better maintenance had asked for the appropriation of the church of Downton, near Salisbury, in his patronage, with which he was thereby authorized to endow the college. The Bishop of Rochester was directed to act on the bull as soon as the endowment of the college had been settled.

On 26 November, 1379, Wykeham founded Seinte Marie College of Wynchestre in Oxenford, then and now commonly called New College, the buildings of which were formally entered on 14 April, 1386. Meanwhile lands were bought for the endowment of Winchester, the site of the college, a messuage and five acres of land in the [Bishop's] Soke outside the city from the priory, and two messuages from private owners. On 20 October, 1382, he sealed the foundation charter of " Seinte Marie College of Wynchestre ", to consist of " seventy poor and needy scholars, clerks, living college-wise therein and studying and becoming proficient in grammaticals or the art, faculty or science of grammar ", the corporate body being the " Warden and Scholars Clerks ", i.e. scholar-clerks. A warden, Thomas of Cranley, S.T.B., a fellow of Merton, and afterwards warden of New College and Archbishop of Dublin, was appointed, and seventy scholars admitted. The school was at first held in the parish of St. John's-on-the-Hill, whence scholars were regularly sent on in their turn to New College. Only on 28 March, 1394, were the present buildings entered.

The Charter stated that the founder had already founded a perpetual college of seventy poor scholars clerks to study theology, canon and civil law and arts in the University of Oxford. But experience had shown that grammar was the foundation, gate, and source of all the other liberal arts, and

SEAL OF WILLIAM OF WYKEHAM
ATTACHED TO FOUNDATION DEED OF WINCHESTER COLLEGE, 1382

that students in the other arts often fell into peril through lack of good teaching and sufficient learning in grammar. There were also many poor scholars who through want of money lacked the means of continuing and becoming proficient in grammar. For these reasons and to assist poor grammar students to pass on to the other faculties he founded the college.

Winchester College was of course no new invention or unprecedented foundation. The statutes of the college, which now exist only in a revised version issued in 1400, show clearly that they were largely modelled on those of Merton and Queen's Colleges; the more immediate model being the Royal College of Navarre at Paris, founded by Joan, Queen of France and Navarre, in 1304, for seventy scholars, twenty in grammar, thirty in arts, and twenty in theology. Both models were improved on.

The French queen had assigned a separate building within the precinct of her college for the grammar scholars : and this was then perhaps the most flourishing part of the establishment, being crowded with paying scholars or commoners, many of noble and even royal birth, who flooded over into adjoining houses. Wykeham made his grammar scholars as numerous as his university scholars, and established them as a separate college with separate endowments, not as a part of the same college, though under its visitatorial authority, nor even at Oxford, but at Winchester, where he himself had been at school. As in the Navarre College, the grammar scholars were to be promoted in their turn to be artist scholars, only instead of passing merely from one part of the college to another, they left Winchester for Oxford.

The chief novelty of Winchester College was in the first place the scale of the foundation. The school of Winchester, which with its scholars, choristers and commoners numbered ninety-six, was not only eight times larger than the schools attached to Merton and Queen's Colleges, but was larger than the whole number of the fellows in all the colleges at Oxford put together. The second and most important novelty was that Wykeham made his school a separate and distinct foundation, independent of, though connected with, the Oxford College. Others had erected collegiate churches for university students.

He erected one for schoolboys. The old collegiate churches had kept grammar schools, and flourishing grammar schools, but they were, though inseparable accidents, still accidents. In the new collegiate churches at the university, called colleges, growing scholars were substituted for grown priests, and study for psalm singing as the essence of the institution, but the schoolboys remained an accident, and a rather unimportant accident. In Winchester College the accident became the essence. The corporate name of " warden and scholars, clerks " stamped the school and the schoolboys as the aim and object of the foundation. The collegiate church form was afterwards adopted, the fellows occupying the place of canons, but instead of the boys being subordinate to the fellows, the fellows were subsidiary to the boys. For the first time a school was established as a sovereign and independent corporation existing by and for itself, self-centred and self-governed.

From the early years of the nineteenth century it has often been asserted that by Wykeham's poor and needy scholars was meant poor children of the working classes or the gutter poor. This is quite untenable. The labouring classes were then serfs, *ascripti glebae*, passing on the sale of an estate to the purchaser. In order to prevent their escaping from this condition by the avenue of learning, it was customary to fine, and fine heavily, those villeins or natives who sent their sons to school without leave from the lord. Thus, on 26 January, 1295, Walter, son of Reginald the carpenter, presented by the manorial jury of Hemingford Abbotts, Hunts, for being ordained without leave, appeared before the lord, the Abbot of Ramsey, and by special grace was licensed to attend school and take all orders, without being reclaimed as a serf, on condition of saying ten psalters (i.e. the whole of the psalms through ten times) for the soul of the late Abbot William. But he was charged nevertheless 10s. fine, or some £40, for this special favour. A striking commentary this on the supposed zeal of monks for education, and an emphatic disproof that the great Abbey of Ramsey, at all events, kept a school for its tenants and subjects. In 1344 the fine of 3s. 4d., or some two months' pay of a skilled craftsman, was inflicted on a villein at Coggeshall in Essex for sending his son to school without licence. The earliest mention of Harrow in connexion with education

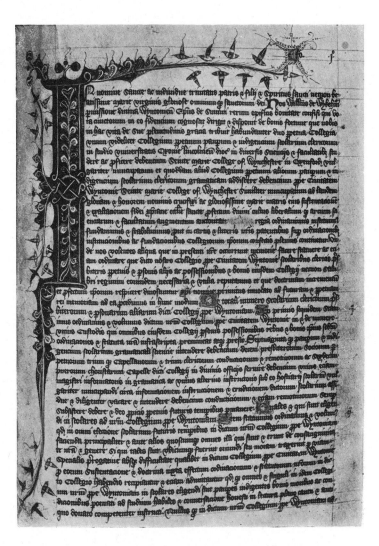

STATUTES OF WINCHESTER COLLEGE, 1400

is in 1384, when seizing of a horse by way of distraint on a villein of the Rectory manor of Harrow who had sent his son out of the manor to school without licence. The fourteenth-century manor rolls all over the country are dotted with fines for sending boys, *ad scolas clericales*, to schools to become clerks. Not until the statute of apprentices in 1406 was this restriction removed. So much for the negative side.

Positively, a vow of poverty was laid down in the statutes. Every scholar had to swear : " I N. (Name), admitted to the college of St. Mary near Winchester, swear that I have nothing whereby I know I can spend beyond five marks a year ". Five marks was the limit of value of church livings for exemption from paying taxes to the Pope or for the support of Papal nuncios. In the diocese of Winchester there were sixty-seven livings below that value. It meant £3 6s. 8d. a year, whereas the pay of a skilled artisan was £1 6s. 8d. a year at the outside. Further, Wykeham, like Merton, was careful to provide for his own relations going to the school as scholars, and actually sent his nephew, Thomas Wykeham, to whom he gave Broughton Castle and estates, which have made the Wykehams and Wykeham-Fiennes among the magnates of the land ever since, to be a scholar first at Winchester and then at New College. Would he have put him and the young "noblemen" who came as commoners, who included the Uvedales or Udalls, lords of the very village of Wykeham in which he was born, to herd with the sons of serfs or the gutter poor of Winchester? In the earliest list of scholars preserved, that for 1394, is one ffarington of the family of that name in Lancashire, whose uncle or other near relative when he came to visit him at the college brought with him a staff of four servants. Of the first list of eleven commoners, who had to pay for their reception, and who were by statute "young noblemen," no less than half passed on into college as scholars, one of them Cranleigh a relation no doubt of the Warden and Archbishop. So far as they can be traced the scholars appointed in Wykeham's own lifetime were scions of county families, and relations of judges and Chancery officials, who corresponded to the bar and the higher civil service of the present day. The poor whom Wykeham wished to help were, as he says, those who had means enough to send their sons to grammar schools, but not enough to send them on to the universities; the younger sons of lords and squires, the landed gentry and farmers in the country, the burgesses and traders in the towns. The notion that the endowments of Winchester or any other school before Christ's Hospital, which was for foundlings and the gutter pauper, have been perverted from the patrimony of the poor into an appanage of the rich, will not bear investigation.

The provenance of the first master appointed by Wykeham, John Melton, is not known. The second, Thomas of Romsey, appointed in 1394, has been traced, through researches as to Sussex schools, as master of Chichester Cathedral Grammar School, receiving presents under the will of the chancellor of that church in 1385. Winchester several times, before the Reformation and after, returned the compliment by sending on masters from Winchester to Chichester School, which, owing to Bishop Story having in 1502 annexed a canonry or prebend to the mastership, is now called the Prebendal School.

The success of Wykeham's school was remarkable. It is not too much to say that in the two generations after Wykeham Wykehamists ran both Church and State and Education. The Yorkist revolution broke their succession and introduced Yorkists to power and place instead. But they in their turn imitated Wykeham, and when the Lancastrian rose flourished again under the Tudors, Wykehamists again took the lead.

Wykeham had some rather humble imitators at the time. Katharine, Lady Berkeley, in her foundation of Wotton-under-Edge Grammar School, on 20 October, 1384, followed the wording of Wykeham as to grammar being the foundation of the liberal arts and information in it being defeated by want of means, and therefore for the exaltation of holy mother church and so on founded her school. But it was only for a master " to teach and receive kindly all scholars whosoever, howsoever and whencesoever coming for instruction . . . without exacting, claiming or receiving any benefit or gain for his pains", except the rents and profits of the land given at the foundation, and two poor scholar-clerks living college-wise therein, who were to be pupil-teachers. This was exactly imitated in the so-called College of Bredgar, Kent, founded by Master Robert Bredgar and other subscribers on 7 April, 1393, for a master and two pupil-teacher scholars from

FAMOUS WYKEHAMISTS, c. 1460

FROM THOMAS CHANDLER'S MS., NEW COLLEGE, OXFORD

seven to twenty-five years old, and two boy-scholars in the almonry at Canterbury. When one of them could read well, sing, construe and make twenty-four verses in one day on a single subject, he was to be allowed to celebrate with the master in Bredgar Church. For the rest of the time he was to attend study reading, song, grammar and the other liberal sciences. The two almonry scholars were by a deed of 3 April, 1398, duly planted in the Almonry of Canterbury Cathedral Priory; of which anon.

The most considerable foundation following on Wykeham's, was that of the College of St. Peter and Paul at Maidstone, founded by William Courtney, Archbishop of Canterbury, under licence of 2 August, 1396. He took over existing institutions, annexing bodily the Hospital of St. Peter and St. Paul, and converting Maidstone parish church into a collegiate church and to it appropriating the endowments of four parish churches. A school had existed there before, as in 1304 Master Ralph, the scolemaistre, had been, with sixty-three others, including Alexander le Chapelayn of Detling, released from Maidstone prison to come up for judgment if called on, for abetting and aiding the death of William Detling and harbouring persons charged with it. The school was now taken over by the college, which had among its later masters William Grocyn, the first "Grecian" in England. On the dissolution of the college, the school resumed its independent existence, the town council buying the right to keep a school from Edward VI.

Schools which first make their appearance in extant records, during the second half of the fourteenth century, are numerous. A school at Dunham, Notts, which formed a prebend or estate of one of the canons of Southwell Minster, is known from a conveyance in 1351 of lands "which belonged to Robert le Taillour, formerly master of the grammar school of Dunham".

Abingdon Grammar School, now called Roysse's school from an Elizabethan benefactor, was in 1372 the subject of a dispute between the rector of St. Nicholas and the vicar of St. Helen's, as to which of them should minister and receive the emoluments for doing so, to "the master of the grammar school of Abendon and his servants, and the scholars living with him" and others. The dispute was settled by the Bishop

14

of Salisbury in favour of the rector of St. Nicholas, the church just outside the abbey gates and just opposite St. John's Hospital, in which the school was held from 1561 to 1870. Master Thomas Weston, *magister scolarum* of Abingdon, occurs in deeds of the Holy Cross Hospital, and in accounts of the abbey, to whom he paid rent for his house, from 1388 to 1415.

At Crofton, Yorkshire, a grammar school is mentioned in Duchy of Lancaster records in 1373.

In 1382 a college, originally founded at Raveningham in Norfolk, was moved by Sir John Walters of Norwich, knight, to Mettingham Castle. The foundation of the collegiate church with its twelve canons or fellows, included, as usual, provision for education. But at first boys were sent for their education to Beccles. This school was not new when, in 1396, the Chamberlain of Bury St. Edmund's Abbey, to which the manor and church belonged, appointed Master Reginald, lector and chaplain, to hold the school at pleasure, proclaiming at the same time that no one else was to presume to open a school there. The college in 1403 paid 5s. for the board of Richard Clerkys at Beccles for two months and four days, i.e. at the rate of 7d. a week, and for the scolage or school fees of Richard and another boy, 1s. 6d., i.e. 2d. a week. A pair of shoes each cost 4d. Was a pair of *galaches* for the clerks of St. Nicholas, at 8d., a pair of goloshes to keep their feet dry? Three years later 6d. a week only was paid for the board of John Melton, with scolage at 2d. a week. He continued to attend school at Beccles till ordained deacon and priest in 1412.

A considerable crop of chantries which were also free grammar schools sprung up in Essex to replace the learned clerks who had perished in the plagues. Thus at Braintree, "a grete and popullus and a market towne" where the St. John Baptist priest taught a grammar school in 1548, the first appointment of such a priest by the Bishop of London took place on 8 September, 1364.

At Bocking the chantry priest of Doreward's chantry founded and endowed under licences to William Doreward in 1369 and John Doreward his son in 1392, in 1548 taught children to read and write. Being elementary only this school was not continued. Bocking had to wait till 1642 for a new elementary school.

Chelmsford Grammar School, continued by the Chantry Commissioners in 1548, and now figuring as one of Edward VI's schools, was founded in 1375 by Sir John Mountney, knight, who endowed a priest to sing in the chapel of Our Lady and also to teach a grammar school there, while the usher was paid by the Morrow Mass or Corpus Christi Gild.

The Gild or Brotherhood of the Assumption of the Virgin in St. Peter's Church, Maldon, from 1388 maintained a chaplain who was also schoolmaster. In 1407 the borough court records show John Scovill, the master, being sued by a townsman on an agreement to pay him half the fees coming from the grammar boys: while on 20 November, 1420, the then master John Trewardyn, who was also an attorney in the borough court, sued for his school fees (*scolagium*) of 12d. for teaching a boy from Midsummer to Michaelmas; or, at the not very extravagant rate of 1d. a week.

A Trinity Gild was founded at Rayleigh under licence of 1 February, 1389, and its priest was to sing mass, help to serve the cure, and teach a " fre Scole," which school was duly kept and continued in 1548. But as the endowment was confiscated and a salary of £10 only paid, the school, in spite of a small additional endowment given in 1640, long ago became merely elementary.

At Coggeshall a chantry was founded in 1392, the priest of which taught school in 1548, and was continued as master. A later master, William Flower, was burnt under Queen Mary for heresy, 24 April, 1555. At Great Baddow a " Coggeshall Priest ", endowed under licence of 1392, and the incumbent of a later chantry founded by Thomas Kille, butler to King Henry V, was master and usher of a grammar school.

The year 1394 saw licences granted for two chantry schools, one founded at Cockermouth by Henry Percy, Earl of Northumberland, the other at Bromyard in Herefordshire, where on a salary of £3 9s. 11d. in 1548, John Bustenall " teachith chyldern and doth brynge up vertuously in redyng, wrythynge and in gramer ".

In 1394 John of Hee, i.e. Hemingborough, Prior of Durham, as Ordinary of the spirituality of the Blessed Cuthbert in Yorkshire, appointed a master to the Grammar School of Hemingborough. The church there was made collegiate in 1426 with a Provost and three canons or prebendaries, when probably the school passed under their care.

There were no doubt many other gild and chantry schools, of this date, but the licences and charters rarely mentioned the schools as part of their objects, the licence not being required for them, even when the school was really the main object of the foundation.

CHAPTER XI

THE ALMONRY OR CHORISTERS' SCHOOLS IN
THE MONASTERIES

THE Almonry at Canterbury, mentioned above in connexion with the Bredgar Exhibition foundation, was the earliest specimen of a new addition to the monasteries, at this time the only contribution by them to lay education. The Almoner, Elemosinarius or eleemosynary officer, alms-giver, was one of the " obedientiaries ", or officers, of most, if not all, monasteries. It was his duty to distribute the broken meats from the monks' meals at the gate of the monastery every day, and on certain days to distribute doles in money or kind among the poor, often as many as 1000 receiving a penny each. At the beginning of the fourteenth century a movement sprung up in connexion with the great increase in the worship of the Virgin Mary, for the establishment of choristers in the Lady Chapels of the monastic churches, and special provision had to be made for their housing and education. As the Almoner's chamber, or house, was, for the convenient performance of his duties, always by the outer-gate of the monastery, and he came in contact with the outside lay world, on him naturally devolved the custody and care of the boys, who thus became inmates of the monasteries, in total defiance of strict monastic rules and principles. In providing board, lodging, and, eventually, teaching for their choristers, the monasteries were, however, only following the example of the great secular churches, which had begun, more than a century earlier, to establish separate endowments and common houses, colleges as they were sometimes called, as at Lincoln, for the choristers. In earlier days the choristers were merely imported to sing in the choir, and either lived at home or were lodged in the houses of the resident canons, who had to feed them and look after them.

St. Paul's seems to have been the earliest cathedral by which separate provision for housing them was made ; a statute dating from the deanery of Ralph de Diceto, between 1180 and 1200, ordering that, "as the boys of the almonry ought to live on alms, they are to sit on the ground in the canons' houses, not with the vicars at table", the resident canons on certain days having to entertain the choir-singers, both vicars choral and choir-boys at dinner. The reason was assigned, "lest they become uppish and when they go back to the almonry despise the food there and blame their master". A later statute made in 1263, ordered the Almoner, besides distributing alms in the method ordained by those who gave endowments for the purpose, and burying gratis poor people and beggars who died in or near the churchyard, to have "daily with him eight boys fit for the service of the Church, whom he is to have instructed either by himself or by another master in matters pertaining to the service of the Church and in literature (i.e. grammar), and good behaviour, taking no payment for the same ".

These almonry boys were the choir-boys, who learnt singing in the choir school, which the precentor had to maintain. As the fourteenth century Almoner records, against himself, in his register : " If the almoner does not keep a clerk to teach the choristers grammar, the schoolmaster of St. Paul's claims 5s. a year for teaching them, though he ought to demand nothing for them, because he keeps the school for them, as the treasurer of St. Paul's once alleged before the dean and chapter is to be found in ancient documents". The attempt thus made by the Treasurer to make the grammar school into a choir school thus early is curious. The allegation that the grammar school was kept for the choristers is historically untrue, though it is probably true that the choristers ought to have been admitted free to it. At Beverley, in 1312, when the grammar schoolmaster wished to make all choristers beyond seven, the original number who attended the grammar school, pay fees, the succentor, the song schoolmaster, contended that he was bound to teach all the choristers free. After inquiry by the chapter into the "ancient customs" of the church, it was decided that the grammar schoolmaster was bound to teach them gratis, but the succentor was not to defraud him by admitting boys to the choir merely for the sake of getting free education in the grammar school. Whatever may have been the choristers' right in the matter, the fact that the grammar schoolmaster at St. Paul's claimed and received payment for them shows with absolute conclusiveness that the grammar school was not a mere choir school, or choir-boys' school.

One of the almoners, William of Tolleshunt, by will made in 1329, gave a shilling to each senior and sixpence to each junior of "the boys of the church whom I educated in the almonry". He also gave his best Hugucio and Priscian major and minor bound in one volume and Isidore "on Ethemology" and all his grammar books but those which Ralph his clerk had, and all his quarterns of sermons on the feast of Holy Innocents which the boy-bishops preached in his time, to remain in the Almonry for ever, to the usufruct of the boys attending it, on condition that they should not be removed or sold. He bequeathed also his books on the art of dialectic, of which John of Stanground had the Old and New Logic, with books on Natural History and other like books on the same art, that these books might be used by boys fit to become scholars, when they left the almonry, but under a caution to restore them that they might not be lost. For the use of the same boys he left his books on physic and also on civil law, namely Institutes, Codex, Ancient Digest and Authentics and other legal writings. He left also two marks to provide the almonry boys with shoes, in return for which they were to say, on getting up and going to bed, the psalm *De Profundis* with the Lord's Prayer and Ave Maria for the souls of the testator and friends.

This will shows that the almonry school was a distinct foundation and intended only for the eight choir-boys in the almonry. That these eight boys, afterwards increased to ten, were the choir-boys, is shown by the fact that, in 1315, Bishop Richard of Newport gave to this very William of Tolleshunt, almoner, one of his executors, and to the Almoner for the time being, a house near St. Paul's, "for the support of one or two of the almonry boys for two years after they have changed their voices".

Lincoln, probably at that time the next largest town to

London, was also the next to provide lodgings for its choristers, in direct imitation of St. Paul's under the influence of Richard of Gravesend, who came from St. Paul's to be Dean of Lincoln in 1254, and bishop in 1258. In the first year of his deanery he acquired the first separate endowment for the choristers, then described, not by that name, but as "the 12 boys ministering in Lincoln church, namely, candle and incense bearers (*cero ferariis et turribulariis*)". At that time, it is stated, the boys of the choir of Lincoln lived on the alms of the canons, and their admission, instruction, and discipline was in the hands of the Precentor. In 1264 Richard of Gravesend ordained that the twelve boys, of whom two were incense bearers, should dwell in one house and live together in common under a master, and appropriated certain revenues for their support. He gave the dean and chapter the right of admitting them, and placed their teaching and discipline in the hands of their master, subject to the supervision of a canon, called Warden (*custos*), appointed for the purpose. It was specially provided, in words borrowed from St. Paul's, that whenever they went for a walk or to play they were to go and come back under the leadership of a grown-up person. At first the choristers attended the City Grammar School for their ordinary education and the song school to learn singing. But in 1351 the Precentor, who had somehow recovered the right of appointing the choristers, agreed with the chapter that he would also present a fit pedagogue, and, after examination by the chapter, appoint him to instruct the chorister boys in singing and grammar. This appointment, which at first was only that of a private tutor in grammar, developed later into a separate grammar school or "choristers' college" in the close, in the choristers' house now occupied by the organist, who, in the course of centuries, managed to evict his fellow-lodgers and pupils.

At York there were seven choristers only, corresponding with the original number of the canons. The first-known notice of their being housed together is on 6 May, 1307, on which day the chapter made an agreement with one Richard of Craven, that he should maintain them in board and learning (*mensa et erudicionibus*) for 4s. 8d. a week, or 8d. a week each, charged on Brodsworth church. Whether there was any fixed house for them is not clear. On 23 August, 1346, Sir Stephen, a chaplain of one of the canons, was ordered to take care of the choristers and that they should live with him.

At Salisbury it is not yet ascertained whether the choristers previously enjoyed separate endowments and a house to live in, before, on 6 May, 1314, Bishop Nicholas Longespee obtained licence in mortmain from Edward II to appropriate the rents of some new shops in the Fish Shambles to the chapter, for the maintenance of fourteen chorister boys and a master to teach them grammar. In 1322 Bishop Roger of Morteval made statutes for their living together in a house in the close, the rectory of Preshute being given for endowment. In 1448 the chapter got John Lane, M.A., who was teaching grammar in the city of Winchester, to come to Salisbury to teach the choristers and altarists. The grammar school thus established in the close proved a serious rival to the ancient Glomery or grammar school under the chancellor. In the seventeenth century, during the commonwealth, the ancient payments to each of them were continued by Parliament, but in the eighteenth century the better-endowed though later and narrower school survived, while the other perished, and the chapter had forgotten their own history to such an extent as to inform the Cathedral Commission of 1854 that the only cathedral grammar school was that of the choristers.

In the monasteries, almonry schools seem to have been supported not by the general monastic funds, but by special endowments given by the abbots or priors or by outsiders. Thus, by deed of 16 February, 1319-20, at Canterbury, Prior Henry of Eastry founded, probably out of a royal grant, a chantry of six priests to pray for the soul of Edward I, with the usual attendant clerks and choristers. It is implied that they had to attend the Cathedral Grammar School by the provision that on feast days, when the schoolmaster does not lecture, they are to attend all the canonical hours. Also it is laid down that no scholar shall be admitted to the almonry unless he knows how to read and sing, and is ten years old at least, and has a decent surplice commensurate with the size of his body.

Though the almonry boys were only fed on the broken meats from the monks' table, yet being one was regarded as a valuable form of scholarship, as is shown by a letter of Queen Philippa to the prior in 1332, asking him to take Richard of Bedingfield into the almonry "to be maintained like other poor scholars of his estate". The prior consents, hoping in return that the Queen will prevent the King's purveyors from seizing the provisions he had collected for his own use while attending Parliament.

In 1364 we hear of the schoolmaster of the almonry being appointed master of the public school of his native town of Kingston-on-Thames. So by that time a separate schoolmaster, though probably only as a private tutor, had been provided for these almonry boys.

St. Alban's Abbey seems to have been the first monastery to follow the example of Canterbury, an "Order of living of the poor scholars in the Almonry" there, being made 4 April, 1339. The scholars were to stay five years at most, "as that time is sufficient for becoming proficient in grammaticals". They were to "shave an ample crown, as choristers", and daily say the seven psalms for the convent and its founders. The sergeant, or servant of the almoner, to whom their care was deputed, took oath to collect the broken meats of the monastery and faithfully distribute them to the boys of the almonry and to friars and other beggars, and to instruct the boys to the best of his ability in morals and learning.

Almonry boys were soon after provided at Reading Abbey. An extant account of the Almoner for 1345-6 contains items of expenditure, "on the garments of 10 clerks, 36s. 3d., on additional food for the boys and others at table (*ad mensam*, i.e. boarded in the Almonry), the schoolmaster, yearly, 3s. 4d., a bishop's mitre for the [boy] bishop on St. Nicholas' Day 5s." The small sum paid to the schoolmaster probably represents a payment to the grammar schoolmaster of the town for teaching these Almonry boys. It is obviously too small for a separate schoolmaster in the abbey. In 1383-4 the schoolmaster's pay had been raised to 9s. 9d. for three-quarters of a year. The clerks or boys had been increased in number from ten to eleven; their clothing cost 35s. 8d. An item of 3s. 6d. for extra food, for the boys and others serving the abbot, while staying at the manor of Bere, illustrates the use of these boys as pages. In 1462 the *clerici* are called throughout simply "boys"; twenty-four yards of cloth for them cost 34s. 4d., and bread 3s. 8d., presumably extra bread bought beyond the leavings from the monks' table. Their expenses and those of other servants (the phrase may be noticed as evidence of their status) at Advent, Shrove Tuesday, and St. Nicholas' Day (6 Dec.), came to 3s. 4d., while new cups and plates for them cost 7d., a new table-cloth, 20d., a new table for the Almonry hall, 3s. 4d., candles for the boys in winter, 8d., and "the expenses of 2 boys living wholly on the alms of the monastery 13s. 4d." This last item suggests that the other boys were not wholly maintained by the abbey. The schoolmaster received 13s. 4d. The *Valor Ecclesiasticus* of 1535 for Reading is missing, so we do not know whether the Almonry boys were maintained to the Dissolution, but there is no reason to doubt that they were.

At Durham, an almonry school appears first in 1350, when a payment is made for the "Almonry bishop", the boy-bishop of the almonry boys. A master of the boys in the almonry is first mentioned in 1352, and in 1372 he is first called schoolmaster of the almonry and paid £1 14s. 3d. for his salary and gown.

It was only on special feasts the boys had anything to eat but the broken meats from the monks' table; 7s. was paid for fresh meat for them for Advent, 1419, at Durham. They were set to menial tasks. In 1448, one pennyworth of bread and beer was given them for tossing hay, and in 1457, 1s. 5d. was spent in beer for them for getting stones. The Elizabethan "Rites of Durham" tells us how the broken meats for them were handed out of the pantry window of the refectory, whence the boys carried them to the almonry just outside the great gate. When a monk died, the children of the almonry spent the night by the corpse "sitting on their knees" and reading the Psalter till 8 a.m. In 1535 these children were described as thirty poor scholars studying the art of grammar in the school of the same monastery, at a cost of £21 13s. 4d. When the priory was turned into a cathedral, which had to keep eighteen King's scholars, the last master of the almonry school became usher, or second master, of the cathedral grammar school, the first head master being the master of the city grammar school.

The first payments for boys in the Almoner's accounts at

Westminster appear in an account roll for 1355 : " For the expenses of 2 boys, 2s. " and " For clothing the boys in the Almonry, 30s." Their numbers were increased from that time, as in 1363 the cloth for their gowns alone cost 24s. 5d. No master for them appears till 1367, when one gown was bought for the " Master of the said boys ", which with his stipend came to 26s. 8d. Two years afterwards there was paid " To the sub-Almoner for boys of the Sub-almonry against St. Nicholas' Day", the day of the boy-bishop's ceremony, " 9s. Cloth for the boys of the Almonry, 46s. 8d. ; for fur for the Boys' Master, 2s. and to the tailor for making the clothes of the boys of the Almonry, 2s. ; for shearing the cloth, 16d. ; and in the stipend of the Master of the boys this year, 13s. 4d." In 1380, the master is for the first time called a grammar master, when there were twenty-eight boys. From 1388 onwards he is called schoolmaster, and is paid " For teaching the boys by the year according to agreement, 13s. 4d." In 1394 a new agreement was made by which his salary was doubled, and at this rate, £1 6s. 8d., he was paid till 1479. He had board and lodging as well. A school-house was provided, items for its repair occurring in 1414, and a complete account for re-building in 1422. With four chambers and four chimneys, it cost £22 9s. 9d.

The payments for cloth enable us to determine with tolerable certainty the status of the almonry schoolmaster and the size of his school. The five yards of cloth allowed him was the same as the allowance to the usher at Winchester College, three yards less than the head master's, and his fur cost 16d. or 18d., while the head master's at Winchester cost 3s. 4d. He was sometimes a married man, and therefore not in holy orders. The number of boys can be deduced from the amount of cloth. Three or four pieces were bought, of twenty-four yards in the piece, which at four yards a boy, would give eighteen to twenty-four boys. This estimate from the almoner's account is confirmed by other accounts. In 1373 the treasurer of " Queen Eleanor's manors" paid to the boys' master and thirteen boys 2s. 2d. ; and in 1385 to the master 6d., and to each of twenty-eight boys 2d. ; while in the next year there were twenty-two boys.

The master's salary was raised to £2 in 1479, and among

the " wages of servants " appears " Paid to William Cornysshe for teaching the singing boys for half a year, 6s. 8d.". A singing-master with a salary of 13s. 4d. regularly appears after this down to the Dissolution. Soon afterwards, the entry of the payment to the schoolmaster "for teaching the boys" is changed, first, by the addition of the words " of the Almonry " ; and from 1510 onwards by calling them "grammar boys". During the reign of Henry VIII, the entry as to cloth for the boys is enlarged by an extra sum of 30s. paid " to the Underalmoner for cloth for the singing-boys ". It seems, therefore, that in later years the singing-boys and the song school were an addition to, and not a selection from the ordinary almonry boys and their grammar school.

At Bardney Abbey, in 1379, the bishop ordered the monks, instead of wandering about the country, to observe their rule, stay at home, and maintain six boys to learn grammar.

At Worcester Cathedral Priory two " boys of the chapel " first appear in the accounts of the master or warden of the Lady chapel in 1395. In 1432, 8d. was paid for cups and bowls for " boys in the Almonry ". An organist, not a monk, first appears in 1475. The chapel boys numbered four in 1480 and five in 1483. In 1486 in the Almonry accounts these boys are first called scholars. In 1489-90 the organist "and instructor of the boys of the Blessed Mary's chapel " received an augmented salary of £8, and the amount spent for necessaries and cloth for the boys' gowns shows that they had been increased in number to ten or twelve. But it is not till 1498 that a schoolmaster for them is mentioned, who on 17 October, 1501, received formal appointment by deed to teach the " brethren and also the scholars of our Almonry the art of grammar and logic indulgently, well and faithfully " at £2 13s. 4d. a year. In 1504 he was promoted by the bishop to the mastership of the Worcester City Grammar School. He had no successor in the Priory; the boys having only a singing- and music-master thenceforward to the Dissolution. In 1535 the poor scholars of the Almonry numbered fourteen, and were given eighty gallons of beer, ninety-eight monks' loaves, and nine yeoman's paste loaves every week.

At St. Mary's Abbey, York, the almonry school, in which fifty boys boarded in a house called the conclave or chamber, attending the cathedral or city grammar school (the terms are convertible), is said, in 1535, to have been founded by William Rufus. But we may put this down to false history. On its dissolution, the same number was provided for in the hospital annexed by Cardinal Pole to the cathedral school, but this boarding-house was soon discontinued.

One of the latest of English monastic foundations, the Coventry Charterhouse, or Carthusian monastery, begun about 1382, was ten years later largely endowed by Richard II out of alien priories for a Prior and twelve monks. One of these priories was subject to a charge of sixty-five marks, or £43 6s. 8d., a year in favour of the King's Hall, now part of Trinity College, Cambridge. It is typical of the change of attitude to the monastic ideal that on 21 May, 1399, the king released the monks from this payment in consideration of their keeping in the monastery twelve poor scholars between the ages of seven and seventeen, to pray for his soul ; an assistance very soon required. The monks profited a good deal by the change. For, in 1535, when they claimed allowance for the "maintenance and exhibition of 12 poor scholars in their house so ordained by the foundation and ordinance of kings of England, their founders", they put the cost at only £30 a year ; more than a third less than the charge for the King's Hall. The monks, of course, did not teach these boys, or have anything to do with them, as the Carthusian was the strictest of orders. The monks lived in separate cells, and theoretically were cut off from all intercourse, not only with the outside world, but with each other, even at meal times ; their food being handed in to them through a hatch contrived like a turnstile, so that they might not even see the hand that fed them. The boys, therefore, probably went, as at York, to the city grammar school for their education.

This the Almonry boys certainly did at Sherborne Abbey, Dorset, where out of the income of the property assigned to the office of the Almoner, " alms " were " yearly distributed for the maintenance (*exhibicione*) of three scholars in the grammar school at Sherborne on the foundation of Alfric Thorncombe, 78s.", or at the rate of £2 6s. a year each ; a valuable form of exhibition, since that of the scholars of Henry VIII's cathedral grammar schools on a sumptuous scale was £2 13s. 4d. Who

Alfric Thorncombe was or when he lived, in the absence of chartularies and registers, has not been discovered.

At Thornton Abbey, Lincolnshire, there ought to have been fourteen boys in the Almonry, but the bishop in 1424 had to order twelve at least to be admitted.

At Ixworth in Suffolk, according to the *Valor Ecclesiasticus*, the Priory paid "in alms given for the keeping and teaching of 6 boys according to the laudable and ancient custom ordained by the seniors of the said priory" £10. The real antiquity of the custom may be doubted. It cannot be earlier than the fourteenth century.

On the other hand, fourteen poor scholars kept on alms in the Almonry of Coventry Cathedral Priory at a cost in clothes, food, and money paid by the sacrist of £12 11s. 4d. a year, had a school of their own. This Almonry school seems to have been first started in 1439, for, on 3 October of that year the city ordered the Mayor and six of his council to go to the Prior "wyllyng hym to occupye a skole of Gramer, yffe he like to teche hys brederon and childerun off the aumbry". But this was not to prevent every man of the city having free choice to set his child to school "to what techer of gramer he liketh, as reson askyth". Evidently the citizens were afraid of this new Almonry school competing with their old city or Cathedral Grammar School, for which a new building had been provided in 1303, and of the Prior exerting his authority as ordinary to make the people send their children also to this new school. Let him keep a school for his own young monks and the charity chorister boys, if he liked, but he was not to interfere with the children of the townsfolk.

A similar innovation, met with similar opposition by the city, took place at Canterbury when the Abbey of St. Augustine set up a separate school. The monks in a petition to the Pope admitted that "in the city of Canterbury there exists by ancient approved and hitherto observed custom a school (*scole* in the plural) for instructing boys in grammar", but, they say, it is far from their monastery, and they desire to set up another school within or near their own precinct for the poor boys who are brought up on their alms, and for other scholars in grammar, lay and wretched (*miserabilibus* but, query, whether the word has not been misread) folk, wishing to be instructed.

They undertook ꞌto provide a master or rector—the school-master at Canterbury was nearly always called rector—at a proper salary and to build the school outside the city walls—the monastery itself was outside the walls, though only a couple of hundred yards from the cathedral. They asked that all scholars should be allowed to go to the school freely without hindrance from the rector of the city school, or any one else, notwithstanding the said custom or any other obstacle. The Pope, ever ready to favour the monks, issued a bull, 28 December, 1431, authorizing this rival of the old school. Whether the Almonry boys were the thirteen poor, on whom, according to the *Valor Ecclesiasticus* 100 years later, £19 13s. 4d. a year was spent in daily doles at the monastery gate, and whether the chaplain in the chapel of the Almonry, who received £6 a year, was their master, does not specifically appear, but it seems probable.

At the beginning of the fifteenth century we first hear of an Almonry School at Norwich, in somewhat peculiar circumstances. In 1403 John Hancok, priest, was collated by the bishop to the Grammar School of Norwich. According to F. Blomefield, the eighteenth-century historian of Norwich, he was succeeded by John Seguard, an excellent poet and rhetorician, who was deprived for too freely reproving the monks for writing filthy verses; but Blomefield does not state his authority for this. At all events, next year, John Hancok was again collated to the school. Nine years later, in 1423, he leased the grammar school for his life to John Rykkes, rector of Wood Norton, at nine marks a year, Rykkes undertaking to teach the boys, Hancok reserving a right to enter the school at pleasure, and correct or reform in decent language any deputy employed by Rykkes. Rykkes was to repair the school and master's house, and might walk in a private garden attached, which was otherwise to be solely for the use of Hancok and his friends. Hancok reserved to himself the right to teach in the Almonry school, of which he was also master, any scholars dwelling within the precinct of the monastery or its neighbouring dependency of St. Leonard's, and any other boys of the city or country round sent by their friends, not exceeding twelve: but he was not to tout for boys to the damage of the Grammar School. The boys dwelling in the

NORWICH GRAMMAR SCHOOL. MASTER AND BOYS. c. 1420
MISERICORDS UNDER MASTERS' STALL IN NORWICH CATHEDRAL.

THE ALMONRY OR CHORISTERS' SCHOOLS 225

precinct were the Almonry boys, and it seems probable that, as at Coventry, this was the first attempt of the Prior and monks to set up a school for them, and the appointment of Hancok was an ingenious device for avoiding the opposition encountered at Coventry and Canterbury in the interests of the ancient Grammar School. In 1520, when Bishop Nikke or Nix held a visitation of the monastery, the Sub-prior complained only that "by ancient custom" fourteen boys ought to be kept in the Almonry and there were then only eight. The monks at this time had a complete contempt for learning, as in 1514 the same bishop had found that they had no grammar school for the young monks, but only a Master Wheteacre, who taught grammar twice a week, that a monk named Dersham, instead of attending the school "pursued other arts", and that the monks generally, as soon as they had been ordained priests, gave up study altogether. In 1535 there were "13 boys yearly living in the monastery to be taught in the grammar school, called 'Le Almery Scole,' out of charity (*ex elemosina*), at the rate of 26s. 8d. each for living and clothing, with £2 13s. 4d. for the wages of a master to teach them, and 20s. a year for the wages of a servant waiting on them". It is stated that this school was "so founded of Hilbert, formerly bishop, founder of the monastery by his own charity," meaning, apparently, Herbert de Lozinga, the first Bishop of Norwich. But this is romance.

At Ely Cathedral Priory, an organ was first made in 1396 in the south part of the church, at a cost of £4 8s. 5d. In 1407 a layman taught the Precentor's clerk to play the organ for 30s. a year. Choristers appear in 1409, when a singer taught "the boys" at a salary of 10s. a quarter. It was not till 1448 that the Prior licensed one John Downham, junior, to teach grammar in a grammar school within the monastery, and nowhere else, to five Almonry boys, and perform Divine service three days a week in the Almonry chapel, and three days in the Lady chapel, and on Sundays and feast days, where the Prior chose; and also to teach the younger brethren (monks) for an hour and a half before Tierce every day. For the Almonry boys the master received £1 6s. 8d. a year, and for the rest a monk's loaf and a gallon of the best ale foaming (*sub spuma*) every day, a monk's mess from the kitchen daily,

15

and pittances when the monks had them, a gown of the best cloth, a chamber and 17s. 4d. in silver. So that the employment of the Almonry schoolmaster for the double duty of teaching the charity boys and the young monks themselves was a cheap way of complying with the insistent demands made during the fifteenth century by episcopal visitors for the education of the monks.

Another illustration of this is found at Evesham Abbey, where the Bishop of Worcester, John Alcock, founder of Jesus College, Cambridge, and of Hull Grammar School, appropriated by deed of 6 July, 1462, the parish church of Eyford (which, it is stated, had no parishioners) to the monks to enable them to "have a master or informer (*informator*, the official title of the masters of Winchester and Eton) in grammar, or in the other primitive sciences, very necessary and much in request to teach the monks, especially the novices, and other boys and youths in the said monastery". These "other boys" were the Almonry boys who, according to the *Valor* of 1535, were only six in number, and cost "on food, livery, and other clothes £6", and a part of the further sum of £25 spent "on alms . . . for the . . . poor in the house of the Almoner . . . viz. $\frac{1}{10}$th of the bread baked in it or bought for it, and the tenth gallon or collection of beer brewed there or bought for it ".

A witness in an Exchequer suit under Queen Elizabeth in 1582 says that at Furness Abbey in Lancashire, where the abbot ruled almost a principality of his own, some children of the tenants of whom he was one were educated and boarded in the abbey, and a grammar and song school kept in it.

That St. Augustine's Abbey, Bristol, had its quota of Almonry boys appears from an account produced to the Bishop of Worcester on a visitation in 1493, in which a payment occurs to John Austin, vicar of St. Augustine the Less, of 13s. 4d. "for teaching the junior canons and other boys in the grammar school in the abbey", and 3s. 4d. "more for his diet for doing so". The number must have been very small.

At St. Peter's Abbey, Gloucester, now the cathedral, the first-known mention of anything like an Almonry school is on 16 April, 1515, when John Tucke, B.A., was granted a salary of £6, £3 paid by the cellarer, £3 by the master of the [Lady] chapel, with a gown, two cartloads of fuel, two courses at dinner the same as a monk, and one "myech" loaf and one gallon of beer a day, in the chapel house where the singers dine with the boys. For this he was to teach the junior monks and thirteen boys in the clerks' chamber the science of grammar, and also five or six boys who were apt for it plain and divided or broken song and discant, and with these boys to sing the Blessed Virgin's anthem daily, and on Saturdays the antiphon of the name of Jesus, and on Sundays and Saints' days to play the organ at vespers and high mass. It is clear that, so far as grammar was concerned, this was an elementary sort of teaching, and the choir boys were the main object. There may have been an earlier provision for the Almonry boys, if not for their education. In the *Valor Ecclesiasticus* the monks had the audacity to attribute the institution to the ordinance of King Barnulph of Mercia.

At Tewkesbury Abbey, according to the *Valor Ecclesiasticus* of 1535, the Almoner paid " in alms distributed to certain poor scholars to the number of 16, as in woollen cloth to clothe them, £7 13s. 4d. ; and to certain poor boys in the same office (the Almonry), limited by the ordinance of foundation as well in eatables and drinkables and other necessaries as in maintenance (*exhibicione*) of the same boys at school (*ad studium*) in ordinary years, £3 11s. 8d.". The wording leads to the inference that these boys, though lodged, boarded, and clothed, were not taught in the Almonry, but sent to the public grammar school of the town. How old the ordinance was which provided for this we are not told.

In the neighbouring abbey of Winchcombe, the date of a similar ordinance is known and it was only fourteen years old. The *Valor* shows " In alms and payments by foundation of the lady Jane Huddilston, relict of Sir John Huddilston, knight, yearly to the master of the Grammar School of Winchcombe, to the master of the boys singing in the monastery and for the maintenance of 6 boys in the said monastery being instructed and taught in the art of grammar and in song " with payments for obits and the poor, "£21 6s. 8d.". This foundation was by a deed of 13 September, 1521. Lady Huddilston gave the abbots of Winchcombe and Hailes £400 to buy lands of the value stated, out of which a schoolmaster was to keep a Free Grammar School, and to receive £6 13s. 4d. a year, a gown or £1, a chamber with fuel, and meat and drink in the monastery, the school itself being outside. The six boys maintained in the monastery were not the grammar school boys, but " six boys or choristers of the Blessed Mary's chapel ", for whom the master of the Lady Chapel, a monk, paid out of his separate estate, valued at £19 14s. 7d. a year, £3 2s., " the price of 6 tunics and making and doubling the same, and of 24 pairs of shoes and 12 shirts according to a composition and ordinance of Richard, late abbot of the monastery, made and confirmed under the common seal of the monastery ". This abbot was Richard of Kidderminster, who resigned in 1525, so that this Almonry school was one of the latest.

At Winchester the introduction of Almonry boys was probably due to William of Wykeham. Five years after he founded his college there, at a visitation of the Cathedral Priory, he rebuked the monks for their ignorance of Latin, and consequent false quantities in singing and reading and per- verting the meaning of scripture, and commanded the Prior to provide a grammar master for the " novices and others not adequately learned ". On 29 September, 1402, the Prior's Register shows the appointment of John Dyes to serve for twenty years in the daily Lady Mass at the Virgin's altar, singing and playing the organ, and on high days in the choir, " he shall also teach the Prior and Convent's boys, not more than five in number, singing ". For this he was to receive a salary of £5 6s. 8d., a furred gown of the clerks' suit and a chamber, and dinner with the Prior whenever he played the organ in choir. On 16 August, 1404, Wykeham formally founded his beautiful chantry chapel in the nave, endowing it largely, the Prior contracting that " every evening the boys of our Almonry, living on the charity (elemosinis) of our Priory, shall sing at the chapel, in honour of the Blessed Virgin, the anthem Salve Regina or Ave Regina, and say the psalm De Profundis with the prayer Fidelium or Inclina ", in return for which the Prior was to pay half a mark, 6s. 8d., for the benefit of the boys on Lady Day. The boys of the Almonry are clearly the same as the chorister boys to whom John Dyes was teaching singing. Under Wykeham's successor, Cardinal Beaufort, the Prior, in asking the bishop to send back one Robert Bygbroke, a secular priest, whom he had taken from the cathedral for his own chapel choir, describes Bygbroke as song-master of the boys and organist and their best singer, "of no great mark among the nightingales of your lovely choir but necessary to us country-folk, in whose absence the choir of psalm-singers is mutilated, the melody of the organ silent and your church in danger of derision". So that the choir-monks by this time were even incapable of adequately conducting the services, the performance of which was the primary object of their existence. In 1482, when Edmund Pynbrygge was appointed song-master, the salary was raised to £6 13s. 4d., the "boys of the Prior and Convent", whom he was to teach in "chant and discant", being now increased to eight. On his retirement with a pension of £4 6s. 8d., his successor in 1511 reverted to the old salary of £5 6s. 8d., though the boys, now called "boys of the Lady chapel", had crept up to "not more than 10". In 1538 the next song-master, Matthew Fuller, syngyng man, received only £4 6s. 8d., but the "boys of the chapel" were reduced to eight. This seems to have been because the bulk of the teaching of the boys had been transferred to another and higher teacher. In 1497 Master Peter Druett, M.A., had been appointed to "inform the monks in grammar, but no secular boys at the same time without special leave". In 1510 Master William Porthous, clerk, combined teaching the young monks "dialectic", or logic, with being physician to the Prior and Convent. In December, 1538, under the stress of the Cromwellian injunctions, John Potinger, who was Second Master of the College, succeeded Druett as master, to teach grammar not only to the young monks, but also to "the chyldren of the chapell" and "the chyldren of the Almery". This is the first indication that the choristers, or such of the Almonry boys as were not choristers, but probably probationary choristers, were thought worthy of being taught grammar. They may, however, have been sent for grammatical instruction to the old city High School, which we know was still flourishing in 1488, when a scholar of Winchester College and fellow of New College was appointed to the mastership; it was close to the monastic precinct on the west.

There were no doubt many other monasteries which maintained Almonry schools, or at least Almonry boys, whom they sent to school. Taking them all together, and putting the average number of boys at ten for a monastery, upwards of a thousand children of the lower classes altogether may have received their board and lodging in the monasteries during the last century of their existence ; and most of them learnt to read and sing and some got a more or less good grammatical or general education there. This of itself would perhaps hardly justify the space devoted to the exposition of the precise facts as to these Almonry schools, were it not that there is reason to think that the common legend that the monasteries afforded the main provision of education in medieval times, so far as it has any foundation in fact at all, and is not the product of mere interested assertion by monasticizing writers, is founded on these Almonry schools. Unfortunately a new currency was given to this legend by the treatment, which these schools received in the paper, which ushered in a publication, with the sounding title of *Oxford Studies in Social and Legal History*, edited by Professor Vinogradoff in 1909, entitled " English Monasteries on the Eve of the Dissolution ", a study of the *Valor Ecclesiasticus* of 1535. This paper was originally published as a Russian thesis, by Alexander Savine, Professor of History in the University of Moscow, and it is to be regretted that it did not remain in its original language. Though the *Valor* extended to all ecclesiastical revenues, not those of monasteries only, for the purpose of ascertaining what were the First-fruits, or first year's income, and Tenths, or 10 per cent of the yearly income, payable to the Crown, which Parliament had recently imposed on ecclesiastical benefices in lieu of the annates and other payments previously payable to the Pope, the paper is limited to the monasteries, and is mainly concerned with their estates. But in an unfortunate moment Professor Savine set himself to estimate the amounts as disclosed in the *Valor* expended by the monks in charity and especially on education.

This expenditure only appears in the *Valor* at all because the Commissioners who took it were directed to exempt compulsory alms given according to the foundation to outsiders ; which were to be treated as an outgoing to be deducted from gross income before arriving at the net taxable revenue accruing to the monks. The Professor expresses surprise that " the Commissioners occasionally did not recognize some expenses that were most undoubtedly compulsory. For instance, the Winchester Commissioners refused to exempt the monastic expenditure upon poor children and poor scholars in spite of the remonstrances of the monks, and of the fact that the 'scholar' of those days was little better than a beggar"—a preposterously untrue generalization by the way, indeed a very reversal of the truth. "The monks pointed out that the expenditure upon poor scholars was called alms, but the Commissioners did not listen to them ; and Gardiner explained to Cromwell that there was 'a great difference between the relief of the poor and the education of children ; the poor would die without the alms, but the children could do without a school'".

It sounds incredible, but it is true, that the poor children and poor scholars mentioned were not the charity or chapel boys in the monastery, but the scholars of Winchester College, specifically called the "Newe College besyds Winchester" in the record. They were, of course, no more monks or kept by the monks than they are now. As for its scholars being little better than beggars, one would like to know how the Says, Cecils, Kingsmills, Phillpotts, Whites, Tichbornes, and other county families, who contributed scions to the school at the time, would have relished this description of their sons. The confusion of Winchester School, with its seventy scholars and ten commoners in college and an indefinite number of oppidans, with the little handful of charity boys who were kept in monasteries, and the warden and fellows of the college with the monks is a confusion so confounded as to show that the Professor had not the least conception what sort of institutions English schools were and are.

The fact is that the college, being well provided with lawyers among its fellows, claimed exemption for every item of their expenditure they could think of. "The seid College askyth to be alowed of, and that notwithstandyng the Kynges Commyssyoners (as yet) haue not alowed them", not only the "livery", or gowns, of the seventy scholars, the payments for oil and candles in their chambers, £11 18s. 5d. for the stipend of the schoolmaster and payments given him at obits, but also the stipends of the warden, the fellows, the "conducts" or chaplains, the wages of the servants, the commons or food of the whole 122 persons living in the college, and even the feed of the warden's eight horses (very like a beggar that scholar-warden was: he was a brother of Lord Mayor White). They actually claimed exemption of what they spent for the entertainment of guests, because Wykeham in his statutes had enjoined hospitality on the college. The total amount of the allowances claimed came to over £634 a year, besides some items not specifically estimated, out of a total gross income of £710 a year.

Naturally the Commissioners, though they were headed by Bishop Gardiner, who lived just opposite the College, and the county gentlemen who had friends and relatives in it, could not make such allowances as these. If allowed in this case, every monk's and abbot's living would also have had to be excluded, as their maintenance, too, was ordered by foundation. Gardiner's reply was more sensible than the Professor represents it: "The tithe of almes . . . we understand it, and have made allocations in the finding and nourishing of old and impotent and lame men. . . . We used herein a distinction of 'finding,' which in poor and impotent men is without other shift necessary to live by. But in children no such necessity to find them to school." It is obvious that the distinction is a real one, especially when as at Winchester College, the children at school were themselves the college, the foundation, its object and the recipients of its revenues, the very people to be taxed. The College managed to get off a good deal, as they were allowed "reprises in alms, fees, and other payments" to the extent of £81 a year, while they also managed to get their property grossly undervalued at £710 a year whereas in the Chantry Commission return thirteen years later the value was shown to be £947 a year.

It is not wonderful that the Russian Professor did not know what a "howler" he was perpetrating in thus treating the first of the "Great Public Schools" of England as a petty monkish charity school. Professor Vinogradoff might have known better than to put forth in the name of his adoptive *Alma Mater* such a derogatory misrepresentation of what was, till 1854, a member of her own body, a part of the University itself.

Professor Savine's further remarks on educational payments in the *Valor* show that he as completely misunderstood the

Almonry schools as he did Winchester College. He remarks that "the Commissioners do not mention schoolboys even in those places where there was no doubt of their existence. When the monasteries of Lilleshull, Garendon, and Ulverscroft were suppressed, children were found there, but the *Valor* does not mention them". But the reason is plain. At Lilleshull the children were "4 gentylmens sones and their scolemaster", who, of course, were no charge on the foundation, but private wards of the abbot, who paid him for their board and for their education, which, it may be observed, was not given them by the abbot or any monk, but by a private tutor hired for the purpose, who is ranked among the servants. As likely as not there were none there at the time of the *Valor*. On the other hand, at Ulverscroft Priory in Leicester the boys were specifically described as "chyldren for the chapel there, 14", and at Garendon as "chyldren founder of almes, 5", i.e. they were choristers and charity boys kept in the almonry of the monastery to wait on the canons or monks and sing in the Lady Chapel. Being inmates of the monasteries for the comfort and benefit of its inmates, the expenditure on them was naturally not exempted from taxation. The Professor repeats his wonder at the alms of St. Peter's, Gloucester, to some adult poor being allowed, while the expenditure upon thirteen poor schoolboys was crossed out, though the monks asserted that they originated in ordinances by King Barnulf of Mercia. We may give the Commissioners credit for not crediting this precious invention.

The Professor, on the other hand, expresses his surprise that while at Gloucester £6 13s. 4d. paid to a lecturer on divinity in the monastery was not exempted, at Worcester the "fee of Master Roger Neckham, professor of theology, warden of the carnary near the palace of Worcester," £10 16s. 8d., which he calls "an expense in Worcester cathedral", was exempted. But the reason is that at Gloucester the lecturer was to lecture in the monastery for the monks themselves, while at Worcester the carnary or charnel-house was, as we saw above, not in the cathedral or monastery at all, but was a separate and independent institution, not monastic, but a chantry chapel of seculars. The payment to its Warden for theological lectures was charged by a definite deed of a bishop of Worcester on the monastery, who had for greater security vested its endowment in the Sacrist, and was as much an outgoing from the monastery as any rent-charge to a secular landowner.

Professor Savine, therefore, who has been cited as the latest authority in support of the theory that the monasteries did the education of England, and that " in the monastic schools not only the children of the poor but also those of gentlemen were educated ", cannot be accepted as of any authority. He started under the prepossession, sedulously inculcated by Abbot Gasquet and other monkish writers, that not only would he find a school in every monastery, but that every school he did find was monastic, and so he made the appalling blunder of representing the *doyen* of our " Great Public Schools " as monastic, and totally failed to realize the humble position and the recent origin of the Almonry boys and their schools.

CHAPTER XII

THE FIFTEENTH CENTURY AND HUMANISM

THE fifteenth century has commonly been decried as a period of decadence in learning owing to the contempt poured by Erasmus, Colet, and other sixteenth century writers on their more immediate predecessors, which has been accentuated by the *odium theologicum* of the Reformers for the reactionaries of their own day. So far as education is concerned, the fifteenth century was not one of decadence but of progress. A great development of educational foundations took place, alike in the re-endowment and enlargement of old schools and the erection of new schools and colleges.

Even in the first years of the century, during the much-troubled reign of Henry IV, new educational developments were not wanting. Oswestry Grammar School is one of the earliest instances of a school entrusted to a mixed body of laymen and clerics, and not part of, or dependent on, an ecclesiastical foundation, college, hospital, or chantry. Its foundation or endowment, perhaps intended to strengthen the English elements in the border county of Shropshire against the ever-rebellious Welsh, was due to a pardoned Welsh lawyer, David Holbeach, who is credited by Leland with the foundation of Davy's or Davies Inn, one of the Inns of Chancery, in London. The school has often been credited to his wife, Gwenwhyvar, though her grant of a corn-mill and lands for the maintenance and sustenance of a schoolmaster in the town of Oswestry for ever are expressly said to be in pursuance " of the intent " of David Holbeach ; whose feoffment of school-lands in 6 Henry IV, i.e. 1404-5, is mentioned in the seventeenth century " School-book ". In 1548 the school endowment of £6 a year was augmented by £2 a year out of the " service of Our Lady " founded by Thomas, Earl of Arundel, also in the early years of the century.

Throughout the century a similar desire to spread education, and that generally free education, is shown. A notable instance appears in the Statute of Apprentices in 1406. While the unfortunate labourers on the land were forbidden to raise their children in life by apprenticing them to trades and manufactures in the towns, unless they owned land worth £1 a year—not less than £30 or £40 a year now,—an express exception was made, that any man or woman of any estate should be free to send his son or daughter to learn literature, i.e. Latin, at any school they pleased. Hence we no longer find in the Manorial Court Rolls, as in the fourteenth century, the villeins being fined for sending their sons to school without the lord's leave; a notable social and educational advance.

A curiously modern difficulty appears in an incident which took place at Lincoln at this time. In spite of all attempts to give choristers a good school education, a difficulty has always arisen in satisfying the conflicting demands of song and grammar, and reconciling the necessary attendance of the choristers at choir practice and choir, with the ordinary grammar-school hours. It was summed up in a famous jest over a similar difficulty as to choral scholars at New College about 1860, that it was impossible to find men " et cantare pares et respondere parati ", able to sing and also pass responsions.

In December, 1406, the Dean and Chapter of Lincoln solved it by starting a separate grammar school for the choristers. They appointed two masters, one of the " General Grammar School of the city " and another of " the grammar school of the college of choristers ". This formal appointment of a choristers' schoolmaster as a rival to the master of the ancient school produced friction. So in January, 1407, the chapter ordered that the choristers and the commoners with them (*commensales*, boarders in their house) should go down to the General Grammar School as in times past. But a week later they agreed that the master of the choristers and their teacher might admit commoners and might teach relations and boys of the canons in the school freely, but that boys from outside he was on

A FIFTEENTH CENTURY GRAMMAR SCHOOL

BRIT. MUS. MS. BURNEY 275 f., 176 b.

no account to admit or to teach. This admission of other than choristers was an innovation, resented by the city, the grammar schoolmaster and the chancellor of the cathedral, who appointed him. Eventually a compromise was recorded in a Chapter Act of 12 February, 1406-7, which ordained that the teachers of the choristers were to be at liberty " to teach grammar to the commoners with them, also to the relations of the canons and vicars of the church, or those living at their expense and charity, or dwelling in their family, on every day and time at which lessons are given . . . on condition that once in each school-term they are bound to go down at the ordinary and accustomed hour to the general school under its own master, and at these times to be under the teaching and chastisement of its master". The actual result was that the two schools competed with each other until, in 1560, they were re-united as one school in the dissolved Grey Friars' house, then converted into a school-house. By a concordat, 18 January, 1583-4, under which the chapter appointed and paid the master, and the city the usher, the bishop covenanted to allow " no other gramer schole " in the city or for three miles round.

A reported case in the Common Pleas in 1410, shows what a demand there was for schools at the time.

We saw that the government of Gloucester School and the exclusive right to appoint the masters and maintain the monopoly of the school had been handed over to the Prior of Llanthony. This seems to have been a cause of continual dissatisfaction. Entries in the diocesan registers of the Bishop of Worcester show that he was called on in 1287 and in 1380 to enforce the monopoly of the authorized master, while in 1340 the priory had to obtain from the Crown a new confirmation of the school to them. In 1410 another attack on this monopoly was made by " Thomas More, that was Scolemaster atte Hereford " who had set up a grammar school (*scolas gramaticales*, a typical use of the plural schools for a single school) in Gloucester, close by the authorized grammar school. So the Prior for himself, and the master and usher, John Hamlyn and Richard Darcy, for themselves, brought actions of trespass on the case, their count being that " whereas the collation to Gloucester Grammar School belonged to the

Prior of Llanthony, and the Prior had made collation to them to have the governance of the said school and to inform children and others . . . the defendant had set up a scole in the same town, by which, whereas the plaintiffs used to make of a child 3s. 4d. or 3s. a quarter now they could only take scarce 12d., to their damage ", which they assessed at £40.

The argument turned on two points, first, whether, though there was undoubted damage, there was any wrong, as keeping school was not a matter of heritable property, like keeping a market. " The teaching of children is a virtuous and charitable thing, and beneficial to the people and is not punishable." Secondly, whether there was not free trade in schools, as it was unreasonable that a master should be disturbed in keeping a school where he pleased. Eventually neither point was decided, a demurrer being allowed on the ground that " the teaching and informing of children is a spiritual matter (chose *espirituel*)" and therefore for the ecclesiastical courts, and not triable in the King's Court. It is interesting to note that the Richard Darcy of this case passed on to be head master of Winchester College, from 1418 to 1424; a sign that there was no marked line drawn between the great collegiate schools and the principal grammar schools. On his retirement the then master of Gloucester Grammar School, Richard Davy, was invited to Winchester as a candidate for the head mastership, and though an old Wykehamist was preferred to him, received the large solatium for his expenses of 6s. 8d. for himself and a shilling for his clerk.

It is possible that the real gravamen in the Gloucester case was that Thomas More was suspected of Lollardry. One of the constitutions of Archbishop Arundel in Convocation in 1408 provided that, " because what a cask holds when it is new it tastes of when it is old", no schoolmasters or anyone teaching boys in arts or grammar or instructing anyone in the primitive sciences (grammar, rhetoric, and logic), should dare to meddle with teaching the faith or the sacraments of the altar or even with expounding scripture except the plain text, or allow his scholars to dispute on them. In 1414 the Statute of Lollards gave all justices power to hold inquisitions into Lollard schools, conventicles, congregations and confederacies. But whether there ever were any Lollard schools, except in

JOHN KENT, A WINCHESTER SCHOLAR, 1434

FROM A BRASS IN HEADBOURNE WORTHY CHURCH

the sense of conventicles to preach Lollard doctrines, seems open to doubt.

A rather pathetic example of the essential connexion of collegiate churches with education is seen in the beautiful little church built on the picturesque tongue of land, surrounded on all sides by river and marsh, which gave its name to Tong in Staffordshire. Here Isabel, wife of Fulk of Pembridge, "chivaler", provided in the near neighbourhood of the castle for a warden and four secular chaplains or fellows, two clerks, and thirteen poor almsfolk. The whole endowment only amounted to £45 a year, of which the almshouse took £20. The statutes of the college, made 9 March, 1410, are fortunately preserved, or it might well have been doubted whether so small an establishment would maintain a school in such a small and unimportant place as Tong was and is. But it is duly provided that one of the chaplains, or, if a chaplain cannot be found, one of the clerks of the college, competently instructed in reading, singing and grammar, should be appointed by the warden and saner (*sanior*), which was construed in effect as senior part of the college, diligently to instruct the clerks and other ministers of the college, and beside them the youths of the town and of neighbouring towns. The schoolmaster's stipend was not very large, being only in fact half a mark a year beyond his pay as chaplain or fellow. The warden received £6 14s. 9d.; the other fellows £2 13s. 4d.; the schoolmaster, the second person in the college, £3; a sum augmented no doubt by the voluntary offerings on Shrove Tuesday and Christmas, which custom made obligatory.

At his native place, Middleton in Lancashire, the Palatine Earl and Bishop of Durham, ex-Chancellor of England, Thomas Langley, founded a grammar school in 1412, which, owing to its having been re-founded and re-endowed by one of its pre-Reformation pupils, Alexander Nowel, afterwards Dean of St. Paul's and Principal of Brasenose College, has been usually reckoned as an Elizabethan foundation.

Another work of the same bishop, in re-organizing and endowing the schools of his own episcopal city, has also been wrongly assigned to others, his own agents. He built a grammar school and song school side by side on the Palace Green between his castle and his cathedral, which under two letters patent of 13 June, 1414, granted by him in the dual capacity of temporal lord and spiritual pastor, were next day founded and endowed by his two chaplains who have been thereupon mistaken by careless historians for the real founders. Each master was to teach and instruct all willing to learn or study under him, the poor indeed freely for the love of God, if they or their parents humbly ask it, but taking from those who by themselves or their friends were willing to pay, the moderate fees accustomed to be paid in other grammar or song schools.   The bishop's accounts show that he maintained exhibitions not only in this school but also thence to the University; e.g. in 1419 one William son of John Ingleby, studying at Oxford, received £2 13s. 4d. for maintenance there, *ad exhibicionem suam.*

If Henry IV's reign was troubled within the realm, Henry V's was troubled without.   Yet to the hero of Agincourt is assigned by John Rows the Warwick historian, a design for a "noble college" at Oxford, in which there should be "deep research in the Seven Sciences", to be endowed out of the Alien Priories, finally suppressed at this time.   Rows asserts that he had himself in his youth seen the Ordinance for this college, but had forgotten its provisions.

The King's good intentions were partly carried out in the foundation of a nobleman who was almost a prince of the blood, the College of St. John the Baptist at Stoke-next-Clare, by Edmund, Earl of March and Ulster, Lord of Wigmore and of Clare, in Suffolk.   By deed of 19 May, 1415, he re-converted an alien priory, which had been a college of secular clerks till 1089, again into a college of a dean and six canons, eight vicars choral, and five choristers with an income of close on £400 a year.   Statutes made 25 January, 1422, ordained a schoolmaster to teach the boys of the college reading, plain song, and descant.   In 1537, Matthew Parker, the future archbishop, when dean, built a new grammar school, in which the tenants' children and young gentlemen were taught grammar, and "other exercises"; he increased the choristers to thirteen, and provided university exhibitions for them.   We find John Crosier, clerk, "scoolemaster" of the "Free Scoole", receiving pay at the high rate of £10 a year.   School and college were destroyed by Edward VI.

A great college founded or projected by a nearer prince of the blood, Edmund, Duke of York, was translated from his Castle of Fotheringhay by Edward, Duke of York, killed at Agincourt, under patents of 1412 and 1415, to the Parish Church. The establishment included a master and twelve fellows, eight clerks, and thirteen choristers. The statutes made on the translation, largely taken from those of Winchester and New College, provided that for the diligent and continuous information of the clerks, choristers, and other poor boys of the said college, and the manifold proficiency and speedy advancement of the same, the Master, Precentor and three senior fellows should depute one of the fellows to celebrate specially for the founder and teach the choristers grammar at a salary of 12 marks (£8); while a song master was to receive £2. When the college was dissolved, the Chantry Commissioners in 1548 said that "a free school had been kept in Fotheringhay, which is now dissolved; it was therefore expedient that there was a new erected in the town of Oundle", three miles away. In fact the school was continued at Fotheringhay and throve until 1814, when the master, becoming vicar, taught no more, but appointed an elementary teacher as his deputy, and elementary it has since remained.

More interesting than the foundation of great lords and ladies, as showing the spread of educational activity in the middle and commercial classes, is the development of schools in connexion with the gilds. As typical of this we may take notice of the development of Stratford-on-Avon school, which, recovered from the despoiling hands of Edward VI and therefore wrongly dubbed by his name, gave Shakespeare the opportunity of sharpening his wits in the acquisition of his little Latin and less Greek. The school existed as we saw in 1295, and was almost certainly conducted by or in connexion with the College of the Trinity by the old church. The business of the town had in the fifteenth century shifted away from there southwards towards where the "birth-place" now is, and the school followed the business.

Three existing gilds in connexion with the old church were in 1400 consolidated as the Gild of the Holy Cross, and removed to the beautiful gild chapel in the new town, which still forms one of its main ornaments, and in its gild hall hard by, the

16

townsmen and the brethren, who were recruited from all over England and Wales, feasted at the hands of many cooks.

In the first account of the consolidated gild, from Michaelmas 1401-2 to Michaelmas 1402-3, appears: "received of John Scolmayster for a chamber, by the year 6s. 8d.," and among the "allowances" is "20d. for rent of a new chambre in the Hall which John Scolemayster held for a quarter". The schoolmaster is referred to again in 1412-13, when the account contains an allowance of "4s. for the rent of St. Mary's house in the Oldetown which the master and aldermen [of the gild] pardoned to the schoolmaster yearly as long as he wished to teach children and keep school in it". St. Mary's house was the gild hall of St. Mary's Gild, and was in Church Street by Trinity Church in the Old Town. This allowance continued till 1417. The school was then moved. A new schoolhouse, the present picturesque Latin School in the new town by the gild hall, was built in 1426-7 at a cost of £9 17s. 11½d. A magnificent feast was given at its opening, at which the Bishop of Worcester was present; seven cooks, with four assistants, preparing the dinner, which included a swan, venison, herons, geese, fowls, capons, rabbits, pigs, mutton and marrow bones.

There was at first no separate endowment for the school, though there are frequent entries of the masters being admitted members of the gild without, or at a reduced, entrance fee. One of these, Richard Fox, B.A., B.C.L., admitted in 1477-8, seems to have been no less a person than the future Prime Minister of Henry VII and founder of Corpus Christi College, Oxford. The first step towards its separate endowment was taken 6 October, 1456, when John Webbe, alias Jolyf, and his wife delivered to Master Thomas Jolyf, chaplain, probably the master, and the Vicar of Snitterfield, ex-master, and others certain lands, to hold according to their deed. Whether the deed gave the lands to Thomas Jolyf, no doubt their son, personally or in trust for the school does not appear. Probably, as in other cases, the Wars of the Roses stayed the proceedings. At length by deed of 7 July, 1482, Master Thomas Jolyffe gave "all his lands" to the master, warden and proctors of the gild to "find a priest fit and able in learning to teach grammar freely to all the scholars coming to him

STRATFORD-ON-AVON LATIN SCHOOL, BUILT IN 1426, AND GILD CHAPEL

to school in the said town, taking nothing from his scholars for his teaching ". The said priest was to be admitted one of the five priests of the gild at the next vacancy, receiving £8 stipend till admission and £10 after. Twice a week the " grammar priest " and his scholars were to sing the anthem of St. Mary, and then say *De Profundis* for Jolyffe's soul. The first appointment of a schoolmaster under the new terms was made on 24 June, 1482, when the gild granted " a priestly service " to William Smyth, clerk, on the condition that he would conduct a free grammar school.

Among other schools first mentioned, though certainly not first founded in Henry V's reign, is Darlington, which had certainly been maintained by the collegiate church there since the thirteenth century, and now appears in a payment by the Almoner of Durham Priory, of 14s. to the schoolmaster coming from Darlington to teach the boys of Durham during a vacancy in the mastership. In 1417 is found a bequest to Master Roger, Master of Bruton, by Richard Bruton, Canon of Wells, thus ante-dating Bruton school a century before its usually re-puted foundation under Henry VIII. The school and chantry in St. Mary's Chapel at Worsborough, Yorkshire, was founded in 1418 by Sir Robert Rockley. In 1420 occurs the earliest evidence of the school at Henley-on-Thame (commonly at-tributed to James I, who chartered it in 1604), in the election of Robert Symon, Scolemayster, as clerk of the " cominalte " or Town Clerk. It is noteworthy that John Longland, last Bishop of Lincoln before the Reformation, was at this school, a commentary on Lily's Grammar for the use of Henley School being dedicated to him in 1532.

When we pass to the reign of Henry VI educational activity took two directions, the orthodox and unorthodox, or rather the sacerdotal and the anti-sacerdotal. In 1423 occurs the first mention of Buckingham Grammar School, which must have existed long before, in the very large rent of 40d. or 13s. 4d. a year paid by the schoolmaster for his house to John Barton the elder, Recorder of London; while John Barton junior, his brother, re-endowed a chantry at Thornton in Buckinghamshire by his will in 1443, the "prieste to teache the children of the said towne " and to give for the livery of six poor children, to every of them 4s.

At Stourbridge, Worcestershire, the service of the Trinity was founded in 1430 by subscription to maintain a stipendiary priest, who, as found in 1548, "hath always used and yett dothe vse to kepe a scoole".

A distinctly anti-sacerdotal tendency appears, however, in the first known school founded by a London citizen, that of Sevenoaks, provided by William Sevenoaks, grocer, of London, by will of 4 July, 1432, by which he gave the vicar and church-wardens lands in London to provide "a master, an honest man, sufficiently advanced and expert in the science of grammar and a Bachelor of Arts, but by no means in holy orders, to keep a grammar school in Sevenoaks, and to teach and instruct all boys whatsoever coming there for learning, taking nothing of them or their parents or friends for teaching them". It may be merely that he did not want the school-master to be wasting his time in performing masses for the dead as a chantry priest, or holding a living and neglecting his school. But the provision has a distinctly Renaissance ring about it as putting education before religion. A noticeable feature about the schoolmasters of the fifteenth century, also pointing in the anti-monastic and anti-sacerdotal direction, is the large number of instances of married men among them. Thus we find in 1421 Ralph Strode, schoolmaster in the city of Winchester, and Diana his wife suing William Coventre of North Okebourne, Wilts, Esquire, for 40s., probably for boarding fees for his son. At York the epitaphs or wills of three successive masters of St. Peter's School, Gilbert Pynchebeck, died 1457, Roger Lewsay, died June, 1465, and John Hamundson, died July, 1472, show that they had wives.

The example set by Sevenoaks was quickly followed and improved upon. A mercer, John Abbott, on 19 June, 1443, not only founded a free school, but made a city company, his own "mistere" of the mercers, trustees of it, giving them lands in London for a master to teach *libere et quiete*, free and quit of all charges, at Farnynghoe, now Farthinghoe in Northamptonshire. He thus anticipated by sixty-seven years the supposed innovation of Colet in entrusting his new endow-ment for St. Paul's to the same Company, because, "while there was no absolute certainty in human affairs, he found less corruption in a body of married laymen like the Mercers, than in any other order or degree of mankind".

We are not aware of any other City Company being made trustees of a school at this time. The Wars of the Roses put a stop to progress. But, to anticipate a little, as soon as things had quieted down again, we find on 20 March, 1487-8, Sir Edmund Shaa (Shaw) "cytezen and goldsmyth and alderman and late mayer of the citee of London" by his will directing a " lyvelode", enough land to provide a livelihood, to be bought by his executors to be "amortisyd (i.e. put in mortmain) unto his felliship of the craft of goldsmythes" to provide amongst other things for finding two honest priests, the one to pray for his soul at Longdendale, and the other " a discrete man and connyng in gramer and able of connyng to teche grammer and pray for his soul in Stopford (Stockport) church" and "kepe a gramer scole contynually, and that he frely without any wages or salarye asking or taking of any person except onely by salarye here under specified, shall teache all maner persons' children and other that wode com to him to lerne as well of the said town as of other townes thereabout the science of gramer . . . into the time that they be covenably instruct in gramer after thair capaciteys that God will give them". The salary specified was £10 a year, the Longdendale priest being merely a chantry priest, only getting £4 6s. 8d. a year out of the "lyvelihood" of £17 to be provided. The company made the executors in fact provide a livelihood of £40 a year so as to secure them against "empties" and other deficits, and the school was in working order with Sir John Randal, " prist and scolmaister", by 1492.

Incited perhaps by this example, in 1502 Sir John Percyvale, Merchant Taylor and ex-Lord Mayor, founded a " Fre Gramer Scole" at Maxfeld (Macclesfield), also in Cheshire, " fast by which he was born", "for gentilmen's sons and other gude men's children of the towne and contre thereabouts". It was made a free school, free from tuition fees, expressly, because " God of his habundant grace hath sent and daily sendeth to the inhabitaunts there copyous plentie of children" but not plenty of money to maintain them, while "right fewe techers and scolemaisters ben in that contre, wherebye many children for lacke of such techyng and draught in connyng fall to idlenes and so consequently live disolutely all their dayes". He did not make his own Company but seventeen local laymen trustees.

Another goldsmith and Lord Mayor, Sir Bartholomew Read, in founding a school at Cromer, 9 October, 1505, imitated Shaw by making the Goldsmiths' Company the governing body, and copied Percyvale in saying that for a salary of £10 the priest was to "kepe a fre gramer scole" for gentlemen's sons and good men's children and especially poor men's children of the said town and of the country thereabouts. How highly he thought of his foundation may be gauged by his directing the company to choose the priest-schoolmaster with the advice of the Provost of King's College, Cambridge, or of Eton College, and that he should be a master graduate or a good grammarian "especially such as had been brought up in the college of Eton or of Winchester, if such might be had". The company proved hard stepfathers; for they still in 1820 paid only £10 a year to the master. They had long ceased to consult the Provost of Eton, and the school on the model of Eton and Winchester had long sunk into a bad elementary school.

The spirit of the Renaissance was indeed abroad in the land, not only among the heretical and revolutionary Lollards, and the trading and commercial classes, but now in the highest and most orthodox clerical and political circles. Through an unfortunate misrepresentation by the self-lauding reformers of the sixteenth century, the Renaissance has in the educational sphere come to be considered as synonymous with the introduction of Greek into the curriculum of schools, and particularly with Colet's statutes for the " newe Scole of Powles " in 1510, in which for the first time Greek was suggested as a desideratum, though not demanded as a *sine qua non*, the High master being required to be one who knew Greek "yf swyche could be gotten ". It is one of the *idola fori* about the Renaissance that it was due to the introduction of Greek. The revival of Greek was an effect, not the cause, of the Renaissance. Petrarch is hailed as the morning star of the Renaissance, but Petrarch's star had set a generation before there was a single Greek teacher in Italy, while he himself had tried to learn Greek and failed. The earliest of the Renaissance educators, Vergerius, was born in the year of the Black Death, and was a man of fame at fifty when in 1397 he began to learn Greek grammar with boys of fifteen under Chrysoloras at Florence. Peter Paul Vergerius, for whom Purgatory would have been too good for introducing the pernicious practice of having two Christian names, published his work on a Liberal Education, *De ingenuis moribus*, in 1404. Full as it is of educational platitudes, borrowed from Quintilian and Cicero, it never suggests that Greek is an element of a liberal education. Indeed, it laments that Greek was utterly lost to Italy "except for one or two who are tardily endeavouring to rescue something from oblivion". Vittorino da Feltre, who started his famous Palace School at Mantua in 1414, was likewise born and bred and had finished his education before Greek was introduced. The first to advocate Greek as not indeed a necessary, but a desirable, part of education was Battista Guarino in 1459. The warden of New College, Thomas Chandler, introduced Greek lectures there by an Italian, Cornelio Vitelli, in 1465, and William Grocyn, the first "Grecian" in England, who left Winchester for New College in that or the following year, learnt the rudiments from him. Grocyn, after travelling abroad, became the first English teacher of Greek in Oxford in 1491. It was studied and presumably taught also at Magdalen College where Lily, the first head master of Colet's school, learnt it about that time. Nicholas Harpsfield, and other Greek scholars and advancers of the study of Greek, almost certainly learnt Greek at Winchester. William Horman, scholar of Winchester in 1468, head master of Eton 1485 to 1494 and of Winchester 1494 to 1502, must have taught Greek in both schools. His *Vulgaria*, a sort of *Delectus*, published in 1519, but reproducing exercises given when he was head master before 1502, is full of Greek phrases and references to Greek, even to the performance of a Greek play. Sir Thomas Pope, writing in 1556, bears specific testimony that when he was "a young scoler at Eton, the Greek tongue was growing apace, which is now much decayed". William Rightwise or Righteous, the first surmaster of St. Paul's School, who knew Greek, was an Etonian, a little before Pope.

But it was not the introduction of Greek at Winchester and Eton, New College and Magdalen, and its appearance in the statutes of St. Paul's School, which made them the great schools and colleges of the day, and their scholars the leading humanists of their age.   On the contrary, Greek was introduced in those colleges and schools because they were the advanced institutions of the day.   Because they were scholarly and literary they took to Greek.   It was not Greek which made them scholarly and literary.

The very term Renaissance is misleading.   There was no new birth of learning wanted, because learning had never died—in schools at all events.   The learning of Latin was the whole aim and end of education in schools.   The authors read may have differed, though Virgil from first to last formed the staple.   Otherwise Horace and Juvenal may have given way to Prudentius and Juvencus, and Cicero to Augustine, and vice versa.   But it is by no means clear that the latter were not better stuff for the schoolboy than the former.   There may well have been more interest in a poet who believed in the God of whom the boy knew than in Horace's sceptical references in a mythological and antiquarian vein to the dying divinities of Greece and Rome.   If it be said that the Latin of the Christian authors is inferior to that of their predecessors, we must ask what is the standard of inferiority.   To all alike Latin was their native tongue.   Is English as spoken to-day "inferior" to that spoken by Shakespeare or Chaucer?   It is certainly very different.   For people who wanted to know Latin, not to write Latin verses in imitation of Virgil, but to speak it or to read the latest work on theology or tactics or geography, the Latin of Prudentius and Augustine, or even of Duns Scotus, was as good or better than the Latin of Horace or Cicero.

The true virtue of what is known as the Renaissance is much better expressed in the term Humanism.   It is not the introduction of Greek or the imitation of Cicero, the preference for the study of grammar over dialectic, or for the details of philology instead of the niceties of logic, which constitute the Renaissance.   It was the substitution of humanism for divinity, of this world for the next, as the object of living, and therefore of education, that differentiated the humanists from

A UNIVERSITY LECTURE, EARLY FIFTEENTH CENTURY

their predecessors. For a thousand years the attention of educated mankind had been concentrated on its latter end, or on what was feared to follow it. Not life but death had been the subject of culture. Not how to prepare for life but how to prepare for death was the sole object of education. The humanists' progress consisted in the adoption of the dogma, "The noblest study of mankind is man". In preaching and practising Cicero in place of Lactantius, Petrarch substituted political for theological study. His own Ciceronian Latin, of which he and his age were so proud, is spoken of by Erasmus with almost the same contempt with which he spoke of his predecessors, or as our scholars speak of Erasmus. "He wants full acquaintance with the language, and his whole diction shows the rudeness of the preceding age", said Erasmus. An Italian writer, quoted by Hallam, describes Petrarch's style still more unkindly, as "scarcely bearing the character of Latinity".

The methods of the humanist educators show little difference from those of their predecessors. Though the Roman politician, very much idealized, is substituted by Vittorino da Feltre and P. P. Vergerius for the starving monks and ascetic unwashed as the ideal, the means of approaching the ideal were not greatly altered. Asceticism still shed its baneful shade. Vergerius' *Liberal Education* lays it down that "dancing should be kept at a distance and the society of women carefully avoided". "Never is it allowable to eat, drink, or sleep up to the point of complete satisfaction."

Æneas Sylvius, afterwards Pope Pius II, brought up himself in the humanist atmosphere, advising the King of Bohemia and Hungary "On the Education of Boys" in 1450, still speaks, in the words of Wykeham in 1382, of grammar as the doorway to all knowledge. Vittorino da Feltre recommends "old Donatus", as did Wykeham, and puts the *Doctrinale*, the grammar in doggerel Latin verse, of Alexander de villa Dei, a Dominican friar of 1240, into the hands of Cecilia Gonzaga, daughter of the tyrant of Mantua, at the age of six. The results of humanist education in her case, by the way, do not seem to have been very different from those of the theologians, as the poor girl became a nun, Vittorino himself aiding and abetting, and indeed instigating her, against her parents' wishes. Nicholas Perotti, a pupil of Vittorino's, first tried to oust Alexander. Grammar was now defined as "ars recte loquendi recteque scribendi scriptorum et poetarum lectionibus observata", and as being "initium et fundamentum omnium disciplinarum". But this was no new definition or description. It is as old as Dionysius Thrax, *c.* 166 B.C., and through Quintilian, Donatus and Priscian descended to Alcuin and all the schoolmasters of the Middle Ages.

The pedagogic works of Vergerius and Æneas Sylvius and others were not new in substance. If based on Quintilian on the one side, they were borrowed on the other from Friar Vincent of Beauvais' *Education of the Sons of Nobles*, addressed about 1250 to Queen Margaret of France, wife of Louis IX, and this was itself largely borrowed from Hugo's *Scholastic Discipline*. The main difference consists in the object laid down. Whereas the thirteenth century friar says that "all the studies of learners ought to be for theology, that is, to tend to the knowledge of God", his fifteenth century followers aim at moulding " the nature of man as a citizen, an active member of the State". Oddly enough both refer to Aristotle in support of their doctrine. There appear to be two novelties in the means used and two only ; one, that in Vincent and his predecessors little or nothing is said about bodily exercise and training, while in the humanists this, with its corollary of spacious grounds and handsome school buildings, becomes prominent. But it may well be that environment accounted for that difference. The sons of the king of France in the first half of the thirteenth century were not likely to lack space for hunting and instruction in the art of war. The children of a city tyrant, the sovereign Lord Mayor of an Italian city, cramped within its walls, might well lack the same opportunities. Vittorino's school, or rather collection of private pupils, was placed in La Giocosa, a converted "pleasure-house" with a large enclosed meadow, bordered by the river, exactly like Meads at Winchester or the Playing-fields at Eton. This innovation was probably an unmixed good.

Chaucer was *par excellence* a product of the Renaissance and breathes the humanist spirit in every line. But he was no isolated phenomenon. Many Englishmen besides him were brought into direct contact with the Italian humanists and Italy, whether bishops and archdeacons and canon

A PALACE SCHOOL OF THE FIFTEENTH CENTURY

(ALEXANDER THE GREAT AT SCHOOL)

BRIT. MUS. MS. ROYAL 20, B. XX, f. 10 b.

lawyers or traders and merchants. The Council of Constance was almost a school of humanists. Henry V, though from political motives a persecutor of the Lollards, yet designed, according to John Rous, the Warwick historian, a great college at Oxford for the Seven Sciences, to be endowed with the vast possessions of the alien priories. "The good duke Humphry" of Gloucester, the Protector of Henry VI, made the Council of Basle in 1432 a means of getting from Italian scholars translations of the Greek philosophers and the Greek fathers into Latin, and of Boccaccio into French.

Henry VI, far more than Edward VI, deserves to be remembered as a founder of English schools and as an eminent promoter, though by no means creator, of English education. Like his successor, the boy-King suffered personally from over-education. On 1 June, 1428, his education, which since 1424 had been in the hands of Dame Alice Boteler, was transferred from the lady to Richard, Earl of Warwick and Albemarle. "Whereas", says a writ of Privy Seal in French, "it is expedient that in our youth we should be taught and indoctrinated in bons meures lettrure langage e nurture et courtoisie et autres vertus et enseignements, (translated in annexed articles in English as 'nurture, lettrure (i.e. grammar), language and other manere of connyng'), "and, above all, 'de nous faire traire a vertues et eschuer vices', (to draw us to virtues and to eschewing of vices)"; therefore the earl was given power, "if we estrange ourselves from learning or do wrong, to reasonably chastise us as other princes of our realm and of other realms are accustomed to be chastised". The earl must have found the young King a difficult pupil to flog. For four years later, on 29 November, 1432, when the King was eleven years old, the earl laid before the council a series of articles. In one he said that the King "is growen in stature of his person and also in conceit and knowlech of heigh and royal authoritee and estat, the which naturally causen him more and more to grucche [grudge] with chastising and to lothe it". So he asked, not to leave off chastising him, but for the support of the council in doing it, and in appeasing any indignation the King might feel against him for doing it, with power to remove those whom he knew "at part and in prive not hering ye said Erle" had "stured" Henry "from his lernyng". The whole council promised to tell the King that it was their advice that he should be chastised for his " defaultes ", so that " for awe thereof he forbere ye more to do mys and entende ye more busily to vertue and to lernyng ".

That Henry did not resent the Spartan training which Warwick thought necessary, is shown by his making his quondam tutor and chastiser Duke of Warwick, the first duke in England not of royal blood.   Henry was not educated alone, as the tenants-in-chief on the royal estates were invited to send their sons to be brought up with him in the palace.   His experience of this school, an arrangement almost certainly made in imitation of the Casa Giacosa established by Gonzaga, the Marquis of Mantua, for his son and his nobles' children under Vittorino da Feltre in 1423, was no doubt largely responsible for Henry's foundation of Eton College, within view of his birthplace and favourite residence at Windsor Castle, with its twenty sons of noblemen.

Eton was by no means the first of Henry's educational foundations.   He, or rather the Duke of Bedford, the Regent of France, in his name, had already established a university at Caen in 1432, at first only for civil and canon law, which was not allowed at Paris, but extended, after the English were expelled from the capital, to theology and medicine, in the hope of keeping the subjects of the English King away from Paris. In 1441 another university was established for Henry's southern dominions at Bordeaux.

By letters patent of 11 October, 1440, Henry, then eighteen years old, having just taken on himself the government, declared his desire " as a sort of first-fruits ", to " show like his ancestors his devotion to the Church ".   But whereas this devotion had in them taken the shape of monasteries, in him it took almost as a matter of course the form of a college or collegiate church, in which a school was a leading, in this case a predominant, feature.   So by the patent he founded in the parish church of Eton " the King's College of Oure Ladye of Eton besyde Wyndesore " to consist of a provost, ten priests (the fellows), four clerks, " six chorister boys, daily to serve at divine worship, and twenty-five poor and needy scholars to learn grammar there ", and " twenty-five poor and disabled men to pray for the souls " of his father and mothei

HIGHAM FERRERS GRAMMAR SCHOOL, c. 1422

and all his forefathers and all the faithful departed ; also " a Master or Informator in grammar to teach the said needy scholars and all others from any part of England coming there, *gratis*, without exaction of money or anything else ".   In other words Eton was a free grammar school, but from the first non-local, open, free from tuition fees, to the nation at large.   The college was licensed to hold property up to the value of 1000 marks (£666 13s. 4d.) a year, equivalent to at least £20,000 a year now.   Shortly after, on 12 February, 1441, King Henry founded another college, in Cambridge University, con-sisting of a rector and twelve fellows, by the name of King's College of St. Nicholas, so called because 6 December, the king's birthday, was the day of St. Nicholas of Myra, the patron saint of schoolboys.   There was in Eton church before 1425 a chantry of St. Nicholas, and it is quite possible that the chantry priest of this church was also a grammar schoolmaster, and that this partly suggested the choice of Eton for the site of the college school.   There was at first no organic connexion between Eton and the Cambridge college.   The immediate model of the two colleges was the college school at Higham Ferrers in Northamptonshire and the College of All Souls at Oxford, founded by Henry Chicheley, Archbishop of Canter-bury, Henry's godfather, in 1422 and 1438 respectively.   But these were only copies on a smaller scale of the two colleges of St. Mary founded by William of Wykeham at Oxford in 1379 and Winchester in 1382.

In his college school at Higham Ferrers, Chicheley incor-porated two pre-existing foundations, the grammar school and a Bede-house or almshouse.   In the school he had no doubt been himself educated before getting a scholarship at Win-chester.   The deed in French has just been published from John of Gaunt's Register, by which, as Duke of Lancaster and Lord of Higham, he on 21 April, 1372, appointed Henry Barton of Great Billing master of the grammar school (*les escoles de gramoir*) to teach all those scholars and children (*escolers et enfaunts*) who wished to train in the faculty of grammar there, to have and to hold in manner heretofore used for term of his life, provided that he behave himself well and duly in the said office.   Barton was a married man, for when he died in 1399, after having served the office of mayor and other public offices several times in alternation with Chicheley's father, Agnes late relict of Henry Barton, schole mayster de Higham Ferrers, did fealty on 1 October, 1399, for a burgage which she held for her life with reversion to the children of the said Henry, and next year, Thomas, son of the late Henry Barton, scholemayster, did fealty by his mother, as he was under age, for another burgage.   The appointment of Barton's successor as schoolmaster by Henry IV in May, 1400, is also preserved.   Chicheley improved on Wykeham by providing that one of the eight chaplains or fellows of which the college consisted might be the grammar schoolmaster and another the song schoolmaster, thus making the masters integral members of the governing body of the foundation instead of stipendiary officers only.   So in the reign of Henry VIII the grammar schoolmaster, Nicholas Stere, was the best paid of the fellows, the warden receiving £14 13s. 4d. a year and the grammar schoolmaster £10 13s. 4d. while the other fellows only received £7 12s. 2d.

A foundation which probably had a considerable influence on Henry was that of Michael de la Pole, one of the Poles of Hull, who in three generations had risen from being merchants of that seaport, a new foundation of Edward III's, to the Earldom of Suffolk.   He founded in 1432, at his wife's place, Ewelme in Oxfordshire, an almshouse and grammar school, the outside of which retains all its ancient picturesqueness though the inside has suffered from the vandalism of the Education authorities, converting the ancient grammar school into a wretched apology for a new elementary school, for the sake of saving a few shillings to the ratepayers' pockets, instead of building them a new one.   De la Pole provided for a master who was to be a preacher, and is now the Regius Professor of Medicine at Oxford, to whose office the mastership was annexed by James I, and a master in grammar "a wele disposed man, apte and able to techyng of gramer, to whose office it shall longe and perteyne diligently to teche and informe chylder in the faculte of gramer; provyded that all the chylder of oure chapelle, of the tenauntes of our lordshyp of Ewelme and of the lordshypes perteynyng to the sayde Almesse Howse, now present and at alle tymes to com, frely be tawt withoute exaccion of any scole-hire".   No less

ARCHBISHOP CHICHELEY, FOUNDER OF HIGHAM FERRERS COLLEGE
AND SCHOOL, 1422, AND ALL SOULS' COLLEGE, OXFORD, 1438

FROM A WINDOW IN ALL SOULS' COLLEGE, OXFORD

than three lordships or manors were given for the endowment. The "Techer in grammer" received the same pay as the "Maystyr", viz. "for his pension and stipende termely, 50s. that is to say £10 in the yere". To prevent slackness on his part it was provided that if it so fortune, he have not "ore four childer that actually lernes gramer besides pettites and reders, that thanne he shal say matyns and evensonge dayly in the said churche of Ewelme with the seide mayster before the seide pore men" that is, become an ordinary chantry priest.

The Earl of Suffolk was the only layman among Henry's principal agents in founding Ewelme with its almshouse attached.

Another college and school foundation on similar lines to that of Higham Ferrers may well have influenced Henry; the College of St. Gregory and St. Martin, founded at Wye, Kent, by John Kemp, Archbishop of York, who, like Wykeham, had been twice Lord Chancellor of England. Born at Wye, he was a fellow of Merton College, Oxford, and a canon lawyer, and became Chicheley's Vicar-General and Dean of the Arches, and Chancellor of Normandy. The date generally attributed to his college is 1447; but in point of fact he obtained the royal licence for it on 10 February, 1432 (not 1431, as given in the local history through the usual confusion of the year of the Lord and the year of the King) and actually founded the college very shortly after, asking Battle Abbey, the impropriators of the living, to sell the vicarage and a site for a college of a "maister and six priests, two clerks and two queristers, and over that a maister of gramer that shal frely teche withoutyn anything takyng of hem al thos that wol come to his techyng". Like Chicheley, he bought from Henry the possessions of an Alien Priory, Newington church, which belonged to the Abbess of Guisnes, for endowment, thus giving more archiepiscopal sanction to the appropriation of monastic property to secular clergy and education. When he, then a cardinal, finally made his statutes, 14 January, 1448 (not 1447), he provided that the provost should be a fellow of Merton, and that the second person in the college should be the master or instructor in grammar. As "the rudiments of grammar are the first foundation for the understanding of the other liberal arts and sciences, lest its study should be omitted and the sons of poor people be driven to desert it through lack of means", he ordered that there should be a master diligently intent on teaching it. He was to be a master in that faculty or a graduate in some other faculty, or some other member of the University of Oxford or Cambridge, fully instructed in grammar, who, if he was a priest, should be admitted a fellow of the college, and for more honour sit next to the provost or his deputy at table. He was to teach freely (gratis), exacting nothing and taking nothing from his scholars whether poor or rich. Then follows a somewhat remarkable provision for that time for private pupils. "If, out of school and at times when he is not obliged to be occupied in school, he wishes to give greater attention to the teaching of any, we do not forbid his being paid for that labour only, provided that, as his oath requires, the common (i.e., public) teaching is in no way diminished by the private". Among the causes for his dismissal, besides negligence in teaching and incapacity through age or illness, is "if he shows any partiality in college or school". If he was merely infirm he might retain his fellowship, giving up the mastership, the pay for which was to be matter of arrangement. In the admission oath of the master it was expressly provided that he was to teach the poor and the rich indifferently, and to take nothing except what was voluntarily offered, except as aforesaid, "besides the customary offering of cocks (i.e., on Shrove Tuesday) and of St. Nicholas 'pence' (the offerings on the boy-bishop's day)"—a striking testimony to the prevalence of those two customs.

Another college of the same kind was founded at Tattershall in Lincolnshire by Sir Ralph Cromwell, an ancestor of Thomas Cromwell, the hammer of the monks, under licence of 14 July, 1439, with a warden and six fellows, priests, six clerks, six choristers and thirteen alms folk and the very large income of £536 a year. Here the grammar master had £9 a year, while the organist and master of the choristers had £4, and each of ten choristers received £3 6s. 8d. a year.

A striking manifestation of the new humanist spirit is seen in the Letters Patent granted in 1439, giving leave to William Byngham, rector of St. John Zachary in London, to found the College of God's House in Cambridge, at first an annex to Clare Hall, and afterwards incorporated with Christ's

College. In his petition for the licence Bingham had said that he had found no less than seventy grammar schools, formerly flourishing, over the east part of the way leading from Hampton [on-Thames] to Coventry and so forth no farther north than Ripon, that were occupied all at once within fifty years past, now fallen into abeyance for lack of proper teachers, "so great scarstee of maistres of Gramer". He therefore asked for leave to found a College of a master and twenty-four scholars for the training of grammar school-masters who were to issue thence to teach school all over the country—the first secondary-school training-college on record. In the patent the importance of the classics was insisted on, not merely as in the days of Wykeham and the foundation of Win-chester because grammar was the key which unlocked the Holy Scriptures and was the gate to the liberal sciences " and theology the mistress of all", but because " it was necessary in dealing with law and other difficult matters of state and also the means of mutual communication and conversation between us and strangers and foreigners ".

Here spoke the citizen of London and the man of the modern world.

It is probable that as Henry imitated Chicheley in adding an almshouse or Bedehouse to his college, he also meant by the original charter to make the master a part of the governing body. He imitated Chicheley also in endowing his college with the alien priories confiscated to the Crown by his father and great-grandfather. A good many of them had been sold or leased to great persons, and Henry had, just as much as William of Wykeham and Chicheley, to buy them for his college; the first instalment being given on 5 March, 1440-1.

In 1441, Henry visited Winchester to see the working of the school, and, as a result, seems to have resolved to depart from the Higham Ferrers precedent and remodel his founda-tion on a larger scale and more closely after the fashion of Winchester. He took William Waynflete, who had been head master of Winchester for eleven years, away from Winchester at Michaelmas, 1441, and made him provost. A Winchester scholar, William Westbury, was brought from New College to be head master in 1442. New statutes were made for Eton and the Cambridge college on 10 July, 1443 ; and five scholars,

17

one ex-scholar and one commoner of Winchester were admitted among the first eleven scholars of Eton, by way of giving it a good start on approved Public School lines.   So large a part did Winchester play at Eton that the first three provosts, twelve out of the first twenty-five head masters and eight of the ushers or second masters, and probably a good many more, came from Winchester.   The new statutes amounted to a complete new scheme.   They brought the two colleges of Eton and King's into the same organic connexion which existed between Winchester and New College.   Each college was enlarged to the same size as Winchester and New College, i.e. to a provost and seventy scholars, besides the ten fellows, while there were also added commoners (*commensales*), who were to be sons of noblemen or special friends of the college, only their number was doubled, being twenty instead of ten as at Winchester, and thirteen outside scholars of the kind known afterwards as servitors, who got their education and board in return for acting as servants to the fellows and head master. Henceforth, King's College, Cambridge, was to be exclusively manned from, and to be the Visitor of, the "College Roiall" of Eton.

Perhaps the most striking proof of Henry's regard for his foundation was his issue on 3 June, 1446, of a signed warrant, by which he recited his grant to the college that "it might always have in its precinct a public and general grammar school"—the first time the term public school was used of Eton—"and that the same school as it surpasses all other such grammar schools whatsoever of our kingdom in the affluence of its endowment and the pre-excellence of its foundation, so it may excel all other grammar schools, as it ought, in the prerogative of its name, and be named therefore the King's General School, and be called the lady, mother and mistress of all other grammar schools : and we have granted to it further that it shall not be lawful for any one of whatsoever authority he may be at any time to presume to teach, set up or found any such public grammar school in the town of Windsor or elsewhere within the space of ten English miles from our said Royal College".   To ordinary conceptions of a public school as a different and superior order of creation to a grammar school this "bill" is illuminating.   The extravagant self-as-

LORDS AND COMMONS PETITIONING FOR ACT TO CONFIRM ETON
COLLEGE CHARTERS. 1447

sertiveness and boastfulness of this language, contrasted with the somewhat pettifogging conclusion of the establishment of a legal monopoly for ten miles round, as if this lady, mother and mistress of all grammar schools, with the largest endowment in the kingdom, could not maintain its superiority without the forcible extinction of rivals ; the remarkable invasion of ecclesiastical jurisdiction, to which alone the grants and still more the enforcement of the monopoly of endowed schools belonged, surely show that Henry was already suffering from megalomania. The curious thing is that this bill, though delivered to the chancellor in the usual way for execution, that is for issue as letters patent, does not appear on the Patent Roll. To megalomania point also the enormous sums spent, chiefly out of the Duchy of Lancaster, on building and rebuilding, on an ever-increasing scale, the college and particularly the church of Eton, with the deliberate intention of making it larger than New College chapel, and finally than Salisbury Cathedral. Though a gorgeously illuminated Act of Parliament in 1447 confirmed all its possessions, the college remained unfinished when, in 1452, Henry first became insane.

During the Wars of the Roses a great part of the Eton endowment was taken away by Edward IV, and in 1463, by Papal Bull, the College was annexed to St. George's, Windsor, and for some four or five years the school, if it did not cease altogether, received no fresh scholars. In 1467 it was restored by the efforts of Westbury and Waynflete, then Bishop of Winchester, with Edward IV as founder instead of Henry VI, though in the days of the Tudors Henry VI was reinstated. The revenues were so diminished that the provost only got £30 a year instead of £75, and the head master £10 instead of £16, and there were only seven fellows instead of ten. This perhaps hastened rather than retarded the development of the school into a great public school for the upper classes and the aristocracy, who, while paying nothing for their education, paid large sums for boarding in the houses of the fellows, and in the town of Eton, whence they came to be called Oppidans. As at Winchester, so at Eton, the " poor and needy " scholars were scions from the first of the noble classes and the country gentry, relations of judges and civil servants and well-to-do people ; and the labouring classes were expressly made ineligible by the proviso that no villein *nativus* or illegitimate was to be admitted.   As early as 1479 a young Paston, of the family of the Paston letters, was an Oppidan, and in 1529 Richard Lord Grey of Ruthyn, probably a commoner, died at the school.

The earliest indication of the number of the Oppidans, who, rather than the scholars, have made the school famous, is in the will of Provost Lupton, provost from 1504, dated 23 February, 1540, by which he gave to " a hundredth children of the town ", i.e. oppidans, " 4d. a piece ", the " three score and ten children of the college ", i.e. scholars and " queresters ", receiving double that sum.   Most of the college buildings and the whole of the great quadrangle, except the chapel, were built by him or in his time, including, in 1504, " Long Chamber ", in which all the seventy scholars slept in one long room, instead of being divided, as in the original buildings, into seven chambers.   Indeed, except the chancel of the chapel, the hall, and the underpart of three sides of the cloister quadrangle there is nothing of Henry VI's building now visible at Eton.

Contemporaneously with the foundation of Eton another school, which for 200 years was the chief school of London, was in progress—St. Anthony's School.   The credit of this foundation is due to Henry VI and his Wykehamical advisers.   It has, however, never been given them owing to the erroneous account of its origin by one of the most famous of its "old boys", John Stow, who in his *Survey of London* attributed the school to the original foundation in 1231 of the Hospital of St. Anthony in Threadneedle Street, in which it was placed.   This Hospital was founded as a cell to the great St. Anthony's Hospital of Vienne, for the cure of St. Anthony's fire, a terrible form of erysipelas due to ergotism, arising it is surmised, from the use of bad rye as bread.   The English hospital was almost entirely maintained by a system of touting for donations and subscriptions all over England which would do no discredit to a modern London hospital, and was in the hands of the Brethren of St. Anthony, an order of regular or monastic canons, under a Preceptor, not a teacher but a governor.   A large part of the collections went to the mother-house abroad.   As an Alien Priory it was seized in the reign of

Edward III and in 1377 was separated from the foreign house and made immediately dependent on the Pope. From 1385 secular preceptors were appointed, and its conversion into a secular hospital, practically an almshouse—St. Anthony's fire having long been quenched in England—was legally sanctioned by a Papal bull in 1441.

John Carpenter, Provost of Oriel at Oxford from 1425, had become master of St. Anthony's in 1434,—the dates given in the *Dictionary of National Biography* are wrong. He was concerned in the foundation of Eton, and it is probably to his initiative that St. Anthony's school was due. He obtained, in 1441, from the Bishop of London the appropriation to the Hospital of the church of St. Bennet Fink next door to it, in order that the revenues of the rectory, worth sixteen marks a year, might be applied to the maintenance of "a master or fit Informer in the faculty of grammar, . . . to keep a grammar school (*regere scolas gramaticales*) in the precinct of the hospital or some fit house close by, to teach, instruct and inform gratis all boys and others whatsoever wishing to learn and become scholars (*scolatizare*)".

A song school was also established with a tavern as its endowment to pay John Bennet, clerk, eight marks a year and four yards of cloth of gentlemen's suit for teaching singing. The grammar schoolmaster received £16 a year, the same as the master of Eton, and there was an usher and twelve "children", six of whom seem to have been choristers and six grammar scholars. All these had board, lodging and clothing as well. In 1451 the school was brought into connexion with the university by the grant of lands to Oriel College, "for the exhibition of certain poor scholars in St. Mary's Hall", a dependency of that college according to ordinances to be made by Carpenter. The ordinances have disappeared. But the accounts of St. Anthony's and Oriel College show that scholars were duly taken from St. Anthony's School.

There is extant a letter from William Selling, Prior of Canterbury, to Thomas Bourchier, Cardinal-Archbishop of Canterbury, in 1472. "Please it your good fatherhood to have in knowledge that, according to your commandment, I have provided for a Schoolmaster for your 'Gramerscole' in Canterbury, the which hath lately taught grammar at Winchester and

S. Anthony's in London, that as I trust to God shall so guide him that it shall be worship and pleasure to your lordship and profit and increase to them that he shall have in governance ". As Archbishop Bourchier's own nephew, the heir to the Earldom of Essex, was a commoner at Winchester College, this reference to the master of St. Anthony's as having been also a master at Winchester, probably usher or second master there, shows that St. Anthony's School already stood high in reputation. Dean Colet and Sir Thomas More are claimed to have been educated in it.

Stow, born about 1525, tells us in a passage which is a *locus classicus* in the history of schools that, in his youth, which, for this purpose, we may take to be from 1532-4, the arguing of the schoolboys as to the principles of grammar of which Fitzstephen wrote, was still continued :—

"For I myself in my youth have yearly seen on the eve of S. Bartholomew the Apostle, the scholars of divers grammar schools repair unto the churchyard of S. Bartholomew, the Priory in Smithfield, where, upon a bank, boarded about under a tree, some one scholar hath stepped up, and there hath apposed and answered, till he were by some better scholar overcome and put down, and then the overcomer, taking the place, did like as the first, and in the end the best opposers and answerers had rewards ; which I observed not but it made both good schoolmasters and also good scholars diligently against such times to prepare themselves for the obtaining of this garland. I remember there repaired to these exercises amongst others the Masters and scholars of the free schools of St. Paul's of London, of St. Peter's of Westminster, of St. Thomas Acon Hospital and of St. Anthony's Hospital ; whereof the last named commonly presented the best scholars and had the prize in those days."

It is very doubtful whether Stow's memory was accurate when he brought scholars from Westminster and the Mercers' School to St. Bartholomew's before its dissolution. However that may be, Stow goes on :—

"This Priory of S. Bartholomew being surrendered to Henry VIII these disputations of scholars in that place surceased ; and were again, only for a year or twain, in the reign of Edward VI, renewed in the cloister of Christ's Hospital, when the best scholars, then still of S. Anthony's school, howsoever the same be now fallen both in number and estimation, were rewarded with bows and arrows of silver given to them by Sir Martin Bowes, goldsmith."

Under Elizabeth, on Stow's own showing: "Nevertheless however the encouragement failed. The schollers of Paules meeting with them of S. Anthonies, would call them Anthonie pigs and they againe would call the other pigeons of Paules, because many pigeons were bred in Paules church, and Saint Anthonie was always figured with a pig following him, and, mindfull of the former usage, did for a long season disorderly in the open streete provoke one another with *Salve tu quoque! placet tibi mecum disputare. Placet.* And so proceeding from this to questions in grammar, they usually fall from wordes to blows, with their satchels full of bookes, many times in great heaps that they troubled the streets and passengers; so that finally they were restrained, with the decay of St. Anthonies schole." Yet as late as 1560 a church brief was issued on its behalf by Queen Elizabeth for collections in support of "its ijc. (200) scolers and pur men" who "praye upon ther knise tweys euery daye for the Quenes estate and the realeme of Englande", and "the scolers found in Oryall College within the Uneversite of Oxforde". It is expressly repeated that the "Scoleres of the grammer schole" are "comunly to the number of towe hundreth".

Strype, in his edition of Stow a century later, gives further evidence :—

"This school kept equal credit with that of Paul's: both which had the greatest reputation in the city in former times.

"I meet with a merry retainer at Queen Elizabeth's Court, giving an account of the great entertainment she had in her progress anno 1575 at Kenilworth Castle by the Earl of Leicester.

"I went to school forsooth both at Polles and also at S. Antonies! In the 5th forme, past Æsop's fables, I wiz read Terence, *Vos ist haec intro auferte*, and began with my *Virgil Tityre tu patulae*. I could my Rules: and could consterue and pars with the best of them."

Strype tells us also how this school used to go in procession: "Thus I find in the year 1562 on the 15th day of September there set out from Mile End 200 children of this S. Anthonies School, all well be-seen, and so along through Algate down Cornhill to the Stocks and so to the Freer Austins with streamers and flags and drums beating. And after, every child went home to their fathers and friends." This September outing was an old custom in schools. It was for a nut gathering. It appears in the accounts of St. Anthony's on 3 September, 1510, when "a sporting day in the cuntre" cost the hospital 18d., the almsmen and choristers being entertained at home for 7d. William Malim mentions it as one of the Eton holidays in 1560. The drums and flags strongly suggest the Eton "montem". As late as 1711 "nutting-money" was one of the regular payments exacted from Winchester scholars to be expended on an outing in the woods, gathering nuts.

Stow's story of the suppression of the street-shows of the scholars is borne out by the curious injunction issued by the Lord Mayor on 20 August, 1561 :—

"Item yt was agreyd that precepts shall forthewith be made to every one of my maisters the Aldermen for the stayinge of all skolemaysters and teacher of youthe within this cytye from makynge of eny more musters or commen and open shewes of theyr skollers, within the said cyttye or without, in ryche apparrell or otherwyse, eyther on horseback or on foote, upon payne of imprysonment".

An illustration of the humanist or Lollard spirit of London may be found in the attempts now made to free it from the monopoly of the three ancient schools. During the Lollard period, at the end of Richard II's reign, this had been tried in vain. It was met by a petition presented to the King in Parliament in 1393 by the Archbishop of Canterbury, the Bishop of London, the Dean of St. Martin's-le-Grand, and the Chancellor of St. Paul's, to assert the privileges of the three old schools, both in London and in the suburbs, and to put down " certain strangers, feigning themselves Masters of Grammar, not sufficiently learned in that faculty, who, against law and custom, hold general Schools of Grammar, in deceit and fraud of children, to the great prejudice of your lieges and of the jurisdiction of Holy Church ". The petitioners say that the three masters of the schools of St. Paul's, of the Arches, and St. Martin's " had proceeded against the said strange masters in Court Christian, who had gone to the secular courts for an inhibition ".   The secular court in question was the Mayor's Court.   So the petitioners asked for letters under the Privy Seal directed to the Mayor and Aldermen to command them, that, " as well in consideration of the king's interest in the case by reason of his Free Chapel (St Martin's-le-Grand) as of the prejudice to the archbishop, bishop, and others before-mentioned, they do nothing to stay the proceedings in the ecclesiastical court ".   Thus, the attempt of the City Corporation to interfere with the exclusive jurisdiction of the ecclesiastical courts over schools and to break the monopoly of the three schools failed.

In Henry V's time, however, the Crown itself broke in on the monopoly by sending to Roger Keston, master of the grammar school at Cornhill, in 1419, Master Walter House, one of the King's wards, the Treasury paying for his board, teaching and maintenance from Michaelmas to 18 July following, £4 11s. 6½d., or about 2s. 2d. a week.

The foundation of St. Anthony's School making a further breach in the monopoly must have provoked further agitation. An interesting attempt at making the famous Hospital of St. Bartholomew, like that of St. Anthony's, a partly educational establishment is to be found in the will of John Stafford, chaplain, 9 September, 1444, by which he gave lands near Paul's wharf to the Master and Brethren, on condition of making certain payments to his relations, and to find a chantry priest at the altar of St. Nicholas, who, besides his chantry pay, was to receive 33s. 4d. more for teaching boys grammar and song ; poor children, and especially the founder's kin, to be taught free.   It is said that the Hospital records show no trace of this school, which, even if the Hospital desired it, might have been refused as infringing the monopoly of the old schools. For in 1446 a writ of Privy Seal, addressed to the Chancellor, stated that the Archbishop and the Bishop of London, " considering the great abusions that have been of long tyme withinne our citee of London that many and divers persons not sufficiently instruct in gramer presumynge to holde comune [i.e. public] grammer scoles, in greet deceipte as well unto theire scolers as unto the frendes that fynde them to scole," had " of their greet wisdome set and ordeigned 5 scoles of

gramer and no moo ".   The five were the three ancient ones,
with St. Dunstan's-in-the-East and St. Anthony's.   The Chancellor was accordingly ordered to issue letters patent to command all liege subjects not to "troble nor empeche the maisters
of the said scoles, but rather helpe and assiste them inasmoch
as in them is".   Letters patent issued accordingly three days
later.   Next year, however, 1447, a petition was presented to
Parliament by the parsons of four London churches: Allhallows
the Great; St. Andrew's, Holborn; St. Peter's, Cornhill, and
St. Mary's, Colechurch—the latter of whom was also Master
of the Hospital of St. Thomas of Acon, now the Mercers' Hall
—for leave to establish permanent grammar schools in their
respective parishes, under the patronage and government of the
parson for the time being.   The preamble to their petition is
extremely interesting, both as demonstrating beyond all doubt
that St. Paul's School was not a mere choir-boys' school, and
also as showing how widespread was, or had been, the provision
for secondary education.   They refer to "the great number of
grammar schools that some time were in divers parts of the
realm, besides those that were in London, and how few be in
these days, and the great hurt that is caused of this, not only
in the spiritual part of the Church, where oftentimes it appeareth
too openly in some persons with great shame, but also in the
temporal part, to whom also it is full expedient to have competent knowledge for many causes. . . . The City of London
is the common concourse of this land, wherein is great multitude of young people, not only born and brought forth in the
same city, but also of many other parts of this land, some for
lack of schoolmasters in their own country for to be informed
of grammar there, and some for the great alms of lords,
merchants, and others, which is in London more plenteously
done than in other places of this realm to such poor creatures
as never should have been brought to so great virtue and
cunning as they have, had it not been by means of the alms
aforesaid."   So they submitted that it was "expedient that
in London were a sufficient number of schools and good informers in grammar, and not for the singular avail of two or
three persons grievously to hurt the multitude of young people.
. . .   For where there is great number of learners and few
teachers, and all the learners be compelled to go to the same

few teachers, the masters wax rich in money and the learners poor in cunning as experience openly sheweth, against all virtue and order of the public weal."

After this powerful attack on the system of monopoly the petitioners got their Bill. "The king wills that it be so as it is desired, so that it be done by the advice of the Ordinary or otherwise of the Archbishop of Canterbury for the time being." This private Act is said to have been the origin of a school established in St. Thomas of Acon's Hospital, which in 1540 became the Mercers' School. No evidence has been found of schools in All Saints', Holborn St. Andrew's, or St. Peter's, Cornhill. The archbishop and bishop probably nipped them in the bud, being assisted by the deaths of two at least of the petitioning rectors within a year of their petition.

Among other schools founded at this time was that of Newport, Shropshire, where Thomas Draper, by licence of Henry VI in 1442, founded a College of our Lady of one warden and three fellows and an organ-player. One of the fellows kept the grammar school, and at the time of the dissolution was receiving £5 a year for doing so.

At Wokingham, the chantry-grammar-school of St. Mary was founded by Adam Mullen, or Moleyns, Dean of Salisbury, in 1445. The chantry-priest-schoolmaster's living was worth £12 2s. 6½d. a year.

The widow of Robert Greyndour, Esquire, obtained a licence in mortmain, 6 November, 1445, for the foundation of a chantry-school at Newland, in Gloucestershire, and endowed it with £12 a year. A striking feature of this foundation was that it was to be both a grammar-school and a reading school, and only half free; " to th 'entent that there shuld be an honeste and discrete preste, being sufficientlie lerned in the arte of gramer to kepe and teache a grammer scoole ther half free for ever; that is to saie, to take of scolers lernynge gramer, 8d. the quarter, and of other lernynge lettres and to rede 4d. the quarter," and also that the priest was "to kepe a scoller sufficientt to teche under hym continually, gyvinge him meate, dryncke, clothe, and all other necessaries ".

Edward VI has heretofore had the credit of Chipping Norton School, because in 1548, when the lands of the gild, producing £16 a year, were confiscated, a payment of £6 a

year to the schoolmaster was continued.   If any king is to
have the credit of the school, it is Henry, not Edward VI.
The credit really belongs to the inhabitants of the place; this
like most other gilds being founded by joint-stock enterprise,
the subscriptions and donations of many.   The gild founded
under licence of 1451 maintained not only a schoolmaster but
a morrow mass priest, i.e. a priest to say mass at dawn for the
benefit of the early and pious workman on his way to work,
and other "almes deades".   At the dissolution, the inhabitants
petitioned for the continuance of the school, "as ther ys muche
vght (youth) in the said towne".   Though the commissioners
reported the gild priest-schoolmaster, Sir Hamlet Malban, as
"well lerned in gramer", Chipping Norton only obtained the
usual order for the fixed payment out of the Crown lands.
Thanks to additional endowments given in Elizabeth's reign
by William Avenell and later by others, the school was maintained as a grammar school till 1824.   In 1859 a County
Court scheme devoted all the endowments to saving the pockets
of the parson and landowners by applying them to the National
School.

   The mention in a deed of 1453 of a street called Schole-
house-gate witnesses to the existence of the Grammar School
at Appleby.   On 25 March, 18 Edward IV, 1478, an indenture
was made between the Mayor, bailiffs, and commonalty of
Appleby and Sir Thomas Whynfell, chaplain, by which they
granted him the chantry of the Blessed Virgin Mary founded
by Thomas Goldyngton and his son John [in 1286] in St.
Laurence Church.   Seeing that the said chantry was not
sufficient for the maintenance of a chaplain, they further
granted him two other chantries, namely, that of St. Nicholas
[which in other documents is called Threlkeld's chantry,
and was founded by one Threlkeld in 1336] in St. Laurence
Church, and that of Sir William Yngliche [English in another
deed], knight, anciently founded in St. Michael's Church.
Further, the said Thomas covenanted that he would keep,
or cause to be kept by a fit person, yearly at all fit and proper
times a sufficient grammar school (*unam scolam gramaticalem*,
in the singular) in the said borough, without ceasing at any
time, in which it ought to be kept, during his life, taking from
the scholars of the school aforesaid the school fees and cus-

tomary payments (*scolagia et custumas*) according to the ancient custom of the school aforesaid. The reference to the ancient custom of the school shows that it was not then new. Nor was this the first time the chantries had been united in the same hands, since, among the town muniments is a lease by Richard of Pathnell, chaplain of the chantries of St. Mary and St. Nicholas, dated 24 June, 1397. The patron saint of St. Nicholas' chantry suggests that it was founded definitely to provide a grammar school. On 5 March, 1534, the same three chantries were granted to Edward Gibson who "wills and grants to keep the grammar school and to teach, instruct, and inform in the best way he knows how scholars there". On the dissolution of chantries in 1548, the property was confiscated, but Edward Gibson continued as master with the salary of £5 10s. 8d., charged on the Crown revenues. Payment was stopped during the Marian reaction from Michaelmas, 1555, till Gibson obtained a new grant from the Court of Exchequer on 17 May, 1557. It is probable that he continued master till the school was re-founded under a charter of Queen Elizabeth, 22 March, 1574, who is now called in consequence its founder and is said to have given £5 10s. 8d. a year; in fact, merely continuing that payment. Fortunately private benefactors added new endowments or the school would not have continued to our time and attained the flourishing condition it now enjoys.

In 1448 a chantry for two priests was founded at Alnwick, his native place, by Bishop Alnwick of Lincoln, who was a Percy, brother of the Earl of Northumberland. One priest had to keep a grammar school and the other a song school and they received £12 3s. 4d. between them.

William Sponne, Archdeacon of Norfolk, by will of 4 September, 1447, founded a chantry at Towcester for two priests. He obtained letters patent, 17 November, 1448, but it was only after his death that the endowment was legally settled and the foundation made effective, 8 July, 1451. One priest was to be a preacher, with a salary of £8 13s. 4d. and the other a schoolmaster, whose salary was £7 6s. 8d. The school still lives though sadly in need of endowment.

The growth of the interest of the laity in the schools may be seen in the licences granted to two Trinity gilds in Oxfordshire to maintain schoolmasters, one at Deddington in 1446, and the other at Chipping Norton in 1451.

William Wayneflete, the greatest schoolmaster, was also the most prominent educational founder of the era. In direct imitation of William of Wykeham, he founded Magdalen College, when Bishop of Winchester, at Oxford, and attached to it not one but two schools, one at his native place, Wainfleet, in Lincolnshire, in 1459, the other Magdalen College School, by the gates of the college at Oxford. He had been carrying the latter on from 1448 and the college from 1456 though, through the Wars of the Roses, the final establishment and formal statutes for both were postponed to 1480. At Oxford there was to be a master with £10 a year and an usher with £5 "to teach all comers freely and gratis without exaction of anything". The humanist tendency came out most strongly in the provisions as to the thirty "demyes", so-called apparently because their commons were to cost half those of the fellows, or poor scholars, distinguished from instead of being merely junior fellows. "Because a weak foundation destroys the work, as experience teaches, and as we understand some of our 30 scholars are in the habit of passing to logic and sophistry immaturely before they are sufficiently instructed in grammar, the mother and foundation of all the sciences, we order that none of them be admitted to sophistry and logic or any other science before he is able and sufficiently instructed for it in the judgment of the President and the Grammar master." The old schoolmaster and the humanist also show themselves in the additional direction that two or three of the thirty demyes are to be insistent and work hard at grammar and poetry and the other humanist arts so long that they may not only be profitable to themselves but also become able and fit to instruct and teach others. In fact Magdalen was to serve to a certain extent, like God's House at Cambridge, as a Training College for Secondary School teachers.

Preference of the classics and grammar to logic is characteristic. The humanists made a dead set at dialectic in the schools. Rhetoric or the art of oratory they encouraged, but dialectic or the art of argument they discouraged. The reason apparently was that dialectic had become indissolubly connected with scholastic theology, and had little to do with the

WAINFLEET GRAMMAR SCHOOL, LINCOLNSHIRE, 1484

poets who formed the main study of the humanists. Like mathematics it presented too severe a study for those who found the whole end of life, literature and education in *belles lettres* and the art of expression. Petrarch had inveighed against dialectic. Niccolo dei Niccoli of Florence, c. 1430, apparently sees something peculiarly English in it. "What is there in dialectic which has not been disturbed by the sophisms of the British? What which has not been separated from the true and ancient way of disputing and transmuted into emptiness and trifles?" No doubt dialectic had been carried to excess and converted into a somewhat solemn trifling. But the humanist educators were one and all churchmen and papalists, holders of Church preferments, possible papal secretaries, like Petrarch, or Popes themselves, like Æneas Silvius. This reference to Britannic sophisms savours of dread of Wicliffe, who was, like Socrates, the greatest sophist of his age. Frightened orthodoxy, jealous of the superior repute of Oxford, played a part in this hostility to dialectic. It is at least greatly to be regretted that when the school age was being extended—Vittorino's pupils stayed till twenty-one—dialectic, which had been too early inculcated on boys of fourteen, should have been dropped. Logic, especially since the creation of Inductive Logic, is after all a more humane and human study than grammar. Even the puerilities of dialectic were better than the puerilities of grammar as a preparation for the politician and the citizen. The art of argument has more bearing on human life than the minutiæ of the use of enclitics in a twice dead language.

Waynflete's moderate reform, however, was no doubt useful. Magdalen College School became the most advanced school of the day. The Grammar of John Stanbridge, a Winchester boy who was usher at Magdalen College School, and became head master in 1487, was the first rational English-Latin grammar, and superseded the doggerel Latin verse of Alexander de Villa Dei. Stanbridge's grammar was adopted by his brother in the famous school at Banbury, which Sir Thomas Pope at Reading and Bishop Oldham at Manchester equally prescribed as the model for teaching their scholars. It was as Head master of Magdalen College school that Thomas Wolsey got his first start in life, and it was from Magdalen that Colet got the first master of his re-endowed school of St. Paul's, William Lyly, whose grammar, with unessential modifications, ruled the schools of England to the middle of the nineteenth century.

Another educational foundation, the completion of which was delayed by the Wars of the Roses, was that of Heytesbury Hospital in Wiltshire, on the model of Ewelme Hospital, and the first foundation of Eton.   Licence was granted 20 February, 1472, to Margaret, widow of Robert, Lord Hungerford, to found an almshouse, to consist of a chaplain, twelve poor men, and a poor woman, an attendant and nurse.   But a memorandum annexed to her will shows that she was not the real founder.   Walter, late Lord Hungerford, her father-in-law, she says, had builded an almshouse for twelve poor, and a schoolmaster, being a priest able to teach grammar, to have the rule and oversight of the same, and directed by will certain manors to be "amortised" for the purpose: but as it was not performed in his days—a modest way of stating the fact that he was killed and attainted as a traitor—she had now obtained the licence in mortmain at a cost of £200.   Her deed, dated 2 April, 1472, incorporated "the Custos (warden, or keeper) of St. John the Baptist, poor men and woman of the Hospital of Walter and Robert, late lords of Hungerford and Heytesbury".   The statutes, only preserved in a Jacobean transcript or translation, make it plain that the school was the first object. For it was provided that the Chancellor of Salisbury, the educational officer of the diocese, "he shall do present an able keeper and a sufficient teacher of grammar at every avoidance". On every "feastful" day the keeper was to attend the church and perform service.   But "all other days that he intend and do his diligent labour to teach and inform all such children and other persons that shall come to the place, which is ordained and deputed them to teach in within Heytesbury, and . . . shall teach from the beginning of learning until such season as they learn sufficient or competent [knowledge?] of grammar; no school hire take of no person or take [save of] such as their friends may spend £10 or above, or else that will give freely; and that he daily attend and keep his school". So that this Free Grammar School of Heytesbury was even more prominently the first object of the foundation than even

MAGDALEN COLLEGE GRAMMAR SCHOOL, 1480

FROM DRAWING MADE IN 1806

that at Eton or Ewelme, where the Free Grammar Schoolmaster
was only the second person in the establishment, not the first.
This is emphasized by a proviso that if the Chancellor could
not in two months find a "sufficient teacher" he was tempor-
arily to put in "a convenable and honest priest . . . unto
such season that an able keeper and sufficient teacher may be
provided". Another statute provided for an usher to teach
in the school and be Deputy overseer of the poor men. The
keeper's oath was to keep all the ordinances made for the
conservation and good rule of the school and almshouse;
putting the school first. The then usher "called Park Miles,
now blind and may not see" was received as a poor man.
No future usher was to be so received, "for by the receiving
the usher into the said house the schoolmaster . . . would think
that such as be usher should have meat and drink of the said
almshouse, the which we would in no wise they never have,"
says the lady, piling on her negatives with both hands. The
Chantry Commissioners of Edward VI reported that the
hospital was founded "for the sustentacyon of a scolemaster"
and poor. The schoolmaster received £10 a year, but this was
besides perquisites, such as two cart-loads of wood a year, and so
forth : but they said there had been no schoolmaster for five or
six years, only the poor, and an absentee master Sir William
Sharington (miscalled Skarington in the Charity Commission's
Report in 1833), a fraudulent master of the Mint at Bristol,
took the whole surplus not spent on the poor. Cardinal Pole
in Mary's reign put in a new warden, John Lybbe, B.C.L.,
ordering him to teach the Grammar School there. The
historians say erroneously that the hospital was confiscated as
superstitious at the Reformation. This is not so. Hospitals
or almshouses and schools were not within the Chantries' Act
of Edward VI. It was not till James I's reign that some
informers wrongfully alleged that it ought to have been confiscated to the Crown under that Act, because the poor had to
pray for the founder's soul. In the result a new charter was
obtained from the King in 1633, under which new statutes
were made. These separated the schoolmastership from the
wardenship, making the schoolmaster what the usher had been
before, a deputy or vice-warden, and assigning a salary of
£15 a year only to him. The school, however, flourished till

18

1765, when the whole place and sixty-five houses in the town were burnt down. Through gross neglect of the trustees the school was never reopened. The Commissioners of Inquiry in 1833 only remarked that "as the instruction was principally in Latin Grammar, and this sort of learning has long ceased to be in request among the common people of the parish, the appointment was suffered to go into disuse". As the income, £42 in 1548, had then risen to £1372, there were ample funds for the provision of a proper school, which might have become an Uppingham or a Sedbergh. But though the case was sent into Chancery, where it stayed for some twenty years, the Court in its scheme in 1859 entirely ignored the original primary object, the school. Though several schemes have been made since, and the income exceeds £2220 a year, of which, if the original proportion were observed, at least £740 should be educational, nothing has ever been done for education since 1765.

As soon as the confusion caused by the Wars of the Roses was over the march of education was resumed. Two of the most interesting and humanistic of the colleges modelled on Winchester and Eton were founded by two of the Yorkist lawyer-clerics who superseded Waynflete and the Lancastrians in the government of the kingdom, Acaster and Rotherham, both in Yorkshire. The former was founded by Robert Stillington, Bishop of Bath and Wells, no doubt while he was chancellor, between 1467 and 1475, but the original document of foundation is non-existent, and our knowledge of it is derived from a private Act of Parliament in 1483, which recited the foundation but not its date. There were three schools attached to the College of Nether Acaster "three divers Masters and Informators in the faculties underwritten; that is to wit, one of them to teach grammar, another to teach Music and Song, and the third to teach to Write and all such thing as belonged to Scrivener Craft, to all manner of persons of whatsoever country they be within the Realm of England . . . all the said Masters and Informators to teach . . . severally, openly and freely without exaction of money or other things of any of their such scholars and disciples ". The Act does not tell us, but we learn from a Chantry Certificate in 1548 that the three masters were the three fellows of the college, and with the provost formed its governing body.   Their stipends were then £10 for the provost, £6 each for the two masters and only £5 for the grammar schoolmaster, but this seems to have been because at the time of the certificate he was much younger than the other two.

The foundation of Jesus College at Rotherham, by Thomas Rotherham, Archbishop of York, was on a grander scale, consisting of ten persons, that, as he says in his will "as I have offended God in his 10 commandments, those 10 might pray for me".   Rotherham had been one of the first scholars of King's, Cambridge, admitted under Henry VI's second charter of 14 July, 1443.   He founded the college at Rotherham in gratitude, because he had "been born and passed his tender age there . . . without learning, and so should have remained for many years, had not by the grace of God a man learned in grammar come there, from whom as from a spring through God's will I have arrived at the estate in which I now stand, and several others have come to great things".   The licence for the foundation was granted 22 January, 1483, and ten days later, 1 February, 1483, Rotherham made his statutes.   They provided for a provost and three fellows, who were also schoolmasters, and six scholar-choristers, to-gether with the chantry priests of Rotherham admitted to free lodging, but not free board, and not part of the foundation. The first fellow was to keep a grammar school, the second a song school, and as Yorkshire produced "many youths endowed with the light and sharpness of ability, who do not all wish to attain the dignity and elevation of the priesthood, that these may be better fitted for the mechanical arts and other worldly matters, we have ordained a third fellow, learned and skilled in the art of writing and accounts".   The college was named the College of Jesus of Rotherham.   The provost was to receive £13 6s. 8d., the grammar master £10, the song schoolmaster, £6 13s. 4d., and the writing schoolmaster £5 6s. 8d.   They were all to teach in schools provided in the college, "without exaction of money or anything else".   The six scholars were to be chosen by the provost from the poorer boys of those parts most fit and apt for learning, with preference to founder's kin, and they were to be entirely maintained till eighteen years of age, and taught grammar, writing and song.   The schools were all free from tuition fees and open to the world. John Bocking, the grammar master, who died six months after the foundation, was a married man, as he gave by his will the residue of his estate to his wife Margaret for life, and then to the college, and desired to be buried by the pew in the south chancel of the church in which his wife and the wife of the bailiff of Rotherham sat. When Rotherham died, by his will made on his seventy-sixth birthday, St. Bartholomew's Day, 1498, he gave a large quantity of plate and vestments to the college, including twelve silver spoons and "a mitre for the barne bishop (the boy-bishop) with two knoppes of silver gilt and enamylled ", and 105 volumes of MSS. They included Lives of Tibullus and Seneca, Terence, Poggio's letters, a commentary on Seneca, Ovid, including, sad to say, three copies of the *Art of Love*, Claudian, Lucan, Sallust, Cicero's Speeches and Letters, Pliny, Josephus, and Isidore of Seville's Etymologies ; and some Chronicles. When a later grammar schoolmaster died in 1509, administration was granted to his wife Jane, showing that he too was no priest. With the college the song and writing school perished under Edward VI, but the grammar school was continued with a fixed salary of £10 15s. 4d. a year, charged on the royal revenues in the county. Subsequently assisted by the feoffees of Rotherham Common Lands, it is now flourishing on an ample site and recently-acquired buildings.

One of the chief Yorkshire schools, Giggleswick Grammar School, commonly attributed to Edward VI, can trace its existence at least to the year 1499. On 12 August, 14 Henry VII, James Carr, of the Carrs of Stackhouse, founder and incumbent of the Rood chantry, leased some of its land. Seemingly he then taught school in hired premises. But on 12 November, 1507, he took from Durham Priory on a building lease for 79 years, perpetually renewable, at a rent of 1s. a year, half an acre of land by the church garth of Giggleswick, covenanting to build "at hys awne propyr charges and costes, in which beildyng he shall kepe or cause to be kept one gramer scole ", and when he "change his naturall lyfe" the vicar and churchwardens to elect his successor. On completing the school Carr inscribed on it the Ennian verses shown in the illustration.

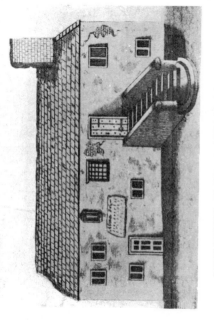

GIGGLESWICK GRAMMAR SCHOOL, BUILT 1507-12

INSCRIPTION ON GIGGLESWICK GRAMMAR SCHOOL, 1512

CHAPTER XIII

HENRY VIII AND THE SCHOOLS

HENRY VIII was, perhaps, the most highly educated person for his time who ever sat on the throne of England. Whether Lord Herbert had any authority for saying that as a younger son Henry was originally destined for a clerical career and the throne of Canterbury, it is certain that he was educated like the most learned clerk. Under John Skelton, Bernard Andre, and others he received the best grammar school, song school, and university education of the day, in Latin, literature, rhetoric, dialectic, and music, besides knowing French, Italian, and Spanish. Hence it was that he became the excellent speaker and writer, the eminent theologian and the expert musician he is admitted to have been. Hence his zeal for learning and for education. No king ever showed more desire to promote learning and learned men, and none was more impressed and desirous of impressing on others the advantages, or did more for the advancement of education. Whether in the statutes of the realm or in the ordinances and statutes of the many foundations of his time, he was never tired of expatiating on the necessity of education and the benefit that educated men were to church and commonwealth.

The reign of Henry VIII has a far better title than that of his son to be regarded as an era of educational development, though it has no more title than the latter to be regarded as the starting-point of an entirely new system of schools or of any great educational advance. The notion that it was, seems to have been chiefly derived from Samuel Knight's *Life of Colet*, published in 1724, in which a most exaggerated account is given of Colet's supposed foundation, really only a re-endowment, of St. Paul's School. Colet's foundation is not really a product of Henry VIII's reign at all. He tells us himself that he " in the year A.D. 1508 began to edify in the East end of the churchyard of Paul's a schoolhouse of stone for children to be taught, free, to the number of 153 ".   The whole design was therefore made and its execution begun in the reign of Henry VII ; though it is of course true that the endowment and legal foundation were given and completed in 1510 to 1512 under Henry VIII.   But in everything he did in regard to the school, Colet followed, and did not set, a fashion.   His new school he placed only a few yards north-ward of the old school, which as we saw was placed there about 1111.   He obtained the royal licence in mortmain for a school in the Churchyard, 6 June, 1510, and on 27 July he, as Dean, with the Chapter granted William Lily, of Magdalen College, Oxford, then appointed first master of the " New School of St. Pauls ", all the privileges of the master of the old school, in-cluding a stall in the choir, and " took him into their bosom ". On 28 March, 1511, he got the Chapter to join him in con-veying to trustees for the new school, the old school, " lately called Poules schole ", and three shops underneath it, and on the same day the Chancellor of St. Paul's released to the same trustees all his rights over the old school ; while the same day the Dean and Chapter conveyed to the same trustees the land on which the new school and master's house were built. Colet also asked the Pope for a transfer of all the rights and privileges of the old to the new school.   In July, 1511, Colet granted a large amount of land in Buckinghamshire and some property in London, being his whole inherited patrimony, to the Mercers' Company, of which he was a member, for the " con-tinuation of a certain school in the cemetery of St. Paul's church". On 10 June, 1512, the three trustees bargained and sold the two school buildings, the old and the new, to Colet, who the same day made his will giving them to the Mercers' Company, in trust for "the newe scole at Poules ".   On 17 June, 1512, he produced to the company his " Boke of Ordinances of the Scole of Poules " under which they were to act as governors, and on 27 July the company took possession of the schools and the foundation was legally complete, or, as Colet puts it, he " in the yere of our lord a thousand fyve hundreth and twelff, full accomplisshed and fynysshed the same scole and mansion in every poynt ".   These first

statutes are not extant, having been superseded by a new
edition on 18 June, 1518.   The steps of this foundation have
been particularized because the school was represented as an
entirely new foundation, with no connexion with the old
school, which was represented as having disappeared, whereas
Colet himself told the Pope in asking for a Bull to place his
new school in the position of the old one that the old one was
going on "though of no importance".   He was careful to
place the new school exactly in the position of the old, except that the Mercers were substituted for the Dean and
Chapter and the Chancellor of St. Paul's as governors.   Nor
was Colet, as was also represented, making a new departure
in entrusting the school to a lay body of governors. and that
a city company, for, as we have seen, there had been a constant stream of schools with city companies as governors from
1443 at least.

A great deal has been made of the curriculum laid down
in Colet's Statutes and particularly of the mention of Greek
and the lay head master, as showing that Colet did initiate a
new educational movement, if not a new system of schools.
As for the lay head master, the novelty of that is sufficiently
refuted by William Sevenoak's foundation at Sevenoaks in
1432, that the master should by no means be in holy orders, by
the fact of there being three successive lay head masters of
York Cathedral Grammar School in the same century, and by
the provision in several foundations of Obits at Winchester
College by which the head master, was paid less for his
attendance at the Obit if he was a layman than if he was
a priest.   As to the curriculum, or as Colet expressed it,
"What shalbe taught", he laid down none.   "What shalbe
taught it passith my wit to devyse and determyn in
particuler".   But "in generall" he would they were taught
"all way in good litterature with laten and greke and goode
auctors such as have the veray Romayne eliquence joyned
withe wisdome, specially Cristyn auctours that wrote theyre
wysdome with clene and chast laten other in verse or in prose".
For he says his great aim is to increase knowledge and "good
Cristen lyff and maners"—conduct and character being with
him, as with his predecessors, the first object.   So he puts first
the English catechism, which he had himself written, then

Erasmus's *Institute of a Christian*, and then "other auctoures Christian ", and reels off the names of those Latin Christian poets of the third to the fifth centuries, Lactantius and the rest, mentioned in Alcuin's School Library at York, adding Baptista Mantuanus, the friar who, only some twenty years before, wrote Eclogues in imitation of the great Mantuan, Virgil, intended to supersede those of his predecessors because they were chaste and Christian.   He was still used as a school-book in Shakespeare's time, who makes Sir Hugh Evans quote the good old Mantuan.   Colet adds such other authors as most conduce to true Latin speaking, and goes on to abuse " all Latin adulterate " which "ignorant blynde folis " brought into this world and poisoned the old Latin speech and the "varay Roman tongue".   But he shows his incapacity as a critic of the very Roman tongue, by speaking of its being used by Cicero and Terence and Virgil, as well as St. Jerome and " seint Austen".   This was, however, not progress but re-action ; it was not promoting humanism, but reverting to theological prepossessions.

It is true he adds such other authors " as shalbe thoughte convenyent and most to purpose unto the true laten spech ". Finally he says, in a passage which has made the statute world-famous, " that fylthynesse and all such abusyon which the later blynde worlde brought in, which more ratheyr may be callid blotterature thenne litterature I utterly abbanysh and exclude oute of this scole ".

As we have shown, there is reason to believe that both Winchester and Eton had taught Greek before this.   The odd thing is that there is some reason to suppose that Greek was not taught at St. Paul's after this, or at least not after Lily's time.   For, while copious efforts in Greek appear in the verses with which Winchester saluted Edward VI and with which Winchester and Eton saluted Elizabeth, the only Pauline effort of the same kind preserved, which greeted Elizabeth on her entry into London in 1560 or 1570—the date is disputed—are much less in quantity and contain no Greek, but only Latin.

The fame of Colet's re-foundation was really due to its transferring the government of the oldest and most famous school of the city and the cathedral from the Dean and

Chapter to a city company of lay and married men; to its being made by far the largest free school in the city, for a hundred and fifty-three boys instead of only twenty-five at the Mercers' own school, or twelve at St. Anthony's; to its being the richest, and, above all, to the encomiums of Erasmus, who boomed it, as the German reformers a few years afterwards boomed the similar re-foundation of Strassburg School by Sturm.

A great many of the other schools credited to Henry VIII's time were, like Colet's, not new foundations but revivals, augmentations or conversions into free schools of old schools which were not free. It may be strongly suspected that this was the case with Wolverhampton Grammar School, for the erection of which Sir Stephen Jenyns, Merchant Taylor and ex-Lord Mayor, had obtained a charter on 22 September, 1511, having previously bought the ground " for the education of boys and youths in good manners and literature and for the better maintenance of a master and usher of the same ". It is impossible to believe that the ancient collegiate church of Wolverhampton of Saxon foundation had not, like Warwick and other ancient collegiate churches, kept a grammar school, though probably its endowment was some anciently fixed payment of £2 a year or so, and therefore inadequate for the sixteenth century and free education.

So when we find the " scolemaster " at Stafford, reckoned as but denied by the inhabitants to be a chantry in the collegiate church of St. Mary there (which church is said in the certificate at its dissolution to have been founded by King John but in fact appears in Domesday), we may feel sure that the scolemaster-chantry was a later and additional endowment of the school always maintained by the college.

Similarly with the Morrow Mass-priest and Schoolmaster at Tamworth in the chapel of St. George in the collegiate church of St. Edith "founded by King Edgar", whose duty was " to teche a free scole ", the endowment of £12 10s. 3½d. must have been a comparatively recent one in substitution for, or in augmentation of that of the foundation grammar school.

The same remark applies to another school, of some fame

because it was founded by Henry VIII.'s own grandmother, the Lady Margaret Tudor, who instituted the first free theological lectures at Oxford and Cambridge through the Lady Margaret Professors of Divinity, that of Wimborne Minster, Dorset. This was to be a free grammar school for all and singular coming there to be instructed in grammar, to be taught freely and gratis in the form and manner and at all and singular such times as is, was or shall be used in the Grammar School at Eton or Winchester, and the master was to be appointed by the master and fellows of Christ's, her College at Cambridge. But though the ordinances for it were made by Bishops Fox of Winchester and Fisher of Rochester on 12 March, 2 Henry VIII., i.e. 1511 (not 1509 or 1510 as the Endowed Schools Commissioners said) the licence for it had been given by Henry VII in 1497, and the endowment granted 3 February, 1504. Nor can we suppose that this ancient Saxon collegiate church had not always maintained a grammar school in some form. The Lady Margaret merely created a new chantry which is returned in the valuation of 1535 as the "Scole maisters chauntrey" and annexed it to the schoolmaster's office permanently. She was in fact only doing permanently and by a new foundation what the Chapter of Southwell did in the same year 1504. The pay of the grammar schoolmaster there from the college was only £2 a year, having been settled at that in the twelfth century or thereabouts. So when St. Cuthbert's, the richest of the fifteen chantries in the minster, which had been founded by Archbishop Booth in 1479, fell vacant on 3 December, 1504, and the senior vicar choral asked to be given it by customary right, the Chapter answered that his petition was just, but requested him to abandon it this time for the public benefit and his own, so that they might present a fit chaplain able to teach the grammar school. Finally he acceded to their request, whereupon they instituted, invested and installed Sir William Babyngton, who then of his own free will and not under compulsion swore on the holy gospels that he would undergo the charge of teaching the grammar school the whole time that he held the chantry. This he held for at least thirty-six years, until the surrender of the college to Henry VIII in 1540, to be refounded by Act of Parliament in 1543.

Oddly enough when Southwell Minster was again dissolved under the Chantries Act in 1548,—the school being continued with a payment of £10 a year charged on the Crown revenues of Notts—this chantry endowment was in 1553 annexed to Guildford Grammar School, then refounded, one of the schools quoted by Mr. Mullinger in the *Cambridge Modern History* in 1910, in teeth of the evidence, as one of Edward VI's creations where no school had been before.   In fact Guildford Grammar School is the earliest school endowed under Henry VIII, for founded it probably was not.   But by will of 3 November, 1509, Robert Bekyngham, citizen and grocer of London, gave all his lands in Bromley and Newington "to make a fre scole in the towne of Guildford or other works and deeds of charitie".   By deed of 4 May, 1512, the lands in Bromley were conveyed for that purpose, the appointment of the master being vested in the mayor and four "of his most sadd and discreete brethren", and the school was established.   Master Nicholas Elyott appeared as master in 1520.   The only complete account of the old school endowment, preserved among the Corporation Records for 1545, shows an income of £8 15s. 6d. of which only half was derived from Bekingham's Bromley lands, the rest from lands in Guildford, possibly the endowment of the previous school which must have existed there.   By patent of 27 January, 1553, Edward VI, refounded the school and gave his name to it, and, by way of endowment two rent charges which formed the endowments of a chantry at Stoke d'Abernon and the Southwell chantry above mentioned.   Under Mary, Archbishop Heath, being chancellor, recovered the Southwell chantry for Southwell Minster, then re-established, by forgery, making five distinct erasures and additions on the rolls in his custody.   By Act of Parliament under Elizabeth, when Heath was deposed, St. Cuthbert's chantry endowment was restored to Guildford school.   Being unfortunately a fixed rent charge on the manor of Battersea it has not proved of much value in later times.   Its chequered career is a striking instance of the Edwardian School foundations, so-called, robbing Peter to pay Paul, and of the looseness of historians in dealing with them.

Another school, which dates from the first year of Henry VIII, though commonly attributed to Queen Elizabeth, who

gave it only a new charter, is Blackburn Grammar School,
Lancashire.   A deed in English of 4 April, 1514, states that
the church reves (churchwardens) and parochyens had bought
(in the first year of King Henry, according to a later bill in
Chancery) lands for an " honest, seculer prest, and no reguler,
suffyciently lerned in gramer and playn song, if any such can
be gettyn, that shall kape contenually a Free Gramer Scole ".
To the lands so bought by the parishioners, the Earl of Derby
contributed a piece of land worth 14s. a year, in consideration
of which he was by the deed called founder and patron, and
given the appointment of the chantry-priest-schoolmaster.   A
rather remarkable provision was that if a man sufficiently
learned to teach grammar could not be found, at least one who
could keep a Free Song School should be put in.

The next two schools credited to Henry VIII's reign, those
of Lewes and Nottingham in 1512, were certainly not wholly
new creations.   We have seen that the school at Lewes was
flourishing in the thirteenth century.   So when Agnes Morley,
widow, made her wills on 20 November, 1511, and 24 May, 1512,
giving a scolehouse, and a rent charge of £20, which she had
bought 16 December, 1508, for a " scole maister and usher
to the use and performacion of a fre scole", the master to be
"a prest able to teche gramer having no cure of souls or other
lette whereby he might draw his attendaunce from the said
scole" she was augmenting and perhaps freeing, not founding,
a school *de novo*.

The same was the case with Nottingham Grammar
School, similarly endowed as a free school by Agnes Mellers,
" wydowe and vowesse" under licence of 22 November, 1512, by
deed dated 2 February, 1512-3, with strict injunctions against
either master or usher having or using " any potacions,
cocke-fight or drinking with his or their wiffe at wiffes' hoost
or hoostices, but onely twise in the yere, nor take any other
giftes or avayles whereby the scholers or their frendes should
be charged ".   This school as we saw appears in records of
the Archbishop, of Southwell Minster, and of the borough of
Nottingham from the thirteenth century, though struggling
with debt and rival schoolmasters, through insufficient endowment.

In like manner at Bruton in Somerset, endowed by

Richard FitzJames, Bishop of London, and his nephew the Lord Chief Justice, by deed of 27 September, 1519.   There are clear indications of a school before, in wills of 1417, 1507 and 1515.   Yet this is one of the schools usually quoted as a product of the generosity of Edward VI, because he restored the old endowment in 1550.

Another school, that of Saffron Walden in Essex—of some note in educational history, since it had been claimed through an egregious blunder as the first school in England in which Greek was taught, and by another blunder its supposed curriculum was quoted as the earliest known—has been attributed to Henry VIII as founded in 1525 by Dame Johane Bradbury, sister and heir of the Vicar of Walden, John Leche, and by the Trinity Gild, itself founded by Henry VIII in 1514. The dates are correct enough as far as they go.   John Leche did in fact by deed of 3 December, 1517, give lands to the Trinity Gild, in order that when they could find £10 a year their second " preest shall be a profound gramarion to the intent that he may teche gramar within the towne after the fourme of the scole of Wynchestre or of Eton ".   A new schoolhouse was built by Leche and his sister.   The gild was not, however, founded by him or by Henry VIII.   It existed before 1389, when in the return made into Chancery in consequence of the panic about gilds due to the peasants' revolt, it is stated to have been begun by John Rote, William Haveryll and others to find fifty torches to be burnt in honour of the Trinity at the elevation of the host on Sundays and feast days and a priest at the Trinity altar in the parish church.   It had then no endowment but was maintained by yearly subscriptions.   There were two other gilds, the Corpus Christi Gild, founded in 1377, which had an endowment of £1 a year in land, and All Saints' Gild.

On 23 December, 1423, Sir John Bernard and William Brynge, chaplains, were summoned before John Hatfield, abbot of Walden, to show why and on what authority they practised the exercise of teaching small boys of Walden, and instructing them in the alphabet, the graces and other higher books, without asking or obtaining leave from the abbot, though they had previously been reproved for their presumption in doing this, and though according to the statutes and customs of the monastery the faculty of granting and conferring schools on grammar masters in the town of Walden and preferring masters to such schools belonged wholly and solely to the abbot and convent.   The two chaplains confessed their offence and submitted themselves to the abbot, who interdicted them from teaching any boys of Walden in the alphabet or graces or other higher books.   But eventually on the instance of the approved and more substantial men of Walden then present who wished their boys to be taught the alphabet, the chaplains were allowed to teach one boy of each inhabitant the alphabet and graces but no higher books.   The "graces" in question were the graces before and after meat, usually included with the alphabet in primers and horn-books.   They were not the graces taught by a master in deportment, though a certain learned lady was barely prevented from alleging this as an instance of the progress of civilization and manners among the lower middle class in the towns of the fifteenth century.   Still less was the licence one to teach the Greek alphabet as Lord Braybrooke stated in his *History of Audley End*, reading *alphabeticis graecis* for *alphabetis et graciis* and claiming Saffron Walden as the first school in England to teach Greek, nearly half a century before the first lecture in Greek given at Oxford. The licence granted to the chaplains, who were no doubt the chantry priests of two of the three gilds, was a limited licence, confining them to the function of a song or elementary schoolmaster, to teach reading and singing only, and intended to prevent their poaching on the preserve of the grammar schoolmaster, whose existence was guessed from the record of this incident.   It is now capable of exact demonstration, thanks to the researches of Mr. E. and Mr. C. H. Emson. The transcripts by the former from the records, till now tossed in dust and confusion in the room over the church porch, show Walter scolemayster witnessing a deed in 1401 and a Walter, clerk of Walden, a grantee with others, evidently as a trustee of land in Walden, while a croft conveyed in 1407 is described as abutting on a messuage of Walter, scolemayster, and others.   He is probably the same person who in 1416, 1418, 1425, 1436 and 1440, appears as Walter Payn of Walden, scolemaister, in 1431 as scolemeaster, and in 1447 as Walter Payn of Walden, scolmayster, deceased.   Walter Payn then was the master who in 1423 instigated the abbot to suppress the chantry priests who were trespassing on his domain of grammar. Nor was he the first of his tribe. In the Walden Abbey chartulary of the fourteenth century there appears as witness of many deeds from December, 1317, to 20 April, 1337, Master Reginald of the school (*de scolis* and *de scola*) or, as he is more usually called, Reginald Schoolmaster (*magister scolarum*) of Walden; while in the municipal records from 1342 to 1345 the same person apparently appears as Reginald of Crek, probably Creyk, Norfolk, schoolmaster of Walden. It is probable that both of them drew the deeds they witnessed, as was certainly the case with James Rogerson, described in a deed of 6 July, 1511, in which with a number of others he was grantee of land in the market-place, as " instructor of the grammar school and notary public ".

The so-called foundation of the Trinity Gild in 1514 was a consolidation of the three old gilds and augmentation by " Master Leche " who in the earliest extant account of the gild, for the year 1546-7, is called the founder. Master Leche's gift for the school had partly failed through defect of title, so his sister by deed of 18 May, 1525, substituted a rent charge of £12 a year out of the manor of Willinghall Spain, belonging to Walden Abbey, which she bought from the abbey, for the original gift—much to the loss of the school in the result—as the fixed rent has remained fixed while the rent of the original lands would have grown with the growth of riches.

Master Leche having directed his school " use " to be that of Winchester and Eton, the alderman obtained from the masters there, a statement of their curricula, copies of which were entered in the alderman's, now the mayor's book. The first page of this document, which would no doubt have shown its origin, is unfortunately lost, and so when it was printed in *Archæologia* by that industrious antiquary Thomas Wright, he gave it as the time-table of Saffron Walden School, and as such it was quoted even in the *History of Eton*.

There were, however, a good many schools founded in Henry VIII's reign at places where, so far as is known, no school existed before; but most of these schools, being planted in places selected because they were the founder's birthplace or abode and not because there was a population with a real demand for a school, have, except when they have become boarding-schools, not been very successful.

One of the earliest of these was Pocklington in the East Riding of Yorkshire, founded under a patent of 24 May, 1514, as a Gild of the Name of Jesus, the Virgin and St. Nicholas, by John Dowman, LL.D. of Cambridge, a Chancery lawyer, arch-deacon, and so on. To it were added by deed of 1 December, 1525, five scholarships for boys from the school at St. John's College, Cambridge. The master was endowed with the mag-nificent stipend of £16 16s. 4d., that of Henry VI's founda-tions of Eton and St. Anthony's, London. Fortunately there was some flaw in the conveyancing, and this school retains its old endowment through being re-founded by Private Act of Parliament in 1549, after being confiscated to Edward VI under the Chantries Act.

Another new school was that founded in 1520 by Bishop Robert IV of Chichester, Robert Sherborne, at Rolleston, Staf-fordshire, "where I was born and by the grace of baptism re-born", as he says. Sherborne had been a scholar of Winchester and of New College, and then a canon lawyer and Chancery official, Master of St. Cross Hospital and Dean of St. Paul's before being made Bishop, first of St. David's, then of Chichester. He tried to make his foundation a smaller Win-chester, giving the appointment of the master to the Warden of New College and directing even the prayers in school to follow those of Winchester, which he sets out in his beautifully illuminated statutes for the purpose. They form one of the most interesting educational documents of the date. They are not confined to a bare legal definition of the schoolmaster's salary and method of appointment, and the government of the school (which was vested in Mr. Thomas Rolleston of that ilk and his heirs male, together with the churchwardens), but also give the founder's views on school methods. For in-stance, they direct that the master is to pay attention to and often ask where in men's judgment is the grammar school of best repute for advancement of learning, what style of teaching and what authors it uses; and as far as he can to imitate those whom he understands by results are most proficient in teaching. Sound advice, not always followed! Among other

nice directions is one that the master is to look after the boys'
manners and dress as well as learning, and particularly that
"their bodies are free from worms and their clothes whole".
The clever boys he is to press on, so that they may act as pupil
teachers (*pedagogos*) to teach small boys who may be brought
to him, the alphabet and first rudiments. He is to take particular care of the clever boys, while the stupid, the lazy, and
those in human judgment incapable of learning he is to sharpen
as far as he can by reading, writing and casting accounts, lest
they should seem to have come to this our school for nothing.

If the master gets in a "bate", as Mr. Horman says, he is
to follow Plato's example, and dropping the subject which
makes him angry, pass on to some other boy or another subject until he has cooled down. For the master must set a
good example, and that is a "vulgar",

Turpe est doctori cum culpa redarguit ipsum

On the teacher the shame
When his is the blame.

"And indeed this age has seen teachers who had far better
have been asleep than teaching like maniacs." Sherborne
would have his master remember that blindness is to be enlightened by skill, not by force, and imitate Ipocrates, the
prince of doctors, with his aphorism "that we ought to lead
nature where it wishes to go".

If a boy at the beginning has grasped even one thing he
is to praise him vehemently with this or the like good saying:

Omni bina die si discam verba sophiæ
De parvo puero clericus aptus ero,

which may be Englished :—

Two words of wisdom mastered every day
Make clever clerk, and drive dull boy away.

But all those words of wisdom were thrown away. Not
being able to find any land for sale near Rolleston for the
endowment of the school, Sherborne gave £500 to the Dean
and Chapter of Chichester for a perpetual rent charge of £10
a year. That is still duly paid. The result is that the school
which was to take Winchester for its model is now a public
elementary school.

The next school was founded not by a successful cleric but

19

by a prosperous citizen and took as its model not Winchester but Eton.

Edmund Flower, " citizein and marchaunt tailor", of London, in his will, 11 July, 1521, said "I for certeine years past at my costs and charge have caused a free Gramer Scole to be maintained and kepte at Cukfelde for the erudicion and lernyng of pore scolers thedur resortyng ". As he had made his fortune by 1504, he probably started the school soon after, and endowed it on his death by will, which was proved 13 August, 1521, for a graduate "beyng a secular prest and suffi- cient man to teche Gramer " to be " always resident there to teche gramer" with lands to the value of £5 a year. A further endowment was given by William Spicer, parson of Balcombe, on 1 October, 1528, who expressly provided that the schoolmaster " shall teach the scholars in the said school grammar after the form order and usage used and taught in the Grammar School at Eton near Windsor from form to form ". To this end, a time-table was sent from Eton, which is fully set out in the Cuckfield statutes, and it was enjoined that these " acts and orders " were only to " continue until such time as the Controlers be certified of others being used and taught in Eton more profitable to scholars ". Unfortu- nately we have only a corrupt copy of a later date of this, the earliest specimen of an Eton time-table preserved.

Another school in Sussex, Horsham, was founded by a man of the same type, Richard Collyer, citizen and mercer of London, by will 23 January, 1532-3. A house was to be built for a free school, " in which house to be threescore scolars", the master to have £10 a year for his " wagis," the usher £5. The said "scolars were to be at noo charge of their scole hire, but freely without any money paying therfor", and preference was to be given to the poor of Horsham and the neighbourhood, " for consideracion gentilmen and other men be in better habilitie than poore men be", but no one from the parish was to be refused. The appointment of master and scholars was given to the vicar and inhabitants, but the management of the estates to the Mercers' Company, which did not prove of advantage to the school, as they took all surplus income for themselves.

In 1523 the inhabitants of Berkhampstead agreed to

devote all the lands of their brotherhood to finding a school-master to teach their children and to the building of a school to teach in. John Incent, Dean of St. Paul's, being president of the fraternity, gave all his lands there to be joined with the brotherhood lands for the same purpose. Further, on 14 October, 1541, John Incent obtained a licence to found a chantry and also "one Free Scole within the towne of Berk-hampstedde, of one mete man being a scolemaster, and one other mete man being an ussher for the techyng of children in grammer frely, withoute any exaccion or request of money for the teaching of the same children, not exceeding the nombre of one hundreth fourty and four". After the founder's death, the King "as principal founder" was to present the chief master and teacher, and the Dean of St. Paul's the usher. An Elizabethan account of the school which the dean built, and which still stands, says "Th'ole building is so strong an faire that the like Grammar Schoole for that point is not to be seene in the whole realme of England". An ex-fellow of All Souls' College himself, he made Richard Rive, or Ryves, a fellow of that college, the master, with an usher and a chap-lain, or petties' master, as at Colet's new school at St. Paul's.

This school has been lately selected for special notice by a Professor of History in the University of London as one of three schools founded by Edward VI, where no school was be-fore, and as thus effectually disproving the wanton assertion, made by the present writer, that none of the Edwardian Gram-mar Schools were really his creation. Professor Pollard cited as proof an Act of Parliament for Berkhampsted School passed in 1548. Had the professor, however, looked at the Act he professed to quote he would have seen that it recited In-cent's foundation and alleged a flaw in the conveyancing of the property, which was therefore claimed by Andrew Incent, the founder's cousin and heir. The Act negatived this claim and corrected the alleged flaw by a re-foundation; Rive and his usher and their successors being incorporated as "Master and Usher of the Free School of King Edward VI in Berk-hampstead", a title which has deceived the unsuspecting pro-fessor.

Another case, that of Stamford Grammar School, cited in

the same connexion by the same professor to support the same allegation of Edwardian initiative, showed even greater abstinence from research and regard for facts on the professor's part. The Act of Parliament of Edward VI for this school in 1548 recited the endowment by William Radcliff's will and the fact that "for 17 or 18 years since his death an honest learned schoolmaster had taught according to the mind and intent of the same William Radcliff greatly to the benefit of the same poor towne and to the other townes thereto adjoyning." It did not even profess to found or re-found the school, or call it Edward VI's Grammar School, but only made the Alderman of Stamford (a mayor had not yet been created) ex officio trustee and governing body of the school, vesting in him the property bequeathed by Radcliff. The professor need not even have taken the trouble to read the Act he professed to quote. For in the very book which he was attacking, *English Schools at the Reformation*, the certificate of Edward VI's Commissioners was printed, which showed the pre-existence of the school. The certificate gave the date, 1 June, 1532, and terms of the will of William Ratclif (so they spelt it) for the maintenance of a fit secular chaplain sufficiently learned, to celebrate for the soul of the said William and freely teach the art of grammar in "Staunford", with a power to get a licence in mortmain for the Alderman of the Corpus Christi Gild to hold it, and also a finding that the school was being carried on under Libeus Byard, who enjoyed for his salary or stipend the rents of the lands given, amounting to £10 3s. 1d. gross, and £9 5s. 5d. net. The Commissioners actually directed this school to be continued, charging the salary on the Crown revenues, the chantry lands being confiscated. But the school had a friend at court in the person of one William Cecil, an "old boy", who was M.P. for Stamford in the Parliament which passed the Chantries Act, and it cannot be doubted that it was through his influence, being Secretary of State, that the Act of Parliament was procured, which saved to the school the endowment, which it still enjoys, without, as usual, substituting the name of the cuckoo King for that of the previous benefactor. Ratclif, however, was not the creator of a new school. As we saw, there was evidence of the school's existence in 1309, in 1327, and 1389, and the Henri-

cian founder was therefore at the best only reviving and probably only refreshing an ancient institution.

An interesting school which may, or may not, have been
first founded at this time is Basingstoke Grammar School.
The Holy Ghost Gild "the brotherhodd of the chapell of the
Holly goost", was, before 1244, founded to maintain a priest
in the picturesque chapel, the ruins of which are seen from
the South-Western railway station.   A chantry certificate in
1548 said that "sythens", that is, at least since its legal in-
corporation under a licence of 16 November, 1524—of which
Bishop Fox has had the credit, though he apparently only
lent his name as a petitioner for it—the endowment was "employed to fynde a scole master to teche children grammer";
the master receiving £5 17s. 8d. a year.   As no continuance
order of Edward VI had been found, it was assumed by the
present writer in the *Victoria County History of Hampshire*,
that the school ceased by virtue of the Chantries Act, and was
only resumed under the new charter or letters patent of Philip
and Mary, 24 February, 1557, whence it is now called Queen
Mary's School.   This assumption now turns out to be wrong,
the Ministers' accounts, since made available, disclosing the
payment from the Crown revenues throughout Edward VI's
reign of £5 17s. 3d. to Thomas Browne, "schoolmaster of the
grammar school founded by a certain gild called the Fraternitie
in Basingstoke" under a warrant or continuance order made
by Sir Walter Mildmay in 1548.   The school therefore never
ceased, and if any sovereign, rather than the people of Basingstoke, is to be regarded as its founder, that sovereign is Henry
VIII, not his daughter.   She, indeed, did on the request of
Cardinal Pole, refound the gild, and restore its lands for a
priest to celebrate in the chapel "and for the instruction and
education of the youths and boys of the said town".   The
accounts of the resuscitated gild mention a schoolmaster in
1559, but not his name.   In 1560 the vicar taught the school
for £1 a quarter, and the vicar was the same Thomas Browne,
a student of Christ Church, Oxford, who had been schoolmaster in 1548.   He still taught occasionally during vacancies
till 1567, what was always called, down to 1852, The Holy
Ghost School.   The continuity of this now flourishing school
from at least 1524 is therefore definitely established.

Another of the schools which has been put down to Edward VI's foundation, Sedbergh in Yorkshire, was in fact founded in the earlier part of Henry VIII's reign by Roger Lupton, one of the successful much-beneficed lawyer-clerics of the day, and Provost of Eton, as we have seen, and Master in Chancery.   He founded it as a Chantry-Grammar School, consisting of a single Chantry-priest-Schoolmaster, in his native place.   The date has been wrongly assigned to 1528.   The true date is fixed as between 23 July, 1523, and 24 March, 1525, by two deeds of these dates.   In the first a dispute was settled as to the ownership of the Loft-house, which Lupton gave for the master's house, showing it not then to be his.   On the other hand, the deed of 24 March, 1525, made by the Archdeacon of Richmond as to seats in Sedbergh Church, says "a place shall always be kept free for the chaplain and scholars celebrating the Lady Mass and anthem in the said chapel"; clearly showing that the school was already going on.   This is further shown by a deed of 26 May, 1527, by which Lupton granted £600 to St. John's College, Cambridge, for six scholars to be incorporated among the other scholars of the college, and receive the same emoluments with £1 6s. 8d. more to pray for his soul.   The scholars were to be born in England [i.e. not Scots] sons of freemen (*libere condicionis*)—a striking late testimony against the notion that colleges and schools were intended for the working classes, who were still mostly villeins—"and who have issued well learned from my Grammar School of Sedbergh", with preference for founder's kin, natives of Sedbergh, Dent and Garstall, especially those whose friends had been benefactors to the foundation.   In order that the college might get more learned scholars from his school he gave the appointment of the schoolmaster to the college, with preference for ex-Lupton scholars.   To bring the school under the supervision of the college, as Winchester was under that of New College, he requested the master of the college, if he happened to go that way, to call and question the schoolmaster on the condition of the school, and examine the most advanced scholars and select the best for St. John's.   If the master could not go, "a fellow is to be elected, who because it is his native country or for some business is going there".   The deed concluded with a proviso that if "through the fraud and malice of men, which God·avert, his Chantry and Grammar school at Sedbergh should be injuriously treated so as to come to an end", the endowment should go over to St. John's College for four more Lupton scholars on the same terms as far as possible, but with preference only for founder's kin.

The school is again spoken of as already existing in a deed of 12 August, 1527, by which Lupton obtained from the Abbot and Convent of Coverham, to whom Sedbergh Church and Rectory were impropriated, a grant of the site of the school, "a little close by the churchyard called the school-house-garth, of,the yearly rent of 1s. 8d., on which a school-house has been built by the same Master Roger Lupton for the institution of a free (*gratuitam*) school there for ever". The later foundation deed of the school, long assumed to have been lost, but produced by the present Master of St. John's College, Cambridge, when bursar, from among their muniments, a deed poll·of 9 March, 1528, distinctly refers to a prior establishment of it in a provision that the chantry priest was to find at his own cost all things sufficient for the celebration of mass "with that sufficient ᵢ stuff I there left at the first endowment". In this deed, Lupton recites that he has bought lands of the yearly value of £12 7s. 9d., besides a messuage called the Lofthouse, "in the which Syr Henry Blomer, nowe chauntery pryst, dwellith", the rents of which are to be used for a chantry in the parish church, and for a chantry priest, who is to be "sufficiently lerned and instructe to fulfyll the chauntery duteis and habyll to teche a gramer Scole". He is to be continually resident, explained to mean not absent more than thirty days in the year, and during that time he is to provide "ᵢone of hys Scolers sufficiently lernyd to teche hys Scolers in hys absens". He is to say mass every day in the church and pray for the souls of the founder and others, and to "rule and order the grammer Scole as master, and teche frely gramer, after the maner, forme and use of some lawdable, notable and famous Scole of England, and in especiall my kynsmen and theym of Sedber, Dent and Garstall, and then all other, without ony exaccion or calenge of theyr stipend or wages besyde my allowaunce". "But", Lupton continues, "the sayd mayster of the grammer Scole shall not be bounde to teche, ne cause no scoler of hys to teche any other thyng but gramer to any chyldern, except the frends of the sayd chyldern wyll gyffe to the seyd Scolemaster, or to the Scoler, with the masters assent, that shall teche theym, for theyr labour as they can agree with the sayd Scolemaster and Scoler that shall teche theym, so that the sayd Scolemaster or sayd Scoler be no letted to teche grammer". A further endowment was given by Lupton to St. John's College for two more Lupton scholars there, making eight in all, by deed of 7 June, 1535. A few months later he retired from the provostship at Eton, to his canonry at Windsor, where he died in 1540. He did not mention Sedbergh School in his will.

Henry Blomer, the first master, held office till his death. By his will, 5 November, 1543, he gave £6 13s. 4d. to St. John's College for the Lupton scholars, on condition that all the scholars were elected from Sedbergh School, that proviso having been omitted from Lupton's deed of 7 June, 1535. Blomer also gave to his successor for the use of the " Free School at Sedbergh, 6 silver spoons, with such certain of my books as shall be delivered by indenture, at the discretion of my executors to remain as heir looms to the said foundation".

He was succeeded by Robert Hebblethwaite, a fellow of St. John's College, who gave him a testimonial on 27 January, 1543-4. Some difficulty about his admission arose with the feoffees at Sedbergh, and the rents being withheld from him, the College appealed in a letter written by the celebrated Roger Ascham, then in residence at St. John's, to Robert Holgate, Bishop of Llandaff, and President of the Council of the North, "to prevent any violence or injustice being offered to the school, and to so repress and punish the greed of these men that the rest may learn what is the result of making an attack on the schools and ease" (*otia*, a Latinization of the Greek *scholas*) " of youth, which are the very foundations of all that is best in the commonwealth". Hebblethwaite was in possession when the endowment was confiscated and sold by Edward VI in 1548.

Manchester Grammar School can hardly be ascribed to Henry VIII's reign, though it received a great increase in endowment then. It was probably part of the collegiate church

THE MANCHESTER GRAMMAR SCHOOLMASTER SLAYING THE DRAGON OF IGNORANCE, 1508

THE MANCHESTER GRAMMAR SCHOOL USHER LICKING HIS CUBS INTO SHAPE, 1508

MISERICORDS IN MANCHESTER COLLEGIATE CHURCH, NOW THE
CATHEDRAL

founded in 1420, as stalls, erected in the choir of the church between 1506 and 1512, assigned to the Archididascalus and Hypodidascalus, are strong evidence of the existence of the school before that date. A chantry founded by Alexander or Richard Bessike in 1506 for two priests, "thone of the two" to teach a free school, was its first separate endowment. Hugh Oldham, a Chancery official and pluralist cleric, afterwards Bishop of Exeter, gave corn-mills in 1515 to the warden and fellows of the college by a Latin deed for the endowment of a "fit person, secular or regular, learned and able, to be schoolmaster to teach and instruct grammar in the town of Manchester, according to the form of grammar now learned and taught in the school of the town of Banbury in the county of Oxford, which in English is called Stanbridge Grammar, and an usher as a deputy or substitute of such person". They covenanted to pay the master £10 and the usher £5 ; and the master took oath to "teach and correct all their boys and scholars equally and impartially" and not to take " any presents, gifts or any kind of thing by colour of their service or office or teaching, except their stipend only, without any fraud, cunning and device". They were to attend choir in surplices, "like other fellows of the college", and every Wednesday and Friday go in procession with their scholars before the warden round the cemetery or church or otherwise. Oldham died, 25 June, 1519. Six years afterwards Ralph Hulme, gentleman, one of the trustees, turned out to be a fraudulent solicitor and claimed the mills and lands as his own, and it was only by special efforts on the part of John Lord Warr, who said he had only sold the mills for the free school (*libere scole*) of Manchester, that the endowment was saved. For some obscure legal reason, perhaps because there was no licence in mortmain, a new settlement of the endowment was made, this time in English, on 1 April, 1525, which is commonly reputed the original foundation deed. It constituted, instead of the college, an entirely new body of twelve lay trustees, and the master was to be appointed by Corpus Christi College, Oxford, instead of by the chapter of the collegiate church. He was to be a " syngilman ", priest or no priest "so that he be no religiouse man ", i.e., no monk, regular canon or friar, "able to teche childeryn gramyar after the maner and forme of the Scole of Banbury, wiche is called Stanbryge gramyer". Most of the provisions as to the school are adapted from the statutes of St. Paul's, and the head master has retained, like him of St. Paul's, the name of high master.

The chief educational foundation in Henry VIII's reign was that of Cardinal's Colleges at Oxford and at Ipswich by Cardinal Wolsey. Ipswich was an already existing school, and had been endowed on 2 January, 1482-3 by an ex-"Portman" or Mayor, Richard Felar, the master receiving £5 a year, in addition, however, at least from 1420, to the chaplaincy of the Corpus Christi Gild. When in 1528 Wolsey built his beautiful college of red brick, of which only one gateway now remains, and endowed it out of eleven Priories suppressed for the purpose, for a dean, twelve fellows, eight choristers, and fifty children or scholars, a schoolmaster and two ushers, he was careful to get a grant from Bailiffs, Portmen and inhabitants of Ipswich of the old school and its endowment. But on 19 September, 1530, the college was declared forfeited to the Crown and only a fragment of the endowment afterwards given to the school.

Space does not permit an account of all the other schools founded, or which first occur under Henry VIII, before the meeting of the Reformation Parliament. We can but afford them that which in the Roman breviary is directed to be given to a saint whose commemoration falls on a day dedicated to some greater saint, *memoria tantum*, a mere mention. There were founded chantry schools at Rock in Worcestershire, by Sir Humphry Connysbie, knight, 1509; Chesterford, Essex, by William Holden, 1514; Owston, Yorkshire, by Robert Henryson, 1514; Houghton Regis, Bedfordshire, by William Dyve, mercer of London, by deed 1515; also in 1515, Liverpool, a priest "to say masse afore the ymage of Saynt Katherine within the chappell of Liverpool" (St. Mary del Key or Quay) and "keepe gramer scole", free for all "whose names be Crosse and poor children", by John Crosse, a London rector; chantry schools at Kinver, Salop, by John Perot the same year; Cannock, Staffordshire, about 1518; East Retford, Notts, school built by Thomas Gunthorpe in 1518, supported out of chantry lands; Earl's Colne, Essex, by deed of Christopher Swallow, vicar of Messing, 1519. There was set up

DOORWAY, CARDINAL COLLEGE, IPSWICH, 1527

at Warrington a "fre gramer scole", by will of Sir Thomas Boteler, 16 August, 1520, "to be the very clear lanthorn of good example in virtuous living to all the country thereabouts", according to Ordinances, to be made, which were made in 1526; at Milton Abbas, Dorset, a "fre scole" was founded by Sir John Leder, priest, 1521 ; at Tenterden, Kent, by William Marshall, the same year.   At Hornby, Lancashire, a school and hospital were directed by will of Lord Monteagle, 1523 ; at Leyland, Lancashire, by deed of Sir Henry ffarington, knight, 1524 ; at Bolton-le-Moors, a grammar school was endowed by grant of William Haigh to parishioners, 4 March, 1524, further endowed in 1623, 1642, by Robert Lever, and in 1895, 1902, and 1913, by W. H. Lever, of Port Sunlight fame.   At Kneesall, Nottinghamshire, the will of John Chapman, notary public, citizen, and mercer of York, Count Palatine of the holy palace of the Lateran, and registrar of the Cardinal-Archbishop, 4 March, 1527-8, established a school.

At St. Michael-upon-Wyre, Lancashire, St. Katharine's chantry school, founded by deed of John Butler, 3 December, 1528, is not heard of after 1642.   At Winwick, a free grammar school was founded by Gwalter Legh, ancestor of Lord Newton; at Kirkoswald, Yorkshire, a collegiate church with Grammar and Song Schools was founded by deed of Lord Dacre in 1530.

Schools of unascertained date appear in the *Valor Ecclesiasticus* of 1535 at Higham, Kent, a chantry with income of £6 13s. 4d. ; Kingsley, Staffordshire, a chantry or priest's service founded by Hugh Adderley, clerk, daily to celebrate at the Altar of Jesus and "to kepe scole and to teche pore men's children of the said parishe grammer, and to rede and sing", yearly value £6 1s. ; Orford, Suffolk, chantry at our Lady's Altar and school, income £5 9s. 9¾d. ; Shenston, Staffordshire, a priest at the altar of Thomas à Becket in a chapel attached to the church, founded under the will of James Keyley, receiving £7 0s. 4½d. a year, "to teche yong children of the parish grammer, or otherwise accordyng to his knowledge" ; Thirsk, Yorkshire, chantry of Our Lady, founded by divers well-disposed persons, to help service and teach a grammar school, income £5 10s. 4d.; Weobley, Herefordshire, the priest in chapel of St. Nicholas in the church, founded by John Chapman and Alice Baker, "to kepe a scole and teache chyldern, and brynge them upe in vertue", clear income £6 13s. 1d.

Childrey, Berks, where a school and almshouse were placed under the tutelage of Queen's College, Oxford, by Sir William Fettiplace on 20 July, 1526, calls for special notice, as it is an early instance of an elementary school, with an "upper division" for those who want grammar or "secondary" instruction. The foundation deed gives the full programme of a Song or Elementary School, which goes far to explain why the Reformers were disposed rather to destroy such schools as promoters of superstition than to preserve them as advancing education. The priest was indeed to be skilful and well used and sufficiently instructed and learned in grammar. But he was to teach in the first place, the alphabet, the Lord's Prayer, the Angel's Salutation, the Apostles' Creed, and all other things necessary for serving the priest at mass, together with the Psalm *De Profundis*, and collects and prayers for the dead; also to say grace as well at dinner as at supper; then, in English, the Fourteen Articles of Faith, the Ten Commandments of God, the seven deadly sins, the seven Sacraments, the seven gifts of the Holy Spirit, the seven works of mercy as well corporeal as spiritual, and the manner of confession, necessary not only for the boys themselves, but in order that they might instruct others who were ignorant. Also he should teach them good manners, especially not to lie, and to honour their parents and in church to serve God devoutly. This curriculum savoured to the Protestant more of superstition than of religious education. One would like to know what proportion of the boys went on to the upper division. For this provision was made that if any were apt and disposed to learn grammar, the priest should instruct them in grammar in the best and most diligent manner he could, and especially teach them what was most useful to them, and what was most expedient according to his true estimation and the sound counsel of learned men. He was to exact nothing from the poor or parishioners, though he might take anything freely offered.

The darkness of our ignorance of the curriculum in our ancient schools is lightened for us first in 1528 by Wolsey's statutes for his short-lived college and by the Eton time-table, set out as noticed above for Cuckfield Grammar School, in the same year, and a year or two later by the curriculum of Eton and part of that of Winchester as preserved at Saffron Walden.

Wolsey ordered his school to be divided into eight forms, the lowest learning the parts of speech and pronunciation. In the second form the boys were to talk Latin and turn into Latin " some common proposition, not dull or inappropriate ". Their books, " if any ", were to be Lily's *Carmen Monitorium*, and the so-called Cato's *Precepts*, better known as the *Moralia*. In Form III. they were to read " Æsop, who is wittier ? Terence, who is more useful ? "—for talking Latin be it understood—and Lily's Genders. In Form IV they went on in Lily's Grammar to preterites and supines, and in authors to Virgil, whose verses they were "to give out with sonorous voice ". Form V was to read Cicero's *Select Letters ;* VI, Sallust or Cæsar ; VII, Horace's *Epistles*, Ovid's *Metamorphoses* or *Fasti ;* VIII, Valla's *Elegantiae*, Donatus' *Figura*, and any ancient authors in the Latin tongue, while Terence is to be studied with lectures on the life of the day, style and so forth. The boys were also to learn précis-making and to write essays.

At Eton in 1528 Stanbridge's *Accidence* was the first thing learnt ; then " after repeating the rules the Master shall cause them to make small and easy Latins, proper and such as the children may understand and delight in ". In the second form they read Whittington's Genders and Heteroclites besides doing Latins with the first form. Whittington was the master of Lichfield Grammar School, augmented by Bishop Smith, in connexion with St. John's Hospital there, about 1495. He re-edited and improved on Stanbridge's grammar. " After their breakfast a lecture of Cato after the new interpretation shall be read to them, which they shall construe again at afternoon." In the third form Whittington's Preterites, Supines, and Defectives were learnt by heart. Their " books " were Terence, Erasmus's *Similitudes* or *Colloquies* and Virgil's *Eclogues*. The fourth form did their " Latin constructions and other things, except rules, with the third form, to the intent that the better learned may instruct the less learned " ; " their rules were the Regiments of Whittington which he called Concinnitates Grammatices ". In the fifth they learnt the Versifying Rules ; and for books read Sallust, Virgil, Horace and Ovid's Epistles, and every week made verses and epistles.   Horace and Cicero were added to these in the Sixth, which "have for their rules Copiam Erasmi".   From the Order sent to Cuckfield in 1528 we see that there were only six forms at Eton, but in that sent to Saffron Walden only two years later, seven forms are mentioned both at Eton and Winchester.

At that time Eton had in the higher forms discarded Whittington's grammar for Lily's, long afterwards re-edited as the Eton Latin grammar, but used Stanbridge's grammar for the lower forms as did Winchester, patriotically, as he was a Wykehamist.   The Winchester scheme of work has lost its first page and so starts in the middle of a sentence, "Ovide Metamorphosesos the Thursday, Salust the Fryday, with the vij forme, and at afternone rendering of there rulys.   The Saterday lyke as the vij forme.   The Sonday lykewise."   Next comes the heading "the Vth forme", to be followed by headings of "the Third", "the Seconde" and "the Fyrst forme".   To any one acquainted with Winchester School or its history this was startling.   For from time when the memory of man runneth not to the contrary up to the present day Winchester has known only three forms, called Sixth, Fifth and Fourth Book.   It has been a subject of much discussion whether there ever were any other forms, and if so when the others disappeared.   We learn for a fact that at Winchester, as then at contemporary Eton, and as at Westminster now, there was a Seventh Form above Sixth Book and three forms below Fourth Book.

The work of the Fifth and lower forms may be thus summarized.   On coming into school at seven o'clock, from Monday to Thursday inclusive, the first business was the giving out of grammar rules.   In the Fifth to Third Forms these were taken from Sulpicius, a schoolmaster at Rome, of Veroli in the Campagna, who published many grammatical works in Latin between 1487 and 1506.   One of the Sixth Form gave them out to the Fifth, and one of the Fifth to the Fourth, but the usher gave them out to the Third.   Form V did "versifical rules" or rules for making verses; Form IV the rules for preterites and supines; and Form III, the rules for genders and heteroclites or irregular declensions, all of which were

separate works of the most heart-rending detail.   Forms II
and I took their rules from the *Parvulorum* and *Vocabula*, the
Babies' Book and Word Book of Stanbridge.   On Friday
morning they were examined on these rules, and Friday afternoon " rendered " them, which appears to mean said them by
heart.   After rules were given out, Forms V-III were
examined on a verb which they had "set up" overnight, and
made "vulgars" on it, i.e. Latin phrases, as in Horman's
Vulgaria.   V and IV together then "write down the Latin
that one of them shall make by the assignment of the Master ",
or as it is phrased for III, " they have a theme to be made in
Laten, the which Latyne one of the said forme at the pleasure
of the master makith openlie dyverse ways.   And after that
they write the master's owne Latyne ", that is, the master
dictated his own version of the piece.   Form V also learnt
by heart Sallust on Monday, Tuesday and Wednesday, and
four verses of Ovid's *Metamorphoses* on Thursday.   For translation, or "construction " as it is called (which was apparently
done not " up to books ", i.e. in form, but in " books chambers ",
sitting at their separate "toys " or desks in chambers), they
did Virgil's *Eclogues* every day except Friday and Saturday.
On Friday they translated Tully's or, as we say, Cicero's
Letters.   On Wednesday they composed Latin verses ; on
Thursday, Latin Epistles.   On Saturday, V and VI said
twelve verses of Ovid "without book " and were examined on
them and showed up their Latin prose.   In the afternoon they
construed Cicero and showed up their epistles.   The Fourth,
instead of doing Virgil, did Terence from Monday to Thursday
inclusive, which the master construed to them in the morning
and they construed and parsed (*parce*) to the usher in the
afternoon, and were examined in it on Saturday afternoon.
Form III construed *Æsop's Fables* on Monday and Wednesday, and Lucian's *Dialogues*, presumably in Latin, on Tuesday
and Thursday ; while Forms II (and I ?) construed *Æsop's
Fables* every day except Saturday, when they had repetition
of four verses of Cato and examination of it.

On Sunday the Sixth Form did "lykewise " to the Seventh
Form, and the Fifth Form did "as the other hie formys
dothe "—but what they did is denied us through the loss of
the first page.   It was certainly not a day of rest.   For the

Fourth Form on " the Sunday with other low holy dayes " did
" an English of an epistle to be made in Latyn diverse wayes,
and somtyme Tullie's paradoxes to be construyd ", the Third
Form had " a dialogue of Lucyane or a fable of Æsop to be
said without book and construed ", and the First, and presumably the Second, " a fabull of Æsope ".

The books used in the two higher forms can only be inferred from the Eton list.   They were Horace or Cicero every
day from Monday to Thursday, and on Friday and Saturday
the *Æneid* of Virgil.   For grammar they read Mosellanus'
Figures of Speech.   They made verses and epistles and
read *Erasmus Copiam verborum* to help them.   The most interesting thing about the two curricula is that both schools
used Sulpicius, the recent Roman writer, the one for " versifical
rules", the other for his " Quos decet in mensa " or table
manners.   Eton used the French schoolmaster Despautier's
Method of writing letters or *Ars Epistolica*, first published at
Strasburg in 1512, and a second edition at Antwerp in 1529,
when he was master of the School of St. Ginnocus at Bergen-
op-Zoom ; so that it was quite the latest foreign school-book.

The school-books of the day were still under the influence
of the over-refining spirit of dissection and classification, which
had been imbibed from the schoolmen.   Epistles, for instance,
are divided by Despautier into three classes, the descriptive,
the political and the familiar, while each letter is said to consist of a salutation, a statement, a petition, and a valediction
or conclusion, though, as he naïvely remarks, all these characters are not always found together.   All letters, in fact, were
not begging letters.   The treatises on versification dwindle
down into the most appallingly minute rules, with ex-
ceptions more numerous than the rules, as to the quantities
of the various vowels in different locations.

The medieval grammar was not made less maddening by
being almost invariably in verse.   In these late fifteenth and
early sixteenth century writers the verses meandered like
slender rivulets of text through meadows of marginal notes and
prose commentary.

> Arte novata aliqua dicendi forma figura est,
> Sunt ejus species metaplasmus, schema, tropusque,
> Schemata dant species tibi lexeos et dianeas.

Such is the exordium of the excellent Mosellanus, who is very scornful on his predecessors for occasionally sacrificing metre to sense, but as he can only avoid the fault by interlarding his discourse with Romanized Græcisms, the learner might well prefer the sacrifice.   No doubt it sharpened the wits for such encounters as those theological controversies which soon overwhelmed the nation.   But the practice of distinctions without differences and classifications without contents was responsible for a great deal of the word-splitting that sent men to the stake or the gallows on theological minutiæ.   The Quos decet in mensa of the Italian Sulpicius out of which the schools learnt at once manners, morals and Latin verse, is a much superior work.   It got its name from its beginning :—

> Quos decet in mensa mores servare docentes
> Virtuti ut studeas litterulisque simul.
>
> Good manners for the table here we tell
> To make our scholars gentlemen as well.

In elegant elegiacs are set out all the good old nursery rules as to behaviour.   Boys are to have clean gowns, and before meals wash hands and face, clean their teeth and blow their noses.   Part I then goes off into general maxims of conduct and morals.   Never return abuse or lose your temper, avoid gluttony and idleness, do not be morose nor get too easy in your manner, and so forth.

Part II returns to manners strictly speaking.   Spread the tables neatly, see that the trenchers (*quadrantes*) are clean. Don't champ your jaws when eating, sit upright, don't put your elbows on the table, take your food only with three fingers and in small mouthfuls.   Remember that you eat to live and do not live to eat (*Esse decet vivas, vivere non ut edas*). Did Sulpicius invent this famous epigram ?   Use your napkin often (napkins were supplied at Winchester, as appears in the first account roll), don't bite your food but cut it, nor gnaw your bones.   Only lift the cup with one hand, unless it's of the kind that Theseus or Bel used to hurl at an enemy ; don't look over it while you are drinking, don't swallow it too fast or drain the pot, or whistle when you drink.   Wipe your mouth after it, and wash your hands and mouth when you leave the table.   Bend your knee, join your hands and say " *Prosit* " for grace.

20

This book of Sulpicius is by no means original. *The Babees Book*, which gives its title to the amusing collection of English, Latin and French books on manners, published by Dr. Furnivall for the early English Text Society, was translated from the Latin somewhere about 1475. They all appear to be derived from a common original written by Facetus, a pseudonym of Johannes de Garlandia, an Englishman who wrote a Latin-English vocabulary and a treatise on manners in the thirteenth century, copies of which were in Winchester College Library *ab initio*, and which was frequently printed by Wynkyn de Worde and Richard Pynson from 1500 and onwards.

The Eton "Order" gives besides the curriculum an interesting general account of internal organisation. The only questions asked of a proposed new boy were "whens he comyth, what frends he hathe; whether there be any plage". School began at 6 a.m.—they got up at 5—with prayers, ending at 9 with De profundis, and then to breakfast. In a quarter of an hour come again, i.e. 9.45, and school till dinner at 11 o'clock. Afternoon school 1 to 5, and then supper after another De profundis. The prefect system was in full vogue. Two prepositores, now called prepostors, to take the names of the absents in every form; two in the body, i.e. nave of the church, two in the choir. In every house a monitor. They go home two in two in order and have a monitor to see that they do till they come to their "hostise" or Dame's door. Privy monitors—to spy on the others—"how many master the will". Prepostors everywhere; in the field when they play, "for fyghtyng, rent clothes, blew eyes or sich like" prepostors for "yll kept hedys, unwasshid faces, fowle clothis and sich other". If there are four or five boys in a house "monytors for chydyng and for Latyn spekyng".

The prepostors were not themselves to keep order or punish so much as to report delinquents to the master. That the reports were not without results we may gather from the character given of Cox, the master who supplied this account, by Walter Haddon, in the conversation on flogging in schools reported by Roger Ascham, which was the occasion of his *Scholemaster*. The Secretary of State, Sir William Cecil, having expressed himself against flogging, Mr. Peters had argued that it was both necessary and useful: "the rod was the sword of justice of the school". "Then", writes Ascham, "Mr. Haddon was fullie of Mr. Peter's opinion and said 'That the best scholemaster of our time was the greatest beater', and named the person. 'Though', quoth I, 'it was his good fortune to send from his schole unto the university one of the best scholers indeede of our time, yet wise men do thincke that that came so to pass, rather by the great towardnesse of the scholer than by the great beating of the master; and whether this be true or no, you yourselfe are best witness.'" This "best scholemaster" and "greatest beater" is commonly said to be Udal. But it is quite clear that Ascham was referring to Haddon's master, Cox. If Haddon had meant Udal, who was then dead, Ascham would not have hesitated to give his name; but Cox was still alive and a bishop, and therefore for obvious reasons the name was suppressed. The mistaken reference to Udal was originally made by James Bennett, "master of the Boarding-School at Hoddesdon in Hertfordshire", in his edition of Ascham's *Works* in 1761, and has been blindly repeated ever since. Udal was no sparer of the rod. But Cox must have the credit, or otherwise, of being reputed by an old pupil the best schoolmaster and greatest beater of his age.

Cox's Elizabethan successor Malim, gave a time-table of the year as well as the week, an account of the feasts and holidays as well as the work. The net result was that hard as the whole schooldays were, each a ten-hours' day, there were only five or indeed four of them a week; and there were so many feasts that hardly a week could have passed without at least one whole or half holiday. For every greater feast day was a whole holiday, and on every eve of the "greater doubles", feast days on which double rations were enjoyed, there was a partial holiday, no work being done after dinner at 11 a.m. Ash Wednesday was given up, not to lessons, but to confession to the fellows or conducts, each boy choosing his own confessor. On the *obit* of William Wayneflete, 13 January, every boy received 2d.; on 7 February, the *obit* of Provost Bost, there was a half holiday; on 27 February, the *obit* of Roger Lupton, every boy received 1d. and there was a holiday from dinner-time (11 a.m.); and on 26 May, the *obit*

of Henry VI, every boy had 2d.   On Saturday before Easter
"while the custom flourished" of the Easter Sepulchre, three
or four of the eldest boys chosen by the master at the request
of the sacrist watched round the sepulchre with wax lights and
torches, "lest the Jews should steal the Lord".   At Easter the
school did not break up, though, to judge from Winchester,
there were extensive *exeats* for those who could go home.
For all there was a ten-days' holiday (*cessatum a publicis
studiis*).   On May Day, St. Philip and St. James, those who
wished got up at 4 a.m. to gather boughs of may; but with a
curiously grandmotherly care, which shows a very different
spirit from that commonly imputed to our scholastic ancestors,
the licence was coupled with the proviso "that they do not
wet their feet".   The windows of Long Chamber were then
hung with may and herbs.

"St. John Lateran before the Latin gate", 6 May, " brings
many advantages, for from now after dinner they had a siesta
in school, until the prepostor of hall and the *ostiarius* call out
'Get up' (*Surgite*) at 3 p.m., when they have beavers or
bever," an interval for drinking beer, the equivalent of the
modern afternoon tea.   Malim recalls the line: "Porta Latina
pilam, pulvinar, pocula prestat", i.e. "St. John Lateran's day
brings the ball, the bed, the beer".

Ascension Day began the summer holidays, which lasted
till the day before Corpus Christi Day, the Thursday after
Trinity Sunday, anyone not present at evening chapel on that
day being flogged.   On St. John the Baptist's birthday, Midsummer Day, all the scholars went after evening prayers to a
bonfire, made in the open space at the east end of chapel, and
then, after the choir had sung their anthems, to a bever.   On
the eve of that day the boys adorned their chambers with
pictures and verses on the "life and gests of the Forerunner",
which they wrote out with illuminations and stuck at the foot
of their beds.   As it was nearly nine before they went to bed,
they were allowed to lie in bed till six on the feast itself
instead of getting up at five.   The same custom was observed
on 29 June, St. Peter and St. Paul.   The custom of the Eton
and Winchester match being always held on one of those two
feast days is perhaps ultimately due to this celebration.   On
7 July, the Translation of St. Thomas (Becket), there was also

a bonfire, but no verses.   At Eton, as at Winchester, the boy-bishop was directed by the statutes to perform divine service on St. Nicholas's Day, 6 December, and not on the usual day, that of the Holy Innocents; to avoid clashing with the established boy-bishop celebrations of the choristers of the cathedral and of St. George's respectively.   Originally mixed up with the boy-bishop was the custom that on St. Andrew's Day (30 November) the schoolmaster used to choose the best and most appropriate stage plays, i.e. plays of Terence or Plautus, "which the boys perform sometimes in public during the Christmas holidays, not without the elegance of the games (sc. of Rome), before a popular audience".   Altogether the sixteenth-century schoolboy before the Reformation did not have such a bad time of it.

It is curious that at the very time when these curricula showing a diversity of grammars were sent to Saffron Walden, steps were being taken by Convocation, under Henry's guidance, to enforce uniformity in the school equally with uniformity in the Church.   In 1529 it laid down, as often before, and with as little effect, that schoolmasters should be orthodox as well as learned, and teach the rudiments of faith as well as of grammar, and prohibited books likely to infect boys' minds being read in school.   Convocation broke new ground, when it proceeded to complain that, often through the plague raging in places where public schools were, or through a master's death, a boy who had learnt grammar for a year or two under one teacher had to continue under another who had a different method, and was laughed at or put back accordingly.   For remedy Convocation directed that only one grammar should be put before boys, and that one to be prescribed within a year by the Archbishop, and a committee of four bishops, four abbots, and four archdeacons.

This was probably the first step towards the universal, or at least general, adoption of the grammar, the joint con position of Colet, Lily, and Erasmus, issued in 1513 by Colet to Lily, commonly known as Lily's Grammar, and adopted by Cardinal Wolsey for his school at Ipswich.   It contained the Accidence in English and the Syntax in Latin.   The preface to Wolsey's book dated 1528, printed by Peter Treveris in 1529, states that this grammar was already "prescribed not only for

Ipswich School, happily established by the Lord Thomas, Cardinal of York, but also for all the other schools of the whole of England". This seems to show that Convocation was only adopting what was perhaps already enunciated by Wolsey's legatine authority. The exclusive use of this grammar was later prescribed by the King in a proclamation, the date of which has never been exactly ascertained, first mentioned in a copy printed by Bartlet in 1542. So successful was the prescription that for thirty-four years this grammar, slightly revised in 1758 and re-christened the Eton Latin Grammar, reigned without a rival in the schools of England, and was only superseded by the Public Schools Latin Primer in 1867.

Another example of Henry's zeal for education was the strenuous attempt made, in ushering in the reform of the Church, to enforce the duty of promoting education on wealthy ecclesiastics. Through Thomas Cromwell, Privy Seal, Vice-gerent of the King in causes ecclesiastical, at a general visitation held in 1536, he put forward the following quaintly-worded injunction :—

"And to the intent that learned men may hereafter springe the more, every beneficed man having yerely to dispend in benefices and other promotions of the church £100, shall gyve competent exhibition to one scolar", and for any additional £100 another scholar "in the universitie of Oxford or Cambridge or some grammer scole". The object is stated to be that after these scholars have profited in good learning they may be partners in their patrons' cure and charge as well in preaching as otherwise in the execution of their offices. But the lawgiver did not forget the State, for he adds "or may otherwyse profite the common wealth with their counsell and wysdom".

Henry VIII's chief work in education consisted in refoundation and improvement, not in creation of new schools, but he did it on a scale which entitles him to the praise of being, in a sense, the greatest of school founders.

It has been commonly assumed that in abolishing the monasteries he abolished a large number of schools, and a saying of an Elizabethan Speaker to the effect that 100 schools had disappeared has been cited as referring to monastic schools. This assumption is founded on the erroneous notion that the monasteries were or kept schools. There were of course, as we have seen, a large number of schools under the government and trusteeship of monasteries. But as far as is known the payments made by them in respect of their mastership was continued. Thus at Reading the grammar school which we saw handed over to the abbey on its foundation had been, by some obscure arrangement in which Robert Sherborne was interested, planted in a decayed hospital for widows and given ten marks a year. At the dissolution the master was Leonard Cox, an Etonian, who wrote the first English text-book on Rhetoric and a preface to a school-book on French. When the abbey was dissolved on 10 February, 1541, the King granted him by patent the office of master or preceptor of the grammar school of Reading, and an annuity of £10 a year, charged on the royal manor of Chelsea. A similar course was taken at Bruton. So at Evesham, the school which, according to nineteenth century historians, was founded in 1546, but according to the chantry commissioners of 1548 had existed and been endowed with £10 a year from the reign of Edward III, was continued. This payment was now charged on the Crown revenue of Worcestershire. James I, incorporating the borough in 1605, confirmed the payment to the corporation, and seized the opportunity of calling the school after his son, " Prince Henry's Grammar School " by which name it is still known—a name which induced a recent clerical historian of the English Church to assert that Henry VIII had destroyed the old school. So at Sherborne, imputed to the wise system of Edward VI's schools, we found Thomas Copeland, a secular, master of Sherborne School, living outside the abbey and subscribing handsomely to the rebuilding of the hospital or almshouse of the two St. Johns in 1437. The school went quietly on after the dissolution of the monastery and the master was made the first master of the re-endowed school in 1550. The schools which Henry abolished in abolishing the monasteries were the small and insignificant almonry schools of a few charity boys, and these he more than replaced by the great schools which he established in the new cathedral foundations.

The abolition of the greater monasteries in 1540 resulted in the refoundation of twelve grammar schools as part of the cathedrals " of the new foundation ", in which the monks who had

600 years before turned out the canons were now in turn turned out to make room for canons. In all the new cathedrals established in 1541, including Westminster but excepting Winchester, " because of that noble school of Wykeham's foundation ", a grammar school, with a master and usher paid on the highest scale of the day, was included.

At Canterbury, Carlisle, Ely, Norwich, Rochester, and Worcester, the new cathedral grammar schools were but the old cathedral schools, which had been under the patronage and government of the archbishop or bishop, in concert or not with his archdeacon, re-established in a glorified form, far more amply endowed, and placed under the patronage and endowment of the new and more continuously resident deans and chapters. Norwich, however, soon ceased in consequence of the school placed in the re-created Great Hospital. At Bristol, Chester, Gloucester, Peterborough, Westminster, the new cathedral grammar schools also replaced old grammar schools, of various origin and government, also in a much glorified form, and as part of the endowment of the churches under the government of the secular deans and chapters instead of that of the abbots or others. But at Bristol and Gloucester these cathedral schools competed with old grammar schools which had passed under the control of the city councils and were eventually eclipsed by them. At Westminster, though the church soon ceased to be a cathedral, and bishop and chapter alike disappeared to be replaced by a restored abbot and monks, the school remained endowed, and when the monks were again expelled and the church was restored as a collegiate but not as a cathedral church by Queen Elizabeth, the school was made an integral part of it and placed under its dean and chapter ; but Henry must still be regarded as its real founder in the more glorified form which replaced the old Almonry School. All the statutes were in the same form, beginning with the recital :—

" Whereas it seemed good to us and the great men of our realm and to all the senate whom we call Parliament, God thereunto as we believe moving us, to suppress and abolish and to convert to far better uses for the true worship of Almighty God and the far greater benefit of the Commonwealth the monasteries which existed everywhere in our realm, both

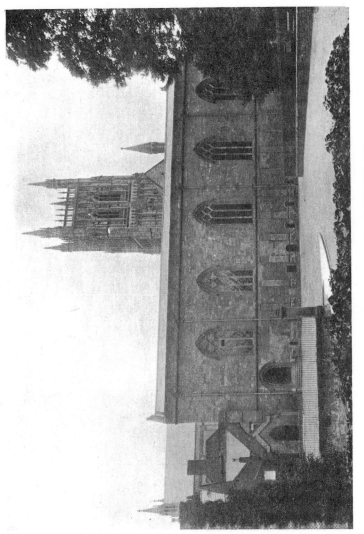

WORCESTER CATHEDRAL GRAMMAR SCHOOL, 1541

THE REFECTORY OF THE DISSOLVED PRIORY

because the sincere and most ancient religion, the most admired uprightness of life and the most profound knowledge of languages and learning, the praise of which virtues it appears flourished in the earliest monasteries, now in the progress of time have become corrupt and deficient, and changed to the foulest superstition and the most disgraceful idleness and lust and the grossest ignorance of Holy Scripture, and because of their 'grave and manifold enormities, as for other just and reasonable causes; Wherefore we, thinking it more in conformity with the divine will and a more Christian thing that where ignorance and superstition reigned there the true worship of God should flourish and the holy gospel of Christ be assiduously and in purity preached; and further that for the increase of Christian faith and piety the youth of my realm may be instructed in good literature and the poor for ever maintained, we have in place of the same monasteries erected and established churches, some of which we will shall be called cathedral and others collegiate churches; For the rule and governance of which churches we have caused to be drawn up the laws and statutes which follow."

Chapter 27 of the Canterbury Statutes deals with the grammar boys and their teachers :—

"That piety and good letters may in our church aforesaid for ever blossom, grow and flower and in their time bear fruit for the glory of God and the advantage and adornment of the commonwealth, we decree and ordain that there shall always be in our church of Canterbury, elected and nominated by the Dean or in his absence the Sub-dean and Chapter, fifty boys, poor and destitute of the help of their friends, to be maintained out of the possessions of the church, of native genius as far as may be and apt to learn : whom however we will shall not be admitted as poor boys of our church before they have learnt to read and write and are moderately learned in the first rudiments of grammar, in the judgment of the Dean or in his absence the Sub-dean and Head Master."

The boys were to be maintained until they had obtained a moderate knowledge of, and had learnt to speak and write Latin, for which four years, extendible to five at the discretion of the head master, was considered enough.   No boy was to be elected under nine or over fourteen years of age, unless he had been a chorister of the cathedral or of the chapel royal, if he was fit and proved proficient in music, and having well served the choir was to be preferred to others.   If any boy turned out remarkably slow and stupid or naturally unfit for learning, he, after long trial, was to be expelled "that he may not like a drone consume the bees' honey", and the conscience of the masters was solemnly charged to use their best diligence to get all the boys on, and not to suffer any of the drones to linger uselessly among the rest, but straightway report him to the dean so that another might be admitted in his place.

The head master was to be learned in Latin and Greek, of good character and pious life, endowed with the faculty of teaching, to instruct in piety and adorn with good learning those fifty boys of our church and all others whatsoever who come to our school to learn.   He shall hold the primacy in our school (*primas obtineat*) and be called the head master or chief teacher (*Archididascalus sive pracipuus Informator*).

The usher need only be learned in Latin to teach the boys, under the head master, the first rudiments of grammar and therefore to be called the lower master or second teacher (*Hipodidascalus sive secundarius Informator*).

If found "idle, negligent or unfit to teach", they might be deprived after three warnings.

The grammar school, it will be observed, was entirely free and open to all.   The masters were to instruct any who came to learn grammar.   There is not a vestige of foundation for the notion, sedulously inculcated by some writers and carelessly accepted by the public, that the school was solely or primarily or in any substantial degree intended for the choristers.   The choristers were separately provided for by chapter 24 :—

"Of the choristers and their master.   We decree that there be . . . by the election of the dean eight choristers, youths who have good voices and are inclined to singing, who may serve, minister and sing in our choir.   For the instruction of these youths and training them up as well in modest behaviour as in skilfulness of singing we will that . . . there shall be chosen one who is of a good life and reputation, skilful both in singing and in playing upon the organ, who shall diligently spend his time in instructing the boys in playing upon the organs and at proper times in singing divine service."

That there might be no mistake as to what was meant by " maintaining " the scholars on the foundation, another statute provided for a college hall.   In his rhetorical way the statute-framer made preamble: " That those who come together and praise God together in choir, may also sit together and praise God together at table", and he then proceeded to order that " as well the Minor Canons and all ministers of the church in the choir, as the teachers of the grammar boys and all other ministers of the church, the boys too learning music and grammar, if it conveniently may be, shall eat together and dine in a common hall ".   In hall the precentor or senior minor canon was to preside at the upper table, next came the head master, then the minor canons.   At the second table were the deacon and sub-deacon, otherwise called epistoller and gospeller, eight clerks and the under master.   At the third were the grammar boys and the choristers. The servants dined afterwards (*secundo prandio*). The precentor as *censor morum* looked after the behaviour of the men ; but only the masters were to correct the boys.   One of the canons or minor canons was to be steward for the year, and provide " all necessary store, as they call it ", while a minor canon was to act as steward of hall for a month and order dinner.   The amount allowed for commons of the head master, minor canons, and choristers' master was 6s. a month or 1s. 6d. a week ; for the clerks and under-master, 4s. or 1s. 2d. a week ; and for the grammar boys and choristers, 3s. 4d. a month or 10d. a week. The masters and scholars, like the minor canons and others, were to have their livery, i.e. cloth for their gowns.

In cathedral the head master and second master had stalls assigned them, and it was provided that the former should rank next above and the latter next below the minor canons, just as the head master at Winchester and Eton ranked next above the fellows but below the warden or provost, and the second master next below the fellows and chaplains.

In pay their position was the same. Thus, at Peterborough, while the dean got £100, a canon £20, minor canon £10, the head master got £16 13s. 4d., the usher £8, and each grammar scholar £2 13s. 4d.

Provision was also made for exhibitions at the University from the schools, but this provision was taken away in 1545, part of the endowment being surrendered in consideration of the relief, to the grievous damage of the schools.

A Method of Teaching formed the last chapter of the Statutes. It provided for six classes, three under the usher and three under the head master. The lower books were Cato, Æsop and *Familiar Colloquies* In Form III, Terence and Mantuanus' *Eclogues ;* in the Fourth Form, they began to practise writing Latin letters ; not until the Fifth Form did they begin to write Latin verses, and polished themes and translated poets and historians. In the Sixth Form, they read Erasmus's *Copia Verborum* and made " varyings ", that is, turned sentences of Latin from the *oratio obliqua* to the *oratio directa,* and from one tense and mood to another, " so as to acquire the faculty of speaking Latin as well as is possible for boys ". They were to read Horace, Cicero and other authors of that class. It is strange that no Greek author is mentioned, nor any Greek composition, but it is provided that whatever they are doing in earnest or in play they shall never use any language but Latin or Greek. Declamations are insisted on " so that they may leave school well learned in the practice of argument ".

The schools thus refounded did the greater part of the education of England till the eighteenth century, and one of them, Westminster, developed into what was throughout the seventeenth and eighteenth centuries, admittedly the greatest of the public schools, taking the lead even of Winchester and Eton, alike in its numbers, its aristocratic connexion and its intellectual achievements.

At Coventry and Bath alone were the cathedral priories destroyed and not converted into colleges, because, in both cases, the dioceses had already secular cathedrals at Lichfield and Wells, while new sees and cathedrals were carved out of them at Chester and Bristol. The episcopal or city grammar school at Coventry, for which a new house had been provided by a private benefactor in 1303, was now endowed by planting it on St. John's Hospital, worth £95 13s. a year, sold to John Hales, a chancery official, clerk to the Hanaper, for £400, subject to the condition of finding a free school. A patent for the foundation of the school was issued on 23 July, 1545. " The basis and safety of every state are the teaching (*informatio*) of boys from their very cradle in piety and the humanities (*humanitatem*), and, if this is neglected, it is impossible that the crowd of idolaters, manslayers, thieves, and idle mendicants"—a hit at the friars—"which stalks everywhere should disappear.   In order that the army of the wicked should be quickly removed we have already established colleges of theologians and schools of faith."   Coventry, however, had hitherto been left unprovided.   Now John Hales, in the name of the whole city, having asked for a faculty, licence was given him "to found in honour of Jesus Christ who wished little children to come to him, a perpetual and free school which shall be called Our (i.e. King's) school", and licence in mortmain was given for the grant of lands to the value of 200 marks (£166 13s. 4d.) to the corporation "for the support of the schoolmaster, teachers, pupils, and servants of the same".   At first Hales maintained the school, not in St. John's Hospital but in the White Friars' Church, allowing the chief master £30 a year, the usher £10, and the music master 20 nobles (£5 13s. 4d.) and their board—a very generous provision.   Owing, however, to some difficulty about the title to the White Friars, the school was removed to the chapel of St. John's Hospital, a fourteenth-century building 80 feet long, where it remained till 1885.   The endowment not being legally completed, the school was in abeyance under Mary, as Hales had to fly abroad for his life, but was finally effected by deed of 5 March, 1573, the Hospital and lands in the city and other property bringing in £43 11s. 2d., being conveyed to the city council.   The salaries of the masters were, however, reduced to £20, £10, and £2 12s. a year.   The income from the Hospital lands has now risen to £1100 a year; so that the school is much better off than the cathedral schools, the incomes of which were not augmented by the deans and chapters when they augmented their own incomes.

Bath School was refounded by a grant to the Corporation of all the lands of the dissolved Priory in Bath, including some which by their name of "school land" sufficiently testify to the existence of the school before the dissolution ; but this was not till 12 July, 1552, and the school was therefore dubbed the Free Grammar School of King Edward the Sixth.

The cathedral statutes spoke of collegiate churches—and collegiate churches were actually established in place of mon-

asteries at Burton-on-Trent, Brecon, and Thornton in Lincolnshire, where the schoolmasters and scholars were given the same
important position as at Rochester or Worcester.   At Thornton
what the father planted the son pulled up by the roots, and
this church fell under the Chantries Act of Edward VI.

At Burton-on-Trent the late monastery of St. Mary and
St. Modwenna was replaced on 14 August, 1541, by the collegiate church of Christ and St. Mary with a dean and four
canons, and a grammar school master, at the high pay of £20
a year.   But the founder of the noble house of Beaudesert and
of the Marquises of Anglesey, built on the spoils of the monasteries, hankered after Burton, and after four and a half years of
existence the King was persuaded to suppress the college, and
grant it to Sir William Paget by patent of 31 January, 1546.
On 3 March, 1546, Richard Harman, late schoolmaster, was
paid £10 for his half year's pension to Lady Day following,
"but no further as the king has provided for him otherwise".
Christ's College, Brecon, is still one of the chief schools of Wales.

Some collegiate churches were dissolved by Henry under
the Acts of 1540 and the Chantries Act of 1545—among them
Warwick, Ottery St. Mary's and Crediton.   The policy here
pursued was different.   The endowments, or a portion of the
endowments, of these churches were by letters patent granted to
incorporations of the inhabitants, to provide for the vicar
and one or two assistant clergy, and the grammar school on
the same enlarged scale as in the cathedrals.   Thus Warwick
was surrendered in 1544 and the bulk of its endowments
granted, 15 May, 1545, to the inhabitants " for the good of them
all and their common advantage ", they being incorporated to
hold it as " one body and community of themselves by the
name of ' Burgesses of the town of Warwick in the county of
Warwick ' ".   They were to maintain a vicar and an assistant
and to pay the master or pedagogue of "our" school to be
incorporated £10 a year and provide him a convenient house,
habitation or mansion to live in.   The King then, "moved by
his love for the ungrown ups (*impuberes*) of the country, that,
henceforth imbued from their cradles with more polite literature than was usual before our time, when they have come
to a more advanced age they may turn out better instructed,
thinking assuredly that so the church of England, whose im-

mediate vice-gerent we are, may be adorned and glorified not
only by learned men in the world of literature but by wise
men for the commonwealth of the kingdom", proceeded to
erect and found " to endure for ever a Free School to be called
in the vulgar tongue ' The King's Newe Scole of Warwyke' ".
By the very fact of calling it the new school he thus preserved
the memory of its being an old school.

At Ottery St. Mary instead of all the inhabitants four
" Governors of the hereditaments and goods of the church ",
in fact, the church wardens, were incorporated and the school
was founded in almost identical terms as at Warwick, called
" the King's Newe Gramar Scole of St. Mary of Ottery".

A less advantageous course was pursued at Higham Ferrers
where the college estates were granted to Robert Dacres on
condition of maintaining the vicar, the almshouse and the
grammar schoolmaster, but the deed unfortunately specifying
the amount to be paid, £10 to the schoolmaster, has been
treated as a fixed charge by the Fitzwilliam family, into whose
hands the property came, and the school is now in abeyance
for lack of endowment.   The same was done at Wye, where
the college possessions were granted to Walter Bucler on condition of maintaining a sufficient schoolmaster, paying him
£13 6s. 8d. a year.   In the reign of Elizabeth the property
was resumed by the Crown for failure to comply with the condition, but Charles I regranted it in 1630, and actually renewed the condition, only raising the amount to £16 a year.
Fortunately in 1724 another endowment was given.   But this
too proved inadequate, and after struggling along in a half-
starved condition the school has now become an Agricultural
College maintained by the County Council.

A more successful effort in the same line was the sale of
St. Thomas à Becket's College of Acon to the Mercers' Company for £969, on condition of their maintaining a free
grammar school with a sufficient master to teach twenty-five
children and scholars freely for ever—this was the origin of
the Mercers' School.

The example of dissolution proved contagious.   The
mesne lords, following the lord paramount, began to dissolve
the hospitals, colleges, and chantries, of which by virtue of
their ancestors' foundation they were patrons, while in many

cases, particularly hospitals, and more particularly leper hospitals, the object of which for lack of leprosy had failed, the masters appropriated the incomes to themselves, or sold the property, or granted long leases on fines and pocketed the fines.   A curious instance of illegal suppression of a school was reported at Malpas in Cheshire, where, about 1538, "there was a gramer scole erected" with endowment of £12 a year, the same lands being resumed and taken away by one Sir Roger Brereton, Kt., so that "there is no school there kept albeit it were very necessary to have a school there".   To meet such cases, and also to supply sinews of war against France and Scotland, the Parliament which met in November, 1545, passed the Chantries Act, "An Acte for the dissolution of Colleges Chantries and Free Chappells at the Kinges Majesties Pleasure".   It vested in the King absolutely all "colleges, fre chappelles, chantries, hospitalles, fraternities, brotherhedds, guildes and stipendarie prestes havinge perpetuitye for ever" which had been illegally dissolved before Christmas, 1545, and enabled him during his life to issue commissions to enter into any others and take them into his possession.   The King, according to the chronicler Hall, then M.P. for Bridgnorth, made a speech expressing his surprise and gratitude at this unexpected and unsolicited present.   In the Act, Parliament had expressed its belief that he "of his most godlie and blessed disposicion entendeth to have the premises used and exercised to more godlie and vertuouse purposes".   So Henry said, that if contrary to their expectations he suffered "learning, which is so great a jewel, to be minished" he were "no trusty friend . . . or lover of the public weal", and assured them "their expectations shall be served more godly and goodly than" they dared to hope.

Commissioners were appointed for every county on 14 February, 1546, to survey and certify what property fell under the Act.   Their certificates first revealed, to the present writer, the large number and the great antiquity of the Pre-Reformation grammar schools, and showed that in these secular foundations and not in the monasteries were to be found not merely the precursors of most of our existing endowed schools, but the schools themselves.   It has been commonly assumed, and many historical blunders are due to the assumption, that most of the colleges and chantries were abolished by Henry VIII under this Act. This is an almost entire mistake. No action could be taken under the Act till the certificates were returned into Chancery, which was not till the summer of 1546. Henry died, and the Act expired with him, on 28 January, 1547. So there was very little time for dealing with them. So far only four colleges, one hospital, and three chantries are known to have been seized under the Act.

The colleges were St. Edmund's, Salisbury, which was, as we saw, one of the earliest University colleges in England; Tong, Staffordshire, and Hastings, Sussex, the schools of which have been mentioned, and Pleshey, Essex. This last was founded by Thomas of Woodstock, Duke of Gloucester, son of Edward III, under licence of 25 January, 1394. Its statutes, confirmed 20 February, 1394-95 and revised in 1441, contain no reference to a school. But there were lands given by Edward Stafford, Earl of Wiltshire, "to find a priest to sing mass and teach a school there", and in 1548 Sir Henry Rutter, clerk, "teachythe a scole there and haythe to the nombre of 35 scolers". As this endowment was distinct from that of the college, the seizure of the college did not harm the school. The seizure of the school endowment was left for Edward VI. The one hospital seized, St. Bartholomew's, might, as we saw, but it is uncertain whether it did keep a school. Of the three chantries, Aldwinckle, Northamptonshire, had, as we saw, "a syllable school"; Lufwick was a chantry of two chaplains, which looks suspiciously like a grammar and song school. Of Bakewell, Derbyshire, owing to the loss of the chantry certificates for that county, we know nothing. Its seizure was apparently due to Sir Richard Manners, ancestor of the Dukes of Rutland, whose fortunes were built on church and monastic endowments, to whom it and Tong College were sold for £486 in January, 1547. Henry's death prevented his showing how he would have "godly and goodly" served the institutions which he did dissolve. The cases of the college of Crediton and St. Giles' Hospital at Norwich, surrendered to him only a few months before the Act, the foundation of the schools of which have been credited to Edward VI, though in both cases the arrangements are stated to have been made by Henry VIII, show us pretty clearly what he would have done.   At Crediton of eighteen prebends, three were before the dissolution already being treated as exhibitions, being held by William Hermon, described as "scoler of Excetor", and two others as scholars, and most of the rest were held by canons of Exeter.   By patent of 2 April, 1547, the church, vicarage, and "scole house" and other property to produce £62 a year, half the income of the former possessions of the college, were granted to twelve governors of the church, and in words copied verbatim from the charters at Warwick and Ottery St. Mary, "The kyng's newe gramer scole of Crediton" was established, and the governors were directed to pay the master £10 a year.

At Norwich letters patent of 7 May, 1547, which re-granted to the Corporation the whole of the possessions of St. Giles' Hospital, and planted on it what has been called King Edward VI's School, are expressly stated to have been issued in pursuance of an arrangement made by Henry VIII. Indeed the most perverse upholder of the title of Edward VI as founder of schools could hardly suppose that at the age of nine, within four months of his accession, this boy could have conceived and carried out such a scheme as this, which made the school an integral part of and thereby gave it a share in the endowments of foundation.   In 1547 the lands produced £133 19s. 2½d. a year net.   In 1858 they were apportioned by the Court of Chancery, the school share producing £1278 a year, while the hospital share produced £5000 a year.   Such was the benefit of getting lands in specie, instead of the fixed stipends which Edward VI assigned in the continued chantry schools.

Many other schools and exhibition foundations appear in the chantry certificates of 1546 or 1548, which, though un-doubtedly some existed long before Henry VIII's accession, can, owing to their date of origin not being ascertained, be claimed only as existing in his reign.   Thus, to take them geographically, there were grammar schools in Northumber-land, at Morpeth, a chantry in All Saints' Chapel, the whole endowment of which, worth £6 8s. 2d. a year, was, after being confiscated by Edward VI, with other chantry lands, restored by him and the school re-founded in 1551 ; in Durham, at

Barnard Castle, maintained by the Trinity Gild, with £4 1s. a year; in Cumberland, at Cockermouth, under a stipendiary priest with an income of £5 16s. "used to kepe and teche a grammer schole there".

In Yorkshire there were schools;—at Richmond, of unknown antiquity, maintained in 1546 in connexion with Trinity Chapel by the bailiff and burgesses, who paid the master £6 13s. 4d. a year; at Bradford, out of "lands given for the use of a scolemaister" declared by a commission in 1601 to have been so employed from time whereof the memory of man runs not to the contrary, producing £2 8s. 8d. a year, which were seized for the Crown under the Chantries Act of Edward VI, but restored as not under the Act by a decree of the Duchy of Lancaster Chamber in 1552, and which still form the endowment of the present school with its over 500 boys, and a girls' school of 350 girls; at Boroughbridge in Aldborough, which was also a chantry of Our Lady, net rent £4 13s. 11d.; at Keighley, kept out of lands in feoffment to find a priest to say mass and teach children, producing £3 1s. 6d. a year; at Normanton, which was the chantry of Our Lady, income £2 19s. 2d., founded for a Fre Scole for the "good educacion of yongthe as well in grammar as wrytinge"; at Pickering, kept by the Lady Gild, the master being paid £1 15s.; at Romaldkirk, the monastery paid out of a stock of money remaining in the hands of the parishioners, £2 16s. 8d. In Lancashire, at Whalley, a schoolmaster had long been kept with a salary of £13 6s. 8d.; at Winwick, the school was founded by Gwalter Legh, ancestor of the present Lord Newton, *temp.* Henry VIII; at Clitheroe, the school was chartered by Queen Mary, 9 August, 1554, and endowed with Almondbury church, part of the property of Rotherham Colege, and with the lands of St. Nicholas Chantry Skipton, may be inferred from the terms of the charter to have existed before the dissolution of chantries.

In Lincolnshire, at Holbeach, a chantry for a chaplain founded by Sir Laurence Holbeach, knight, was appropriated as an exhibition for a scholar at Oxford and Cambridge, and held in 1546 by Richard Thorpe at Queens' College, Cambridge. In Nottinghamshire, at Mattersey, the "stipendarie prieste", Robert Buttie, swore there was no chantry, but only lands given to feoffees to find a priest at will of the parishioners to help the vicar and teach children.

In Staffordshire, at Eccleshall, two gilds of Our Lady and of St. Katherine, founded by licence of King Henry VIII, maintained two priests, one of whom always kept school and taught poor men's children, freely; at Cannock, Our Lady's Priest, income £4 14s. 5½d., for thirty years had kept a grammar school and taught children of the parish "for the most part, freely"; at Paget's Bromley, a priest receiving £1 5s. 6d. a year from lands "given of long tyme past, by whom it is not knowen" always kept a school, but not freely; naturally, for the endowment was not enough to enable him to dispense with fees.

In Suffolk, at Stowmarket, " by common consent of the lord of the manor of Abbots' Hall and diverse inhabitants" the Gildhall was at some time before 1547 converted into a schoolhouse; at Lavenham, the priest of St. Peter's Gild taught children.

In Northamptonshire, the chapel of St. John Baptist on Stamford bridge, originally a hospital, had been converted into an exhibition for Thomas Stoddard, thirteen or fourteen years old, at school; at Wellingborough the gild probably kept the school which was restored after a struggle in Chancery in the reign of Elizabeth.

In Warwickshire, at Nuneaton, the endowment of a chantry, founded in 1508 by John Leke, amounting to £2 13s. 4d. a year, was about 1541 "with more gyven of theyr devocion, convertyd" (by the parishioners) "to the mayntenance of a scoole master".

In Worcestershire, at Bromsgrove, the grammar school was maintained out of lands producing £11 11s. 8d. a year, of which £7 had been always employed towards the finding of a schoolmaster, being a priest, who was not only bound to keep a school but also to assist the curate, the balance going to church repair, " setting of sodijers (soldiers) forwarde to the warres", highways, bridges and " such like charitable dedes". The schoolmaster was continued at £7 a year and the school chartered, but not founded or endowed, by Queen Mary; at Lye, a stipendiary priest at £2 2s. 8d. a year used to teach a free school.

In Essex, a school at Finchingfield was taught by the priest of the Trinity Gild, " foundation cannot be shewid ", who had thirty scholars; at Hornchurch, school was taught by the priest of another Trinity Gild, who was paid £5 4s. 11d. a year; at Great Chesterford, the school was kept out of lands given by William Holden " to find a priest to sing mass " and the mass priest " had twenty scholars and more ".

In Buckinghamshire, at Great Marlow, the chantry priest of Our Lady paid £6 13s. 4d. a year, was admitted to teach and did teach children ; at Aston in Ivinghoe, the chaplain of St. James' Chapel taught school.

In Oxfordshire, at Burford, the gild of Our Lady, which if the same as the Merchant Gild dated from the end of the eleventh century, maintained a priest at least from 1507, who received £7 a year out of a total income of £16 10s. 10d., the rest going on taxes, bridges, and highways, and at Deddington, the priest of the Trinity Gild, William Burton, paid £6 a year, was "a good scole master, and bryngyth up yough very well in learnyng ".

In Gloucestershire, at Cheltenham, the priest of St. Katharine's service, by special covenant between the parishioners and him, was bound always to teach their children at £5 a year; he was paid till 1554, and the chantry funds were then granted to Richard Pate, 7 January, 1574, to endow the present grammar school.

In Herefordshire, at Ledbury, the stipendiary priest of the Trinity service, Sir Richard Wheler, at a salary of £4 1s. 4½d. kept a boarding school; and " the inhabitants of the same have not only had profit and advantage by the keeping of a grammar school there as in boarding and lodging his scholars, but also the country thereabouts in uttering their victuals there by means of the said scholars "; at Bosbury, the schoolmaster was found out of lands producing £2 19s. 9½d. a year, given " with no use declared but always employed to bring up youth in learning and to play at the organs "; at Leominster, " a scole " was " ever before thys tyme kept "; at Dilwyn, the chantry of St. Nicholas was about 1542 " converted to be a school " in which were sixty scholars; at Kinnersley, a stipendiary priest, wages £6 2s., had sixty scholars ; at Yardsley, now regarded as being in Worcestershire, a sti-

pendiary was receiving £4 13s. 10d., founded by Sir John Basker-
vyle, Kt., to instruct and bring up his children and other men's
" in learning of grammar"; at Bromyard, lands producing
£3 9s. 11d. were given to maintain service and bring up
children born there in reading and writing and grammar; at
Bucknill, a stipendiary and scolemaster received £5 6s. 8d.
wages from divers men of the parish out of a certain stock of
money of £32, to teach poor men's children their grammar.

In Kent, at Ospring, a stipend of £6 13s. 4d. was paid by
St. John's College, Cambridge, to a priest to sing in the chapel
and teach children freely; at Tenterden, the chantry of Peter
Marshall, income £10 a year, was also a school.

In Hampshire, at Odiham, a stipendiary priest was paid
£6 13s. 4d. to assist in the ministration and teach children
grammar; in the Isle of Wight at Godshill, John Griffith, M.A.,
priest of a chantry founded by Sir John Ligh, Kt., " teachithe
there grammer to many yung children".

In Dorset, at Netherbury, was a " gramar scole " endowed
with £5 6s. 8d. a year; at Blandford, the free chapel of
Westhamsworth, worth £2 8s. a year, was " ordained " for a
schoolmaster, and held by Dr. Benet.

In Wilts, at Malmesbury, the stipendiary priest in West-
port, receiving £5 14s. 9d. a year, " doth occupie hymself in
brynginge uppe yonge children in learnynge "; at Bradford,
Horton's chantry, valued at £10 12s. 7d. a year, was founded
purposely for the maintenance of a Free School and no other
intent, and kept accordingly; at Dorchester, St. John's free
chapel, worth £10 4s. 6d. a year, was held by Edward Welden
by grant from Henry VIII of 3 August, 1540, " towards his
exibicion at the Universitie of Oxford "; at Trowbridge, the
priest of Terumbere's chantry, Robert Whetacre, a very
honest man, and well learned, occupied himself in teaching a
school ever since he came first thither; at Endford was a
chantry, founded by John Westley, who gave 1000 sheep to
find a priest to sing for ever; but 692 died, so " one parson
Burde " gave 578 sheep to increase the stock, which in 1548
numbered 886, priced at 6d. each, let to divers persons for
£7 14s. 6d.   " The Incumbent hathe alwayes occupied hym-
selfe in teaching of children."   Four free chapels and chantries
in this county founded for priests were held by laymen as

TENTERDEN OLD GRAMMAR SCHOOL

exhibitions for educational purposes; Cryour's chantry in Fisherton Anger worth £5 15s. 2½d. a year was given to John Powell, age thirty-six, a very honest man, "for and to his exibytyon to scole, albeit he is no preeste"; the chapel of Asserton in the parish of Berwick St. John was held by Gyles Chestellthwayte, age twenty-six, a layman, who also had it for his exhibition at school, and had sold a chalice and vestments belonging to it; the priory or free chapel of St. John in Colne, worth £4 4s. 11d. a year, was held by Robert Blake, aged twenty-six, "to fynde hym to scole"; a chantry in North Wraxall, worth £2 4s. 8d., was held by William Spenon, age twenty, "a student in Oxforde but no prieste, and furthermore a very poore man, havyng no parentes or any other lyvinge to kepe hym to scole"; while the free chapel of Backhampton in Avebury, worth £4 5s. a year, was held by John Warner, aged forty, warden of All Soules College in Oxforde.

In Somerset, at Yeovil, was a chapel in the churchyard, covered with lead worth £4, which "the habitants ther desire to have for a scole house".

In Devon, at Barnstaple, a chapel of St. Nicholas, with freehold lands bringing in £7 18s. 3d. "was founded to kepe a grammer scole"; at Marldon, the chantry was for the maintenance of two poor men at 8d. a week, and for the maintenance of a grammar school.

In Cornwall, at Saltash, from lands worth £9 13s. 2d. of the gift and feoffment of John Smith and others to the Mayor and burgesses for a priest to pray for them and their fathers and mothers, and to teach children born in the borough £7 was paid to the schoolmaster; at Truro, the stipendiary and scolemaster received £6 13s. 4d. from lands worth £9, found by the benevolence of the Mayor and burgesses, to find a priest to minister in the church and keep a school there.

It must not be supposed that this list, long as it is, is exhaustive.

It will be noticed that there are no schools in it in Cambridgeshire, Huntingdon, Surrey, and Norfolk, there being no chantry certificates for those counties, while in the Derbyshire certificate schools are not noticed: and in several counties the certificates are meagre.

The suppression of monasteries and colleges was by no

means regarded by Henry's contemporaries as discouraging education or educational endowments.

In 1527, Sir George Monoux, draper and ex-Lord Mayor, bought a plot of land at Walthamstow, on which he built a free school and almshouse and completed the foundation with ordinances in 1541, for the "almese prest scolemaster" at a salary of £6 13s. 4d. to "teche without taking of any hire or benefit the childerne of the parisshe to the nombre of 20 or 30". By his will in 1544 he bequeathed £42 more to assist to maintain the priest "to sing masse and teche a free scole for 20 yeres". Walthamstow school still flourishes.

John Stow recounts that the first building at Ratcliffe Highway, then a beautifully timbered country lane " near unto London", was a "fair free school and almshouse" founded by Avice, wife of Nicholas Gibsson, grocer and ex-sheriff; the school for sixty poor men's children, the master's pay £10 and the usher's £6 6s. 8d. The Coopers' Company were made governors.

Berkhampstead we have already noticed. The very end of Henry's reign was signalized by the birth of triplets from one founder; three free schools in Yorkshire of Robert Holgate, ex-head of the Order of Gilbertine Canons, Archbishop of York. On 24 October, 1546, "for the good education and instruction of children and boys of the realm of England in good manners and the art of grammar and other liberal learning (*liberalis scientia*)" he obtained licence to found three free and perpetual schools at York, Hemsworth, and Old Malton. Only that at York was actually established by deed of 10 January, 1546-7, in Henry's reign, eighteen days before his death. The master was to be " convenientlie seen and have understandinge in the Hebrew, Greek and Latin tongues",—the first appearance of Hebrew in a school programme. Its foundation close by the cathedral emphasizes the fact that the Cathedral Grammar School, with only its thirteenth century endowment of £5 a year, was not free but charged fees. The archbishop himself, not the Chapter, was to appoint the master, who might be a married man or a layman. At Old Malton, established by deed 24 May, 1547, Holgate named his own father-in-law as the first master, with a stipend on Henry's highest cathedral school scale of £20 a year.

So with the death on 28 January, 1547 of Henry VIII, earnest
to the last in the furtherance of education, having done more
to bring the Middle Ages to an end by the swift, wholesale and,
on the whole, peaceful dissolution of those fortresses of
medievalism, the monasteries, than all the half-hearted humanists
like Erasmus and Sir Thomas More, who could not bear to see
their principles put into practice, we bring our survey of the
Medieval Schools of England to an end.

It may be interesting, in conclusion, to attempt some sort
of statistical summary of school supply in England before the
Reformation.   It is clear from the number of schools mentioned,
which are by no means all that could be named, that the supply
was more than ample.   It may be said broadly that wherever
there was a cluster of houses which could be dignified with the
name of town, there was a grammar school in the midst of
it.   Indeed, a grammar school might almost be taken as the
test of that corporate, or quasi-corporate, activity which justified
a place in calling itself a town.   It was an institution without
which no community could consider itself respectable.

It is difficult to arrive at a precise estimate of the proportion of schools to population, because, while it is hard to ascertain the exact number of schools, it is even harder, and perhaps
impossible, to ascertain the population of England at any given
date in the Middle Ages.   Professor Thorold Rogers puts the
population of England and Wales at not more than a million
and a half before the Black Death of 1349, and says that " it
is certain that the rate of production precludes the possibility
of its being more than two and a half millions".   In 1377 the
poll-tax, levied on all persons fourteen years old and upwards,
gave an indirect census, showing 1,376,442 lay people and
29,161 ecclesiastics who paid the tax.   It is assumed, in es-
timating the population, that one-fifth of those who ought to
have paid did not (a very large proportion indeed); and that
one-third of the whole population was under fourteen, and
therefore exempt.   This would give just over two and a quarter
millions, which it is pretty certain would be an over—rather
than an under—estimate.

Forty-two towns appear in the poll tax returns, which
ranking, in modern parlance, as county-boroughs, were assessed
separately from the counties they were in.   They had a total

population of 166,000.   Of the eight most populous towns, six were cathedral cities; and the whole of the cathedral towns mentioned amount to seventeen.   Each of these had its cathedral grammar school.   London, with 44,000 people, had at least five grammar schools.   York, with 13,500, had its cathedral school, with its abbey boarding-house and smaller schools in St. Leonard's, and the Trinity or Fossgate Hospitals.   Bristol, with 12,000, had its grammar school, besides one in Redcliffe Church, and there is evidence that there was teaching in connexion with St. Nicholas Church.   All the other towns had a population under 10,000; and twenty-six of them had a population under 4000.   Yet, with the possible exception of Dartmouth, with its petty 949 people, every one of these towns, which would not make a decently sized twentieth-century village, had its grammar school—some of them, like Canterbury, certainly two or three.   Nor is there any doubt that the numbers attending these schools were large. Whenever we get any numbers mentioned, they are (outside the cloister or novices' school of a monastery) reckoned not by units but by scores.   Even in a tiny little place like Wollaton, near Nottingham, we noticed that a strict limit was being imposed when the master was allowed to teach twenty-six scholars only, and no more; and at Bruton there were 120; while a small place like Kynnersley in Herefordshire had sixty.

To take this single county.   The population of Herefordshire was some 25,000; that of Hereford city, 3568; and of Ludlow (then seemingly reckoned in Herefordshire) 2198, or, say, in round figures, 30,000 in all.   Hereford had its cathedral grammar school; Ludlow its gild school; Ledbury its collegiate church grammar school.   Besides these, there were fourteen grammar schools in the county at the time of the suppression of colleges and chantries, of which only three or four survived.   That is, there were seventeen grammar schools for a population of 30,000.

The supply of schools in Herefordshire may have been rather over the average.   But taking one county with another, the number of grammar schools per county was certainly not less than ten.   This figure would give in forty counties 400 schools for 2,250,000 people (a probably too high estimate of population), or one grammar school for every 5625 people.   Moreover, at least half, and that the most important half, of these schools were not confined, like modern schools, to an endowment of fixed amount; but, having to be adequately maintained by the collegiate body, or the gild, to which they were attached, could, and did, draw on their endowments at large.   These endowments were confiscated by the State, and many still line the pockets of the descendants of the statesmen of the day.   The contrast between one grammar school to every 5625 people, and that presented by the Schools Inquiry Report in 1864 of one to every 23,750 people, and even to the enlarged provision at the present day, is not to the disadvantage of our pre-Reformation ancestors.

In spite, however, of the ample and continually growing supply of schools, the results were disappointing.   So long as the monasteries furnished a safe and easy refuge from the struggle for existence, and monasticism enforced celibacy on churchmen, who largely depended on the patronage of the monasteries for their chances of promotion, education made little impression on society at large.   It was in vain for clever boys to be educated and to be promoted to the chief offices in church and state, when they were doomed to die without issue ; or worse, produce the "scholars" who filled the papal purse by obtaining the innumerable dispensations from the bar sinister, which recent Calendars of Papal letters have revealed to us.   The advancement of science and learning comes from a cultured middle class.   No such class could be formed when the cultured individual established no family to be a centre of culture, and left no sons behind him to inherit his ability and widen the circle of culture, by founding more educated families to hand on the lamp of life.   The success in life of the child of the parsonage and the manse has become proverbial.   While monasticism prevailed, that source of national energy was cut off.   The extension of education to the laity, in the prince, the noble, and the merchant, which was the distinguishing mark of the Renaissance, produced great results, and Henry VIII himself was not the least of them. But as long as the clergy was sterilized, and yet monopolized a large and ever-increasing proportion of the territory and wealth of the world, progress was checked.   The quiet thinker was lured into the cloister, the progressive thinker was under a ban, originality was a crime, and repression prevailed especially in the region, in which it is most dangerous, of religion and philosophy. In Italy, Spain, Portugal, Flanders, the most populous and naturally the richest countries, the Renaissance was strangled almost in its cradle by monasticism in its most formidable development, the Inquisition: while its growth was stunted in France and Germany by the prolonged series of wars and massacres between the upholders of monasticism and the friends of free thought. Its full development was reserved for England and Scotland, where the monasteries, and with them clerical celibacy, were suddenly and wholly swept away.

The expansion of Elizabethan England, which took the world by surprise, not only in navigation, in commerce, in colonization, but in poetry and the drama, in philosophy and science, was due to the immense extension of lay initiative and effort in every department of national life; and not least in the sphere of education and the schools. The crop was reaped by Elizabeth in a Spenser and a Sidney, a Bacon and a Shakespeare; but it was Henry VIII, aided by the three Thomases of progress (not the *Tres Thomæ* of reaction), by Thomas Wolsey, Thomas Cranmer, and, above all, Thomas Cromwell, who cleared the field and sowed the seed.

INDEX

22

INDEX

339

Free Schools, 119, 132, 156, 208, 243-
6, 254, 255, 261, 270, 274, 275,
281, 284, 290, 291, 295-9, 317,
319, 323, 324, 326, 328.
French, English substituted for, 196.
— talking in schools, 181, 195.
— translation into English, 199.
Fulgentius, 60.
Fuller, Matthew, 229.
Fulmerston, Sir Robert, 123.
Furness Abbey, Grammar and Song
Schools in, 226.
Furnivall, Dr., *The Babees' Book*, 306.

GALENS, 29.
Games, 140, 146, 174.
Gardiner, Bishop, 232.
Garendon Monastery, almonry boys at,
233.
Garlandia, Johannes de, 306.
Garton, Stephen of, 182.
Gasquet, Abbot, 234.
Gaunt, John of, register, 253.
Gelasius, Pope, 25.
Gerontius, 42.
Gibson, Edward, 269.
Gibsson, Avice, 328.
— Nicholas, 328.
Giffard, Archbishop, 171.
— Godfrey, Bishop, 126, 169.
Giggleswick Grammar School, 276.
Gilbert, Abbot of Westminster, 96.
Gild at Bury St. Edmunds, 120, 188.
— — Saffron Walden, 285.
— Schools, 197, 202, 211, 241, 244,
268, 288, 292, 293, 323-5.
Giles, Dr., *Edition of Aldhelm's letters*,
38.
Gilson, Mr., 95.
Giraldus Cambrensis, 130.
Girls' Education, 89.
Glasney Collegiate Church, 152, 166.
Glastonbury Church, 79, 80.
Glomery, Master of, 157, 171, 172, 180.
Gloucester, Bishops of: *see* names
Giffard, Godfrey, Wakefield,
Henry.
— Collegiate Church at, 115, 125.
— Humphrey, Duke of, 251.
— St. Peter's Abbey Almonry School,
226, 233.
— School, 115, 125-7, 237, 312.
— Thomas, Duke of, 321.
— William, Earl of, 128.
Goda, 125.
God's House, Cambridge, 201, 256.
Godshill Chantry School, 326.
Goldsmiths' Company made school
trustees, 245, 246.
— — St. Dunstan patron saint of,
84.

Goldyngton, John, 268.
— Thomas, 268.
Gonzaga, Cecilia, 249.
— Marquis of, 252.
Goscelin, 67.
Graces, the, 286.
Grammar, Ælfric's, 85.
— definition of, 250.
— degree in, 143.
— Donatus', *see* name.
— jests on, 87.
— Lily's, *see* name.
— Priscian's, *see* name.
— Schools, *passim*.
— — attached to churches, 158.
— — class attending, 207.
— — differentiated from Song Schools,
6.
— — function of, 15-17.
— — number of, 266.
— — necessary for religious teaching,
3.
— Stanbridge's, *see* name.
— uniformity prescribed, 309.
— versified, 304.
Grandison, Bishop, 152, 193, 194.
Grantham School, 192.
Gratian, 20.
Gravesend, Richard of, 216.
Great Baddow Grammar School, 211.
Greek, at St. Paul's School, 280.
— — Saffron Walden School, 286.
— — Winchester and Eton, 247, 280.
— disappearance of, 20.
— introduced into schools, 246.
— learning, 21, 22.
— reappearance of, 20.
— schools, 14-18.
Gregorian chant, 6.
Gregory of Nyssa, 9.
— of Nazianzus, 10-12.
— — Tours, 28, 29.
— the Great, 2, 28-30, 60, 87.
Gregory's *Pastoral Care*, 70, 72.
Grey of Ruthyn, Richard, Lord, 260.
Greyndour, Robert, 267.
Griffith, John, 326.
Grimsby School, 192.
Grocyn, William, 209, 247.
Grosseteste, Bishop, 145.
Guarino, Battista, 247.
Guildford Grammar School, 283.
Gundulf, Bishop, 98.
Gunthorpe, Thomas, 298.
Gurney, William of, 192.
Guthlac, St., 50.
Guthrum, 76, 79.
Gymming, 115.

HADDON, Walter, 306.
Hadrian, Abbot, 31, 33, 37, 38, 53.

Smith, Bishop, 301.
— John, 327.
Smyth, William, 243.
Song School, Alnwick, 269.
— — Bury St. Edmunds, 120.
— — Rochester, 6.
— — Rotherham, 275.
— — St. Anthony's, 261.
— — York, 6.
— — Prioress's Tale, 137.
— Schools, 6, 7, 158, 214, 221.
— — curriculum, 300.
Southampton, Priory of St. Denis, 134.
Southwell Minster Grammar School, 282, 283.
— — Statutes of, 162.
Spenon, William, 327.
Spicer, William, 290.
Spirlyng, John, 168.
Sponne, William, 269.
Spurius Carvilius, 15.
Stafford, burh at, 78.
— early school at, 77, 79.
— John, 265.
— schoolmaster-chantry at, 281.
Stamford Bridge (Northants), hospital converted into exhibition, 324.
— School, 78, 192, 291.
Stanbridge, John, 271.
— — Grammar of, 297, 298, 301.
Stanground, John of, 215.
Stapledon, Bishop, 193, 197.
— Hall, 193.
Statius, 61.
Statute of apprentices, 207, 236.
— — Lollards, 238.
Statutes, school, 179-200, 257, 279, 288, 312-6.
Staunton, John of, 199.
— William of, 202.
Stephen, King, 107.
Stere, Nicholas, 254.
Stevenson, Mr. W. H., 69, 74.
Stillington, Robert, Bishop, 274.
Stockport Grammar School, 245.
Stoddard, Thomas, 324.
Stoke d'Abernon, chantry at, 283.
Stoke-next-Clare College, 240.
— — — Grammar School, 240.
Stortford, Richard of, 112.
Story, Bishop, 208.
Stourbridge School, 244.
Stow's Survey of London, 138, 141, 143, 260, 262.
Stowmarket School, 324.
Strassburg School, 281.
Stratford-on-Avon School, 241.
Strode, Diana, 244.
— Ralph, 244.
Strubby School, 192.
Strype's edition of Stow, 263.

Stubbs, Bishop, 34, 45, 53, 54, 79, 80, 84, 111.
Sturm, 281.
Sucuro, 24.
Suetonius, 15, 87.
Suffield, Bishop, 168.
Sulpicius Severus, 43, 302.
— Quos decet in mensa, 305.
Surreton, Nicholas of, 170.
Sutton, Henry of, 177.
— Roger of, 183.
Swallow, Christopher, 298.
Swithun, St., 67, 86.
Symon, Robert, 243.
Synod of Lucus Victoriæ, 1.

Taillour, Robert le, 209.
Tamworth, burh at, 78.
— early school at, 77, 79, 281.
Tatfrid, 44.
Tattershall College, 256.
Taunton School, 178.
Tenterden Chantry School, 299, 326.
Terence, 23, 43.
Tertullian, 8.
Tettenhall, battle at, 78.
Tewkesbury Abbey, almonry boys in, 227.
Theobald Stampensis, 130, 131.
Theodore, Archbishop, 5, 6, 31-3, 38, 44, 46, 49.
Theodoric the Ostrogoth, 26.
Theodosius, 20, 26.
Theodulf, Bishop of Orleans, 62, 85.
Theological lectures at Oxford and Cambridge, 282.
— schools, 158.
Thetford School, 123, 168.
Thirsk Chantry School, 299.
Thomas I, Archbishop, 108.
Thompson, Sir W. Maunde, 68.
Thorncombe, Alfric, 222.
Thornton Abbey, almonry boys at, 223.
— Collegiate Church and School, 318.
— (Bucks), Chantry at, 243.
Thorpe, Richard, 323.
Threlkeld's Chantry, 268.
Thurstan, Archbishop, 109, 131.
Tiberius, Emperor, 87.
Tiberius Victor Minerius, 24.
Tickhill School, 200.
Tobias, Bishop, 33, 38.
Tolleshunt, William of, 215.
Tong Collegiate Church and School, 239, 321.
Toulouse, schools at, 23, 24.
Tour, Hugh de la, 178.
Tours, Gregory of, 28, 29.
— St. Martin of, 28.
— Schools at, 28.
Tovi the Proud, 93.